Municipal Management Series

The Effective Local Government Manager

Second Edition

Edited by
Charldean Newell

Published for the
ICMA Training Institute

By the
International
City/County
Management
Association

Municipal Management Series

Library of Congress Cataloging-in-Publication Data

The Effective local government manager / edited by Charldean Newell. -
- 2nd ed.
          p.   cm. — (Municipal management series)
       Includes bibliographical references and index.
       ISBN 0-87326-090-2 (hrdbk.) ISBN 0-87326-091-0 (pbk.)
       I. Municipal government by city manager—United States.
    I. Newell. Charldean. II. Series.
    JS344.C5A52   1993
    352' .0084'0973—dc20   93-17353
                                                              CIP

Printed in the United States of America

99989796959493
87654321

Municipal Management Series

The Effective Local Government Manager

The International City/County Management Association is the professional and educational organization for appointed administrators and assistant administrators in local government. The purposes of ICMA are to enhance the quality of local government and to nurture and assist professional local government administrators in the United States and other countries. To further its mission, ICMA develops and disseminates new approaches to management through training programs, information services, and publications.

Local government managers—carrying a wide range of titles—serve cities, towns, counties, councils of governments, and state/provincial associations of local governments. They serve at the direction of elected councils and governing boards. ICMA serves these managers and local governments through many programs that aim at improving the manager's professional competence and strengthening the quality of all local governments.

The International City/County Management Association was founded in 1914; adopted its City Management Code of Ethics in 1924; and established its Institute for Training in Municipal Administration in 1934. The Institute, in turn, provided the basis for the Municipal Management Series, generally termed the "ICMA Green Books."

ICMA's interests and activities include public management education; standards of ethics for members; the *Municipal Year Book* and other data services; urban research; and newsletters, a monthly magazine, *Public Management*, and other publications. ICMA's efforts for the improvement of local government management—as represented by this book—are offered for all local governments and educational institutions.

Contributors

The second edition of *The Effective Local Government Manager* contains material adapted from the 1983 edition, edited by Wayne F. Anderson, Chester A. Newland, and Richard J. Stillman II.

First Edition	Second Edition
Wayne F. Anderson	David N. Ammons
F. Gerald Brown	David R. Berman
E. H. Denton	N. Joseph Cayer
Chester A. Newland	E. H. Denton
Joe P. Pisciotte	James J. Glass
Richard J. Stillman II	Patrick Manion
	Charldean Newell
	Joe P. Pisciotte
	James H. Svara

Foreword

Local governments today face unprecedented fiscal, social, political, economic, and technological challenges. To help his or her community meet these challenges, the local government manager must, in addition to possessing all the traditional management skills, be an accomplished and inspired consensus builder, facilitator, negotiator, leader, and visionary.

Like its predecessor, published in 1983, this second edition of *The Effective Local Government Manager* concentrates on management—what local government managers do, how they do it, and how they can do it more effectively. It recognizes that today's manager works in a complex, changing environment, that a primary part of the job is building and mediating relationships, and that the public nature of the job creates special pressures and responsibilities.

This book shows how today's manager fits together the pieces of local government—relating to the community, working with the governing body, creating the organizational climate for excellence, overseeing the delivery of public services, promoting the community's future, conducting relations with other governments, and maintaining personal effectiveness throughout his or her career.

The book is intended for local government managers—a term that includes city, town, and township managers; county managers; directors of councils of governments; and other administrators with a variety of titles who serve local governments. It is also intended for assistant managers, whose responsibilities complement and support those of the manager.

The second edition of *The Effective Local Government Manager* takes its place in a series of distinguished books in local public management published by the International City/County Management Association. The first book in the Municipal Management Series, *The American City and Its Government,* was published in 1935. The pioneering book for the city manager was *The Technique of Municipal Administration*, published in four editions between 1940 and 1957. Among the many persons who worked on successive editions of the book were Louis Brownlow, Herbert Emmerich, Lyman S. Moore, Orin F. Nolting, John M. Pfiffner, Don K. Price, Clarence E. Ridley, Charles F. Rhyne, Herbert A. Simon, and Donald C. Stone. A broader look at local government management was provided by *Managing the Modern City*, edited by James M. Banovetz and published by ICMA in 1971.

The Effective Local Government Manager, like its companions in the Municipal Management Series, has been prepared for ICMA's Training Institute. The Institute, sponsored by ICMA since 1934, offers in-service training specifically designed for local government administrators, and it has prepared a training course to accompany this book.

Creating this volume was a cooperative effort that involved a large number of people. The editors of the first edition, Wayne F. Anderson, Chester A. Newland, and Richard J. Stillman II, contributed valuable suggestions on how to update the book. Suggestions for updating the first edition were also generously offered by the following (listed with their affiliations at the time of their participation): Eric A. Anderson, city manager, Eau Claire, Wisconsin; David Arnold, former senior editor, ICMA; Neal Berlin, city manager, Arvada, Colorado; Louis

Bezich, county administrator, county of Camden, New Jersey; Robert H. Blodgett, deputy city manager, Aurora, Colorado; Terrell Blodgett, professor, LBJ School of Public Administration, University of Texas, Austin; Donald A. Blubaugh, city manager, Walnut Creek, California; James L. Brimeyer, vice-president, Sathe & Associates., St. Louis Park, Minnesota (formerly city manager, St. Louis Park, Minnesota); Beverly A. Cigler, professor, Pennsylvania State University, Harrisburg; Raymond W. Cox, acting department head, Department of Government, New Mexico State University; Ed Daley, city manager, Winchester, Virginia; Delmer D. Dunn, regents professor and associate vice-president, The University of Georgia, Athens; Daniel Fitzpatrick, vice-president, Blasland, Bouck & Lee, Syracuse, New York (formerly city manager, Augusta, Maine); H. George Frederickson, Edwin O. Stene Professor of Public Administration, The University of Kansas, Lawrence, Kansas; Lawrence F. Keller, associate professor, Maxine Goodman Levin College of Urban Affairs, Cleveland State University, Ohio; Norman R. King, city manager, Moreno Valley, California; Robert S. Kravchik, Department of Public Administration, University of Hartford, West Hartford, Connecticut; Kathleen K. Loewy, School of Public Administration, University of Southern California; John Matzer, Jr., formerly city administrator, San Bernardino, California; John Nalbandian, professor, Department of Public Administration, University of Kansas, Lawrence, Kansas; Gary F. Pokorny, city manager, El Cerrito, California; Greg J. Protasel, associate professor, School of Public Affairs, University of Alaska, Anchorage, Alaska; David Ringsmuth, Department of Political Science, California State University, Northridge, California; Barbara Romzek, associate professor and chairperson, Department of Public Administration, University of Kansas, Lawrence, Kansas; Howard D. Tipton, city manager, Daytona Beach, Florida; Martin Vanacour, city manager, Glendale, Arizona; William D. Wagoner, assistant city manager, Berkley, Michigan.

We extend special thanks to our editorial advisors, who helped in the planning and development of the second edition: Wayne F. Anderson, Distinguished Professor of Public Administration, George Mason University, Fairfax, Virginia; Gerald Fox, county manager, Mecklenburg County, Charlotte, North Carolina; Mary Jane Kuffner Hirt, formerly township manager, O'Hara, Pennsylvania; Michael Letcher, city manager, Winooski, Vermont; David Mora, city manager, Salinas, California; Jan Perkins, assistant city manager, Fremont, California; Jacques Perreault, formerly city manager of Quebec City, Canada; and David Warm, executive director, Mid-America Regional Council, Kansas City, Missouri.

We are grateful to the chapter authors, not only for their contributions but also for their responsiveness, patience, and cooperation during the stages leading to publication. In addition, the author of Chapter 7 would like to thank John J. DeBolske for his assistance.

A number of ICMA staff members contributed to the project: Barbara H. Moore, director of publications; Verity Weston-Truby and Eileen Hughes, who served as project editor and copyeditor respectively; Dawn M. Leland, who coordinated production; Melissa Machulski, who designed the cover for the second edition; and Phyllis Brown, who input the manuscript for production.

William H. Hansell, Jr.
Executive Director, ICMA

Contents

On being an effective local government manager

The context in which local government operates has changed and continues to change in dramatic ways. Demographically, the country is becoming more diverse, particularly with the fast growth of elderly and ethnic minority populations. Economically, for the first time in this century a generation may not be able to meet or exceed the living standard of its parents. Fiscally, local governments are beset by state and national mandates, resistance to increased taxes, and the need for creative public-private cooperation. Socially, dual-career families and women executives are now commonplace. Technologically, the revolutionary effect of the information explosion on the workplace is reshaping the manager's environment. Politically, environmentalism, canny consumerism, and governing bodies that are much more active than in the past all affect the setting in which the manager works.[1] The larger and more complex the jurisdiction, the greater the need for a manager who can see the issues, has a vision of what the community can be, takes charge, and manages effectively.

This book is concerned with effective local government management. Its primary purpose is not to predict the unknown future and how unforeseen changes might affect local government managers. Its focus is on the present and the clearly foreseeable future—on examining what public managers are doing and can do to be more effective today and better equipped for tomorrow. It does, however, stress being prepared to cope with tomorrow. The local government manager must look ahead, as the International City/County Management Association (ICMA) 1991 FutureVisions Consortium noted, to future challenges and future opportunities as one century ends and a new one begins.[2]

In 1918, Richard Childs made this prediction at the annual convention of the International City Managers' Association (now ICMA):

Some day we shall have managers who have achieved national reputation, not by saving taxes or running their cities for a freakishly low expense per capita, but managers who have successfully led their commissions into great new enterprises of service . . . The great city managers of tomorrow will be those who pushed beyond the old horizons and discovered new worlds of service.[3]

Someday has arrived. The role of the local government manager is decidedly more complex now than it was in 1918. The contemporary local government manager is still concerned with potholes and sewer systems, but today responsibilities for human relations are far greater. In 1918 the role of the city manager was clearer, and managing the routine business of the city had the highest priority. Today the role is vaguely defined and highly dynamic. As the environment of local government management changes, the people who sit in the local government manager's office must change too.[4]

ICMA surveys its members annually on the state of the profession. A look at the results of that survey during the 1980s and 1990s shows that local government managers are constantly bombarded by the need to deal with change. Issues such as solid waste management and the aging infrastructure continue to be top priorities for local government managers, but other problems such as illegal drug use, the quality of education, and population changes are emerging as major concerns.

When the first city manager was appointed in 1908 and the first city charter incorporating the basic principles of council-manager government was adopted, the mode of professional local government managers was that of the business manager reporting to an elected board of directors. This board—the city council—viewed its service as just another volunteer effort along with that of the Rotary Club. The manager's basic duties were to keep the books straight and the roads passable.

At the close of the twentieth century, the mayor is often elected at large and council members are often elected from single-member districts and represent widely disparate interest and political philosophies. Moreover, although the profession of local government management began in the cities of the United States, it is now found throughout other types of local government.

Local government managers—bearing diverse titles—serve cities, towns, villages, counties, councils of governments, and state and provincial local government associations throughout North America and the rest of the world. They typically are appointed by, and serve at the discretion of, elected governing bodies or an elected chief executive. Whatever the arrangement, the professional local government manager has significant responsibility for the operations of the local government organization and for working with the council to set overall policy.[5]

This book focuses on the people who manage local governments and are in positions to influence the quality of life in their communities. It also focuses on the need for managerial leadership both in helping to set a course of action for the community and in accomplishing the many tasks faced by cities, counties, and regional councils. The book discusses what local government managers do, how they do it, and perhaps most important, how they can do what they do effectively. It is designed to provide a clearer perspective on public management roles and on the skills needed to perform the job well—skills that may include handling heightened political conflict and sometimes extraordinary demands on the manager's time.

Thus, it is a very personal book about managers, their lives, their problems, and the challenges that make their jobs exciting and desirable. The first chapter provides an overview of the meaning of professionalism; of general management roles and responsibilities; of the importance of leadership in local government; and of hallmarks of effectiveness in local government management.

Historical highlights of professional local government management

First professional local government manager—Charles Asburner, Staunton, Virginia, 1908

First city in the United States to adopt a charter incorporating basic principles of the council-manager plan—Sumter, South Carolina, 1912; and in Canada—Westmount, Quebec, 1913

First large city to adopt the council-manager form—Dayton, Ohio, 1914

First county to adopt the council-manager form—Iredell County, North Carolina, 1927

First meeting of the International City Managers' Association, 1914 (name change in 1969 to International City Management Association and in 1991 to International City/County Management Association)

Adoption of Code of Ethics, 1924 (revisions in 1938, 1952, 1969, 1976, 1990, 1992)

Source: Adapted in part from *Who's Who in Local Government Management, 1991–1992* (Washington, DC: ICMA, 1991).

Professionalism

According to Frederick C. Mosher, a profession is a reasonably explicit lifetime career that usually requires a college degree, often at the master's level. He notes that professions have their

own particularized view of the world and of the agency's role and mission in it. The perspective and motivation of each professional are shaped at least to some extent by the lens provided him by his professional education, his prior professional experience, and by his professional colleagues.[6]

Moreover, professions are characterized as having an "evolving and agreed-upon body of knowledge," as promoting socialization among members, and as sometimes reflecting different norms from those of the organizations that employ their practitioners.[7] Other features of a profession are client recognition, professional identity, professional culture, a code of ethics, and sufficient discretion to perform at a professional level.[8] A formal measure of professional competence is also a standard feature.

Local government managers as professionals

Local government management as a profession conforms to the characteristics outlined above. For example, virtually all professional local government managers have college degrees, and increasingly, master's degrees are required for executive positions. The National Association of Schools of Public Affairs and Administration (NASPAA) promulgates standards and accredits master's degree programs on the basis of an agreed-upon body of knowledge and skills, and NASPAA and ICMA have jointly developed guidelines for local government management education.[9] Local government managers are a rather tightly knit group whose members know, consult, and learn from one another, and they are recognized by the public as professionals. Local government managers hold widely shared beliefs on such issues as efficiency, representation, individual rights, and social equity, and they may agonize over the conflicts that sometimes arise between efficiency and other values.[10] Such conflicts illustrate that professional and organizational norms are sometimes at variance. Finally, professional local managers who are members of ICMA place a great deal of importance on personal integrity and adherence to the ICMA Code of Ethics.

The ICMA Code of Ethics

The ICMA Code of Ethics, which has existed since 1924, is a point of distinction for ICMA members, and they take pride in the process established to monitor themselves and sanction members who violate the code. ICMA's Committee on Professional Conduct is responsible for reviewing charges and bringing sanctions against errant members; sanctions include private censure, public censure, expulsion, and a bar against reinstatement. Moreover, as one city manager put it, "Many public organizations have recognized the need to do more than establish standards of ethics . . . [they also give] employees an understanding of why ethical behavior is necessary."[11]

Both ICMA and other professional organizations may have enforcement problems on occasion. For example, although ICMA can affect the behavior of its members, it recognizes that it cannot dictate to governing boards. Anyone can declare himself or herself to be a manager, and any given council, commission, or executive board may hire a nonprofessional person. That fact has led to an ongoing debate about the need for an accreditation or certification process that would require local public managers—like public accountants, physicians, and attorneys—to be board certified.

Tenets of the ICMA Code of Ethics

The purpose of ICMA is to increase the proficiency of city managers, county managers, and other municipal administrators and to strengthen the quality of urban government through professional management. To further these objectives, certain ethical principles shall govern the conduct of every member of ICMA, who shall:

1. Be dedicated to the concepts of effective and democratic local government by responsible elected officials and believe that professional general management is essential to the achievement of this objective.
2. Affirm the dignity and worth of the services rendered by government and maintain a constructive, creative, and practical attitude toward urban affairs and a deep sense of social responsibility as a trusted public service.
3. Be dedicated to the highest ideals of honor and integrity in all public and personal relationships in order that the member may merit the respect and confidence of the elected officials, of other officials and employees, and of the public.
4. Recognize that the chief function of local government at all times is to serve the best interests of all of the people.
5. Submit policy proposals to elected officials; provide them with facts and advice on matters of policy as a basis for making decisions and setting community goals; and uphold and implement municipal policies adopted by elected officials.

6. Recognize that elected representatives of the people are entitled to the credit for the establishment of municipal policies; responsibility for policy execution rests with the members.
7. Refrain from participation in the election of the members of the employing legislative body, and from all partisan political activities which would impair performance as a professional administrator.
8. Make it a duty continually to improve the member's professional ability and to develop the competence of associates in the use of management techniques.
9. Keep the community informed on municipal affairs; encourage communication between the citizens and all municipal officers; emphasize friendly and courteous service to the public; and seek to improve the quality and range of public service.
10. Resist any encroachment on professional responsibilities, believing the member should be free to carry out official policies without interference, and handle each problem without discrimination on the basis of principle and justice.
12. Seek no favor; believe that personal aggrandizement or profit secured by confidential information or by misuse of public time is dishonest.

Source: Abridged from "ICMA Code of Ethics with Guidelines," *Who's Who in Local Government Management, 1991–1992* (Washington, DC: ICMA, 1991), 3–4.

On being a manager

Management often is used as a generic term to cover all individuals responsible for the administration of an organization. Harold Gortner, Julianne Mahler, and Jeanne Bell Nicholson argue persuasively that management consists of a three-part hierarchy of executives, managers, and supervisors. Executives are responsible for establishing the structure of the organization, for having a broad and general view of organizational purpose and effectiveness, for goal setting, for creating the general work environment, and for being the chief contact with the world outside the organization. Managers focus on processes and procedures and on supervising other supervisors; much of their work involves coordination. Supervisors are responsible for achieving specific organizational objectives and, accordingly, they focus on motivation, productivity, and interpersonal relations.[12]

These distinctions illustrate the importance of leadership in the executive's job—not merely in getting a task accomplished but also in setting the whole tone and pace of the organization. Chester I. Barnard in 1938 noted that leadership encompasses both technical functions, such as maintaining effective communication, accomplishing tasks, and formulating goals, and a higher aspect—that of responsibility for establishing an organizational culture and inculcating organizational values in the staff.[13] These observations are still relevant today.

Top level local government managers such as city managers, county managers, and executive directors of councils or associations of governments are executives, whatever their official titles. Consequently, they have broad responsibilities for establishing the organizational culture, solidifying values, and determining the direction of the organization. The breadth of their responsibilities far exceeds that of the duties of the city manager of 1908; consequently, the emphasis in this book is on leadership.

**If you walk around city hall or any city facilities, you hear people laughing . . .
I think that's a great sign—people are enjoying what they're doing.**
Martin Vanacour

Roles of managers

Early writers on organization and management—the classicists—sought to find "one best way" to operate an organization. They believed in universal principles of organization, and their thinking allowed little room for the dynamics of people or politics. Later writers incorporated the importance of interpersonal relations and the organizational environment in developing first the human relations (neoclassical) approach, and then systems theory. A further step in the evolution of the theory of organizations and management revolves around the idiosyncrasies of individual organizations and the values, traditions, and practices that constitute their corporate culture. One aspect of this theoretical development has been the expansion of the concept of what managers do—what roles they play.

Henry Mintzberg, an observer of and frequent commentator on managerial roles and behavior, identified three major sets or categories of roles—interpersonal, informational, and decisional.[14] (See Figure 1–1.)

The three interpersonal roles—figurehead, leader, and liaison—are related to a manager's formal authority. As figurehead, the manager represents the organization and performs ceremonial duties, lending a positive presence in appropriate situations. As leader, the manager is the head of an organization—someone who can hire and assign people and who is responsible for training them and motivating them to perform. Mintzberg explains, "Formal authority vests him [the manager] with great potential power; leadership determines in large part how much of it he will realize."[15] As liaison, the manager works with people outside the formal chain of command—building a network with others who have a relationship to the organization, have influence over it, or have expectations of it.

Figure 1–1 Major categories of managerial roles.

Interpersonal roles	Informational roles	Decisional roles
Figurehead	Monitor	Entrepreneur
Leader	Disseminator	Disturbance handler
Liaison	Spokesperson	Resource allocator
		Negotiator

The three informational roles—monitor, disseminator, and spokesperson—make the manager the "nerve center" of the organization. As monitor, the manager scans the external environment to determine what might affect the organization and brings new information inside. As disseminator, he or she shares information within the organization and makes connections between the external environment and the internal system. As a spokesperson, the manager presents the organizational perspective and shares information with others outside the organization who are interested in or affected by it. The manager is at the "neck of the hourglass," standing between the organization and the outside world.

The four decisional roles—entrepreneur, disturbance handler, resource allocator, and negotiator—focus on how the manager uses formal authority, interpersonal relationships, and information to take action. As entrepreneur, the manager tries to improve the organization and help it adapt to change. This is a *proactive* role. The role of disturbance handler, on the other hand, involves responding to crises; it is *reactive*. The role of resource allocator involves deciding who will get what—for example, money, time, attention, and work assignments. As negotiator, the manager works out problems, resolves conflicts, and develops compromises.

Mintzberg's approach ties it all together. He argues that the three sets of roles overlap to form an integrated and very busy whole. "To sum up, we find that the manager . . . is overburdened with work. With the increasing complexity of modern organizations and their problems, he is destined to become more so."[16]

Leonard Sayles offers another behavioral view that pares down the manager's role to two basic functions—contingency response and reduction of uncertainty. Both functions focus on how managers respond to change—how they adjust the system and keep it going. Contingency responses are necessary to cope with potential or actual threats to the integrity of the routine. Sayles says such threats require managers to develop "unanticipatable, going-into-action-when-needed responses." Reduction of uncertainty is a proactive function similar to that of Mintzberg's entrepreneurial manager. Effective managers, Sayles says, seek to improve organizations by anticipating and adapting quickly to external changes. "In simplest terms, this is the introduction of change—but change with a purpose: to cope with threatening instabilities."[17]

Public sector managers are particularly sensitive to change and frequently observe that change is the one constant in their lives. As local government becomes more politicized—through structural changes such as direct election of mayors and election of councils by district and through the intrusion of single-issue politics—managers become more vulnerable. "Once some managers begin to pick up momentum in carrying out their [own] agenda, they run the risk of forgetting to check the political weather vane periodically. When managers fail to notice and adapt to political changes . . . they risk getting blown away."[18]

Public versus private management

Many similarities exist in management roles found in the public, private, and nonprofit sectors, allowing all sectors to fit Mintzberg's model. Nevertheless, political accountability to the governing board—and indirectly to citizens—casts a somewhat different light on the public manager. Only the public manager bears the major responsibility for carrying out public mandates and working with the governing body to resolve political conflict.

The comments of David Mora, based on his managerial experience, neatly summarize one side of an ongoing argument about whether public management is fundamentally different from private management.[19]

Our constituencies and the demands placed by these constituencies on public management force us not to run as private type enterprises. We cannot run local government with a profit motive in mind.

Public service by its very nature is not meant to always run as effectively and efficiently as private enterprise. The business of government is not business. Rather, we need to recognize that government is not the most efficient and the most effective service provider; if a profit was possible or practical, then the private sector would provide that service. As public service providers, we need to recognize that revenues paid to government through taxes are actually subsidies to keep an operation running that cannot be run effectively in the private sector.[20]

Clearly, Mora opts for the side that says public service has a distinctive quality—that in its goals, funding base, quest for social justice, and responsiveness to citizen demands, it is unique. Moreover, the influence of citizens and interest groups, the quagmire in some public bureaucracies, the turnover in legislative bodies, and the sheer amount of managerial time spent dealing with extraorganizational individuals and groups exemplify additional differences between public and private organizations.

Personnel, including the city manager, must have the fortitude and psychological make-up to be able to operate in an environment of citizen hostility, constant demands that exceed our resources, and greater expectations for customized services. We're increasingly dealing with morale problems due to these stress factors.

Jan Perkins

The similarities tend to be found in the internal operations of the organization and in the more technical aspects of management such as motivation, time management, and benefits administration. For example, public and private managers have struggled equally with the rising cost of health care and the resulting escalation of the cost of the employee benefits package. And managers in both sectors constantly strive to achieve a level of employee satisfaction sufficient to maintain high productivity. County administrator Jan Winters directly compares the public and private sectors:

Although the pressures on local government at times seem enormous, they really are not that different from the wake-up call most American businesses are receiving. Once-invincible giants of industry are now fighting for their very survival.[21]

However, most local government managers perceive differences in public and private management. They see today's public manager as constantly barraged by overtly political events. He or she is buffeted by council fighting over the drawing of electoral districts, the demands of highly organized single-interest groups, contentious mayoral elections, an increase in citizens' use of the initiative power, and special elections to respond to state mandates or court orders. The dean of American city managers, L. P. Cookingham, put it this way:

If the mayor and the manager don't agree, you have to call for a meeting to talk over the friction. If it can't be resolved, then you get rid of the city manager. The mayor and manager have to have a good working relationship for the city to prosper. The city manager is a hired hand. He has to be the one to go.

The two drawbacks to a council-manager system are a poor council or a poor manager. A poor manager is an easier problem to fix. You fire him. A poor council is another story.[22]

Knowledge, skills, and abilities of the manager

Over a twenty-year period, John Kerrigan and David Hinton tracked local managers' perceptions of their changing roles and of the knowledge, skills, and abilities they most needed to cope with their jobs. They found the most important skills to be those with broad application—understanding the values that motivate human behavior, handling interpersonal relations, being able to "size up" the political situation in the community, and assessing community needs. Hinton and Kerrigan point out that managers in the 1970s and 1980s failed to see the emergence of economic development as the preeminent issue of the 1990s and speculate that managers in the 1990s may undervalue the importance of relating to and understanding ethnic minorities and other culturally distinct groups.[23]

Results of the annual ICMA State of the Profession Survey since the mid 1980s show that conflict resolution is the skill that managers feel they most need to build, a finding that testifies to the turbulent political environment in which they work. In contrast, what might be considered more abstract skills, such as decision analysis and economics, have tended to decline steadily in importance. Financial management has consistently been considered important by almost one-third of the respondents. These responses are consistent with the predictions of the ICMA Future Horizons Committee, which in 1979 identified brokering and negotiating as the key skills needed for the 1980s and 1990s.[24]

From 1988 to 1991, the ICMA FutureVisions Consortium further examined the skills required to manage local government and identified the following thirteen important managerial roles:[25]

1. Consensus builder
2. Educator on community issues
3. Translator/interpreter of community values
4. Problem solver
5. Process leader
6. Convener of interested parties and diverse community groups
7. Team builder/mentor
8. Source of empowerment
9. Change agent
10. Champion of new technologies
11. Facilitator of conflict resolution
12. Bearer of ethical standards
13. Champion of leadership development within the community.

As a *consensus builder*, the manager is responsible for gaining staff agreement on tactics and procedures for policy implementation and for helping governing board members reach agreement on policy issues. Without such consensus, local government will have great difficulty coping with the changes occurring now and in the foreseeable future. In one locale, the issue may be traditional: commercial real estate developers versus home owners, each with elected representatives on the governing board. In another jurisdiction, an issue may arise out of cultural diversity, for example when minorities constitute a majority of the population of a municipality but its affirmative action policies have failed to produce a diversified work force.

You can go in as a yes-person . . . you can try to build coalitions, and hope people will follow you . . . or you can knock heads . . . I'm not a head-knocker. So I guess I'm a coalition-builder. I like lots of input.
                                                                            Melinda Carlton

---

The role of *educator on community issues* refers to the manager's part in using and disseminating information wisely. As the FutureVisions report notes, the manager must make sure that everyone in the "community has the training and education to contribute to its economic and social health . . . it is not enough to share the 'what' if the 'why' is unclear."[26] According to long-time city manager Howard Tipton, "The use of knowledge to educate the community is a primary responsibility of the manager . . . [and] Briefing council members on important issues is one of the manager's required duties."[27]

As *translator/interpreter of community values*, the manager must not only discern the values of the community—such as a strong preference for no growth and environmental protection—but also help to guide citizens toward values that benefit the entire community.

The role of *problem solver* is more conventional. From the beginning, managers have addressed problems. In the early days, these were often engineering problems such as building a road or a bridge. Today, infrastructure problems are again rising in importance, but they are only one of the many types of problems that the modern manager faces. For example, San Antonio created Alamo City Heat, a rock band composed of police officers, as a device for reaching schoolchildren with an anti-drug message to which they have been quite receptive.[28] The problem is wide-spread; the solution is innovative.

Managers traditionally have been *process leaders*—those responsible for human relations, communication, and decision making. As local governments struggle to deal with fiscal and economic changes, globalization, multiculturalism, citizens' demands, and complex ethical issues, developing processes becomes more impor-tant. This role cuts across many others. It requires the ability to motivate staff, find meaningful avenues of involvement for citizens, satisfy citizens who view them-selves as consumers, seek innovation and not settle for the commonplace, and find solutions to problems of increasing complexity.

"Do things right" as well as "do the right things" administratively.
Kevin C. Duggan

The role of *convener of interested parties and diverse community groups* requires the brokering and negotiating skills emphasized in the Future Horizons report. It overlaps the role of *facilitator of conflict resolution*. The modern manager must constantly deal with competing viewpoints—for example, labor versus manage-ment, Asian American versus African American, old guard versus immigrant; with complex contracts for services such as solid waste disposal and energy recovery; with myriad demands for additional services with no increase in taxes; with national and state government representatives over compliance with mandates such as air quality controls. For the county manager or state or regional association director, the brokering is often among competing communities—most frequently when sev-eral are seeking the same economic development opportunity—and between gov-ernments and industry to establish partnerships.

The traditional role of *team builder/mentor* becomes more important given some of the real frustrations of public service today—fiscal austerity, heightened citizen demand for services, and calls for greater accountability. In the future, this role will tend to merge with that of *source of empowerment*. James Belasco admonishes:

Empower your people—every day. Show your vision in action—every day. Talk about the vision's success—every day. Or else—your people will forget and your vision will be history.[29]

Both of these roles pertain to relating to the people in the organization in a positive way and encouraging their participation.

Although the concept of PM [participatory management] is frustrating to some American managers, it *can* be extremely helpful in increasing employee satisfaction and productiv-ity, lowering absence rates, and in promoting receptivity to changes. The problem is how to get it to work for you rather than to be merely another fad.[30]

Thus far, this chapter has stressed the constant change that buffets a local gov-ernment manager. However, the manager is also a *change agent* who must understand shifts in community values and demands and perceive internal stresses, then act to bring about needed changes. Warren Bennis states, "People in authority must be social architects, studying and shaping what we call 'the culture of work,' examining the values and norms of organizations and the ways they are transmitted to the individual, and wherever necessary, altering them." He further calls for a "transitive organization" to facilitate the appropriate and timely promotion of people to levels of increased responsibility within the organization.[31]

The modern manager must also be a *champion of new technologies* in order to encourage the rapid development of sophisticated information resources that enable organizations to be more productive and interactive. For example, in Yokohama, Japan, the fire department has equipped its fire stations, offices, and command cars with telefax machines that allow rapid transmission during a fire of such information as building floor plans.[32] Managers also will need to incorporate new technologies as they promote the economic diversification of their communities.

Another role included in the FutureVisions report is that of *bearer of ethical standards*. This role is familiar to local managers, given the primacy of the professional code of ethics. A newer concern is that of the manager's behavior toward others inside and outside the organization. Edward Freeman and Daniel Gilbert call for a humanistic approach to management that acknowledges that "strategy and ethics go hand in hand. Strategy is concerned with purposes and values, and so is ethics."[33]

The final role identified in the FutureVisions report is that of *champion of leadership development within the community*. This role has two dimensions. First, more diverse populations, specialized political interests, and a lack of community consensus all have contributed to the politicization of local government through changes in electoral procedures and the addition of items to the policy agenda. These factors have also created a need for the professional manager to ensure that citizens are prepared to be more active participants in local government. Second, most managers are well aware that they spend more time than in the past dealing with the council and tending to its needs and requests—in essence, helping council members to improve their leadership abilities.

Leadership

Many local government managers are uncomfortable with discussions of leadership. They interpret leadership to mean overt, political leadership that calls for the manager to be the "front person" on controversial local issues and the key individual in reconciling or, at least, refereeing major political disputes. At the other extreme, some individuals may agree with the definition of leadership offered by Mintzberg, whose concept was confined to motivating employees. Both definitions are relevant but too limited. On one hand, managers would be foolhardy indeed to play the part of front person, usurping council and mayoral prerogatives. On the other hand, they would be derelict in their duty if they tried to motivate and empower employees in a vacuum, divorced from the political reality of the community. A broader view of leadership is offered by James McGregor Burns.

Transactional and transformational leadership

Burns examines two types of leadership—*transactional* and *transformational*. He says that, basically, transactional leadership is getting things done and that the bulk of leadership is, in fact, transactional. Managers are comfortable with this half of the dichotomy because it focuses on those procedures and techniques in which they are trained. Burns's other concept is transformational leadership—determining what should be done. Some local government managers are less comfortable with this aspect because it deals with values, political judgments, and even community

---

This world has three kinds of people: those who make it happen, those who watch it happen, and those who do not know what hit them. The time for watching is over.

James Crupi

---

moral standards.[34] Nevertheless, the job of the local executive encompasses both the transformational and transactional dimensions of leadership.

Two conclusions of the Future Horizons study suggest that organizations may come to acknowledge the need for both transformational and transactional leadership by assigning different individuals to develop each type of leadership. These conclusions were that ''local governments will require managers who can lead by being led'' (transformational leadership) and that ''a new profession within the profession—that of internal manager—will emerge in some places'' (transactional leadership). The report continues by emphasizing the

ability to help people see more clearly their own desires and goals. Leadership is continuing quietly to instill in people the belief that they can successfully contend with the future . . . Managers [in the future] will rely much less on fixed legal parameters—much more on political realities and strategic thinking and persuasiveness . . . The manager as broker and negotiator, or unobtrusive leader, will dominate the time and resources of the top professional . . . The more traditional internal management functions—that often require entirely different skills, knowledge, and experience—will fall to a new group of specialists.[35]

The idea of specialized skills among local government managers may cause managers to question whether the days of truly professional management have ended, replaced by a more volatile, politicized model. James Griesemer observes:

Today, managers are often required to be more involved with policy than management, more concerned with equity than efficiency, and more sensitive to matters of due process than tangible results . . . They have moved from a position where contributions were based on specialized knowledge to one where contributions are based more on political or interpersonal skills than technical expertise. They have become actors in an arena that, by definition, is judgmental and not technical.[36]

However, the traditional definition of leadership has not disappeared. When one considers the skills and attributes cited by the FutureVisions Consortium, the emphasis on the interpersonal roles identified by Mintzberg is considerable: consensus builder, team builder/mentor, source of empowerment, facilitator of conflict resolution. Nevertheless, the consortium also called for informational and decisional roles that recognize the changing environment: community educator, translator of community values, convenor of interested parties and diverse community groups, and champion of leadership development. The key for the manager is to exercise this broader leadership without appearing too political.[37]

Commenting on why a modern local government manager cannot remain invisible (but must always be cautious), city manager Camille Cates Barnett states, ''I think it is abdicating for a manager not to tell people what she thinks. But you don't ever want to upstage your council or . . . assume the role of politician.''[38]

Other approaches to leadership

Modern leadership theory emphasizes effectiveness. Originally, this approach focused only on leadership style, which is determined in part by the relative emphasis that an individual places on task performance and interpersonal relations, with effectiveness resulting from a balanced emphasis on each. More recent management literature stresses the importance of situation, or contingency, as the prime determinant of managerial effectiveness. This line of thought might be called the school of "it all depends."[39] Kenneth Blanchard notes that no one style of leadership is always effective: "Successful leaders must adapt themselves to the particular situation."[40] Herbert Kaufman thinks that timing and chance determine effectiveness far more than any management style.[41]

Local government managers are in effect obliged to adopt the contingency approach in order to deal with different types of local governments and electoral arrangements. Managers quickly recognize both the legal and political differences among various forms of government such as council-manager, chief administrative officer, reform county, non-reform county, council of governments, and regional association. Their own authority varies depending on the form of government.

Furthermore, managers certainly perceive differences in cities where the mayor is popularly elected rather than chosen by the council or where council members are elected by district.[42] Every manager also recognizes that changes in the mayor's office or in the council often mean a significant shift for the manager: one group of elected officials may want the manager to be overtly involved in community issues whereas another group may want to limit the manager's role to responsibility for council relations and management, with virtually no community role.

Changes in governmental structure can be overwhelming. For example, in 1990 in New Zealand, the central government turned control of local government over to local authority. Sir Ross Jansen, president of the New Zealand Local Government Association at the time, explained the difficulty of dealing with the reformed New Zealand system this way: "Local government has been willing to meet this challenge and the responsibilities it involves. It is up to the central government to provide the trust and cooperation and an appropriate sharing of resources, which are essential to the program's success."[43]

A manager's effectiveness within the same community can vary considerably from issue to issue. Erwin Hargrove and John Glidewell describe four conditions that may make resolution of a problem virtually impossible: (1) when the clientele

---

Local government in Poland   Perhaps nowhere is the importance of structure—and of time and chance—more evident in the 1990s than in the various countries that were once within the sphere of influence of the former Soviet Union. These governments are faced with the transition from a government dominated by a central bureaucracy to democratic local politics and administration.

In Poland, for example, the key tasks facing officials are to develop their capacity to govern with no recent experience in self-government and to develop their capacity to manage effectively. In the process, they must learn and apply unfamiliar techniques for budgeting, tax collection, program evaluation, and personnel administration.

For forty-five years, local government in Poland was run by national bureaucrats, and little importance was placed on local ability to identify and solve problems, make sure that things worked, or innovate. Moreover, the magnitude of the job to be done is considerable. For example, most of the housing in Polish cities was built just after World War II and is government owned. It is devoid of the aesthetic appeal that the Polish people cherish, and has not been maintained over the years. In addition, water and air pollution are rampant, industrial plants are outdated, and much of the infrastructure is crumbling.

Thus, the end of Soviet domination in Central Europe has created an opportunity for citizens there to develop their own forms of government and management practices appropriate to the job at hand. Nevertheless, the challenges are daunting.

have little political legitimacy (e.g., if homeless citizens are not recognized as a group with significant influence); (2) when many constituencies with conflicting views exist (e.g., if homeowners, taxpayers, real estate developers, and business people have different views on the desirability of bringing in an industry that may tend to pollute the environment); (3) when respect for professional authority is weak (e.g., if social scientists rather than physical scientists are cited as authorities on the physical effects of pollution); and (4) when the organization's "political myth" (public acceptance of its goals and major strategies for accomplishing them) is unstable or controversial (e.g., if a governing body is committed to growth at any cost).[44]

The effective professional local government manager

Local government managers need to be familiar with the leadership theories discussed above in order to reflect on what their own leadership role should be. However, a practicing manager's purpose is not to apply labels to what he or she does or to fit behavior into a theory; it is to be an effective professional local government manager. The roles that the local government manager must assume have changed over time as local governments themselves have changed. Thus, managers of today and tomorrow must be concerned with understanding the dynamics of the environment in which they operate, with adapting their personal style to the idiosyncrasies of that environment, with helping the governing board to effect policies that are of maximum benefit to the community, and with keeping their jobs while behaving responsibly, ethically, and creatively.

Facing [the] challenges [of the future] will increasingly be beyond the immediate skills of elected officials, who generally serve on a part-time basis. The manager then must assume a responsibility for very carefully guiding and leading within the community without being seen as an invader of the policy-makers' position.

Mary Jane Kuffner Hirt

This book defines *effectiveness* in the broadest sense, to encompass both efficiency and economy. Put simply, it involves doing the right things well—whatever the contingencies. The effective manager must not only get the right things done, but must use creative management practices to do so in the context of financial and other constraints. Effectiveness means winning the game—most of the time. And it means knowing when not to play the game. Clearly, timing is crucial. The book also stresses the importance of good interpersonal skills, ranging from brokering and negotiating, to empowering employees and citizens, to being sensitive to multicultural issues.

Definitions of effectiveness are as diverse as definitions of management roles and responsibilities. Peter Drucker says effectiveness is a "habit," or a complex set of practices. He identifies five "habits of mind" that executives need:

1. Managing the portion of their time that they can control and knowing where the time goes
2. Focusing on outward contributions, gearing their efforts to results rather than work
3. Building on strengths they have at their disposal, including their own strengths as well as those of their colleagues, subordinates, and the situations they face
4. Concentrating on the few major areas that will produce the most outstanding results by setting clear priorities and sticking with them
5. Making effective decisions, knowing that a decision is "a judgment based on 'dissenting opinions' rather than on 'consensus on the facts.' "[45]

The distinctions among executives, managers, and supervisors are important in attempting to measure effectiveness. To reiterate, executives are responsible for establishing the structure of the organization, for having a broad and general view of organizational purpose and effectiveness, for goal setting, for creating the general work environment, and for relating to the external environment. Managers are more attuned to processes and procedures. Supervisors are concerned with details of production, personnel issues, and task accomplishment. *A local government manager is all three*—executive, manager, and supervisor—and is evaluated accordingly. Moreover, public managers may be unique in that they often must take responsibility for devising the process by which the governing board evaluates them.

No definition of effectiveness exists that establishes precisely what the public manager can and should strive for, but effective managers display some common traits:

1. A sense of commitment to the job, the goals, and the purpose of whatever the manager undertakes
2. Attention to the broad picture—the overall results for which the organization is striving
3. Personal self-assurance
4. Faith in the people in the organization and a willingness to let them excel
5. Attention to resources, including people, money, and opportunities
6. Awareness of important relationships and institutions outside the organization.

An effective manager is one who causes the organization he or she heads to achieve the "results" goals and "results" objectives that have been set for it and who causes the organization to achieve these goals and objectives on time and with optimum efficiency.

Arthur A. Mendonsa

Looking ahead

The chapters that follow pursue in depth some of the concepts introduced in this chapter and provide guidance on how local government managers can become *effective* managers. The chapters focus on the theaters of operation that shape and lend vitality to the manager's job—community relations, the governing body, the organization, community planning and development, and intergovernmental relations. The manager's own well-being is the subject of the final chapter.

Chapter 2 examines the partnership between the manager and the community that he or she serves, pointing out that the manager cannot delegate responsibility for this partnership. It emphasizes the differences among types of communities and the many political actors in the local arena.

Chapter 3 focuses on how the manager can help the governing body to be effective. It points out likely stumbling blocks in governing body-manager relations and suggests ways to resolve conflicts.

Chapter 4 explores the manager's responsibility to establish and maintain excellence in the organization. It stresses the manager's role in creating an environment that promotes excellence and in empowering employees to be productive and creative.

Chapter 5 is a companion to Chapter 4. It also looks inside the organization, focusing on the manager's responsiblity to ensure that public services of high quality are provided. Key topics include implementation strategies, alternative delivery systems, and performance evaluation.

Chapter 6 looks at the public executive's role in shaping the future of the community. It focuses on the necessity for strategic planning and economic development in any modern local government.

Chapter 7 focuses on the role of the local government manager in relation to other units and levels of government—an area of enormous change since the days of large-scale federal funding. Being an effective participant in the intergovernmental—and sometimes international—arena and an effective representative of the community requires an informed, ''street-wise,'' highly skilled professional.

Chapter 8, the final chapter, focuses on the most subtle influence on performance of these complex roles—the manager's personal identity and well-being. A public manager is also an individual and a family member who needs to manage self as well as the organization to be truly effective.

Recap

This chapter has focused on the knowledge, skills, and abilities that a present-day manager needs to be effective. It acknowledges the evolution of professional local government management, describes the difficulties of professionals in a dynamic and highly charged political environment, and compares public and private sector managers. The hope is that practicing and prospective managers will be made aware of the importance of providing professional leadership in the public sector and that they will be challenged to maximize the effectiveness of their own performance.

Managerial effectiveness checklist

The following checklist may be used by the governing board or executive team to evaluate the manager or modified by the manager to perform a self-evaluation.[46]

Executive leadership

How well does the manager empower others?

Is the manager visible in the community without infringing on the prerogatives of elected officials?

How well does the manager represent the community (to other governments, prospective businesses, etc.)?

Does the manager seem to keep up professionally?

Has the manager been effective in setting an appropriate tone for the organization?

Has the manager created local team spirit?

Management processes

How well does the manager anticipate issues?

How effective are the manager's processes for handling issues?

Is the manager effective in developing management policies, procedures, and systems?

Has the manager built an effective management team?

Does the manager build the capacity of employees through training?

Supervision

Is the manager a good personnel administrator? Does he or she handle hiring, firing, and promoting staff well?

How well does the manager monitor and regulate the performance of subordinates?

Does the manager provide clear direction to subordinates?

How effective is the manager in interpreting council goals and directives for the staff?

How effective is the manager in counseling staff on problems?

Manager's tasks

Does the manager seem to handle complaints effectively?

How well does the manager handle problems?

How well does the manager provide information and analyses to equip the governing board to make decisions?

How effective is the manager in developing the budget? It is a useful policy tool for the council? Is it fiscally sound?

How effective is the manager in preparing the council agenda?

1   See Judith Waldrop, "You'll Know It's the 21st Century When . . ." *Public Management* (January 1991): 2, and Amy Cohen Paul, *Future Challenges, Future Opportunities: The Final Report of the ICMA FutureVisions Consortium*, with an introduction by James R. Griesemer (Washington, DC: International City Management Association, 1991).
2   Paul, ibid.
3   Leonard D. White, *The City Manager* (Chicago: University of Chicago Press, 1927), 149.
4   See Chester A. Newland, "The Future of Council-Manager Government," in *Ideal and Practice in Council-Manager Government*, ed. George W. Frederickson (Washington, DC: International City Management Association, 1989), 257-271 for a useful history of local government as well as a look at what the future holds for the manager.
5   ICMA's "Criteria for Guidelines for Recognition" of council-manager and general management positions set forth in *Who's Who in Local Government Management, 1991–1992* stipulate that the manager must have considerable responsibility for budget, personnel, and operations as well as for policy formulation and implementation, although council-manager and general management positions will vary somewhat in the magnitude of this responsibility. The council is always the final authority on policy issues.
6   Frederick C. Mosher, *Democracy and the Public Service* (Englewood Cliffs, NJ: Prentice-Hall, 1968), 106, 122.
7   Steven W. Hays and T. Zane Reeves, *Personnel Management in the Public Sector* (Boston: Allyn and Bacon, 1984), 437–438.
8   Daniel W. Fitzpatrick, "City Management: Profession or Guild," *Public Management* (January/February 1990): 32.
9   National Association of Schools of Public Affairs and Administration and the International City/County Management Association, *Guidelines for Local Government Management Education*, unpublished report of the NASPAA/ICMA Task Force on Local Government Education, Washington, DC, 1992.
10 John Nalbandian, *Professionalism in Local Government: Transformations in the Roles, Responsibilities,* and Values of City Managers (San Francisco: Jossey-Bass, 1991), 87–89.
11 Stephen Bonczek, "Creating an Ethical Work Environment: Enhancing Ethics Awareness in Local Government," *Public Management* (October 1991): 20.
12 Harold F. Gortner, Julianne Mahler, and Jeanne Bell Nicholson, *Organization Theory* (Chicago: Dorsey, 1987), 291–294.
13 Chester I. Barnard, *The Functions of the Executive* (Cambridge: Harvard University Press, 1962), 217–234, 258–284 (originally published in 1938).
14 Henry Mintzberg, *The Nature of Managerial Work* (New York: Harper & Row, 1973), 92–93.
15 Henry Mintzberg, "The Manager's Job: Folklore and Fact," *Harvard Business Review* 49 (July/August 1975): 58.
16 Ibid., 173.
17 Leonard R. Sayles, *Leadership* (New York: McGraw-Hill, 1979), 27.
18 Anne Amoury, "The 7 Symptons of a Manager in Trouble: or How to Spot/Stop a Pink Slip Before It Hits Your Desk," *Public Management* (December 1990): 8.
19 The classic literature on the issue of differences in public and private management includes the following authors, who argue that differences are minimal: Michael A. Murray, "Comparing Public and Private Management: An Exploratory Essay," *Public Administration Review* 35 (July/August 1975): 364, and Hal G. Rainey, Robert W. Backoff, and Charles H. Levine, "Comparing Public and Private Organizations," *Public Administration Review* 36 (March/April 1976: 233. Those who argue that basic differences exist include John D. Millett, *Organization for the Public Service* (Princeton, NJ: Van Nostrand, 1966); James D. Thompson and William J. McEwen, "Organization Goals and Environment: Goal Setting as an Interaction Process," *American Sociological Review* 28 (February 1958): 23; and Graham T. Allison, Jr., "Public and Private Management: Are They Fundamentally Alike in All Unimportant Respects?", *Public Management: Public and Private Perspectives*, ed. James L. Perry and Kenneth L. Kraemer (Palo Alto, CA: Mayfield, 1983) 727–792.

20 David Mora, letter to the editor, April 7, 1992, as part of the review of prospective chapters for this book.

21 Jan Winters, "Rethinking Local Government," *Public Management* (November 1991): 2.

22 Jane Mobley, "Advice to Managers: You're Expendable," *Governing* (February 1988): 47.

23 John Kerrigan and David Hinton, "Knowledge and Skill Needs for Tomorrow's Public Administrators," *Public Administration Review* 40 (September/October 1980): 469, and David Hinton and John Kerrigan, "Tracing the Changing Knowledge and Skill Needs and Service Activities of Public Managers," in *Ideal and Practice in Council-Manager Government*, ed. Frederickson (Washington, DC: International City Management Association, 1989), 155–163.

24 Laurence Rutter, *The Essential Community* (Washington, DC: International City Management Association, 1980), 126–127.

25 Paul, *Future Challenges, Future Opportunities*, 4.

26 Ibid.

27 Howard D. Tipton, "Response" to Martha L. Hale, "The Nature of City Managers' Work," in Frederickson, *Ideal and Practice*, 178.

28 Alexander F. Briseño, "Managing Local Government with Your Back to the Wall," *Governing* (October 1991): 11.

29 James A. Belasco, *Teaching the Elephant to Dance: The Manager's Guide to Empowering Change* (New York: Penguin Books, 1991), 151.

30 Paul R. Britton and John W. Stallings, *Leadership is Empowering People* (Lanham, MD: University Press of America, 1986), 41–42.

31 Warren Bennis, *Why Leaders Can't Lead: The Unconscious Conspiracy Continues* (San Francisco: Jossey-Bass, 1990), 155, 157–158.

32 *ICMA Newsletter* (November 19, 1990): 8.

33 R. Edward Freeman and Daniel R. Gilbert, Jr., *Corporate Strategy and The Search for Ethics* (Englewood Cliffs, NJ: Prentice-Hall, 1988), 174.

34 James McGregor Burns, *Leadership* (New York: Harper & Row, Torchback ed., 1979), 4.

35 "New Worlds of Service," *Public Management* (January/February 1980): 8.

36 James R. Griesemer, "Restoring Relevance to Local Government Management," *Public Management* (September 1990): 10.

37 For practical tips, see Kevin C. Duggan, "Leadership Without Appearing Political," *Public Management* (February 1991): 12.

38 Alan Ehrenhalt, "The New City Manager is (1) Invisible, (2) Anonymous, (3) Non-Political, (4) None of the Above," *Governing* (September 1990): 45.

39 Although "it all depends" is a common expression, its use to convey the essence of the contingency theory of management dates from Harvey Sherman's book *It All Depends: A Pragmatic Approach to Organization* (University, AL: University of Alabama Press, 1966).

40 Kenneth Blanchard, "Choosing the Right Management Style," *Public Management* (August 1986): 16.

41 Herbert Kaufman, *Time, Chance, and Organizations: Natural Selection in a Perilous Environment* (Chatham, NJ: Chatham House, 1985).

42 See, for example, Robert P. Boynton and Victor S. DeSantis, "Form and Adaptation: A Study of the Formal and Informal Functions of Mayors, Managers, and Chief Administrative Officers," *Baseline Data Report* 22 (January/February 1990) and Charldean Newell, James J. Glass, and David N. Ammons, "City Manager Roles in a Changing Political Environment," *Ideal and Practice in Local Government Management*, ed. Frederickson, 99–113.

43 Ross Jansen, "Rapid Change in New Zealand Local Government," *Public Management* (June 1990): 15.

44 Erwin C. Hargrove and John C. Glidewell, *Impossible Jobs in Public Management* (Lawrence: University of Kansas Press, 1990) 5–9.

45 Peter F. Drucker, *The Effective Executive* (New York: Harper & Row, 1966), 23–24.

46 Adapted from Lyle J. Sumek, "Evaluate or Not: That is the Question," *Public Management* (February 1988): 6.

Achieving effective community leadership

Local government managers have always been leaders in their communities. They may be more or less visible, but by virtue of their position they are at the forefront of efforts to identify and address the needs of the community. Although the role of community leader is not new to managers, changes in local politics—in council characteristics, community demographics, and fiscal conditions—make it more imperative than ever that they bring the distinctive qualities of responsible professionalism to the conduct of community affairs.

This chapter explores the nature of community leadership provided by local government managers and assesses the changing political context in which they operate. The characteristics of the major actors in community affairs are described, and guidelines are offered for assessing community dynamics and the manager's personal style. The chapter concludes with a consideration of key aspects of effective community leadership.

The nature of community leadership

Defining the local government manager's role in the community is challenging and somewhat perplexing. It is as easy to minimize this facet of the manager's position as to exaggerate it. Some argue that the manager's job is to work for the elected officials and let them handle community relations; the manager should focus on internal organization and try to restrict outside interference in the work of local government. This approach is characterized by a "passion for anonymity." A different, but related, view is that community relations can be delegated to a subordinate or treated as a staff function rather than as a primary responsibility of the manager. Proponents of this view may fear that, by engaging in community leadership and being active in the policy role, local government managers lose (or operate outside the bounds of) their professionalism.[1] However, the manager who avoids community leadership runs the dual risk of being perceived as aloof and being blindsided by unanticipated events.

On the other hand, some managers argue that the problems of communities are so great and the number of competing interest groups so large that the manager must be involved in efforts to mediate conflicts and to build support for addressing community needs. These managers may see themselves primarily as community leaders or think that their circumstances require this orientation. They let the departments of local government take care of themselves or leave them to an assistant manager. Such managers must guard against becoming so involved in community affairs that the governmental organization suffers.

A key requirement for effective community leadership is recognizing what it entails for a professional local government manager. Because it involves issues of politics and policy, defining the scope of community leadership has been an elusive goal. When is the manager entering the "political realm"? When is the manager inappropriately involved in policy development or operating outside a professional base? In other words, what are the limits of the public manager's position?

Professionalism in community relations

In 1940, Harold Stone, Don Price, and Kathryn Stone distinguished "community leadership" from "political leadership." They observed that managers were active in the former because they were involved in the community and worked to solve its problems. However, managers avoided involvement in partisan politics, currying the favor of councilmembers, or appealing over the head of the council to the voters.[2]

The type of community leadership described by Stone, Price, and Stone entails an active role in community relations for the local government manager. This role involves taking part in local organizations and civic affairs generally. It includes explaining what local government is doing and proposing new policies. In addition, the manager may be instrumental in helping to forge partnerships between government and the community. The manager negotiates with private citizens and organizations to get support for local government projects and seeks assistance from the community in dealing with problems that government cannot fully address. Managers also mediate differences and help to resolve controversies among groups within the community. The manager's part in community relations, therefore, entails monitoring all aspects of the interaction between the local government and the community.

The traditional way in the U.K. is to appoint an in-house public relations manager to herald the dawn of a new empire of assistants . . . My approach . . . proceeds from the simple proposition that all staff should be involved in publicising their services and it should be a part of the job of all local government managers . . . to develop pro-active PR skills.
Michael Ball

Although this community leadership role is not new, managers are being called upon to engage in increasingly more complex relationships with the people they serve. As they do so, managers are naturally concerned about the professionalism of their actions. A professional approach to community relations involves a distinctive objective, method, and standard of conduct. First, the manager's objective—to increase the capability of government to respond to public needs—is rooted in a professional commitment to advance the public interest. Second, professional expertise is applied to the tasks of community leadership. Methods used may extend from personal involvement in civic organizations to the use of systematic techniques to promote citizen participation, conflict resolution, strategic planning, and community goal setting. Third, the local government manager is bound by the standards of the profession to promote the participation of all citizens in community affairs, to ensure impartiality in assessing demands and seeking resolution of conflicts, and to advance equity in the distribution of resources. Thus, managers operate within a professional framework in their community relations activities. The manager complements the political leadership of the governing board with a professional perspective on the community's needs and ways to address them. On the basis of knowledge, experience, and independent monitoring of community sentiments and conditions, the manager can raise issues or propose alternatives that the board may not have considered.

To be effective community leaders, managers need a "constituency," people in the community who are interested in what they are trying to accomplish and willing to provide assistance. This is not a political following that permits the manager to stand against the council, but rather a network of individuals and groups through whom the manager can communicate and from whom the manager can receive information and suggestions. Through such contacts, a city manager might be able to identify intermediaries who could convince a recalcitrant business owner to take part in a main street revitalization project; a county manager might be able to defuse a conflict between two volunteer fire departments; or a regional council director might be able to persuade a local newspaper to provide adequate coverage of the council's activities. Formal channels of communication, however extensive, are not a substitute for extensive informal channels.

Decisions governments make and "levels of the game"

The community relations activities of the local government manager vary with the level of the decision to be made and the "stakes" involved in the decision. The manager faces a different "game" at each level of decision. The game metaphor is useful because it conveys the "uncertainty, ambiguity, and conflict" that surround decisions in the public sector.[3] Governmental games are particularly challenging because the goals are not always clear; the rules are vague and shifting; participants may switch teams; fans may become participants; there is no umpire (except, at times, the courts); and the game is never necessarily over. Managers should know what game they are playing and follow certain guidelines.

Mission decisions/high-stakes games   Mission decisions involve determining the basic purposes and role of government within the community and clearly have high stakes because of their long-term implications. Establishing the mission defines the scope of programs and services in local government and determines the direction that the government will take for some time to come.[4] Local government managers understand the need for political representatives to resolve such policy issues, but managers often are instrumental in framing the issues through their research and analysis of community conditions. Examples of mission decisions are determining what goals local government should pursue (e.g., developing a plan for downtown revitalization); deciding whether to provide a new service (e.g., public assumption of transit company); deciding whether to shift responsibility for service delivery (e.g., privatizing garbage collection or transferring library operations to the county); or deciding whether to abandon a service. Managers must recognize that it is hard to get serious consideration for major changes of the high-stakes type. Such issues frequently lack sufficient support to get on the political agenda and are often resolved by "nondecision," the refusal to act. The manager must decide whether and how to raise an issue that is unpopular and to assist groups having difficulty getting a matter on the agenda.

Policy decisions/middle-stakes games   Policy decisions in the middle range involve deciding how to spend money, design a program, or develop the details of a plan. Whereas high-stakes games deal with broad and often abstract concepts, middle-stakes games deal with concrete policy proposals. The range of participants expands as the decisions to be made become more specific. Staff play a larger role in designing programs and developing the details of service delivery, and citizen groups may become involved. Positions may shift as well. For example, a group that opposed a new service may still have opinions on how it is delivered. Local government managers must consult with the specific groups that will be affected by a policy decision and ensure that their input is invited. The impact and implications of the policy and its relationship to broader goals should be made clear.

Administrative decisions/low-stakes games   Administrative decisions usually are made by administrative staff according to criteria appropriate to a specific activity—for example, delivering a service, implementing a policy, or undertaking a project. They have a direct impact on citizens who will receive services or are affected by a policy or project. Under the guidance of the manager, the staff in the department involved in the decision must determine what kind of citizen involvement is needed to ensure its acceptance and effectiveness. The police may work more cooperatively with constituents and be more effective if they adopt community-based policing. The permitting and inspections involved in subdivision development may be more efficient and effective if administrators seek input from builders. Consulting residents and establishing fair criteria for siting facilities may reduce conflict over who gets something desirable, such as a community center, or something undesirable, such as a landfill. Ignoring citizen reactions increases the likelihood of controversy and extensive involvement by the governing board.

Management decisions/internal-external games   Management decisions involve the control and coordination of the resources of the organization. They are guided by systems and procedures that regulate personnel practices and purchasing, for example, and by the technical aspects of governmental functions (e.g., engineering standards for street construction). Normally, management decisions are made by staff and handled internally; they can become internal-external games, however, when they affect outside groups or when elected officials or citizens become involved in them. A minority contracting program, for example, can engender support or opposition from firms, depending on whether they are affected positively or negatively by its requirements. The handling of an investigation of alleged police brutality or the dismissal of an employee with political connections can embroil staff in a community controversy. When this happens, the boundary between the internal and external becomes blurred. The manager must be attentive to outside groups while maintaining the integrity of the organization's procedures.

Values that guide community leadership

From the beginning of the council-manager form of government to the present, community leadership has been recognized as a central responsibility of local government managers. Childs called for managers to create "new enterprises of service" (see Chapter 1), and in 1919 the drafters of the second Model City Charter, which endorsed the council-manager plan, expected the manager to exert great influence on "civic policy" and urged the manager to "show himself to be a leader, formulating policies and urging their adoption by the council."[5] C.A. Harrell of Norfolk, Virginia, in his presidential address to ICMA in 1948, endorsed this approach:

The ideal manager is a positive, vital force in the community. He spends a great deal of his time thinking of broad objectives which would greatly improve community life. Why should he hesitate to initiate policy proposals and submit them to the council? Neither the mayor nor individual councilmen can give much time to this task, and if the manager also shys away from such leadership the community stands still and important matters are allowed to pass by default . . . . [The manager] visualizes broad objectives, distant goals, far-sighted projects.

Despite some calls in the 1950s for a more restricted role, this expansive view reflects the attitudes of most practicing local government managers and has prevailed in the organizational values of ICMA, expressed in its Code of Ethics and Declaration of Ideals. Surveys of city and county managers over the years indicate a widespread acceptance of their obligation to provide community leadership and to serve all citizens. Approximately 80 percent of city and county managers agree that a manager should advocate major changes in policies, assume leadership in shaping policies, advocate new services in order to promote equity and fairness for low-income groups and minorities, and actively promote equity and fairness in the distribution of existing services.[6] A majority do not believe that the manager should maintain a neutral position on issues on which the community is divided, and about half think that the manager should work through powerful members of the community to achieve policy goals. Community leadership does not mean getting embroiled in community controversies, nor does it mean standing aside.

Strategies for community leadership ICMA's FutureVisions report recommends that managers facilitate the establishment of a community-based "visioning process" to develop goals and strategies for the future. In response to the shift from representative to participatory democracy and to create consensus on community goals, local governments should

Create new forums for citizens to connect with each other and with local government

Provide systems for broader participation in public policy development

Help elected officials in their efforts to achieve community consensus

Foster consumer- or community-based administration

Seek input from diverse groups and leaders of community organizations.

Source: Amy Cohen Paul, *Future Challenges, Future Opportunities* (Washington, DC: ICMA, 1991).

The ICMA Code of Ethics asserts the manager's obligation to promote the welfare of the community. Members of ICMA are ethically required to "maintain a deep sense of social responsibility" and "serve the best interests of all of the people." In the Declaration of Ideals, adopted in 1984, members dedicate themselves to seeking to "maintain and enhance public trust and confidence in government, to achieve equity and social justice, to affirm human dignity, and to improve the quality of life for the individual and the community." Specific ideals include advocating a "forum for meaningful citizen participation," clarifying "community values and goals," and taking "actions to create diverse opportunities . . . in every community for all people." Building on its traditions, the local government management profession has committed itself to offering multifaceted community leadership.

Local politics in the 1990s

The manager's traditional community leadership role has expanded in response to the changing conditions and challenges of the 1980s and 1990s. Populist politicians critical of government action are more common. Governing boards are more fragmented, and leadership within them is more difficult to achieve. Elected officials are more activist in their orientation. At the same time, fiscal stress has heightened debate over the role of local government and increased conflict over scarce resources. The population has become more diverse, and pressure from interest groups has increased. All these forces put pressure on the local government manager to provide greater leadership.

Changing conditions in local government

Local government managers of the past faced many community leadership challenges. What is unique about the present situation are the simultaneous changes in the purposes of government, the governmental structure, the political climate, and the resource base. Three periods have been identified in the evolution of managerial responsibility in local governments,[7] and it appears that the 1990s signal a fourth. The accompanying sidebar identifies the dominant features of each period in three areas: organizational thrust; policy orientation; and sources of financial support for local government (resource base).

Changes in these features have increased the need for present-day managers to be involved in an increasing number of activities in the community and to communicate effectively with a wider range of groups. Since the middle of the third period, they also have needed to be more energetic and more creative in seeking the resources needed to undertake governmental programs.

During the third period and continuing into the present, a vast change in local government structures and patterns of political participation has occurred. In the 1970s and 1980s, the structure of government was changed in many council-manager cities and counties to incorporate district representation on governing boards.[8] By the end of the period, most cities had mayors who were directly elected and more actively engaged in governmental affairs.[9]

Periods in local government development

Period 1: 1900–1949

Organizational thrust: Create the organization by cleaning up corruption and bringing businesslike efficiency to government.

Policy orientation: Establish and improve modern infrastructure.

Resource base: Local resources, expanding through the 1920s, then severely restricted during the Great Depression.

Period 2: 1940–1965

Organizational thrust: Modernize the organization.

Policy orientation: Control and support the development of rapidly growing communities.

Resource base: Local resources augmented by growing tax base; development capital; modest intergovernmental assistance overall but substantial support through mortgage insurance, funding for urban renewal and public housing construction, and, in selected areas, highway construction and defense industries.

Period 3: 1965–1990

Organizational thrust: Open up and decentralize the organization.

Policy orientation: Promote ideals of equal opportunity, tolerance, and understanding; revitalize central business district and declining and stagnant areas; and improve the quality of community life.

Resource base: Local resources (al-though in some areas constricted tax revolt); sizeable intergovernmental assistance to induce development of new programs, followed by shift to general revenue sharing and block grants, followed by reduction in federal assistance but increased state support; venture capital, tax shelters, and speculative loans to support downtown development.

Period 4: 1990–

Organizational thrust: Consolidate and rightsize or downsize the organization.

Policy orientation: Provide modest infrastructure development (however, maintenance has been deferred and replacement delayed in many localities because of fiscal constraints); accommodate diversity and address the long-term consequences of inequality; protect environment under state and federal mandates; privatize and undertake joint governmental provision of some services and enhance the quality of remaining public services; increase competitiveness and competitive advantage through strategic planning.

Resource base: Continued low level of federal assistance and constriction in state support; moderate to reduced private investment; dependence on local sources with increased use of charges for services; increased reliance on volunteers.

Source: Based in part on David M. Welborn, "The Environment and Role of the Administrator," in *Managing the Modern City*, ed. James M. Banovetz (Washington, DC: ICMA, 1971), 84.

Governing boards and interest groups

In addition to changes in conditions and institutions, more interest groups have spokespersons on the governing board. Their power and the intensity and impact of their activities have increased. More communities—even small ones—have more ethnic groups and immigrants than ever before.

The characteristics and attitudes of members of governing boards also have changed. Council members were once the ''influentials,'' or persons with close ties to influential interests in the community; now more of them are activists. It has been typical to view council members, particularly in council-manager cities, as serving out of a sense of civic duty. It is still true that almost all council members have a desire to serve the city as a whole, according to a national survey of council members conducted in 1989.[10] In addition, serving the neighborhood was very important to approximately half of the council members in small and medium-sized cities, and almost three-quarters of the council members in large cities (more than 200,000 population) cite neighborhood representation as a major reason for running for office. A high level of concern about some specific issue prompted a majority of the council members to become candidates, and the percentage goes up as city size increases. Issue-oriented candidates have become very common in local government in recent years. More council members represent specific groups and promote specific interests than previously. More of them also report that they consider it important to represent a wide range of groups. As a consequence, it is harder to reach consensus among the members of the governing board.[11]

One of the things that I have seen . . . is a tendency toward segmentation of interests. There have always been special interest groups . . . but I think we are seeing those groups become much more defined and narrowly focused.
Jewel Scott

Council members spend more time on their position than previously. They spend much of this time ensuring that citizens receive services, responding to complaints, and helping to secure information—in short, acting as ombudsman (see Table 2–1). The manager and staff, therefore, have extensive interactions with council members over specific matters in community relations.

Governing board members increasingly are interested in constituency service—in representing specific groups and seeking new programs for their constituents. Consequently, more of the responsibility to respond to the needs of the entire community and to balance competing demands falls on the manager.

Table 2–1   City council member workload.

Hours	City size		
	Small	Medium	Large
Average hours per week on council-related matters	16.6	24.4	40.0
Average hours per week on services for people	5.9	10.3	17.9
Service hours as percent of total	36%	42%	45%

Note: 904 council members were interviewed. City size:
  small = 25,000 to 70,000; medium = 70,000 to 199,999;
  large = more than 200,000.

Manager's orientation to the council and the community

There is evidence that the manager is becoming more strongly oriented toward interacting with the council, despite the increasing need to address other groups and attend to community problems. When deciding the relative importance of a management role, a policy role including council relations, and a political role including community leadership, 33 percent of managers surveyed in 1965 indicated that community leadership was most important, compared with 22 percent who chose council relations. By 1985, a dramatic shift had occurred. Over half—56 percent—indicated that council relations was most important, and the proportion choosing community leadership had dropped to 6 percent.[12] (In both surveys, just under two-fifths chose the management role as most important.)

This result does not mean that community leadership is unimportant, but it has become relatively less important to a manager's success than council relations. Whereas many local government managers previously were able to concentrate on community leadership with a clear understanding of the policy priorities of a cohesive council, they now devote considerable attention to working with council members to develop agreement on policy among them and to respond to their demands. Because council members now represent a wider range of groups and receive more demands from constituents, the manager must work more closely with them in the effort to define the broad public interest. (Chapter 3 will discuss in more detail how the manager can work effectively with the governing body.)

Divisions and the dwindling sense of community

A final dimension of the changing politics of the 1990s is change in communities themselves, which display sharper divisions and more intense political activism than before. NIMBY (not in my back yard)-ism appears to be more deeply entrenched as neighborhood groups become more insistent on asserting their interests and more effective at blocking government action.

General support for a broad public agenda has declined. The sense of community that could counteract divisive forces is dwindling. More frenetic lifestyles, greater time at work, more households in which both spouses work, single parents, fewer children, increased relocation at retirement, and a larger population of very elderly citizens all diminish the time, energy, and inclination for involvement in the community.

Less and less social interaction takes place among people because homes have become cocoons. Instead of playing at the local park or even in our yards or socializing on the front porch, we have created recreation rooms . . . We only open our front doors for the pizza man.

Frank Benest

People now work, shop, and pursue a variety of leisure activities throughout urban and suburban areas, not only in the communities in which they live. The products of new technologies, notably the personal computer and the videocassette recorder, permit more to be done at home. These factors, and the disappearance of places for informal gatherings, reduce personal engagement in the community. A progressively greater rootlessness contributes to the "privatization of American public life."[13]

Local government managers face the need to take active steps to strengthen interpersonal connections. They also must deal with the consequences of a weak commitment to a broad public agenda and a weak expression of the general public interest in the face of intense efforts by special interests in issue debates, referenda, and campaigns. Unfortunately, local government managers may expose themselves to attack if they do so.

In sum, responsible managers blend professionalism and community leadership to achieve success. The manager has an obligation to seek to advance the public interest of the community as a whole, and community leadership has become more crucial with the changing conditions of the 1990s.

Evaluating community leadership style

A local government manager needs to assess his or her values, ideals, and qualities in order to be effective in dealing with others. A frank recognition of personal preferences, strengths, and weaknesses is needed in order to handle the responsibility for community leadership. Only through personal understanding can the manager hope to adapt to the characteristics of the community served.

The manager's personal qualities

Four major personality dimensions are especially pertinent to understanding leadership style: internal versus external orientation, innovativeness, technical orientation, and flexibility. Some common types of community leaders can be identified by variations on these qualities.

Internal versus external orientation This dimension is not determined by whether the manager is involved outside the organization; external involvement is unavoidable. Rather, it is determined by whether the manager enjoys, is good at, and is extensively engaged in community affairs. To what extent is the manager energized by relating to other people face-to-face? Those who seek out contact with other people and enjoy the give-and-take of verbal exchange probably find it more natural and enjoyable to have extensive dealings with citizens and groups. Those who prefer to reflect on information they have received, who prefer written reports to discovery through dialogue, and who need time to themselves to recharge their batteries are less inclined to be involved in the community. They also may be drained rather than energized by extensive personal interaction. These contrasting types are labeled *extroverts*—people who are drawn to others—and *introverts*—those who prefer to reflect on the information they have received.[14]

Innovativeness The second dimension concerns the degree of innovation exhibited by the manager. How creative, change-oriented, and visionary is the manager? Some managers focus on the concrete, the here-and-now, and the facts of the situation. These types—the realists—are *sensors*. Others look at the same information and see new patterns and possibilities for the future. These visionaries are *intuitives*.

Technical orientation The third dimension is technical orientation. How much emphasis does the manager place on the use of administrative and managerial expertise? Managers who have a strong technical orientation—*thinkers*—incorporate management systems within the organization and emphasize information collection and analysis in decision making. Managers who are low on this dimension—*feelers*—place more emphasis on the ''art'' of management and their feel for the situation. The former manager is more comfortable with data about community conditions and citizen attitudes and looks for logical analyses and reasoned conclusions about the ''best'' approach or solution to a problem. The latter puts more trust in knowing how people are affected by a decision and how they feel about it. This manager would be comfortable bargaining and compromising to find a basis for agreement and mutually acceptable solutions.

Flexibility   Some people like order and predictability and prefer to bring matters to closure. Others are happier with spontaneity and surprises; they like to keep their options open and postpone decisions. Most managers who like to get issues resolved might be called *closers*.[15] *Processors*, on the other hand, want to delay decisions and keep their options open. The political process tends to produce delays that the processor may be better able to tolerate. Because citizen groups frequently raise new factors or considerations, decisions are often postponed and issues are sometimes reopened after decisions have been made.

Types of local government manager

From these dimensions (particularly the first three), an array of local government manager types can be developed. Managers can have low, medium, or high scores on any of the dimensions. The combinations are not clearly differentiated, and many more types can be imagined. The following descriptions of hypothetical managers are meant to suggest ways in which managers can think about their own characteristics and tendencies.

The complete *community leader* has an external focus, is highly innovative, and has a high technical orientation. For those who feel that the manager should be a creative leader and actively involved in community affairs as well as highly proficient in the technical aspects of the position, this manager is the ideal type. An example is Tom Q., a county manager who has developed extensive contacts with a broad array of community groups and who also maintains close ties with the city managers and other government leaders in his county. Tom draws upon his independent knowledge of what is happening in the county to better understand the pressures that the commissioners experience, and he has a knack for seeing both problems and opportunities before others do. He has a vision of the future that guides his thinking about what should be done in the short run, and he developed support for a community-based strategic planning project to create a shared vision for the county. In close cooperation with his assistant manager and department heads, Tom works to incorporate the best management practices in the operation of the county organization, including the use of user and citizen surveys on service satisfaction. At times, he also finds himself in the middle of community controversies, and some commissioners occasionally grumble about Tom's high visibility. Tom is active and effective on all fronts, but he must be on guard against stretching himself too thin, taking on too many projects at once, and burning out.

The *chief executive* is similar in many ways to the community leader but has a stronger internal orientation. City manager Susan J. prefers working within the organization and with the city council behind the scenes. She is familiar with many leaders in the community, contacts them when necessary, and responds when they seek her out, although she is more comfortable meeting one-on-one with a few community leaders she knows and trusts. She is somewhat detached from the community, and this detachment contributes to an impression of aloofness in some minds, but she also is spared criticism for being excessively involved. She is innovative and technically proficient like the community leader. She puts heavy emphasis on systematically assessing citizen response to services and has put in place a new procedure for handling complaints that carefully tracks their number and distribution and the actions taken to respond to them. Because of her internal orientation, she relies more on her staff to develop proposals.

Two types of manager have a strong external focus, but differ significantly from the community leader. Mary S. is a *coalition builder*. She is happiest working with citizens and community groups to help solve community problems. The details of her job, on the other hand, are dull and uninspiring to her because of her low technical orientation. She gets high marks for the ingenious ways that she brings opposing groups together to support a common goal; she is flexible and does not mind protracted discussion to reach decisions as much as others do. Mary is highly innovative in finding solutions to complex problems, but she is criticized for juggling too many projects at once, for lack of attention to detail, and for laxness in supervising department heads. The *arbiter* is similar but ranks lower on innovation. This manager negotiates with groups and helps them to compromise but does not have a creative approach to problem solving.

The *administrative innovator* has a strong technical orientation and is, as the title suggests, highly innovative when it comes to making the organization work better. However, this manager avoids community involvement even more than does the chief executive. Fernando A. is manager of a medium-sized city. In his two previous positions, he modernized budgeting, capital planning, and personnel systems. He regularly attends state and national manager meetings and conscientiously reads professional publications in order to keep up with new developments in management. He has limited contact with the community beyond his dealings with citizens on the job, and apart from participation in athletic events and the Rotary Club, Fernando is most at ease dealing with other managers in business and nonprofit organizations. The issues he identifies have to do with the organization's performance, and the input he seeks is that of staff and professional colleagues, not citizens. He is somewhat dissatisfied with the city council for ignoring staff recommendations and "giving in" to demands from constituents and community groups. Several major projects have been postponed or derailed because of community opposition that surfaced late in the process of consideration—opposition that might have been avoided if citizens had been consulted at the beginning.

Harry B. is similar to Fernando A. in that both have an internal orientation. Harry is an *administrative stabilizer* or *improver* rather than an innovator. He too likes to work on the inside, but places more emphasis on making existing systems work better than on introducing new ones. He is a pragmatist who is interested in getting the job done. He is most inclined to examine new ideas that have been tested elsewhere in order to adapt them to the circumstances in his city. Like Fernando, he easily gets impatient with "interference" from citizens and is inclined to dismiss a lot of suggestions as impractical, pie-in-the-sky plans that will never work. He is uncomfortable with groups that seem to try to get special treatment or want to deviate from the standard rules.

Both the administrative innovator and the stabilizer/improver rely on the governing board as their channel to the community. They are inclined to view elected officials as the ones who should speak for the community and secure the public support needed to act on decisions.

A manager who ranks low on all dimensions is a *caretaker*. With an internal focus, low innovativeness, low technical orientation, and lack of flexibility, this manager concentrates on the housekeeping or maintenance functions in the local government that he or she serves. The caretaker may be a short-termer asked to fill the slot because no one else could be found for the job or a local politician with the right connections. The caretaker certainly does not make waves in the community.

How to know your style

Local government managers must develop a good sense of their own characteristics and tendencies in order to be effective. Most of the types previously described can be effective managers if they recognize their weaknesses and blind spots as well as their strengths; it is possible to develop attributes that do not come naturally and are not performed with as much facility as others. One approach to self-assessment if you are a practicing manager is to develop a portrait of your own community relations style. You can do this by asking yourself questions such as those in the accompanying sidebar. Future managers can project how they think they would handle the position.

Another approach to self-assessment is to use an inventory that identifies key personality traits, such as the commonly used Myers Briggs Type Indicator.[16] The

Assessing your community relations style What parts of your job do you like most? Least?

How comfortable are you in your dealings with the council? Do you like it when they look to you for explicit leadership in dealing with community issues, regardless of whether it is wise to provide it?

Are you comfortable interacting with groups in the community? Which groups do you like to deal with and which do you not?

Do you look at situations and think about how things can be changed in fundamental ways, or do you concentrate on specific actions that can improve how the organization operates?

Are you interested in identifying the major problems and needs facing the community and developing a vision for the community, or do you consider this the council's responsibility?

Do you pay as much attention to practices that pertain to citizen and community relations as you do to internal operations? Are you committed to using the best available methods and adhering to the highest standards of practice in your organization?

How flexible are you? How do you feel about adapting the decision-making process to include diverse groups and opinions?

---

typical traits manifested by managers who have completed this inventory suggest that managers most commonly would fall into the administrative stabilizer/improver category *if their behavior were determined completely by their preferences.* There are many exceptions, but managers tend to be introverts—reflectors rather than relaters—and therefore are more likely to be somewhat disengaged from citizens and community groups rather than highly involved with them.[17] Rather than being highly innovative and visionary (the intuitive characteristic), they typically are concerned about concrete problems in the present (the sensing or realist characteristic). Rather than being highly empathetic (the feeler), they prefer rational, logical approaches to decision making (the thinking characteristic). Finally, they have a strong preference for being orderly, maintaining control, anticipating and preparing for problems, and bringing decisions to closure (the closer characteristic) rather than for being spontaneous, flexible, and willing to postpone decisions (the processor). The characteristics associated with facility in community relations (e.g., being outgoing, innovative, empathetic, and flexible) are atypical of many local government managers. These managers may need to make special efforts to strengthen those characteristics.

Local government managers adopt a community relations style on the basis of their personal traits and skills, the circumstances they face, and the characteristics and needs of the community, all of which may change over time. They probably have felt the need to manifest most or all of the styles at different times in their careers. The mode of behavior that is closest to the manager's personal preferences will be the most common and the one to which the manager tends to revert. Effective managers need to understand all the modes, however, and adopt them when needed.

Understanding community dynamics

In addition to being aware of their own community relations style, managers need to recognize different kinds of communities. This section first examines four types of community and then explores the varying political configurations of different communities.

Types of communities and constituencies

Some communities, usually small ones, have a dominant character. In others, particularly larger ones, segments of the population differ in what they demand from government in services, degree of activism, and level of expenditures. Managers must be able to understand the expectations and needs of the community and adapt their style accordingly; otherwise, disparities in expectations will diminish effectiveness and produce tension.

In 1961, Oliver Williams supplied a comparative typology of communities based on four kinds of socioeconomic demands that citizens place on their local governments.[18] In these four types of communities, government plays a distinctive role—as instrument of growth, provider of amenities, provider of caretaker functions, and arbiter of conflicting interests. These types still are a useful starting point, and some variations on them will be added and additional types suggested.

Growth communities   Economic growth and development are the key objectives of the growth community, which was once common in the Sunbelt and the West. Public officials serve primarily as catalysts for community and regional growth, and public managers are kept busy promoting population expansion, fostering industrial development, encouraging commercial activities, and building the essential infrastructure—roads, sewers, and so forth—to further business development and economic progress. Their activities therefore entail a great deal of promotion and involvement in planning industrial and residential site development. Managers also are behind efforts to keep costs low, provide tax advantages or other incentives for local business development, and ensure adequate utility, transit, labor, and other services necessary for rapid economic expansion.

Consumption communities   Public managers serving the upper-middle-class suburbs that ring many large cities in the Unites States are pressed with a very different set of demands. In these areas, public managers must offer residents life's amenities and an attractive community in which to live. Consumption—as opposed to growth—is the principal value in these towns and suburbs. In a consumption community, maintenance of the current way of life is preferred over the possibility of attaining a new or better way of life tomorrow. Therefore, a local public manager emphasizes such activities as the provision of adequate parks and recreational opportunities; prompt and courteous response to citizens requiring public services; strict enforcement of zoning; the safe and quiet flow of traffic; and abatement of noise and pollution.

The local government manager in these communities must have the technical competencies required to supply public goods and services in innovative ways at a reasonable cost to citizens. The manager and staff must be prepared to devote a good deal of attention to involved citizens who are interested in particular services (e.g., a library board) and who want special attention given to "their" service, with perhaps little regard to its effect on the total budget.

Caretaker/minimal government communities   Where local government is caretaker, as in some small towns, the demands on a public manager are substantially reduced or even restricted. Here the job entails keeping the size of government as a whole to a minimum and keeping the costs of government down. Hence, managers often rely largely on the private sector or other levels of government to supply such necessary public goods and services as refuse collection and recreation—if these services are supplied at all. Very little innovation ever occurs, and even if the majority of the citizens want something new, such as a library building, private rather than public funding is sought. In short, the manager keeps the government functioning, but does little to innovate. Some citizens may not want to pay for professional management.

The number of local governments that approximate the characteristics of the caretaker community probably have increased as a result of the tax revolt experienced in many states and the increased financial difficulties that many local governments face. Although it may appear that the caretaker type of manager is well matched to these communities, this is not always the case, particularly when the antigovernment sentiment stems from a desire to minimize taxes. The manager then needs to maintain extensive ties with the community as a positive representative of government. He or she needs to be an accomplished organizational leader who looks for ways to cut costs and improve productivity, as well as a good communicator in order to persuade elected officials and the community that the local government is being operated frugally and effectively.

Arbiter/opportunity communities   Many large, declining, and impoverished central cities in the Northeast and Midwest are arbiter/opportunity communities. Here the public manager's job is very different because of pressure on local government to provide extensive services to an increasingly poor, lower-class population and to expand opportunities in an economically depressed area. The job involves managing sometimes quite intense conflict among various groups over scarce public goods and services. In arbiter/opportunity communities, the public manager's community relations skills often are tested to their utmost because much of the manager's time is spent negotiating, compromising, and bargaining in order to find a common ground for action. Symbolic acts on the part of the manager—the "right" gestures, proclamations, or appointments—are frequently more valued than solid managerial results.

Although it is common to associate these problems with central cities, they now are found in an increasing number of suburban communities. Both inner-ring older suburbs and new ethnic enclaves suffer when a major employer shuts down or economic opportunities are limited. They have liabilities beyond those of the central city because their resource base is narrow, services are minimal, and transportation to other parts of the metropolitan area is lacking. These suburbs, like the impoverished communities in central cities, have a very high need and demand for services and few resources.

In these areas, local government managers must not only be adept at resolving conflict but also must develop close personal ties in order to try to offset feelings of alienation and distrust of local government. The local government is expected to promote civil rights and expanded economic opportunities as vigorously as the manager in the growth community promotes economic expansion.

There are two major qualifications that must be stressed in using these four types of communities as a guide to assessing any actual situation. First, the distinctions among the four are diminishing. The traits of one type of community are likely to

---

The other suburbia   Some 500 suburbs across the United States now face problems approaching those of inner cities . . . Unlike poor urban neighborhoods, many of these towns are virtual prisons, with little or no public transit linking residents to city or suburban jobs . . . Those who end up in poor suburbs face special hurdles. Their appeals for new businesses tend to attract only those gritty industries that other communities reject, like landfills. Because they lack the richer tax base cities get from office and factory districts, the suburbs can't afford many of the costly social, recreational, and other services that cities offer.

Source: "The Other Suburbia," *Newsweek* (June 26, 1989): 22–23.

appear in one or more of the others. For example, a high level of services is viewed as important also in the growth community.

Second, a single community often will have the characteristics of two or more types when distinct segments of the population stress different values. Pro-growth forces are countered by those that favor limited growth and enhancement of quality of life. Economically disadvantaged groups press for a wider range of services to meet their needs. All of these interests are opposed by groups that want lower taxes and less government activity. The local government manager in this situation must be multi-faceted. Not only does the manager need the skill and sensitivity required to deal with each group separately, he or she also must be effective at linking dissimilar groups, promoting the identification of common interests, and, of course, resolving conflicts between them without getting caught in the cross-fire. The manager's role is particularly important in this setting because the governing board, which is likely to reflect the divisions among groups, may be unable to serve as a unifying force.

Community political configurations

In addition to differing policy orientations, there are some basic configurations of the political landscape to which managers should be attentive. The degree of fragmentation and stability in the community can shape the scope of local managerial action.[19]

Small, homogeneous community   In the small, homogeneous community, ethnic, racial, and income differences are minimal; hence no highly divisive issues arise and conflict is relatively rare. Public managers usually have considerable latitude for active leadership in the affairs of these communities and find citizens generally willing to cooperate in a broad range of initiatives and activities. In fact, due to the full-time involvement and specialization of managers in public affairs, citizens frequently look to them for leadership and direction. Often, local leaders also may have great confidence in their managers and give them considerable latitude.

Divided community with two factions   The evenly divided community in which control shifts between two factions is frequently a medium-sized commmunity with a diverse population that is divided into two roughly equal interest groups or factions, for instance, pro-growth and environmentalist, Black and White, old ethnic and new minority, established and newcomer, Democrat and Republican, or progressive and conservative. Obviously maneuverability in this type of community is sharply limited because the manager cannot become too closely identified with either group.

The most dramatic example of shifts between the factions is when a council controlled by one group hires the public manager and the opposition wins in the next election. The manager may suddenly be fired or confronted with the challenge of winning the trust of a council whose majority comes from a faction different from the one that hired the manager.

This situation confronted city manager George Bean after he assumed the managership of Peoria, Illinois, during the 1950s. When Bean arrived in Peoria, the old courthouse gang of politicians had been beaten by reformers, who installed the council-manager form of government. Bean went full throttle instituting "good government reforms" in the city. The problem was that, once the manager had been installed, the reform group forgot about the city. In the next election two years later, the old courthouse gang won a majority of seats on the city council, leaving Bean with the enemies of council-manager government and thus effectively stopping his innovations in the community. In short, Bean learned the liabilities of managing with a soft base of support. Unfortunately, he had done little during his tenure to build support in the opposition's camp.

The experience of a county manager in North Carolina illustrates the uncertainties of working with two evenly balanced political parties. Having been hired initially by a commission controlled by Republicans in the late 1960s, he was viewed as a Republican when the Democrats won a majority some years later. He had been able to build sufficient respect and support that community and Democratic leaders squelched the idea that the new majority should "get rid of the Republican administrators." When the Republicans regained control in 1988, he was viewed as a Democrat. He was able, however, to establish a professional relationship with the new members by stressing his continuing commitment to help the commission accomplish its goals regardless of which party was in charge.

Managers should maintain ties with both factions if possible and treat each side fairly. In the case of political parties, they should have no partisan connection with any. The manager must provide information equally to all and not take actions that may be viewed as detrimental to the group that is no longer in office.

Stable community with a dominant faction   By contrast, the stable community with a single dominant faction—the local business community, for example, or a controlling coalition of groups—can create a secure position for the local public manager, as long as the manager retains the respect and confidence of that faction. L.P. Cookingham, the highly successful manager of Kansas City for nineteen years, was installed in 1940 by a reform group of businessmen who ousted the old political machine. These businessmen retained control of the city government for a long time thereafter, giving Cookingham enormous latitude and influence over various aspects of community affairs. His is a classic case of solid and enduring majority support in the community—earned also through his effectiveness on the job and the respect he received from Kansas City citizens.

A variant of this type of community is one with a majority faction but potential for transition. A risk of close association with a single dominant group is that political forces change, and the manager is likely to be viewed as unsympathetic by the newcomers to office. This situation has been common in California where new progressive coalitions are replacing business-dominated city councils.[20] It can also happen when an institutional change, such as the introduction of district elections, brings a new majority onto the council. Efforts by the manager to communicate actively with all groups will not ensure that he or she is retained by the newcomers, but failure to do so is likely to ensure dismissal. Furthermore, the manager will have cut off significant citizen input.

Unstable community with multiple shifting factions   The unstable community with multiple, shifting factions is the norm today for most large central cities, where numerous labor, business, and ethnic groups jostle for control of city hall. This diversity and instability can exist even in small communities. In a decade, many previously homogeneous suburbs in California have become small versions of the United Nations. This type of community presents the local manager with an extremely demanding and volatile situation. The manager must swim in these turbulent waters very carefully, issue by issue, putting together on an ad hoc basis the coalition of interests and groups necessary to achieve effective managerial action. The manager must never move too far ahead of or behind the shifting political currents of community life or get out of touch with council expectations. However, even here ample opportunities for initiative and leadership do exist, especially for a public executive skilled in bargaining, negotiation, and compromise.

The level of political stability varies in council-manager governments and has some impact on managerial turnover. In a study of Florida cities, Whitaker and DeHoog measured the stability of their governments and found that 37 percent were very stable, 44 percent somewhat stable, and 19 percent unstable.[21] As might be expected, city managers in the unstable cities were most likely to leave their position within two years (46 percent), followed by those in somewhat stable cities

(21 percent). Stability was associated with low rates of departure (10 percent) unless managers lacked the full confidence of the council or disagreed with the council about the manager's policy role, in which case most had left in two years. Over half the managers who left stable situations departed under pressure or were fired. Six managers lost support of the council majority after an election brought a new faction opposed to the manager into office. Only two of the six had been aware in advance that change in political control was likely to occur.

To summarize, managers need to continuously monitor community groups and the dynamics of relations among them. They also should assess how conditions in the community match their personal style. In general, the greater the divisions in the community, the more externally oriented the manager needs to be. The more diverse the population, the more carefully the manager needs to balance a strong technical orientation with empathy for others and sensitivity to how groups with different backgrounds and values will respond to actions taken. Innovative managers need to ensure that their vision is widely understood and shared. Managers also should take stock of their community relations skills and their ability to work with specific groups. They may be more effective or have more contact with some than others.

Actors in community politics

Communities are made up of a variety of actors: groups, institutions, and networks. Developing an inventory involves identifying both general patterns of influence and activity as well as the characteristics of specific groups. This section therefore gives an overview of the sources of influence at different stages of community action; it then goes on to discuss various groups and constituents.

Sources of power and influence in the community

The study of community power fascinates both scholars and practitioners. Both want to know who pulls the strings behind the scenes. Sociologists and political scientists doing research in this field—often using different methods—have come up with somewhat different results. Sociologists often found the existence of a "power elite" based in the business sector who exerted control over the political life of the community in ways that were not visible to the public. In this view, public officials were not especially important as the "movers and shakers" in the community. Political scientists, on the other hand, found more dispersed activity. They concluded that the political process was pluralistic rather than dominated by a single elite and that public officials played an important and central role and were more likely than a private elite to be involved across a wide range of issues. The divergence in methods and findings reveals distinct facets of influence, all of which are important for the local government manager to recognize.[22] By putting the approaches together, the sources of influence in the community can be identified.

The first question is that of how ideas originate. What are the sources for change in the community? The answer is that both public officials and interest group leaders as well as the economic elite figure prominently at this stage. Mayors in mayor-council governments are particularly important policy innovators, but, with less fanfare, mayors and board chairpersons, governing board members, and local government managers in council-manager governments also help to identify problems and issues. Major economic interests also originate large-scale projects that have a substantial impact on the public agenda—for example, a developer whose plan for a downtown mall causes city government to take actions to advance the project and subsidize it. Many communities large and small have been "forced" to act to keep a major commercial establishment or employer from moving elsewhere. There is also evidence that networks of economic and political influence (including elected officials) represent a "regime" that originates action and secures support for certain kinds of activities, usually those related to economic development.[23]

The second stage in issue formation is legitimation and approval or opposition. Issues will not secure a place on the agenda or, if they do, are unlikely to receive support, if significant "opinion makers" and "value shapers" veto them. On the other hand, the acceptance of an idea by these sources ensures a full hearing. The opinion makers are typically part of the community's elite, including key figures in the media. Political legitimacy—sufficient support for serious consideration— may be withheld also by interest groups or large segments of the population, as shown by the resistance of Whites to change in the early days of the civil rights movement or by the opposition to multifamily housing in an affluent community.

The next stage is providing resources. When a project needs resources beyond those that government can generate, potential sources of support obviously exert great influence over whether that project is accomplished. The shift in ownership of companies from local families to national or international corporations reduces the likelihood of support for community projects. For a project such as a new hospital or arts center, the support of economic interests is critical because private contributions are usually required. In creating a program that is largely regulatory (e.g., creating a historic district) or a project for which public funds are available (e.g., building a new school) the influence of private resource holders is diminished.

Finally, new ideas need to be implemented. The activists who play the key roles in implementation are likely to come from government, a range of civic organizations and agencies, and interest groups. Although typically these actors are not thought of as being power holders, they usually are crucial to the actual success of a new project or program.

The participants—who may have more or less influence over affairs in the community—vary in their background and prominence. It is the rare community in which an economic power elite exerts comprehensive control, and this occurrence is becoming less common. Local government managers should assess carefully all those whose support and contributions are necessary for specific projects. It is a mistake either to ignore the major economic interests in the community or to assume that they control all decisions.

Public officials

Although the sources of power and influence in a community may vary, the local government manager must always maintain contact with other public officials.

Elected officials   Elected officials on the governing board are not discussed at length here because board-manager relations are the subject of the next chapter. Several points, however, pertain directly to this discussion. First, there has been a shift in the composition of the governing board from persons who come from or have ties to influential organizations in the community to persons who are more likely to be political activists. In working with the governing board, the manager does not have as much access to the community elite—the key groups for legitimizing and providing resources for activities—as he or she once had. Furthermore, council or board members are more likely to be single-issue candidates or to be elected from a district with a homogeneous population than to be elected at large. They also, as noted previously, represent a larger range of groups than before. The manager in his or her interactions with governing body members also is dealing indirectly with interest groups. The manager should be familiar with these connections not only to be sensitive to elected officials' concerns but also to be aware of potential biases and blind spots in their thinking.

In view of these characteristics of the governing body, a leader who can make it more cohesive is an important asset. The mayor or chairperson of the board can make a substantial contribution as a "facilitative leader."[24] Such leaders promote communication and effective interaction between the council and manager and between the local government and the public. They empower other officials rather than seek power for themselves and develop a shared vision of the local government's goals.

Other officials　In addition to governing board members, the manager should also be attentive to other officials in the area. It is useful to foster a network with managers from a variety of jurisdictions. Indeed, it is at the professional level that much informal communication and cooperation among neighboring governments is achieved. Either directly or through the governing board, the manager should maintain lines of communication to other local elected officials and to members of the state legislature and U.S. Congress from the area. The local government manager's relations with other jurisdictions and levels of government are discussed more fully in Chapter 7.

I want to make people comfortable with the way they receive information and have them participate in the process—more than is required in the public hearing process. They shouldn't feel that we are springing anything on them.
Janet M. Dolan

Constituents and groups

Most citizens do not participate directly in community affairs. Those with higher education and income and professional occupations are more likely to feel that they have a duty as citizens to take part and to feel that their participation makes a difference. As a consequence, they represent a larger proportion of the minority of citizens who vote than they do of the general population. Typically, only 15 to 25 percent of the adult population vote in local elections. Those who have fewer resources and weaker motivation to take part are not likely to participate in community affairs in the absence of special efforts to involve them or events that have a direct impact on their lives. When local government managers work with organized interest groups, they are dealing with a small minority of the population. They should always be aware of the differences among the activists in interest groups, the attentive electorate that chooses the governing board members, and the general citizenry. They should therefore be inclusive in their approach to community relations. For example, they need to directly solicit input about the quality and impact of local government services from consumers and not rely solely on the opinions of activists or voters to determine whether programs are being run well. (Additional aspects of citizen participation are discussed in Chapters 4–6.)

However, a wide range of groups is active in local affairs. The larger the community, the more groups present and the better organized they are likely to be. Table 2–2 presents a general picture of the relative influence of certain major types of group provided by the results from a National League of Cities survey of the attitudes of city council members conducted in 1989.[25]

Neighborhood and business organizations were viewed as very influential by a majority of council members in cities of all sizes, and elderly citizens were viewed similarly by almost two-fifths of council members. Although other groups had less impact overall, some were more influential in larger cities (e.g. racial minorities) and many others had considerable influence in the opinion of some council members. Even groups that are not generally perceived to be influential (e.g., "pro-choice" or "right-to-life" organizations) can exert substantial pressure if they are able to mobilize allies regarding a concrete issue in a particular community. Similarly, groups and organizations that are peripheral to local government can be galvanized into action over a specific issue (e.g., churches over zoning for adult entertainment establishments or garden clubs over removal of trees). The challenge

Table 2-2   Council members' attitudes about group influence in their cities, 1989.

Group	City size			
	Average	Small	Medium	Large
Neighborhoods	66	61	66	69
Businesses	56	50	57	59
Elderly citizens	39	38	40	40
Realtors/developers	27	16	26	38
Racial minorities	26	18	20	39
Environmentalists	22	19	25	23
Labor unions	22	9	21	32
Municipal employees	21	21	20	22
Ethnic groups	17	12	14	23
Women	16	13	14	21
Good-government organizations (e.g., LWV)	13	14	13	13
Anti-pornography/anti-vice groups	10	9	12	10
"Pro-choice" groups	5	4	3	8
"Right to life" groups	4	4	3	4

Note: The figures indicate the percentage of council members who felt that each group had **considerable** influence on council decisions. 904 council members were interviewed. City size: small = 25,000 to 70,000; medium = 70,000 to 199,999; large = more than 200,000.

to local officials is to be accessible to all groups and to reach sound decisions despite the pressures and counter-pressures. The following discussion describes certain of these groups in more detail.

Business community   The business community is divided roughly into two groups: those businesses whose markets are national and those whose markets are local and who therefore have a vital stake in local development because their livelihoods directly depend on it. Businesses in the latter group, especially when they are locally owned, normally are active in the local chamber of commerce and other such organizations for promoting local growth. Members include department store owners, utility companies, real estate developers and sales people, and small-business owners whose economic survival requires them to press local government for downtown redevelopment, better roads, improved trash collection, mass transit, and better all-around services to bring customers to their places of business. Thus, business leaders often are great supporters of physical improvement projects and initiatives to improve municipal management. Chambers of commerce and city governments commonly form close partnerships.[26]

Because the business community has great influence on the economic prosperity of any community, the local public manager has extensive interactions with it. Considering the influence that businesses have, local government managers must take care that the actions they take reflect need rather than acquiescence to business demands. In a study comparing the response of city governments to demands for assistance from businesses and developers, there is some evidence that managers have done so. The study found that action in council-manager cities depended on indicators of economic need, whereas in mayor-council cities, assistance was likely regardless of need.[27] The demands of business always must be justified and balanced against the broader needs of the entire community.

Local government employees   The employees of local government have three important functions: (1) as the work force, they implement programs and deliver

Sound employee relations make good citizen relations   If employees are not appreciated, do not have adequate resources, are not empowered to make decisions appropriate to their position, do not understand and accept the rationale for rules and policies, and feel that they are treated arbitrarily, they have difficulty in achieving good relations with citizens and are likely to project a negative image of the local government in their private comments to friends and neighbors. Such conditions also are likely to push employees into acting as a voting bloc which

seeks to go over the head of their managers to get more sympathetic bosses. On the other hand, when employees feel that they are given responsibility and are appreciated for using it well, involved in setting organizational objectives, treated with respect, and able to get grievances handled fairly, they are likely to relate positively to citizens.

Source: Tom L. Kaleko, "Good Citizen Relations Plus Good Employee Relations Equals Good Management," *Public Management* (March 1989): 25–27.

services; (2) as organizational members, they influence internal decisions about pay and work conditions, and, when covered by a collective bargaining agreement, they engage in bilateral negotiations to determine these matters; and (3) as voters who are particularly interested in what local government does, they constitute a pressure group that often supports the election of favored members of the governing board. In general, employees are the government's representatives in the community, both on and off the job.

When collective bargaining is used, the local government manager may find that standard approaches to promoting cooperation such as team building, consensus building, and facilitation do not work well. The perception of opposing interests precludes the mutual trust required for these methods to be successful. There are some principles, however, that are effective in negotiating with employee unions: (1) look at the perceptions, fears, and motivations behind the actions of the union representative; (2) think of a mutually beneficial action for the representative to take; and (3) make it easy for the representative to take that action. When these principles were followed in one city, the union president moved from simply giving input to providing advice to participating in a program to train negotiators, along with other union representatives.[28] This approach does not ask for complete cooperation at the start but moves forward incrementally to greater areas of agreement.

Neighborhood groups   Neighborhood groups are among the most numerous and, in the view of council members who responded to the NLC survey, the most influential in local government affairs. Many of the most intensely felt issues that arise deal with the characteristics of neighborhoods (e.g., what kind of housing will be permitted); providing services that will make the neighborhood more attractive (e.g., a community center); protecting it from threats (e.g., drug trafficking); and resisting changes that will have an adverse impact (e.g., widening a street and increasing traffic). Not only do residents seek to protect the lifestyle of their neighborhood, but also, for homeowners, the value of a major property investment is at stake.

The increased use of district elections has increased the influence of neighborhoods. Also, many local governments have created formal mechanisms for input, such as neighborhood-based citizen advisory committees. For example, the city of

(*continued on page 41*)

The Neighborhood Team Process (NTP) in Richmond, Virginia The NTP is driven by the philosophy that local government in the year 2000 must dramatically change the way it does business. Therefore, it seemed only natural to include the most credible "experts"—the residents whose neighborhoods are affected by the city's decisions—in efforts to restructure the traditional, top-down decision-making process. This approach called for inviting representatives from *all* neighborhoods to participate.

An unlikely assortment of residents from more than 100 diverse neighborhoods was transformed into nine working teams. These teams included a tremendous cross-section of interests represented by city officials, business people, nonprofit organizations, and civic associations, as well as citizens. It was not unusual to find a business owner with a six-figure income seated next to an elderly retiree whose fixed income barely covered the cost of groceries. But in the team meetings they became equal partners in the endeavor to solve problems and set priorities for the city on the basis of the individual needs of their neighborhoods.

The new approach has been enlightening for public administrators. One resident who had been trying for two years to get a manhole cover replaced decided to attempt to get this seemingly impossible task accomplished through the NTP. The effort involved provided a real education for the NTP coordinator—the city's deputy director of community development—in just what working through the system means from the citizen's point of view. The coordinator had to cut through red tape wrapped around a number of players, including the power company, the telephone company, the sewer department, and the property owner. She finally offered to pay for the manhole cover, and ten days and $15 dollars later, she had achieved what the resident had tried to get done for two years. The resident was happy, and the coordinator's perspective on the reality of problem solving was broadened considerably.

Other concerns surfaced during NTP meetings. Six pay phones on one street corner had become a hot spot for drug dealing. Because the NTP included representatives of the Police Bureau and the telephone company, participants were able to come up with a creative solution to the problem. The telephone company began working with the city to convert the pay phones to rotary phones—which the drug dealers could not use with their beepers—and to alter the phones so that incoming calls could not be received.

One citizen was impressed by the cooperative effect of the program. "One of the most positive aspects of the process is that it places citizens and city staffers side by side, which tends to do away with the 'us versus them' mentality and eventually leads to a 'we' frame of mind," said this individual, an architect and one of the chairpersons for the neighborhood districts.

The city manager proved his personal commitment to the NTP by attending two team meetings a year for each district. He also attended regular meetings to bring all the team leaders together to talk about their common problems and concerns. The city manager's willingness to commit his time and to listen directly to the concerns of the participants contributed greatly to their enthusiasm and to the credibility of the process.

In a survey to assess citizen reaction to the NTP, one resident wrote that what she liked most about the process was that it "allows residents to really feel that their concerns about their neighborhoods are being heard. When we come to these meetings, we know there will be someone from the city who will hear us and can be held accountable."

Source: Adapted from Anne Amoury, "A Neighborhood Revolution Hits Richmond City Hall," *Public Management* (August 1990).

(continued from page 39)
Richmond, Virginia, created the Neighborhood Team Process (NTP), a program that brings residents from over 100 neighborhoods into nine working teams to help address service complaints from citizens, provide ideas for the operating and capital improvement budgets, and find ways to help the police counter drug sales (see accompanying sidebar).[29] In large cities, neighborhood groups are being included in strategies to reclaim parks, gyms, community centers, and other municipal facilities in high-crime areas.[30]

Principles for resolving NIMBY disputes NIMBY (Not In My Backyard) disputes are sources of increasing concern for the local government manager. These conflicts occur when the community needs a facility, but no neighborhoods are willing to have the facility located near them. Keeping several principles of conflict resolution in mind may help the local government manager in these situations.

Those who have a stake in NIMBY disputes should be involved in solving them. The local government manager often is confronted with the irreconcilable demands of competing groups who never confront each other. Representatives of the conflicting groups should sit down face to face to craft a solution. Negative perceptions may shift in this face-to-face interaction, especially if the local government manager encourages participants to abide by two other important principles listed below.

Respect the opposition. If the local government manager is a skilled communicator, he or she can facilitate the interaction. Rules of procedure should require active listening, a joint assessment of the situation, and the development of shared solutions to the problems. In some cases, especially when the jurisdiction is or is perceived to be one of the disputants, the manager may want to involve a professional facilitator.

Seek solutions that honor diverse values. Increasingly, the local government manager is confronted with situations in which people of different ages and religious, cultural, ethnic, and socioeconomic backgrounds must co-exist in the same community. In these

cases, people may fear each other without valid reasons. For example, older people may fear that teenagers in the neighborhood will lead to increased crime although statistics do not bear this out. In these situations, it is important that the manager respect the concern, even when it has no realistic basis. The following case, related by David Stiebel, a lecturer on municipal dispute resolution at the University of California, illustrates this point, as well as the principle of resolving a NIMBY dispute through face-to-face contact of the opposing groups.

A county wanted to locate a probation facility across from a shopping center in the county's largest city. The chamber of commerce was pressuring the city to sue to block the facility because the shopping center merchants were afraid it would contribute to the growing problem of drug dealing in the neighborhood. There was no evidence to support these concerns.

The city, however, did not focus its efforts on trying to convince merchants that their concerns were unfounded. Instead, it involved the merchants in a face-to-face dialogue with the county. In professionally managed negotiations, the disputants were able to agree to locate a sheriff's substation in the shopping center at the same time the probation facility was located adjacent to the shopping center. This resolution avoided a costly lawsuit, improved overall relations between the city and the county, and led the merchants to support their local government.

Source: Frances Cooper, Vice-President, Communication Technologies, San Francisco.

Neighborhood organizations can form the base for resisting changes that are viewed as actually or symbolically detrimental. The NIMBY phenomenon is a powerful force to be reckoned with in making siting decisions. It is imperative to consult with residents of the neighborhood before a decision is made, recognize their concerns, and take action to address those concerns. Taking these and other measures to resolve conflicts discussed later in this chapter will not assure acceptance. Failure to take these actions, however, will certainly lead to strong resistance from those in the area affected.

Racial and ethnic groups   Communities are experiencing a transformation of their racial and ethnic composition. "Old" European ethnic groups continue to be important participants in the local politics of cities, primarily in the Northeast and Midwest. African-Americans, who once lived primarily in the rural areas of the South, are a major segment of the population in communities throughout the country. Large numbers of immigrants from Latin America and Asia are adding "new" ethnic groups to the populations of communities. This transformation has been compared to that brought about by the influx of Europeans into the United States in the late nineteenth and early twentieth centuries.

The presence of diverse groups in communities always has created dynamic forces for change and renewal. It also has produced tensions over different values and conflict over how resources are distributed as new groups seek a share. Members of minority groups often have suffered from discrimination, although it is easier for members of European ethnic groups to avoid than it has been—and continues to be—for those in identifiable racial groups.

Different organizations within minority communities emphasize different strategies (or combinations of strategies) for improving the position of the group. For example, among African-Americans, certain groups have emphasized the use of the courts to advance their right to jobs and participation in the political process. Some have stressed political action, including demonstrations and protest, to speed up the pace of change. Others have stressed self-sufficiency and community development through neighborhood corporations and self-help projects.

Although Asian groups exhibit a low level of political participation, they are making an effort to secure increased representation on elected and appointed bodies. The current experience of Asian groups, a large proportion of whom are immigrants, highlights concerns local government managers should have regarding the experience of all ethnic and racial groups. Value and life-style differences may arise between these groups and the established community. For example, there have been disagreements with neighbors and local officials over the removal of trees for garden plots in some Asian communities. Nutritional programs for the elderly may not be sensitive to the dietary preferences of Asian-Americans. Access to jobs is a concern. There have been disputes over economic activities (e.g., between Vietnamese and Anglo fishermen or between Korean shopkeepers and residents of Black neighborhoods). Asians also have been the victims of hate crimes.

In states along the southwestern border of the United States, county governments have become central to the development of unincorporated communities of newly immigrated Hispanics who lack the language and political skills to achieve access to services. They especially need help in securing infrastructure and social services.

Local government managers need to promote recognition and opportunities for inclusion of all groups in the governmental process. They also should determine whether there are problems in the community that relate to race and ethnicity. These include the following: systematic bias in living conditions and opportunities along racial or ethnic lines; discrimination against and exclusion of any groups; tension and conflict among groups; and acts of intolerance and violence directed toward members of minority groups. Local government managers are committed by professional values to promote equality, fair provision of services, service delivery that is sensitive to the characteristics of citizens served, affirmative action to expand opportunities, full participation by all groups, and protection of minority rights.

Civic groups   Communities have a wide variety of civic groups and social clubs. Groups such as the Kiwanis Club, League of Women Voters, Lions Club, Junior League, Rotary Club, and Jaycees provide an opportunity for members to be informed about community affairs, undertake common projects, contribute to community activities, and network with each other. They usually are not influential community actors as organizations (although the people who belong to them may

---

Managing in a community of changing demographics   The most important aspect of management's approach to the new demographics is discussing the issues involved in order to understand them and avoid confrontation. Although it is easier to expect new residents to conform to existing rules and procedures, the potential exists for development of adversarial relations that do not contribute to the long-term welfare of the community.

Diversity can benefit the community if respect for it is fostered by local government leaders and integrated into current programs. Managers can familiarize themselves with the cultures and traditions of new residents by reading related materials or by attending cultural programs that can give them a sense of the residents' background and traditional beliefs and practices. This effort can help managers understand why members of the groups take some of the actions they take. Ethnic support groups also can be a valuable tool for local officials who want to learn about different cultures and work with their members.

Managers never should criticize another culture because its norms are inconsistent with theirs. In San Marino, city staff members came to understand the Chinese belief that having an unobstructed entry into the home ensures good fortune. Appropriate steps were then taken to deal with city codes that prohibited the cutting down of trees, resulting in a policy that allowed trees to be removed (which met the concern of Chinese residents) while requiring that new trees be planted on the prop-

erty (which maintained the city's effort to preserve an urban forest setting).

Most ethnic groups have their own social, philanthropic, and religious organizations that can serve as an education medium for anyone who is interested in learning about them. San Marino has the Chinese Club, a strong community organization that publishes a newsletter in Chinese that is mailed to Chinese residents, who constitute about 500 of the 4,200 families in the city. The Chinese Club has helped city staff by interpreting city codes, explaining procedures, and serving as a sounding board for the city manager on issues of concern to the Chinese community.

Something as simple as a monthly lunch with the club's board has had positive results. When the city proposed new commercial sign regulations—which would have the most direct impact on Chinese businesses— the Chinese Club conveyed to city staff the community's ideas about acceptable standards for signs. It also explained the code that eventually was adopted to new businesses. As a result, a broad range of residents and businesses in San Marino supported the regulations, when elsewhere lawsuits were being filed against cities throughout the San Gabriel Valley of Los Angeles County. Confrontation was avoided, and unified support was obtained.

Source: Adapted from John E. Nowak, "Managing in a City of Changing Demographics," *Public Management* (April 1991).

be active and influential); nevertheless, some will take the initiative to propose governmental actions. They are important to local government managers as vehicles for the managers' own involvement in the community, as organizations through which information about local government needs and programs can be disseminated, and as the source of the activists who may be needed to make projects successful. Managers should include these groups in an assessment of their networking in the community. In a similar way, professional associations (e.g., of physicians or accountants) and labor organizations can be important as channels through which information is disseminated or assistance is requested by managers, although typically these groups are not active in local government affairs.

Interest groups   The number of groups that promote broad- and narrow-issue agendas is very large. They may be nationally oriented and take up local issues only when they are relevant to the group's concerns (e.g., the Sierra Club) or organized specifically around local issues (e.g., a save-the-park organization). As noted previously, there is probably an increased number of groups that are actively represented by elected officials, seek to influence decisions made by local officials, or apply pressure to block a local action. A general phenomenon that affects local government (as well as national lobbying or election campaigns) is the increasing ability of organizations to mobilize members to apply intense pressure regarding a specific issue. This may take the form of lobbying as well as of supporting candidates for the governing board. The activity of these groups has expanded the local government agenda and injected many new voices into public discussions. It has also, however, increased the possibility that response to one issue will create imbalances in other areas and that governing board members will be elected who have very narrow agendas. Managers need to communicate more extensively with governing board members to help them be aware of the general needs and policies that should be kept in mind when making specific decisions.

In the future, we must accept the moral commitment to serve all stakeholders in the community. This requires sensitivity to equity as well as efficiency.
G. Curtis Branscome

Elderly citizens   The elderly population—persons sixty-two years of age and older—is growing in size and will increase dramatically in the not-too-distant future.[31] Elderly citizens—who are more active politically than younger people—have distinct characteristics and needs and should be recognized as a distinct group by local government managers. Whereas they once were concentrated in central cities of metropolitan areas, they are now found in rural areas (where young people have moved out); in suburban communities (where they are a larger proportion of the population than in urban areas); and, of course, in retirement communities. For elderly citizens who prefer to live independently in the same area they resided in during their adult lives, the housing (e.g., houses or apartment buildings with more than one story) and community characteristics (e.g., reliance on the automobile for access) may not match their needs if physical limitations develop. Services and facilities of special interest to them may not be as available as they would be in retirement complexes and communities that have developed around an influx of elderly residents. For all elderly people, health costs can impose a strain on budgets, particularly when income is fixed. Elderly residents can nevertheless be highly committed to the betterment of the community and are important sources of volunteer assistance.

Poor and homeless citizens   Poor citizens generally demonstrate a low level of participation in community affairs. Because many of them feel alienated from and excluded by the community, they pay less attention to government and are less likely to vote. As individuals, they often lack the knowledge, skills, time, and resources for effective participation. As a "group," poor people are fragmented into many segments (e.g., single mothers with dependent children and jobless, homeless, ill, disabled, and elderly citizens), and they are divided by race and ethnicity. This group therefore has limited organization and leadership.

Nevertheless, poor citizens have extensive contact with public officials. They are heavy consumers of public services, yet have great unmet needs. The problems of homeless citizens are especially acute. However, local governments are severely constrained in their capacity to respond to the needs of poor and homeless citizens. Restricted budgets and increasing needs in all areas limit their ability to allocate more funds for programs for the poor. This constraint is particularly evident in cities with the greatest problems.

There are, however, general strategies that local government managers can employ in their efforts to serve poor citizens as fairly and effectively as they do other members of the community. These strategies include the following: (1) fair and prompt response to the individual citizen's problems and complaints about local services; (2) effective and impartial delivery of basic services (e.g., fire, police, recreation, refuse collection, and social services) to all parts of the community; (3) equal opportunity for jobs and promotion in the government work force; (4) going beyond an open-door policy to make special efforts to identify, support, and seek input from leaders of groups that speak for poor people; (5) prohibition of discriminatory practices by public employees; and (6) constant monitoring for unintended exclusionary impacts of public policies.

The media

The media simultaneously occupy a number of roles, making them an important and potent force in community relations as well as an interested party affected by the outcome of some governmental decisions. As business enterprises, they have at least an interest in their own economic success, and their handling of news (including how much attention they give to local government) can be affected by a desire to sell papers or air time to sponsors. Nevertheless, local government asks the media to donate advertising space or time for local government activities. The media both relay information from local officials and shape and reflect public opinion. They are participants in and instigators of local political action and interpreters of community affairs who can help to make or break the acceptance of a project or passage of a referendum. These cross-currents make the relationship between local government and the media complex, to say the least.

The greatest amount of interaction with the media relates to news coverage of local government activities. Managers need to recognize that tight deadlines, limited space and time, lack of knowledgeable reporters, and lack of reader or viewer interest in complex, technical subjects all tend to limit and distort local news coverage. The print and electronic media have widely varying perspectives on news coverage and different production methods and schedules. Some guidelines for effective media relations are presented in the next section.

Providing effective community leadership

The effective local government manager brings to community leadership a perspective that reflects the values and methods of the profession of local government management. Those values include fairness, impartiality, inclusiveness, and commitment to the broad public interest. The FutureVisions project of ICMA identified the skills and attributes managers need to be effective (e.g., consensus builder, translator/interpreter of community values, and problem solver). The full list is given in Chapter 1. In this chapter, the emphasis is on the skills that the manager

Principles in conflict resolution

1. Separate the people from the problem. Don't personalize attacks. Don't take cheap shots. Invite the other person to disagree with you when you make a statement. Publicly test the inferences you draw from statements and the assumptions you make about other participants.
2. Discuss interests and concerns rather than positions. Positions usually are well known and mutually unacceptable, but the interests and concerns behind them may not be well articulated or understood. Encourage others to discuss their interests, and do not tell them what their interests are.
3. Invent options for mutual gain.

Identify and agree on shared interests. Think of new options that satisfy the concerns and interests of both sides.
4. Separate the generation of alternatives from decision making. Use brain storming to generate ideas, but do not evaluate them as they are being presented.
5. Develop consensus for solutions. This assures that each side and each participant has an equal role in shaping the agreements of the group.

Source: Adapted from William Potapchuk, "Building Forums for the Cooperative Resolution of Disputes in Communities," *National Civic Review* 77 (July/August 1988): 342.

---

needs to handle key aspects of community relations: conflict resolution, media relations, and leadership in a diverse community.

Resolving conflict

Conflict resolution is divided into two separate tasks. First, the parties must agree or be persuaded to come to the table and engage in dialogue. Second, assistance is required to help them find some basis for agreement. The first task entails "building a forum" for cooperative resolution of disputes.[32] The key participants must be persuaded that the process will be open and fair and that no outcome will be imposed on them. They must agree to a set of ground rules that govern openness of the meetings, media relations, decision making (is consensus required?), and use of a facilitator or mediator. Establishing the ground rules provides an opportunity to form agreements before the groups turn to substantive issues.

The second task involves facilitating discussion according to certain principles designed to change the tone of interaction (from negative to neutral to positive) and to identify common ground.

Using these principles, residents and skateboarders in one community were able to move from an impasse over the construction of a skateboard ramp in a specific site. When they acknowledged their respective interests—maintaining a quiet, pleasant neighborhood and having a safe place to skateboard—they were able to explore alternative methods to meet these interests and develop a mutually acceptable solution to the problem.

Media relations

It is easy for the manager to view the media as the enemy and to feel that is impossible to have any influence on them. However, managers can follow these pointers for effective media relations in news coverage.[33]

Recognize and accept the fact that the public has the right to know what goes on in local government. Respect the spirit and letter of freedom of information laws. Contests with the media over how much to hide and how much to expose are not positive for either side.

Be honest. If you don't know the answer, tell reporters that you will try to find an answer for them, and be sure to follow up. If you cannot answer a question, explain why.

Remember that *nothing* is off the record unless the reporter has agreed in advance to treat the communication that way. Sometimes things need to be discussed in confidence, but managers who go off the record frequently may damage their own credibility as well as circumvent the public's right to know.

Establish a clear policy for press relations, coordinated by one person, that establishes who is responsible for releasing what type of information. Encourage reporters to talk to any officials. Be sure that officials and employees know, however, what information is public and when it is appropriate and inappropriate to comment on policy questions.

Be sure information given to reporters is accurate and complete. Provide them the full agenda packet as well as background reports. Do not make it difficult for a reporter to obtain information.

Take time to orient reporters to local government relations. Explain who does what, what various acronyms mean, and how and why certain decisions are made.

Do your homework before you meet with reporters. Anticipate their questions. Think about your audience and the purpose of the story. Avoid off-the-wall comments that may cause you or the local government embarrassment later.

If a news story is inaccurate, do not hesitate to tell the reporter. However, the manager should respect the reporter's news judgment and ignore minor inaccuracies.

Examples of efforts to involve and promote the appreciation of all groups in the community   The city of Little Rock, Arkansas, brought diverse racial, ethnic, and income groups—including those who had been adversaries of the city—into a community planning process, through programs such as community policing, using volunteers for neighborhood cleanup efforts, and establishing pools of capital funds for which neighborhoods set priorities.

The Neighborhood Revitalization Plan in Minneapolis, Minnesota, empowered residents in all neighborhoods to set priorities for services.

"Leadership Santa Barbara" in California is an on-going educational forum that stresses collaborative planning and facilitation and teaches decision-making skills to develop the talents of existing and aspiring leaders from all segments of the county's population.

"Dallas Together" was created in 1986 by the mayor of Dallas, Texas, with representatives of all local ethnic and cultural groups, to promote communication and cultural understanding.

"Team Abilene" is a grass-roots effort in Texas to involve citizens in community service, increase awareness of the city's diversity, celebrate unity, and build a sense of community.

Allentown, Pennsylvania, created "A World of Difference," a program to reduce prejudice through the celebration of diversity. Acceptance of and respect for differences are taught in workshops that bring people of different backgrounds together.

In Dallas, the police opened a storefront office in an Asian community staffed by reserve officers who are of the same nationality as the members of the community.

Source: Adapted from William R. Barnes, ed., *Diversity and Governance* (Washington, DC: National League of Cities, 1992).

Be aware of differences in their deadlines and recognize the competition between the print and electronic media. Provide equal access and the same information to all reporters. Return calls in time to meet deadlines. Handle news breaks as impartially and objectively as possible among competing media.

Be accessible during evenings and weekends. Reporters generally will respect your privacy, although some may need to check a fact or get your comment in order to complete a story. Frequently, stories are written, edited, or produced long after government offices are closed.

Recognize the pressures on reporters from deadlines, limited time for checking statements, limited space or air time, and competition with other media. All tend to encourage sensationalism and controversial coverage.

Learn to accept the fact that criticism of local government, the manager, and other officials will appear in the media. Learn to live with the skepticism that is part of a reporter's professional perspective. Remember that the media are not in business to quietly inform local government when a problem is discovered but rather to transmit the information to their audience.

Leadership in a diverse community

Effective leadership in a community characterized by ethnic, cultural, and socioeconomic diversity requires the manager to relate to citizens in distinctive ways.[34] When there are large numbers of immigrants, part of this approach is to communicate with at least some citizens in their native tongue, and in many communities, managers will need to be bilingual in the future. In their relationships with these groups, managers should stress inclusion, appreciation of diversity, and representation.

Inclusion   Leadership involves creating a sense of community out of diversity rather than dividing or polarizing groups. Efforts to identify common ground and overarching principles acceptable to all must start with a willingness to encompass all segments of the community. The challenge is to create something more than just an assembly of representatives of different groups. If inclusion is to become a reality, the groups must actually participate in efforts to achieve a broader perspective on the nature of problems and their solutions.

Appreciation of diversity   Group differences and special qualities should be appreciated and celebrated. Appreciation leads to understanding the reasons for behavior and how different cultural traditions—or a group's distinct experience—may affect its values and participation in community affairs. It is one thing to be aware of an ethnic group's traditions in its original homeland; it is more difficult to understand how those traditions and values affect behavior in the group's present circumstances. Frank Benest, city manager of Brea, California, argues that cities should "market diversity" in order to promote it as a positive feature rather than view it as a liability.[35] However, officials must first ensure that the government has embraced diversity internally and in its relationships with citizens in order to achieve the depth of understanding necessary to overcome stereotypic assumptions and prejudices.

Representation of diversity   Despite the fact that more groups are represented on city and county governing boards by the increase in district elections, leaders should also provide opportunities for groups to speak and act for themselves through special channels and forums for expression of diverse views. For example, Phoenix has adopted an urban village system by creating eight city council districts. By increasing decentralization of services, empowering citizens at the neighborhood level, and widely disseminating information about city government activities, the city allows diverse neighborhoods to speak for themselves. The challenge is to ensure that the points of view of all groups are effectively expressed, directly or indirectly. Furthermore, groups must be encouraged to communicate with each other. City manager Don Paschal observed, "We need to remember the necessity not only of sensitizing Anglos to minority culture but also each minority culture to the culture of other ethnic minorities.[36] Inclusion is not achieved one-on-one with each separate group, but by forming a sense of community among all groups with each other.

Recap

The theme of this chapter is that local government managers are and must be leaders in their communities. They do not act as independent agents in providing leadership. They do not seek to achieve any fixed level of involvement, nor do they necessarily undertake any specific activities. Rather they work with other leaders to create and maintain certain conditions: effective two-way communication with all parts of the public; the capacity to identify and resolve issues in ways that meet the long-term needs of the community; broad-based understanding of and support for the work of local government; and constructive relations among groups in the community.

These conditions are not created without contributions from managers. However, local government managers must adjust their level of activity depending on the activism of elected officials and other community leaders. Appointed managers complement the abilities and inclinations of elected officials and fill in as needed to strengthen the government's relations with, and performance in, the community. They do not seek center stage unless the conditions require that the manager be both visible and active.

Professional managers are obligated to ensure that all groups have access to the decision-making process and are treated fairly, whether or not they are directly represented on the city council or participate actively in local politics. Because managers value objectivity and decision making based on complete information, they seek to bring all points of view and a full range of alternatives into consideration, not just those that are promoted by activist groups. They also are increasingly a source of continuity, linking current decisions to past actions and to long-term goals for the community. As governing boards become more diverse and members focus more on specific areas and groups, local government managers must maintain a perspective that encompasses all segments of the community. They must draw attention to problems and initiate proposals to solve them. The politics of the 1990s challenge the manager to be at once an advocate and a guardian of the integrity of the policymaking process.

To meet their responsibilities, local government managers need to have their own ties with a full range of groups in the community. They must be outgoing, or at least capable of communicating effectively outside government, and inclusive. They must have a clear understanding of patterns of influence and participation and know how to get things accomplished in a professionally responsible way. They need their own constituency, a network of contacts to be used both for input and for disseminating information about what local government is doing.

Local government managers must be introspective and assess their strengths and weaknesses. The typical manager is not naturally comfortable with the demands of community leadership and is more inclined to be a pragmatic problem solver than a visionary thinker. Most prefer to be analytical, whereas many people in the community are emotional about their problems and positions. Managers seek to create order and move decisions to closure, whereas community affairs are unpredictable and spontaneous, and decision making is often protracted.

The typical characteristics of local government managers make them well suited to processing information and developing recommendations to the governing board for the fair delivery of services and the efficient management of organizational resources. They must develop their abilities to communicate, empathize, create, and adapt. Their professional commitment to fairness and equity makes them attentive to all groups and to the community as a whole. With these qualities, local government managers become effective community leaders.

Community assessment for project initiation

When local government managers work to get a major project under way, they fill several roles:

The initiator, who helps get an issue on the public agenda and seeks to secure effective action

The catalyst, who brings others into the process and who works through others

The responsible professional, who seeks to ensure that the decisions are (1) clearly related to and advance the mission of the organization; (2) based on appropriate information about needs, alternatives, and impacts; and (3) reached in a legitimate way by the governing board with broad-based participation of all those affected.

The following are questions the manager can use to assess and monitor the involvement in the project of various individuals and groups in the local government and community.

A. Local government

Where did the project originate?

Is there complete and objective analysis of the need and the alternative approaches?

What other departments will be affected? What input do they have or should they have in developing a proposal?

Is there an appropriate level of understanding and support for the project in the organization?

B. Governing body

What is the stance of elected officials with regard to the project? Are they in agreement, divided by constituency, opposed, or waiting for a decision to be presented to them?

If they are supportive, how firm is their support?

How much do they know about the project? (Have you been the only source of information?) Who might sway them in different directions?

What would happen if something goes wrong or a new issue appears?

Are you too far out in front of the governing body? As you venture into the community, is the governing body behind you?

C. The active community
Who constitutes your network of supporters through whom information about the project can be disseminated and general support can be obtained?

Whose support is needed? What kind of support?

1. Non-opposition
2. Approval
3. Endorsements/publicity
4. Participation
5. Resources

How will support be obtained? Who is the best contact?

Who will oppose the project? When? At the beginning, middle, or end of the project? If opposition will occur late in the process, should participation be invited earlier to secure the input of opponents? On what grounds is the opposition based? Is common ground possible? How can it be secured? Are opponents willing to engage in conflict resolution efforts?

D. The inactive community

Who will be affected by the project but not necessarily participate in the decision-making process?

How will they be affected?

Will they support or oppose the project?

Should they be left alone or involved? Are they being left alone to make it simpler to get the project approved? (If so, they should be brought into the process.)

Who should contact them?

To capture the steps and interrelationships in the process, develop a Gantt chart (bar graph plotting of action by start and completion date) or flow chart for the process. Be particularly attentive to the sequencing of actions. Asking the question "Who should be contacted before I take this action?" helps the manager identify people who might otherwise be left out and steps that might be overlooked.

---

1 See Bill Kirchoff, "Babbit Could Have Been a Manager," *Public Management* 72 (September 1990): 2, and James R. Griesemer, "Restoring Relevance to Local Government Management," *Public Management* 72 (September 1990): 7.

2 Harold A. Stone, Don K. Price, and Kathryn H. Stone, *City Manager Government in the United States* (Chicago: Public Administration Service, 1940), 247. This observation is noteworthy because the Great Depression was the period of most constricted involvement by local government managers.

3 Laurence E. Lynn, Jr., *Managing the Public's Business* (New York: Basic Books, 1981), ch. 6.

4 The levels of decisions are defined in James H. Svara, "Dichotomy and Duality: Reconceptualizing the Relationship Between Policy and Administration in Council-Manager Cities," *Public Administration Review* 45 (January/February, 1985): 221. The types of games are from Lynn.

5 Clinton Rogers Woodruff, ed., *A New Municipal Program* (New York: D. Appleton, 1919), 31, 130. For a fuller discussion, see James H. Svara, "Progressive Roots of the Model Charter and the Manager Profession: A Positive Heritage," *National Civic Review* 78 (September/October 1989): 339.

6 James H. Svara, *Official Leadership in the City* (New York: Oxford University Press, 1990), 188–192.

7 James M. Banovetz, ed., *Managing the Modern City* (Washington, DC: ICMA, 1971), 84.

8 Tari Renner, "Municipal Election Processes: The Impact on Minority Representation," *Municipal Yearbook 1988* (Washington, DC: ICMA, 1988), 140.

9 Charles R. Adrian, "Forms of City Government in American History," *Municipal Yearbook 1988* (Washington, DC: ICMA, 1988), 10.

10 James H. Svara, *A Survey of America's City Councils* (Washington, DC: National League of Cities, 1991).

11 Ibid., 28–29.

12 Charldean Newell and David N. Ammons, "Role Emphasis of City Managers and Other Municipal Executives," *Public Administration Review* 47 (May/June 1987): 246.

13 David Morris, "Rootlessness Undermines Our Economy as Well as the Quality of Our Lives," *Utne Reader* (May/June 1990): 88.

14 Terms used in this discussion are drawn from the Myers Briggs Type Indicator, which is discussed further below. See Sandra Krebs Hirsh and Jean M. Kummerow, *Introduction to Type in Organizational Settings* (Palo Alto: Consulting Psychologists Press, 1987).

15 The Myers Briggs types on this dimension are "judgers" and "perceivers."

16 The approximate connections between the types of manager we have just described and the MBTI types follow. (E = extroverted; I = introverted; S = sensing; N = intuitive; T = thinking; F = feeling; J = judging; P = perceiving)
   Community leader—ENTJ
   Chief executive—INTJ
   Administrative innovator—INTJ
   Administrative stabilizer/improver—ISTJ
   Coalition builder—ENFP
   Arbiter—ESFP
   Caretaker—ISTJ

17 Charles K. Coe, "The MBTI: A Tool for Understanding and Improving Management," *State and Local Government Review* 23 (Winter 1991): 37. The percentage of each characteristic among city managers in North Carolina is as follows:

Extroverted	39%	Inverted	61%
Sensing	76%	Intuitive	24%
Thinking	87%	Feeling	13%
Judging	82%	Perceiving	18%

18 Oliver P. Williams, "A Typology for Comparative Local Government," *Midwest Journal of Political Science* 5 (May, 1961): 150.

19 Edward C. Banfield and James Q. Wilson, *City Politics* (New York: Vintage Books, 1963), 177–180.

20 See Rufus P. Browning, Dale Rogers Marshall, and David H. Tabb, *Protest Is Not Enough* (Berkeley: University of California Press, 1984), for an analysis of changing political forces in ten California cities.

21 Gordon Whitaker and Ruth Hoogland DeHoog, "City Managers Under Fire: How Conflict Leads to

Turnover," *Public Administration Review* 51 (March/April 1991): 156. The managers completed a survey in 1986 that included questions about the political stability of the community. Those who left were reinterviewed by phone three years later.

22 For a review of major studies and a multi-method analysis of San Jose, see Philip J. Trounstine and Terry Christensen, *Movers and Shakers* (New York: St. Martin's Press, 1982).

23 See, for example, Stephen Elkin, *City and Regime in the American Republic* (Chicago: University of Chicago Press, 1987), and Clarence Stone, *Regime Politics: Governing Atlanta* (Lawrence: University of Kansas Press, 1989).

24 Svara, *Official Leadership in the City*, 87–88.

25 James H. Svara, *A Survey of America's City Councils* (Washington, DC: National League of Cities, 1991), 32.

26 Alan Ehrenhalt, "For Chambers of Commerce and Cities, The Days of Conflict May Be Over," *Governing* (November 1989), 40.

27 Richard C. Feiock and James Clingermayer, "Municipal Representation, Executive Power, and Economic Development Policy Activity," *Policy Studies Journal* 15 (December 1986): 211. The actions examined were business assistance centers, tax rebates, and Urban Development Action Grant submissions.

28 David Stiebel, "They Won't Cooperate? Reach Agreement Anyway!" *Public Management* (July 1991): 13.

29 Anne Amoury, "A Neighborhood Revolution Hits Richmond City Hall," *Public Management* (August 1990): 2.

30 For examples, see Frank Benest, "Creating Neighborhood Connections," *Public Management* (August 1990): 6.

31 Between July 2008 and July 2009, 3.5 million people will celebrate their sixty-second birthday as the first of the baby boom generation to reach the age for early retirement. This will be 37 percent more than in the previous year and 63 percent more than in 1990. See Judith Waldrop, "You'll Know It's the 21st Century When . . .," *Public Management* (January 1991): 3. See also Fernando M. Torres-Gil, *The New Aging: Politics and Change in America* (New York: Auburn House, 1992).

32 William Potapchuk, "Building Forums for the Cooperative Resolution of Disputes in Communities," *National Civic Review* 77 (July-August, 1988): 342.

33 Many of these points were drawn from Stribling P. Boynton, "A Dozen Tips for Working with the Media," *Public Management* (March 1989): 27.

34 For additional suggestions, see John Nowak, "Managing in a City of Changing Demographics," *Public Management* (April 1991): 3.

35 Frank Benest, "Marketing Multiethnic Communities," *Public Management* (December 1991): 4.

36 Remarks made by Don Paschal at a meeting of the North Texas City Management Association focused on "Future Issues," 15 November 1991.

Enhancing the governing body's effectiveness

A bond exists between the elected governing body and its appointed manager in the form of their common obligation to make local government work for the good of the citizens in the community. Citizens usually judge how well their local government officials meet this obligation on the basis of the community's economic vitality and quality of life and the local government's responsiveness to their needs. Often, the success of the local government in meeting citizens' expectations and community goals depends on the manager's ability to enhance the governing body's effectiveness.

This chapter explores ways in which local appointed and elected officials can achieve a successful partnership in their mutual effort to create and maintain an effective government. It examines the changing roles of both the governing body and the local government manager and explores ways in which the manager can help members of the governing body become more effective policymakers with a broad view of community affairs. In addition, the chapter discusses the importance of the governing body's confidence in the manager and describes possible sources of friction between the manager and governing body. The chapter concludes by suggesting some ways of measuring the manager's and the governing body's effectiveness.

The changing role of the governing body

At various times throughout the twentieth century, intense struggles have occurred to replace centralized dictatorial forms of government with more decentralized and democratic forms. In the 1980s, totalitarian regimes fell in both Asia and Europe, and in the early 1990s, democratically elected governments predominated in South America. Central European countries have attempted to recast their economic systems as they try to revive the dormant roots of home rule in local government, and local governments have assumed broader roles in Canada, Australia, and New Zealand, as well as in the United States.

National governments have begun to delegate some of their authority and the responsibilities that go with it to lower levels of government, and they are likely to continue to do so in the next century. As a consequence, local governing bodies will be required to demonstrate a greater degree of political leadership than they have in the past. As they receive less state and national financial assistance, local elected officials will have to find innovative ways to generate revenue; as they prepare to compete in an increasingly global economy, they will have to develop an international outlook. At the same time, policymakers in rural areas, townships, and smaller municipalities may find it necessary to seek innovative approaches to interlocal cooperation in order to avoid service duplication, improve the quality and efficiency of services and the equity of service delivery, and develop a much-needed sense of community with other localities.

As they confront the challenges that arise from social, political, and economic change, local elected officials must ask themselves the old question of whether they should lead by influencing citizen attitudes and opinions or by faithfully representing public opinion as expressed in polls and public forums. This question was addressed by Edmund Burke as long ago as the eighteenth century. Both he and, in modern times, John F. Kennedy, held that the elected leader must assume responsibility for independent personal action within the framework of democratic principles, with sensitivity to individual rights and freedoms. In Kennedy's words,

The voters selected us, in short, because they had confidence in our judgment and our ability to exercise that judgment from a position where we could determine what were their own best interests, as part of the nation's [or community's] interests. This may mean that we must on occasion lead, inform, correct and sometimes even ignore constituent opinion, if we are to exercise fully that judgment for which we were elected.[1]

For elected officials who agree with Burke and Kennedy, effective leadership is not an automatic consequence of their position and authority; rather, it is an applied art. According to Warren Bennis, leaders should exercise a "transformative power" that does not spring from the structures of governments, but from the ability of the leader to empower others through vision, purpose, belief, and organizational culture.[2] Like appointed local government managers, elected officials need to reinterpret traditional models of leadership and develop the proactive and anticipatory leadership qualities discussed in Chapter 1 in order to meet the demands they will face.

However, the newer models of leadership may increase opportunities for conflict, which, in a rapidly changing world, already are numerous. John Gardner contends that collisions are inevitable and often healthy: "Indeed, one could argue that willingness to engage in battle when necessary is a sine qua non of leadership."[3] In the constant battle over which services local governments are to provide for whom—and over how they are to be funded—the resolution of conflict emerges as a central focus of leadership and management. Despite leaders' efforts to diminish it, conflict will remain a constant as the demand for services increases, resources shrink, and the need for change challenges the status quo.

James H. Svara notes that local governments themselves also may experience persistent conflict, which occurs commonly in mayor-council or county executive forms of government based on the separation of powers and checks and balances. However, in council-manager governments with no separation of powers, "elected and administrative officials have compatible goals, and therefore, do not actively seek to block the goals of others."[4]

Cooperation between elected officials and administrators is perhaps more critical now than ever before. In the face of pervasive social, political, and economic change, successful partnerships between the governing body and the local government manager are essential in sustaining present achievements and maintaining the momentum of progress.

The manager

The institutional role of the local government manager has evolved through adaptation to increasingly rapid and complex social and political change. For better or worse, the local government manager has come a long way since 1908, when Staunton, Virginia, provided by ordinance for the appointment of a general manager. At that time, the primary objective of local government was to provide prompt, effective, and economical administration that was responsive to the electorate. Democratic principles were served by concentrating all municipal powers in a council of elected representatives vested with total responsibility for public policymaking. Administrative efficiency, in turn, was obtained by concentrating all administrative functions under a single manager appointed by and responsible to the council. This arrangement clearly acknowledged a distinction between policymaking and administration.

The appointed professional manager was required to be an expert in matters of municipal administration, summarized in Luther Gulick's famous acronym POSDCORB (Planning, Organizing, Staffing, Directing, Coordinating, Reporting, Budgeting). Once simply a shorthand method of recalling the assigned functions of the local government manager, the acronym now serves as an index of the state of the art of public management in past decades. Managers were largely trained, and success was largely determined by performance, in these seven areas.

In *The Study of Public Administration*, Dwight Waldo traced the changes that took place in management between the 1930s and the 1950s, but most important, he underscored the emergence of a "newly awakened interest in the value side of public administration."[5] The politics-administration dichotomy was being laid aside in response to the realization that effective management meant dealing with the values involved in public policymaking. Management was becoming involved as much in politics as it was in pure administration—not partisan politics of the type that motivated turn-of-the-century reformers, but the politics involved in the conflict of values encountered in allocating public resources in a democratic society.

Of the broad functions of the local government—providing services, creating benefits, and resolving conflict—contemporary managers have had to take an ever-increasing role in conflict resolution. Services and benefits must still be provided, with even greater efficiency, but the manager now is also expected to be a full partner with the governing body in the political side of the policymaking process. The effective manager has been able to adapt to the change.

Managers who are apolitical will not survive in the 90s.
Don Osenbaugh

The role of the local government manager in the 1990s has become ambiguous. No longer can an all-encompassing acronym, a managerial security blanket, be used to give clear direction. The vast and increasing responsibilities of current and future managers are not amenable to easy or precise definition. The job calls for a blend of interpersonal, professional, and technical skills. To say that the managerial function is primarily to administer the council's policies is to neglect a large number of activities that make up a typical day on the manager's calendar. It would be more appropriate to describe the term *the managerial function* as shorthand for everything the local manager is expected to do.

The manager carries out managerial functions when he or she prepares a budget for council consideration, gives a speech to a local community group, fires a department head, meets with officials from other governments, or develops a five-year plan for annexation. In each of these, as in numerous other activities, the manager wears a variety of hats, as the chapters of this book illustrate. The influences and various powers that accompany each of the roles complement one another in such a way that the office of manager amounts to a good deal more than the sum of its parts. Furthermore, there is an ongoing reciprocal relationship among the roles; performance in one affects and is affected by performance in the others. The effective manager wears all the hats at once to make the best use of the legal, administrative, and political power of the office.

The effective governing body

The impact of the political system and of individual managers' values and goals on policy implementation cannot be overemphasized. However, regardless of variations, managers have in common one responsibility that should receive the highest priority: enhancing the governing body's effectiveness. This should be the consideration around which all others revolve and the baseline for setting priorities.

Professional managers in most local governments have help in carrying out their various roles. Depending on the size of the government, a good many day-to-day managerial tasks and more important policy roles are often assumed by others in administrative positions. Thus, the manager can give direction and delegate authority in virtually every task except that of primary responsibility for working with and enhancing the effectiveness of the governing body. Only the manager has the obligation and is in a position to work with elected officials to enable them to fulfill their roles successfully.

The success, professional development, and future of the professional local government manager are tied directly to the council. If the governing body is effective, or is perceived to be effective, generally the manager also looks good. A symbiotic relationship exists between the two, and the effective manager seeks to ensure that the relationship remains mutually beneficial.

Managers considered successful by their peers—in terms of both tenure and far-reaching impact on policy and the community—are those who have effective councils and commissions and have given credit to the elected body for its achievements. Managers gain strength and develop their own effectiveness in direct proportion to the strength, skill, and policymaking ability of their governing body. They have a responsibility to develop the capabilities of the elected officials and to make them aware of their roles and powers. Often governing body members seek office as a public service and without significant experience in local politics. Frequently, they are paid only a nominal sum and have modest, if any, staff support. Accordingly, many are amateurs attempting to cope with the demands of government, politics, administration, and technology while serving part-time. The manager's obligation is to work with the council or commission on a continuing basis to make local government work, not by telling members what to do, but by counseling them and suggesting actions to help them achieve their goals.

Many kinds of manager-governing body relationships exist, either by design or by default, but as Figure 3–1 shows, there are four basic types: strong council-strong manager; strong council-weak manager; weak council-strong manager; and weak council-weak manager. Any of the relationships is determined in part by its legal framework, but the personalities and interpersonal relations of the individuals involved have significant influence.

It is the thesis of this chapter that local governing bodies, if they are to rise to

---

Orientation to increase council members' effectiveness   When John Goss became city manager of Chula Vista, California, the city faced many challenges, ranging from growth management to limited resources. Goss therefore designed the following techniques to increase the effectiveness of the city's elected officials in dealing with these challenges.

In order to give elected officials the background they need to make informed recommendations and decisions, the city provides orientation for council members and candidates.

The city manager meets with candidates for mayor and council before an election to fill them in on city issues. In addition, the city manager offers to provide information as questions arise during the campaign.

After an election, the city manager orients new council members and encourages them to schedule meetings with department heads.

Quarterly tours of the city are conducted for the city council, press, and interested public.

Special workshops are scheduled to allow elected officials and the public more opportunity to contribute to city planning. The workshops are videotaped for other officials and televised for the public.

Source: *Public Management* (November 1991): 17.

Figure 3–1 Manager-governing body relations.

	Council	
	Strong	**Weak**
Manager — Strong	Strong council Strong manager	Weak council Strong manager
Manager — Weak	Strong council Weak manager	Weak council Weak manager

the challenges of the 1990s and beyond the year 2000, have a more important role to play in the years ahead than at perhaps any time during the twentieth century. The federal system has changed in ways that directly affect local governments. "New localism"—the requirement that local governments make policy without federal initiatives or funding—and the continuing necessity to "do more with less" mean that local government will continue to move toward governance by managing conflict rather than governance by consensus. In many respects, the local governing board will serve as the court of last appeal.

It has become increasingly imperative that governing bodies understand their responsibilities and have the ability to assess the needs of a community at any given time. Changing conditions often dictate changing responsibilities, and a strong legislative body has the ability not only to make accurate assessments, but to provide appropriate direction and leadership. For example, a community may have in place policies predicated on growth—the boom model of the 1970s and early 1980s—but find itself with a high unemployment rate and a serious shortfall in revenues. The governing body must be able to alter course and adopt a strategy for recovery.

Structuring effectiveness

Although there has been no systematic inquiry into what combination of conditions makes local legislative bodies effective, three questions related to policymaking constitute a brief checklist: (1) Does the governing body make decisions that are a basis for getting things done? (2) Does the governing body exercise its primary role of formulating policy and overseeing its execution? (3) Does the governing body get sufficient information to initiate policy successfully?

Decisions as a basis for action   Policies determine the nature and extent of government intervention in the regulation of public behavior, the allocation of community resources, and the provision of public services. Policies further determine how and where behavior is to be regulated and services are to be provided. Similarly, policies determine who will be affected by governmental action and who must finance such action through payment of taxes, licenses, or fees. For example, a decision to enhance local revenues by increasing the number and amount of user fees determines who will receive and pay for services.

Policy formulation and oversight   In theory, the governing body assumes responsibility for formulating policy and delegates responsibility for its execution to the manager. However, such clear distinctions are misleading. In practice, policymaking is a shared responsibility of the governing body and the manager. Managers play a significant and often leading role in policy formulation, and governing bodies sometimes intervene directly in policy execution. A decision by the governing body

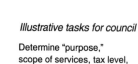

Figure 3-2 Mission-management separation with shared responsibility for policy and administration.

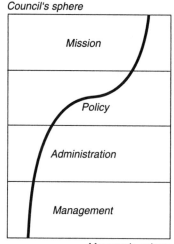

Dimensions of governmental process

Illustrative tasks for council   Council's sphere   *Illustrative tasks for administrators*

Determine "purpose," scope of services, tax level, constitutional issues

Mission

Advise (what city "can" do may influence what it "should" do); analyze conditions and trends

Pass ordinances; approve new projects and programs; ratify budget

Policy

Make recommendations on all decisions; formulate budget; determine service distribution formulae

Make implementing decisions (e.g., site selection); handle complaints; oversee administration

Administration

Establish practices and procedures and make decisions for implementing policy

Suggest management changes to manager; review organizational performance in manager's appraisal

Management

Control the human, material, and informational resources of organization to support policy and administrative functions

Manager's sphere

The curved line suggests the division between the council's and the manager's spheres of activity, with the council to the *left* and the manager to the *right* of the line. The division presented is intended to roughly approximate a "proper" degree of separation and sharing. Shifts to either the left or right would indicate improper incursions.

to increase user fees, for example, would almost surely be based on revenue projections, impact assessments, and comparisons with other revenue sources compiled by the manager with a recommendation for action by the governing body.

James H. Svara departs from the traditional dichotomy by proposing a new model of the relationship between the governing body and the manager that recognizes their "shared responsibility for policy and administration," redefines their spheres of influence, and establishes when one has made an "improper incursion" into the role of the other. Svara's model sets a higher level of involvement for the governing body in setting the mission and general policies of the organization, while the manager assumes the lead in the administration and management of the organization. Figure 3–2 shows the basic elements of Svara's model.[6]

Information   In the local setting, policies are initiated in response to an identified problem or a perceived need. Among the considerations that shape policy are technical feasibility, cost, and anticipated social benefit, as well as long-range environmental and other consequences. Input often comes from special interest groups, other governments, citizen advisory boards, and individual constituents, as well as from elected officials themselves. Yet the manager and staff remain the primary source of information for both policy initiation and oversight of policy execution. Regardless of the source and type of information, an effective policymaker must maintain three levels of awareness, all of which ultimately affect the community:

Knowledge about the local government and its operations

Understanding of trends in local government and of global events that influence local conditions

Awareness of the social, economic, and political changes taking place in society.

Share your knowledge with the governing body even down to the nuts and bolts.

Yvonne E. Coon

Major duties of the governing body

The role of the governing body will vary from one unit of government to another, as does the manager's role, but some duties, functions, and responsibilities apply to all governing bodies in one manner or another, at one time or another. Generally speaking, a legislative body is performing its major duties when it

Sets short-, mid-, and long-range goals and the agenda for achieving them

Defines the kind and level of services to be provided

Monitors effectiveness of services

Exercises leadership in the community

Arbitrates conflicts among competing interests

Serves as facilitator/expediter of citizen inquiries and complaints

Sends members to perform such ceremonial duties as ribbon-cutting, speech-making, and official greeting in their capacity as elected representatives of the community

Supports the "civic infrastructure" by promoting citizens' participation and sense of ownership in the community.

The foregoing are broad activities in which local elected officials may engage, either by choice or by demand, depending on their individual inclinations and the political system of which they are a part. In addition, governing bodies must undertake the following five specific activities mandated by law.[7]

Employing the administrator The appointment of a professional administrator is readily recognized as a primary responsibility of the local governing body. An extreme view of this role is characterized by the tongue-in-cheek pronouncement that a governing body has only two decisions to make: the first is whether to support the manager, in which case the members can adjourn; if the answer to that question is no, the second decision is where to find the manager's successor. Indeed, the manager is the agent of the elected officials, who have the legal responsibility for the local government; the effective performance of the manager is crucial to their own effectiveness.

The governing body can enhance its relationship with the manager by backing the manager as the office becomes the focal point of competing demands and conflicting pressures and by evaluating the manager's performance according to criteria agreed on by both parties. When performance is unsatisfactory and unlikely to improve, a decision to change should be reached before the crisis stage. A quietly arranged departure is more beneficial than a showdown both for the manager and for the long-term effectiveness of the governing body.

Managing the community's finances Local government is in a severe financial straitjacket and will be for some time, a situation that brings into sharper focus the importance of prudent financial management as a major responsibility of governing boards. During the 1950s and 1960s, local governments had become accustomed to growth and anticipated the consequent expansion of revenues and opportunities. However, the 1970s and 1980s brought the painful need to cope first with serious inflation and then with sharp reductions in revenue. Throughout the 1990s local governments will take on greater financial responsibilities as the federal government—bent on addressing the twin problems of debt and annual deficits—continues to retreat from its leading role of the past several decades in initiating and funding policies related to state and local government. Local governing bodies will have to continue to generate more of their own revenue and to balance income and expenditures—that is, to reconcile resources with services. The way in which this reconciliation is accomplished will in turn determine how resources are allocated in the community.

Developing and maintaining the infrastructure   Developing and maintaining the infrastructure involves not only the obvious activities of street and road building and repair, but also allocation of land for development, construction of buildings with public funds, creation of recreational and industrial parks, development of public utilities, and the operation of facilities built with revenue generated either directly by a local government or through state, federal, or private grants. In recent decades the priority given to these activities by governing bodies has fluctuated. Such projects may threaten the resources available for day-to-day operations of the government and for groups whose taxes support the projects but who do not necessarily receive direct benefit from them.

Acting as final arbiter in community conflicts   Increasing social diversity, often combined with political change, may result in conflicts on a broad range of issues that must be resolved by government officials. It is perhaps in fulfilling this role that the elected official is most vulnerable.

When a candidate wins an election, the victory, together with incumbency, confers a certain amount of prestige and power on the individual. However, this state of affairs can deteriorate rapidly. In resolving conflict, the governing body often must decide in favor of one party at the expense of another. It can be difficult for an elected official to recover from the loss of the support of those who did not benefit from the decision, particularly in nonpartisan election systems and in the absence of patronage. The long-term fallout of serving as the final arbiter is the risk of high turnover on the governing body. The manager's role of enhancing effectiveness thus becomes more crucial.

Observing open meeting requirements   "Sunshine laws" are a legal rubric under which public officials must conduct their business. The era of private meetings has come to an end. The legal requirement in some states prohibits private meetings except to discuss a few specified topics related to personnel and purchase of property. In governing bodies with five or fewer members, one elected official literally cannot talk privately to another without running the risk of violating the open meeting law, because three is a quorum and two can conduct business. The manager often becomes the sole conduit of information between the elected officials, and the impact on the manager's relationship with governing body members is profound. What is sometimes lost in this less than perfect means of communication may have a negative influence on the governing body's effectiveness, as well as on the manager's tenure.

Strengthening policymaking capabilities

The manager and his or her staff can help strengthen the policymaking capabilities of the governing body by proposing goals to guide decision making, ensuring that those goals and related decisions are addressed in the budget process, using citizen input and expertise, relieving the council of as much routine business as possible, creating an annual policy calendar, providing a base of operations for the council, keeping in touch with individual council members, scheduling orientation sessions for new members, and aiding in evaluation of appointed officials.[8]

Proposing goals

In order to lay the groundwork for policymaking, the manager can marshal the resources of the staff and the community to help develop a strategic agenda. In small as well as large localities, information should be assembled that will provide the basis for projecting the future of the community. These questions, for example, should be addressed:

What is the community like now?

What are its strengths and weaknesses, its opportunities, and threats to its well-being?

What will the community be like in the twenty-first century if no action is taken?

What will it be like in the twenty-first century if a strategic plan is developed and if positive, informed policies, goals, and service levels are defined and actively pursued?

All things being equal, if given the option, citizens will choose positive change and progress. The governing body is obligated to identify alternative policies and to structure the process for setting goals and determining service levels. The manager is obligated to ensure that the governing body, not the staff, initiates the planning and goal setting process, to be shared with staff and the community. To do otherwise allows staff to set the policy agenda without being held accountable to the public through elections.

Structuring the budget process

Once goals are established, the manager can structure the budget preparation, review, and adoption process in such a way that the governing body understands it and feels that goals and agreed-upon service levels are appropriately addressed. It is important that the manager integrate annual operating and capital improvements budgets, debt service, and state and federal grants so that they are related to the achievement of community goals.

Using citizen expertise

Leaders of local business, community, and service agencies are usually willing to donate time to advise local managers on recent developments in budgeting, financial forecasting, and methods of assessing effectiveness and efficiency. Asking such citizens to serve on a task force to review budget, goal-setting, and productivity levels has several benefits. They frequently recommend changes and improvements based on their experience in the private and volunteer sectors. Furthermore, establishing links with leaders in the community also tends to promote communication between community leaders and elected officials, which can be useful when critical decisions are before the governing body.

Freeing council members' time

Excessive concern with administrative detail, an impediment to effective policy-making, can be overcome. It is widely agreed that governing bodies spend the greater share of their time on routine administrative matters and considerably less of their time on the purpose for which they were elected—to set policy. While such time-consumers as maintaining relations with boards and commissions and responding to citizen complaints are necessary, over-allocation of time to routine activities detracts from policymaking. Local government managers can facilitate the flow of information and shift the balance of the governing body's workload from administrative to policymaking matters by

Shifting the emphasis of the meeting agenda from routine to policy considera-

---

The effectiveness and happiness of the governing body is inversely proportional to the length of the meeting.
                                        Carol Bloodworth

---

tions by limiting a public agenda item, for example, to thirty minutes and speakers to five minutes

Developing a consent agenda of administrative or routine matters that can be acted upon by a single motion, unless individual members call for exceptions for special consideration

Scheduling informal public meetings with staff in neighborhoods to answer questions and resolve problems prior to a formal hearing and action by the governing body

Holding hearings on zoning and property-related matters, as well as traffic engineering and control matters, with citizen boards, whose recommendations can then be reviewed and acted upon by the governing body (if authorized by state statute or local ordinance)

Reducing staff position papers submitted in support of policy recommendations to short executive summaries on an annotated agenda, with documentation available for later review by members of the governing body; using electronic mail and computers, if possible, for instant retrieval

Establishing special biweekly sessions to deal solely with planning issues and/or reserving three- or four-hour blocks of time or one meeting each month to focus attention on one broad policy area of local concern

Delegating non-policy-related duties and responsibilities to administrative staff and appointed citizen bodies, if possible

Including in policy statements formal criteria for exceptions to discourage capricious disregard of adopted policies of the governing body.

In order to streamline staff communications, materials on policy issues submitted by staff should be structured to reduce volume, organized to work with the agenda, and formatted to include at least the following:

A clear identification of an item as a policy issue and a clear statement of the issue

A discussion of feasible alternatives

A presentation of the strengths and weaknesses of each alternative

An identification of the relevant social, economic, political, and environmental implications of various alternatives.

Creating an annual policy calendar

Incorporating an annual policy calendar into the governing body's operating procedures will help coordinate long-range policy issues. The policy calendar should focus on at least the two major policy issues that face the governing body each year: the operating budget and the capital improvements program. Discussions of these issues should be scheduled regularly throughout the year. The governing body should be involved in the process at an early stage and set goals before staff prepare working documents.

The policy calendar should provide for periodic sessions each year to give members of the governing body the opportunity to study particular issues or responsibilities in greater depth. For example, focus sessions or retreats can be used to

Evaluate performance of the chief executive administrative officer and other appointees

Review internal operations and procedures, especially following elections, which generally bring new members to the board

Reconsider and refine community goals and major policy statements

Consider intergovernmental and legislative matters (e.g., joint budgeting, interlocal cooperation, key legislation pending in the state legislature or in Congress).

If retreats are used, they should be held over one or two days in a relaxed setting that will permit participants to get away from "business as usual." All elected officials should be present, along with the manager, but staff should be limited to those members whose presence is absolutely necessary. An outside facilitator can be selected to lead the discussion, giving others a free opportunity to participate. The facilitator should be experienced in leading public organizations through goal-setting discussions and preferably familiar with the background of the government, the governing body, and the issues involved. The media should be invited to attend the retreat and attention given to their logistical needs and respective deadlines. Participation by the media will improve their awareness and understanding of the local government and may increase their support, not only for the retreat as a policymaking device, but also for the issues involved. One caveat is that the governing body must be aware that the issue of propriety may be raised if the choice of retreat location is too distant or elegant to accord with community values or economic conditions.

Providing a base of operations

Insofar as resources permit, the governing body should be provided a centralized base of operations. Effectiveness of the governing body can be enhanced by

Providing a central file, an office or a space to meet with citizens in private, and access to computers if they are available

Furnishing an aide and secretary under the direction of the manager to maintain the central office, handle correspondence and telephone calls, maintain appointment calendars, and receive citizen requests on behalf of governing body members

Establishing weekly office hours for members of the governing body and publishing these for constituents.

Meeting council members individually

As a matter of priority, the manager should spend one hour weekly with each member of the governing body to exchange information and to discuss current issues. At specified intervals, the manager should inventory council members to determine whether their individual goals as elected officials remain unaddressed or, if appropriate, what new objectives or programs are of concern. Failures in individual goal achievement frequently are depersonalized through discussion, which also tends to reinforce confidence in the manager and the decision-making process.

The Lord gave us two ears and one mouth. This means we should listen to the governing body twice as much as we speak.
Joe J. Palacioz

Scheduling orientation

New members of the governing body should be given an orientation soon after election, and refresher courses should be provided for continuing members. Some newly elected members will have had prior experience, while others will be new to public office. In either event, an orientation process should be in place for them and for continuing governing body members; some communities conduct orientation sessions for candidates as well. A basic orientation process should be established that can be customized according to current needs, policies, and issues.

To the extent that time and resources are available, the orientation session should be held in a retreat setting where attention can be given to the business at hand. The session should be sufficiently long to allow policies and programs to be covered and to provide an opportunity for governing body members to get acquainted with each other as well as with the manager and key staff. Local colleges and universities are valuable resources for conducting the orientations and for developing manuals and training sessions related to the duties and responsibilities of elected policymakers. Government, political science, communications, and management departments can be called on for assistance.

Following orientation, one or more members of the manager's staff might be designated temporary liaison with individual members of the governing body in order to facilitate the flow of information, obtain answers to questions, assist with constituent requests, and conduct research.

Institutionalizing annual reviews

The manager can help provide a structure for evaluating his or her own effectiveness and performance and that of others appointed by or under the direct supervision of the governing body (see also Chapter 1). Annual review provides a means for continuing dialogue on the management of local affairs. Elements of the review should include

Review of the past year's performance to see whether the expectations of the governing body and the manager coincided and were realized

Specific feedback to the manager on areas in which the governing body feels the manager could have served more effectively

Establishment of definite objectives and a plan and/or contract for the upcoming year.[9]

Structuring input from citizen participation

A governing body can expand its opportunities for anticipatory policymaking through mechanisms for widespread citizen participation. For example, depending on the size of the community, neighborhood councils can be formed by election at the same time that the governing body is elected, in order to advise on policy matters, convene hearings, and refer citizen service requests. In cooperation with local colleges, some communities are organizing town meetings to create a dialogue on problems of importance to the community. These meetings promote empowerment of citizen groups, and the governing body receives important information

A good manager must be able to tell time by the community's clock.
Leonard Biggs

on policy-related issues. Community groups should be encouraged to schedule their activities according to the annual policy calendar of the governing body.

Governing body confidence in the manager

The foundation of a successful manager-council relationship is confidence. In some countries, this principle is institutionalized at the national level; the prime minister, for example, serves only as long as he or she enjoys the confidence of the parliament, the governing body. Few other comparisons between parliamentary prime ministers and local government managers are valid, but the principle of confidence in the manager is worth noting.

Local managers' future environment

It is essential that the manager provide the governing body with the information it needs to make sound policy decisions. This responsibility goes beyond briefing the council on internal and external developments. The knowledgeable manager must have both a sense of history and a sense of the future.

The following list of responsibilities, skills, and trends of increasing importance in the manager's future environment was generated from discussions based on ICMA's report entitled *Future Visions, Future Opportunities*, which were held among thirty local government managers at the Hugo Wall Center for Urban Studies, Wichita State University, Kansas, in 1992.

Increased emphasis on helping the governing body to

Generate policy initiatives

Identify and focus on goals

Carefully define consensus

Improve capacity for leadership

Be futurists or anticipatory policymakers.

Skills required to enhance governing body capabilities

Flexibility in working with the governing body

Listening

Ability to meet with and negotiate with diverse interest groups

Communication skills for helping the community make decisions

Situational leadership

Adaptability.

Emerging trends affecting local government

More politics

More mandates without money

Less trained/qualified work force

More fragmented perspectives on council

Cultural diversity; need for bilingualism

More exchange of expertise with private sector

Transfer of public sector knowledge

More marketing

Governing body members drawn less from business, highly educated, older; more single-issue candidates

Smaller units of government need more professional manager

Increased professionalism in county government

Demands for reducing the number of governments

Increased cooperation, coordination, and function consolidation

Merged governments

Emphasis on quality of services, employee empowerment, customer.

The governing body's confidence in the manager usually depends on how well he or she deals with key issues and makes critical decisions. Managers will find that really important decisions—those that have a major bearing on the governing body's confidence—are often complex and have long-term implications. They involve labor negotiations, selection of key staff members, annual budgets, capital improvements programs, comprehensive planning, independent audits, and credit ratings. Managers also may be judged on how well they handle the media and interest groups on issues that tend to be highly visible and involve community conflict.

Ironically, as Figure 3–3 shows, it appears that the time allotted to making decisions that involve people, planning, and finances is little more than 5 percent of the total time spent by the governing body. If the time spent on these issues related more directly to their importance, governing bodies would spend 80 percent of their time on them.

Most professional managers are skilled technicians, effective communicators, and often gifted and trusted advisors. But manager-council relationships that are regarded as successful (judged by tenure of the manager) may depend most of the time on how well 5 percent of the business is conducted. As discussed earlier in this chapter, managers should do everything they can to help their governing body spend more time on important policy matters and less time on administrative details.

No quantitative measures exist to gauge governing body effectiveness, but the level of confidence in the manager can be increased by the skillful manager's ability, through a variety of techniques, to maintain the spirit of teamwork needed to assist the governing body in resolving conflict and carrying out its responsibilities.

Techniques to maintain confidence

The following techniques for maintaining the confidence of the council are frequently suggested by experienced managers with stable tenure and by effective elected policymakers.

Prepare good agendas   Agenda items should be accompanied by clear, concise, timely, written evaluations that exhibit careful preparation and competent analysis. A manager who fails to meet this requirement may seriously cripple the ability of the governing body to function in even routine matters.[10] Because of the continuing and often routine nature of agenda preparation, managers may lose interest or the motivation to maintain quality control. Perceptions of the importance of agenda items also may differ between appointed and elected officials, and it is essential that managers monitor the quality of the agenda through frequent and open com-

Figure 3–3   Local government policy decisions.

Type	Impact on	Role of manager	Manager's relationship to council	Council time (%)	Importance (%)
People, plans, money	Future	Executive	Confidant	5	80
Ordinances, resolutions	Standards	Arbiter	Advisor	10	10
Board/staff recommendations	Procedures	Advocate	Conduit	30	5
Routine operations	Functions	Trustee	Technician	55	5

munication with members of the governing body. Weekly agenda communications can be improved if the manager and staff try to do the following:

1. Give all elected officials prior knowledge of agenda items.
2. Deliver all agenda packets at the same time.
3. Give the same information to all elected members; if one asks for something special, share it with everyone.
4. Within the limitations of open meeting laws, discuss key issues informally before formal meetings.
5. Make recommendations, with advantages and disadvantages of each.

Good communication is a two-way street; the effective manager should not be timid in suggesting to elected officials how they too can improve the weekly agenda preparation process. The following guidelines can help elected officials improve communication with the manager and staff:

1. Be prepared; study the issues before, not during, the meeting.
2. Recognize that staff often have little time to prepare the agenda, necessitating last-minute inclusion of perhaps unpredictable items.
3. Do not embarrass the staff in public; if there is a problem with an agenda item, discuss it before or after the meeting.
4. Inform the manager if members of the governing body want to meet with other staff members about agenda items.
5. Tell the manager if the agenda and supporting information meet expectations, and if not, what changes need to be made.

Identify alternatives   In making policy recommendations, the manager should identify all tenable alternatives, and note objective arguments for and against each one. Even though the manager is expected to make recommendations favoring the "best" solution, failure to list alternatives and discuss their advantages and disadvantages brings the motives of the manager into question, entails the risk of converting the manager's role from a professional to a partisan one, and often undermines the confidence in the policymaking process, as well as in the manager as an individual.

Avoid peaks and valleys   The length and intensity of regular governing body meetings will vary by jurisdiction and by issues on the public agenda, but meetings should be planned so that members know what to expect. A schedule of short, routine meetings alternated with marathon sessions conveys the impression that no one is in charge. It decreases the ability of policymakers to give adequate time to some critical issues, while it devotes too much time to others. Short agendas invite excursions into administrative detail, but on the other hand, the manager who stacks the agenda with "heavy issues" is often accused of manipulating the agenda to force the governing body to adopt staff recommendations out of sheer fatigue or frustration. Such practices, even in the absence of a hidden staff agenda, do not build a spirit of teamwork or confidence.

Withdraw from the final decision   Withdrawal of the manager from debate in the last stages of the decision-making process is fair, fitting, and necessary. The manager is in the privileged position of being able to make recommendations without being held directly responsible, through the electoral process, to the people of the community for the decisions made. The governing body does not enjoy this luxury. Staff also have an unusual advantage through their advance communications and greater access to information about any given issue or policy. However, it is finally the right and responsibility of the governing body to make its own decisions, based on all input.

Respect council decisions   It is easy to respect the decisions of those with whom we agree; it is not as easy to respect the decisions of those with whom we disagree. The professional manager who seeks the confidence of the governing body must keep personal opinions private in order to maintain a public and continuous display of fidelity to the democratic process of decision making. Acknowledgement of the right of elected officials to differ vigorously with staff policy recommendations, regardless of whose position prevails, is best stated openly, often, and with conviction.

Lose gracefully   There are floating coalitions in the governing body; last week's winner may be next week's loser. The confident manager is both a graceful loser and a modest winner. It is axiomatic that losing erodes confidence to a greater degree than winning builds it, but battles gracefully lost can increase the stature of the manager. Managers gain stature by trying twice as hard to implement what they did not recommend, thereby demonstrating the professional mettle that builds trust, respect, and admiration. The manager needs governing body support, but equally, the policymakers must be secure in the knowledge that they will have staff support.

Never argue *publicly* with the governing body.
Stan Stewart

Be generous with credit   The manager who gives credit to the governing body when things go right builds confidence on both sides. Except on rare occasions, the manager is not native to the jurisdiction that he or she serves, owns no property there other than a car and house, and has no historical connection to or family position in the community. Success for the manager, then, lies in the reflected glory of the governing body.

More than one manager has lost the council's confidence not because of failure, but because of too much recognition of the manager or of other appointed staff members, whose star outshone that of elected policymakers. But the manager should be aware that recognition may become increasingly difficult to avoid in view of the attributes of a successful manager described in the ICMA FutureVisions report, which calls on the manager to play an expanded and more visible role in the policymaking process.

Members of the governing board usually enter elected politics to pursue personal as well as altruistic goals—if not also to qualify for election to a higher office—and these goals are not served by anonymity. Managers who crave public credit or who ensure high visibility for their own recommendations run the risk of labeling the governing body a "rubber stamp" and themselves dictators, which can be risky for their tenured well-being.

Take the heat   Not only should the manager be free with credit, he or she must also be ready to take the heat when things go wrong. Failure to do so sometimes sends a message of cover-up, if not complicity; however, quick acknowledgement of misconduct, policy failure, or nonperformance shifts the public concern from fixing the blame to correcting the problem. In the normal course of affairs, mistakes are inevitable, but few are intentional. When a policy adopted by the governing body fails, the wise manager remembers that policies usually are proposed by the staff, the manager, or both. The governing body most often reacts rather than acts. Thus, placing the blame for adoption solely on the policymakers under such circumstances distorts the truth and undermines confidence in the manager. The manager's candor and obvious dedication to prompt corrective measures shifts public attention from what action the governing body is going to take against the manager to what the manager proposes to do to solve the problem. The governing body will be more likely to shield its appointed executive when they are confident that he or she will shoulder rather than shift the blame when the going gets tough.

Pay attention to timing In public management, there are three critical factors: timing, timing, and timing. An acute sense of timing is felt, not counted; it is learned, not inherited. Experience tells the manager when it is time to press hard, time to pull back, or time to move on; it is not possible to create a checklist. It is of great importance to recognize the significance of timing in the success or failure of managers, governing bodies, and cities. History is replete with stories of people or institutions that misjudged critical timing and were left behind in the onward rush of progress. It is a gifted leader who can say with conviction, "This is the time, and this is the place."

Barriers to effective manager-council relations

It is well established in theory and in fact that social and political changes have brought about a blurring of the relationship between the elected policymaking body and the appointed administrator. Their roles have blended, making the local government hierarchy a "marble cake."[11] It is not known whether local government works because of or in spite of such a relationship; in any case, the relationship is tenuous and highly personal. It has both formal and informal dimensions, in which the individual values and goals of the several actors are always present. Consequently, the manager-council relationship, although ideally cooperative, has the built-in potential for conflict.

Role perceptions

Perhaps the most subtle source of conflict between elected officials and the appointed executive lies in their perceptions of how the other carries out the job. It is not surprising that their perceptions will concur at times and differ at others. All work in the same political environment, have shared values, and often share in victory and defeat. However, each individual comes to his or her position via a different route, with different motivations, and each has a different perspective toward governing. Each has different relations with and loyalties to the community and its electorate, and each has different needs for interaction with the others of the governmental group.

Don't let honest differences of opinion degenerate into personality conflicts.
E.A. Mosher

Managers and council members often do not fully appreciate each other's roles. Managers have been criticized for possessing a "manager's complex," that is, the inability to think like an elected official or the inability get inside the minds or walk in the shoes of those who came to office through elective politics. Managers often view elected officials as "too political," yielding to popular pressure in order to retain office rather than staying the course on policy matters. These conflicting perceptions can create barriers which, if neglected, may become difficult to overcome. Communication, sometimes in teambuilding retreats, is the key to transforming erroneous into empathetic perceptions that lead to effective manager-council relations.

Citizen demands

As the size and complexity of government increase, members of the governing body as well as citizens may feel increasingly powerless to make changes and get services delivered. Elected governing body members get large numbers of requests from constituents who feel they know an "insider" who will redress government abuse or neglect by the prompt exercise of the power of his or her position. Ironically, many governing body members complain that they have no power at all, particularly where merit systems are involved and appointed employees have longer tenure than elected officials. A majority of the governing body is required in the council-manager form of government to effect a policy change. When the manager is hired by the council, directly elected mayors have little executive power or authority. If the governing body perceives itself as powerless, the working relationship with the manager is in jeopardy.

The ability of the governing body to motivate and move the manager and staff to respond quickly and effectively to requests on behalf of citizens has many positive advantages:

1. Citizens learn that the elected official has status and power in the community.
2. Citizens are assured that staff members are subordinate and responsible to elected governing body members.
3. If properly handled, requests from the governing body to the staff, processed through the manager, demonstrate that the governing body is in control.
4. Community problems and complaints are addressed in an environment where a spirit of teamwork exists between the governing body and the staff.
5. The quality of life and sense of well-being in the community are heightened.

Early in the council-manager relationship, perhaps during performance evaluation, the two parties should discuss what is and is not expected in processing citizens' requests. Figure 3–4 illustrates some of these expectations. The role of expediter and logjam breaker, expected of the legislative body by some citizens, is an important if not a traditional part of policymaking.

The visibility of the governing body in getting things done for constituents is a gauge of effectiveness that is important, if not crucial, in many communities. Of more importance to the manager is the clear demonstration of representative democracy, effective teamwork, and staff loyalty. A responsive, attentive manager and staff project an image of productivity and efficiency.

Centrality of the manager

Some observers, and indeed some managers themselves, may operate on the mistaken assumption that the manager is the key to the operation of an effective local government. This assumption is a source of much manager-mayor-council conflict, and it would be a mistake to leave such an assumption unchallenged. The centrality

Figure 3–4   Council expectations of managers in processing citizens' requests.

Expected	Not expected
Timely action and uniform standards	Referral or buck passing
No favoritism	Putting some citizens ahead of others
Fair treatment for all	Special favors for certain elected body members
Citizen contact and report of action	Costly tailored services without approval of governing body
Report to elected representatives on action taken	Extensive studies without approval of governing body
Full explanation of reasons if no action is taken	Always finding a way to satisfy citizens regardless of cost or consequences

of the manager's office, determined in large part by the manager's control of staff, information, and resources, involves the office in virtually all phases of the administrative and policymaking processes. The level of effectiveness of the local government, for both the manager and the governing body, depends on the manager's ability to keep the governing body members involved and to keep things flowing in order to prevent bottlenecks from occurring. The effective manager will periodically assess the volume and velocity of information and decisions that come through the manager's office in order to address one basic question: Is the manager, as the point of intercept, an expediter or obstacle to effective policymaking?

Sources of conflict

There is some truth in the old saying that the departure of a manager is often caused by illness and fatigue: "The council was sick and tired of him." Managers who attain long tenure occasionally do so because of a lackluster record. Highly competent and energetic managers sometimes depart after a short time because they try to do too much, too fast.

What are the major conflicts between managers and their governing bodies? How can the danger signals be recognized before the conflicts lead to a premature parting of the ways? This section outlines ten common conflicts, concentrating on strategies that the manager can use to resolve them.

Overstepping bounds (manager)

A sure route to conflict with the council is for the manager to overstep his or her bounds and become too involved in policymaking or politics. To avoid misunderstanding of this kind, at the time of hiring, the manager and the governing body should discuss and agree on ground rules about how aggressive an agent of change the manager should be and especially about how visible the manager should be in recommending and supporting policy initiatives. This is not normally the subject of an employment agreement, but a paragraph could be inserted that states categorically the role of the manager and clearly delineates the style of management that the governing body may expect. Refinement of the understanding could become part of annual performance reviews, periodic retreats, or training sessions conducted by local colleges or universities.

Withholding information (manager)

If the manager withholds information essential for policymaking, is secretive, or is supersensitive about contact between staff and governing body members, the potential for another conflict arises. Blind faith in professional credentials and reputation is not sufficient reason for modern governing bodies to ratify management recommendations; information is the basis for action as well as understanding. To ensure open access to information, the manager and key staff should spend time with individual members of the governing body, with the clear understanding that work assignments and policy directions come from the elected body as a whole—not from individual members. A manager must be especially sensitive to council perceptions if he or she shares staff with the council. In summary: err on the side of furnishing too much information.

Failing to anticipate problems (manager)

At least half of management is anticipation, and the remainder is execution; on this successful managers agree. However, too many otherwise good managers spend all their time on execution. If problems are unanticipated, execution becomes putting out fires, which projects the image of government by crisis, creating stress and general discontent. In a well-run organization, goals are set and objectives agreed upon regularly by both the manager and governing body. As suggested earlier, the manager should insist on planning by use of a policy calendar, having regular discussions with individual governing body members about their individual goals and objectives, and scheduling discussion of policy issues at regular intervals when a decision is not needed immediately. If the groundwork is well laid, policymaking can be accomplished in a climate of reason instead of panic.

What goes unchallenged, goes unchanged.
Meryl Dye

Avoiding responsibility (manager)

Sometimes a conflict arises because the council thinks that the manager will not speak frankly or take responsibility for his or her actions. It is helpful for managers to state publicly that they accept full accountability for operations under their control. Some managers include such a statement in their biographical sketch, which is distributed to organizations in advance of speeches. The reassurance that a professional is in charge is probably one of the main reasons for the success of the council-manager plan. As one of the manager's strongest support mechanisms, professionalism must be reinforced by the willingness to confront problems quickly and candidly.

Overstepping bounds (council)

The governing body as well as the manager can overstep its bounds, by getting involved in personnel and administrative matters. The remedies are not unlike those

---

Symptoms of a manager in trouble

How can managers spot conflicts? What are the reasons for managers' difficulties with their councils? Sometimes, the reasons may be strictly political and out of the control of the manager. But the most serious conflicts evolve from managers not understanding what the councils expect. Industrial psychologist Bill Mathis, in his presentation to the 1990 ICMA Annual Conference in Fort Worth, outlined "Seven Symptoms of a Manager in Trouble" as a guide to help managers avoid pitfalls. These symptoms are as follows:

1. *Unwillingness to fire or move a department head*   Councils see a manager who is reluctant to fire or transfer a department head who obviously is not performing well as a weakness or abdication of responsibility. Continued problems from that department head will eventually be perceived as the manager's fault.

2. *Change in personal effectiveness*   Managers who suffer a personal crisis, such as a divorce or an illness, must be careful to minimize the problem's impact on their ability to perform the job. Council members who see a manager preoccupied by personal problems may begin to question his or her competency to lead the organization.

3. *Unwillingness to read or adapt to political environment*   When political changes are occurring in a community, particularly when newly elected officials enter office with a mandate to implement new policies, the manager must adapt. The council will expect the manager to implement the changes they promised the community as soon as possible.

suggested before about setting guidelines at hiring and reaffirming them periodically during performance evaluations. If problems do arise, a direct confrontation is usually most effective. A single member can be approached privately. If group trust is in jeopardy, one solution is to have a frank discussion of the problem in order to arrive at an understanding of expectations. Intervention by governing body members is usually a symptom of information starvation, not a deliberate effort to cause conflict. Keep talking, avoid the temptation to retreat, and appeal to the need for a rational, not an emotional, approach.

Handling appointments and dismissals (manager)

Following the appointment of the local government manager, the selection of department heads has the greatest effect on the nature and quality of local government services and consequently on citizens' perceptions of how the elected officials are fulfilling their stewardship. Members of governing bodies sometimes feel uninformed because occasionally managers are unnecessarily protective or secretive about appointment and dismissal procedures. The power of the manager to hire and fire is well established in most organizations, and in these, elected members are usually more than willing to let managers take full responsibility for their selections—especially when they turn out poorly. The governing body does deserve to be kept informed at critical points in the selection and termination process, especially when trouble develops that could lead to a messy dismissal. Consultation with the governing body in advance of an announcement often avoids unpleasant surprises.

Blaming the governing body (manager)

Some managers are quick to shift accountability to the governing body: "The council set the policy; I just carry it out." Assigning blame is especially hazardous

---

4. *Becoming a target for what's wrong in the community* If a manager becomes too identified with policies concerning a specific issue, for example, growth or war on drugs, then the manager may become the lightning rod for community criticism of those policies. This criticism can set the stage for the council to take action against the manager as a way to address community concerns.

5. *Power conflict* Managers must be careful not to place the council in a politically uncomfortable position by getting too far out in front on policy matters. Managers must understand that their orientation toward long-term goals may be in direct conflict with the council's short-term needs to address immediate concerns of their constituents.

6. *Distancing* In trying to avoid being too far out in front of the council, managers also have to be careful not to become too detached from the issues. Council members may perceive distancing by the manager as a lack of interest or concern about the community or the council.

7. *History of environmental dishonesty* When councils act covertly to decide issues before discussing issues in public, they may tend to make the manager a scapegoat for the community's distrust of their actions.

Source: Ann Amoury, "The 7 Symptoms of a Manager in Trouble, Or How to Spot/Stop a Pink Slip Before It Hits Your Desk," *Public Management* 72 (December 1990): 7–9.

when a subordinate assigns it to the hiring authority. The wise manager will take the heat for the governing body; members then will be more likely to be protective the next time the target of abuse is the manager.

Attacking the manager for political reasons (the public)

From time to time a manager is the victim of a political attack, usually by citizens who feel that their interests are threatened. Such attacks on the manager by council members' constituents can negatively influence the governing body's confidence in the manager. The best defense is strict adherence to a professional code of ethics, augmented by allies in the community who are able to confront attackers. Public political attack on nonelected officials may become more popular as managers become more visible in policymaking. But responsible political leaders respect the manager who makes the system work for all parties. They may be the manager's best allies and most able to effectively neutralize irresponsible political attacks.

Providing weak leadership (manager)

Conflict can arise if the manager is perceived to be a weak leader. Governing body members frequently regard the manager as a source of energy and direction, somewhat like the locomotive of a train. Energy and enthusiasm for the job of leadership are expected and can compensate for the shortcomings and errors of judgment that are bound to occur during any manager's tenure. The manager who is in control of subordinates is one who projects an image of order, security, and well-being. Managers who fail to control and discipline subordinates are perceived to be weak and become vulnerable. Early establishment of a strong internal position is essential if the manager is to be known as a strong leader.

Keys to resolution

Conflicts are as varied and numerous as communities and personalities. Experience is a good teacher, but too many bad experiences can destroy a career. Unresolved differences inevitably worsen if they are suppressed or magnified by fear, or if their original causes are distorted by time and distance. Keys to conflict resolution appear to be self-understanding, awareness of relationships, cultivation of allies and support systems, and a willingness to be open and candid in confronting conflict.

Measuring effectiveness

A theme of this chapter is that a bond exists between the elected members of the local governing body and their appointed chief executive. The council has an obligation to work with the manager on the behalf of the electorate to make government work. Managers have an obligation to enhance elected officials' ability to make government work—that is, to make it effective. But how do we know whether the manager and the council have been effective? There is no one accepted definition of effectiveness, and a manager or council that may be effective in one community at one point in time may be ineffective in another at a different time. However, the manager can use various indicators as a frame of reference: (1) quality of life; (2) revenue; (3) municipal services; (4) political indicators; and (5) governing body self-evaluation.

Quality of life

Numerous composite rankings have been developed by a variety of organizations to determine a community's attractiveness and to compare communities throughout the country. Included in these comparisons are variables related to economic factors; demographic/environmental factors; crime; health care; and recreational, educational, and cultural offerings. Although the rankings themselves may be controversial, the indicators do provide some guidelines for determining how one unit of government is doing in relation to another. Closely related to the quality of life are factors that attract industrial or economic investment in a community: size of market; availability and price of labor, materials, and services; energy sources; and proximity to supportive industry.

Revenue, financial, and accounting indicators

A major share of a local government's activities deal with fiscal matters, and public leaders are often judged on the government's fiscal management and accountability, which determine the level of fiscal trust or distrust in the community. The U.S. Advisory Commission on Intergovernmental Relations has identified various danger signals that are valid forecasters of financial troubles.[12] They can be adapted as follows to indicate fiscal stability:

1. Operating fund revenues in excess of expenditures
2. Assets in excess of current liabilities
3. Absence of a pattern over several years in which current expenditures exceed current revenues
4. Absence of a short-term debt in operating funds at the end of the fiscal year
5. A low rate of delinquency in property tax payments
6. Stability or increase in assessed values
7. A fully or nearly fully funded retirement system
8. Good techniques for accounting, financial management, and reporting
9. Stable or improved credit/bond rating
10. Absence of financial litigation.

Local government services

The Urban Institute and ICMA have jointly published a volume that details procedures and measures for gauging the effectiveness of basic local government services—solid waste collection and disposal, parks and recreation facilities, libraries, crime control, fire protection, transportation, water supply, and the handling of citizen complaints and requests for service. Although the recommended procedures vary by service, generally managers are advised to measure

The degree to which the intended purposes of the services are being met

The degree to which the service has unintended, adverse effects on the community

The adequacy of the service provided relative to the community's needs, desires, and willingness to pay

The speed and courtesy displayed in responding to citizen requests

Citizen perceptions of how satisfactory the service is (even though these may not be in agreement with "factual" observations).[13]

In sum, measures should focus on whatever is involved in answering the question "How well is this service doing what it should do for citizens and the community?"

Political indicators

There are any number of political indicators that managers and/or governing bodies can use to evaluate their individual or combined effectiveness. The following factors are examples:

Turnover in the governing body itself, by defeat or resignation

Turnover on appointed boards and commissions, by resignation or removal

Turnover among key staff, particularly department heads, by firing or resignation

Litigation by or against government units

Success/failure ratio of referenda

Success/failure ratio of state and federal legislation

Disruption in services, particularly from employee strikes

Degree of intergovernmental cooperation to enhance efficient, effective, equitable, and accountable use of available resources.

Governing body evaluation

The local government manager should not overlook the performance of the governing body itself as a test of effectiveness. Periodic completion of questionnaires by the governing body not only will allow members to monitor their own behavior and perceptions, but will provide the manager with valuable information on goal-setting, policymaking, and budgetary processes; boards and commissions; and manager and staff relationships with the governing body.

Other indicators

There are certain to be indicators of effectiveness other than those outlined above, and managers are certain to have their own criteria. The most important criteria, those that provide the best basis for evaluation, are the ones that are worked out with the governing body at the time of appointment and periodically updated. Evaluation of effectiveness may be viewed best in simple terms: What are the goals and objectives of the manager and the elected officials over a given period of time? Have they been realized? If not, can they be, within the present manager-governing body arrangement?

To survive as a city manager you must satisfy the governing body; to survive as a person you must satisfy your own conscience and sense of responsibility and integrity.

George W. Pyle

The answers to these basic questions vary with the answers to others: How long has the manager been in office? How close are the elected members to reelection? Is there a match between personalities and styles? Managers also develop their own score cards. There is no precise point at which effectiveness ends and ineffectiveness begins, but a score of 95-percent agreement with the governing body may mean that the manager did not lead and attempted too little, and 65-percent may mean that the chemistry is poor and it is time for a change. Something in between may indicate that the manager has been effective and in turn has helped the legislative body to be effective.

Recap

This chapter emphasizes the importance of a strong partnership between the manager and the governing body in the effort to create and maintain an effective local government. It noted changes in the institutional roles of the manager and governing body that have led to increased responsibilities for both and a blurring of the formerly clear delineation of their duties.

Today, for example, the manager must assume responsibility not only for implementing policy, but also for strengthening the governing body's policymaking capabilities. The governing body is most effective when the manager understands his or her pivotal role as policy advisor, consensus builder, problem solver, innovator, broker, communicator, and technician. Suggestions were given for specific ways in which the manager can help the governing body fulfill its mandate—for example, by proposing goals to guide decision making, establishing mechanisms for citizen participation, and streamlining administrative functions in order to allow the governing body time to concentrate on more significant issues.

The chapter stressed the importance of the governing body's confidence in the manager and described techniques to gain and maintain confidence, noting in particular the need for the manager to withdraw from the final stage of the decision-making process and to respect the decisions made by the governing body. Barriers to effective council-manager relations and sources of conflict were pointed out. Finally, indicators of effectiveness were described to enable managers and governing bodies alike to evaluate their performance.

Governing body evaluation

The following questionnaire (adapted if necessary to suit individual needs) may be used by governing bodies for self-evaluation or by local government managers as they attempt to assess and enhance their governing body's effectiveness.

Goal setting

1. Are established council goals realistic and do-able within the time frame stated?
   Almost always _____ Sometimes _____ Never _____

2. Do council members participate sufficiently in implementing goals once established?
   Almost always _____ Sometimes _____ Never _____

3. Is the public adequately informed about council goals?
   Almost always _____ Sometimes _____ Never _____

Policymaking

1. Are council positions and policies effectively communicated?
   Almost always _____ Sometimes _____ Never _____

2. Does the council have the capacity to make hard choices and politically unpopular decisions when required or necessary?
   Almost always _____ Sometimes _____ Never _____

Budgeting

1. Does the council clearly understand the city's financial resources in order to make sound decisions on prioritizing public spending?
   Almost always _____ Sometimes _____ Never _____

2. Is there adequate opportunity for a cross section of public participation in the budgeting process?
   Almost always _____ Sometimes _____ Never _____

3. Does the council avoid unbudgeted appropriations?
   Almost always _____ Sometimes _____ Never _____

4. Does the council consider the budget their budget as opposed to the staff's budget?
   Almost always _____ Sometimes _____ Never _____

Council meetings

1. Does the council provide for adequate public input at council meetings?
   Almost always _____   Sometimes _____   Never _____

2. Does each council member effectively participate in council meetings?
   Almost always _____   Sometimes _____   Never _____

3. Does the staff have adequate opportunity for input before making its decision?
   Almost always _____   Sometimes _____   Never _____

4. Is council meeting time well utilized?
   Almost always _____   Sometimes _____   Never _____

5. Are relevant facts and opinions expressed before decisions are made or council position stated?
   Almost always _____   Sometimes _____   Never _____

6. Is direction given to staff clear and concise?
   Almost always _____   Sometimes _____   Never _____

Advisory commissions and committees

1. Is there adequate public participation in commission and/or committee member selection?
   Almost always _____   Sometimes _____   Never _____

2. Are commission/committee members selected based upon ability to serve the community rather than personal friendships?
   Almost always _____   Sometimes _____   Never _____

3. Does the council place sufficient emphasis on balancing commission/committee membership in order to assure the total community is represented?
   Almost always _____   Sometimes _____   Never _____

4. Does the council give sufficient weight to commission/committee recommendations?
   Almost always _____   Sometimes _____   Never _____

Relationship with staff

1. Does the council establish reasonable time frames for staff to accomplish assignments?
   Almost always _____   Sometimes _____   Never _____

2. If it changes its priorities, does the council consider the impact on staff time?
   Almost always _____   Sometimes _____   Never _____

3. Does the council give adequate consideration to staff recommendations?
   Almost always _____   Sometimes _____   Never _____

4. Do council members limit contacts with staff members to inquiries and suggestions as opposed to giving direction?
   Almost always _____   Sometimes _____   Never _____

Council relationships

1. Allowing for differences of philosophy and opinions on given issues, do council members respect one another's opinions?
   Almost always _____   Sometimes _____   Never _____

2. Does the council function as a team?
   Almost always _____   Sometimes _____   Never _____

3. Do individual council members avoid unduly consuming council meeting time?
   Almost always _____   Sometimes _____   Never _____

4. Do council members deal with issues openly?
   Almost always _____   Sometimes _____   Never _____

5. Do individual council members avoid overpoliticizing the public process?
   Almost always _____   Sometimes _____   Never _____

6. Do council members in their attitude reflect a sense of public service over personal interest?
   Almost always _____   Sometimes _____   Never _____

Relationship with the city manager

1. Is the relationship among council members and the city manager open and honest?
   Almost always _____   Sometimes _____   Never _____

2. Does the council function as a unit in giving direction to the city manager?
   Almost always _____   Sometimes _____   Never _____

3. Is there mutual respect between the council and city manager?
   Almost always _____   Sometimes _____   Never _____

4. Is there opportunity for the city manager to offer input into the decision-making process?
   Almost always _____   Sometimes _____   Never _____

---

1 John F. Kennedy, *Profiles in Courage* (New York: Harper, 1955), 16–17.

2 Warren Bennis, "Transformational Power and Leadership," in *Leadership and Organizational Culture*, ed. Thomas H. Sergiovanni and John E. Corbally (Urbana: University of Illinois Press, 1986), 70.

3 James Gardner, *On Leadership* (New York: The Free Press, 1990), 16.

4 James H. Svara, *Official Leadership in the City* (New York: Oxford University Press, 1990), 29.

5 Dwight Waldo, *The Study of Public Administration* (New York: Random House, 1955), 47.

6 James H. Svara, "Dichotomy and Duality: Reconceptualizing the Relationship Between Policy and Administration in Council-Manager Cities," *Public Administration Review* 47 (January–February 1989): 228.

7 Parts of this section are adapted from John W. Nason, *The Future of Trusteeship: The Roles and Responsibilities of College and University Boards* (Washington, DC: Association of Governing Boards of Universities and Colleges, 1974).

8 Parts of this discussion are adapted from Booz, Allen, Hamilton Management Consultants, *Strengthening Policy-Making Capabilities of the City Commission* (Wichita, KS: City of Wichita, 1975).

9 For more discussion of evaluating the manager, see the February 1988 issue of *Public Management*, which is devoted to the topic.

10 The discussion of agenda preparation is adapted from Elizabeth K. Kellar, "Communicating with Elected Officials," in *Effective Communication: Getting the Message Across*, ed. David S. Arnold, Christine S. Becker, and Elizabeth K. Kellar (Washington, DC: ICMA, 1983).

11 Sue Martin Grodzins, *The American Federal System* (Chicago, IL: Rand McNally, 1966).

12 Advisory Commission on Intergovernmental Relations, *City Financial Emergencies: The Intergovernmental Dimension* (Washington, DC: GPO, 1973), 1–55.

13 Urban Institute and International City/County Management Association, *How Effective Are Your Community Services?*, rev. ed. (Washington, DC: Urban Institute and ICMA, 1992).

Promoting excellence in management

Excellence in local government is more than answering police and fire emergency calls promptly. It is more than keeping the streets clean and providing water to residences and businesses. It is more than having beautiful parks and attractive landscaping along roadways. It is more than making sure that the garbage is picked up on time.

Excellence in local government means involving citizens in government to help define and plan the services that are most critical to the community. It means reaching out to all citizens—rich, middle-class, and poor—and ensuring that city services are equitable and affordable. It means creating a dynamic organization that is flexible and responsive to the rapid social and technological changes occurring throughout the world. It means protecting the environment. It means nurturing neighborhoods and making the community safe and livable. It means recruiting and maintaining a well-educated workforce representative of the community. It means establishing and adhering to high ethical standards. It means managing the organization within its financial limitations. It means giving citizens what they want from government.

It is the local government manager who assumes primary responsibility for creating and maintaining standards of excellence in the organization. This chapter explores the challenges facing managers who must react to the fast-evolving social, economic, and technological changes that are shaping citizens' expectations of local government. It emphasizes the leadership and managerial styles that encourage employees to be productive and creative. It provides managers with ideas and approaches that successful local government managers have used to promote the pursuit of excellence in their organizations.

The local government manager's ability to create the conditions for achieving excellence is examined as it relates to his or her

1. Leadership traits and managerial roles and responsibilities that set the executive style for the organization
2. Capacity to generate and facilitate public policy issues with a diverse, highly informed, and involved citizenry
3. Assistance to elected officials in carrying out their responsibilities
4. Success in stimulating employees to seek innovative solutions to organizational problems
5. Skill in establishing and communicating a vision for the organization that inspires and motivates the workforce to set high standards for their work
6. Commitment to customer service
7. Professionalism and ethical conduct, which serve as a model for behavior within the organization.

Excellence in the twenty-first century

In its report, *Future Challenges, Future Opportunities*, The ICMA FutureVisions Consortium observed that the role of the local government manager needs to be redefined. The report noted that the traditional role of the manager—implementing programs and policies—is no longer enough. According to the consortium, the manager of the future must turn away from his or her intuitive inclination to respond to new situations by relying on past experiences; instead, managers "must teach themselves to manage on the basis of likely future outcomes." The report concluded that "the capacity to identify and interpret change is becoming a fundamental responsibility of professional local government managers."

The ICMA FutureVisions report also analyzed emerging trends that will determine what skills and attributes managers must have in order to achieve excellence in coping with the demands on local government in the twenty-first century. (These skills and attributes are described in Chapter 1.) The report contends that the aging of the population, the cultural diversity of communities, and the growing global economy will require local governments to alter drastically their structure and service orientation. For example, local governments will have to shift their service delivery systems to better meet the needs of elderly citizens; adapt the workforce to reflect and encourage sensitivity to cultural, ethical, and gender differences; and become more oriented to regional, national, and international economic markets.

Citizens will be very active in the coming decades in selecting the services they want for their communities; local governments, therefore, will have to become much more oriented to customer service. Service delivery systems structured to meet the needs of individual neighborhoods will be much more common. Community-oriented policing will replace more traditional approaches to crime prevention. Flexible leisure services that accommodate nontraditional lifestyles will be in greater demand.[1]

Low revenues, combined with the growing transfer of federal programs and their costs to state and local governments, have resulted in unbalanced budgets and taxpayer revolts,[2] and local governments—many of which experienced severe fiscal stress in the late 1980s and early 1990s—are likely to see their budget woes continue. As managers strive to help elected officials meet the challenge of achieving financial stability in times of rapid change, they need to be innovative, flexible, and entrepreneurial. In his keynote address to the 1990 ICMA Annual Conference, James Crupi, president of Strategic Leadership Solutions in Dallas, Texas, commented that a new generation of leaders is about to take over as local government managers. Crupi said that the new generation of leaders, people now in their thirties and forties, are fueling the most rapid rise of entrepreneurialism in United States history. These leaders are conservative, but not traditional. For these people, "life is too complex, information too specialized, and society too diverse for dedication to tradition. This generation is people- and information-oriented."[3]

The increasing complexities of modern society also will create fundamental changes in the relationship of the manager and the governing body in council-manager cities. Chester A. Newland, a past president of the American Society for Public Administration, cautions that "automated information systems and related high-tech capabilities are reshaping council-manager relations." He says that "the old rule that council members are to deal with the administrative apparatus only through the manager is out of date when computer terminals in council offices can be routinely used to probe for information—without personal contact with subordinate administrators." Newland believes, however, that despite these pressures and changes, the council-manager form of local government will survive and prosper.[4]

Managerial qualities

What qualities will the successful local government manager of the twenty-first century possess? What skills must young public administrators develop if they want to become city or county managers? In the literature on both public and private sector management, there are many lists of attributes common to strong managers. Although the lists contain useful descriptive information about meaningful skills that managers need, having these skills does not ensure success. However, local government managers who lack them are unlikely to achieve excellence as managers.

Leadership traits

N. Joseph Cayer observed that traditional research focused on finding leadership traits that were common among successful public managers. However, researchers found that managers often exhibited significant differences in leadership styles. Cayers says these studies "have led to the conclusion that leadership is dependent both on the situation and on the traits and needs of leaders and subordinates alike. Thus it is almost impossible to predict leadership success." Nevertheless, Cayer identified four key skills that he says are almost indispensable to anyone who hopes to be successful. They are

Practical skills Ability to complete specific actions required in organizing and accomplishing the work of an agency (e.g., conducting meetings, handling conflicts, maintaining an effective work flow)
People skills Attributes needed by the manager to inspire confidence and trust in others so that they are willing to perform assigned tasks (e.g., communicating effectively with employees, establishing and building trust and confidence)
Political skills Flexibility to handle both internal and external political forces (e.g., balancing viewpoints from different ideological perspectives, facilitating resolution of disputes in order to develop consensus)
Leadership skills Capability to handle task roles (e.g., giving clear directions for accomplishing the work of the organization) and maintenance roles (e.g., nurturing employees, fostering positive interpersonal relations).[5]

In the *Handbook of Public Administration*, James L. Perry also noted many differing leadership characteristics, but similarly narrowed the list to a few key factors that influence a public administrator's effectiveness. Perry's list includes technical skills that reflect proficiency in methods and procedures, human skills that enable the manager to encourage people to work together cooperatively, and conceptual skills that allow managers to see the big picture—how decisions, events, and people are linked in time and space. Perry stresses that managers must be responsive to democratic institutions and comply with the letter of the law; focus on results; network effectively with peers and subordinates; consider the viewpoints of differing interest groups; and maintain the vision of the stategic plan while handling day-to-day operations.[6]

The human and political skills identified by Cayer and Perry are also stressed by ICMA in its list of critical leadership attributes, which are discussed in Chapter 1. As Chapter 1 pointed out, because executives, managers, and supervisors have different responsibilities and functions, their skills vary. A diagnostic tool developed by the U.S. Office of Personnel Management (OPM) provides some insight into the relative importance of specific management skills at different management levels. The Management Excellence Inventory (MEI) was created to help federal agencies analyze their management strengths and development needs. The model was refined following extensive surveys, interviews, and job analyses conducted by OPM in several federal agencies, but it is also relevant to local government. The MEI model identifies twelve "management functions." These are

External awareness
Interpretation
Representation
Coordination
Work-unit planning
Work-unit guidance

Budgeting
Material resources administration
Personnel management
Supervision
Work-unit monitoring
Program evaluation

The model also identifies the following ten "effectiveness characteristics," or managerial skills, attitudes, and perspectives:

Broad perspective   Action orientation
Strategic view   Results focus
Environmental sensitivity   Communication
Leadership   Interpersonal sensitivity
Flexibility   Technical competence

The management functions and effectiveness characteristics are then rated according to their relative importance to the responsibilities and needs of executives, middle managers, and supervisors. For example, all twelve management functions are shown to be of great importance to executives, as are all the effectiveness characteristics except technical competence. For supervisors, on the other hand, only three of the effectiveness characteristics are of great importance (communication, interpersonal sensitivity, and technical competence) and only four of the management functions (work-unit guidance, personnel management, supervision, and work-unit monitoring).[7]

The findings of the MEI model are similar to those of Jeffrey S. Luke. He observed that leaders and executive managers share characteristics that differ from those of the average middle manager and administrator. Leaders, according to Luke, are able to look beyond the daily crises and grasp how the organization fits into the national and international scene. They reach beyond the local organization and influence people far outside their immediate constituency with their ability to envision the future, instill values, and motivate people to follow their ideals.[8]

Crucial skills for managers and assistants

Which of the skills discussed above are most needed by local government managers in the day-to-day business of running cities and counties? David N. Ammons and Charldean Newell surveyed city managers and assistant city managers across the United States to determine how their time typically was spent. Analysis of the survey results showed that city managers devoted 33.9 percent of their time to internal administration; 26.6 percent to council relations; 17.5 percent to policy development; 13.1 percent to public relations; and 9 percent to intergovernmental relations. Results for assistant city managers were significantly different in two areas. Assistant city managers spent considerably less time on council relations (19 percent) and more time on internal administration (44.5 percent).[9]

Ammons and Newell's analysis documents clearly that city managers spend nearly two-thirds of their time on non-administrative matters. The priority skills for city managers necessarily relate to their ability to communicate effectively with elected officials and people outside the organization; the city manager must be able to discuss with them the importance to the community and the city of major policy issues. How effectively a manager defines, analyzes, and explains these policy issues to elected officials, key persons in the community, the media, and the public often will be the single most critical factor to his or her success.

The difference between a manager who uses his or her skills to create an excellent organization and a manager whose organization is in continuous turmoil and conflict is primarily the ability to adjust to change and to be flexible in interpersonal relationships. Often, managers who have been successful run into trouble when there is a change in political leadership or when they take a new position with a different government agency. In either event, networking systems familiar to the manager may break down. The manager's success then depends on his or her ability to establish relationships with new individuals who may expect radically different things.

A manager who has been highly visible in the community may need to blend into the background more. A manager who has focused primarily on internal management may need to become more assertive in community mobilization efforts. A manager who has established a centralized management structure may need to delegate some responsibilities in order to be able to have more time to spend nurturing relationships with elected officials. The manager who can, over an extended period of time, make major adjustments in style and management approach generally will be successful and perceived as an effective administrator. In fact, one recent study identified longevity in an organization as a common trait among city managers with strong national reputations for productivity and innovation.[10]

The assistant city manager requires many of the same skills employed by the city manager, but their specific duties will vary significantly depending on the individual relationship of the persons involved. Before being appointed city manager, Martin Vanacour served for many years as assistant city manager. From this unique perspective, Vanacour wrote about the importance of assistants taking supportive positions and working behind the scenes. He noted that the managers he surveyed considered loyalty, trustworthiness, and competence to be the most crucial qualities of an assistant. Other important characteristics mentioned were supporting the manager's decisions, possessing generalist skills, being a good communicator, and being a self-starter.[11]

Working with the community

Citizen activists and neighborhood associations across the country have become a major political force that increasingly influences how local government resources are allocated. Effective managers cooperate with citizen groups in order to develop programs and design service delivery systems that best meet the needs of the community. The challenge for the local government manager is to make sure that (1) the active citizen groups are truly representative of the whole community; (2) all segments of the community have an equal opportunity to participate; (3) citizen input is timely and meaningful; and (4) citizens have good access to data and information sources related to the policy issues under review.

Citizen participation efforts

Berry, Portney, and Thompson write that managers who want to consider serious citizen participation efforts must comply with four key standards:

Effective outreach   Efforts must be made to provide realistic opportunities for large numbers of the target population to participate.
Equal access   The citizen participation process must provide equal access for all citizens. Citizen commissions and task forces must be representative of the entire community.
Significant policy impact   The input of citizens involved in the public participation efforts must be able to have significant impact on final policy decisions.
Enactable policy   The participation process must be related to a specific government policy or program decision. The citizens should make recommendations on the policy or program directly to the decision makers or be empowered to enact the changes themselves.[12]

It is critical that citizen participation activities not be overwhelmed by single interest or special interest groups. Although these groups have a legitimate right to have their causes heard and considered by decision makers, public managers must make sure that narrowly focused viewpoints do not bias the work of citizen groups. Single interest and special interest groups usually are more organized, have well-documented resource material, and are better financed than neighborhood-oriented grassroots groups. Consequently, the single interest and special interest groups can dominate public meetings and discussions and they may intimidate those who are not as informed as they are.

City managers may want to establish consensus programs to help communities reach agreement on controversial issues. These consensus programs can provide mediation services designed to solve private complaints such as neighborhood property-maintenance violations, or the services of professional facilitators who work with large groups to decide critical issues such as the location of a major new transportation corridor. Characteristics of a well-managed consensus program include making sure that the process involves participation from all affected segments of the community; keeping everyone informed on all key points; seeking a common definition of problems that all sides find acceptable; and offering multiple options for consideration. These options should then be modified until nearly everyone agrees on the best solution to the problem. Consensus also is critical on how the solution will be implemented and monitored for results.[13]

Community mobilization

Another way to get citizens to participate is by getting the community involved in service delivery. Virtually all cities and counties use citizen groups to some extent to assist with service delivery. This approach, referred to as "co-production," takes many forms—for example, neighborhood block watches, trash clean-ups, volunteering in schools and hospitals. As cities face growing budget reductions, co-production of services may expand, become more creative, and move into service delivery traditionally provided solely by the government.

Cayer and Weschler see this trend toward co-production as healthy for the community and the local government. They comment that "these efforts to involve bureaucracies more in community affairs and citizens more in production of services have beneficial effects exceeding cost reduction and improvement of services. They provide more joint understanding and more public support. They tend to reduce both public hostility toward government and bureaucratic cynicism toward the public.[14]

Once a commitment is made by the public manager to empower the public by expanding participation efforts, he or she must assume responsibility to assist those citizens who lack the expertise and sophistication to organize themselves effectively. This assistance may take the form of efforts to conduct public meetings; train people in community mobilization techniques; provide information and referral services to meet social and welfare needs; help prepare reports and presentations; and provide appropriate data and information resources.

Community mowing   The cash-strapped city council of Parramatta (population 132,000) in New South Wales, Australia, has asked local residents to volunteer for lawn mowing duty in local parks. Hit by the recession and declining tax receipts, the municipal budget could no longer absorb the costs of maintaining public green space. Since 1988, a total of 48 parks and nature reserves have been dropped from the regular mowing list, receiving at best only an annual clip.

Making a virtue of necessity, Mayor John Haines told local media represen-tatives that the volunteer mowing scheme, possibly an Australian first, would break new ground in promoting community spirit. Mayor Haines said the council had been forced to appeal to the community because the impact of legislation limiting the property tax had severely reduced expected revenues. The council turned to the community after receiving numerous complaints about the overgrown recreation areas.

Source: *Public Innovation Abroad* (November 1992): 7.

Many cities have highly structured programs to assist community mobilization efforts. For example, in 1991, The Urban Institute highlighted various local government efforts to provide technical assistance to citizen groups working on community development block grant proposals, using examples from Albany, New York; Cleveland, Ohio; Rock Island, Illinois; Cuyahoga County, Ohio; Roanoke, Virginia; and Seattle, Washington, among others. The study summarized that "technical assistance to neighborhood organizations includes making suggestions about potential funding sources or helping them prepare proposals. It can also include providing advice, or identifying sources for advice, regarding projects that neighborhood associations are implementing.[15]

Possible costs of citizen involvement   Thomas Mikulecky, a public management consultant and former city manager, believes that local governments must consider drastic changes in values if they are serious about citizen involvement. Increased efforts to get neighborhoods organized and involved in providing input on city policy issues and service delivery will lead to expanded pressure for more empowerment of neighborhood groups and decentralization of policymaking authority. Decentralization may have the unanticipated consequence of increasing the cost of government. According to Mikulecky, "If municipal officials are to consider true decentralization, values must be reconsidered because responsiveness to citizen-neighborhood needs may not be consistent with the time cherished values of efficiency and economy." He goes on to say that decentralization probably will lead to a different mix of services for different neighborhoods. This approach may raise costs because of inefficiencies and create the potential for serious inequity in service delivery. He suggests, however, that citizens may be willing to pay increased taxes for this approach if they feel they have more control over the services they receive.[16]

Controversial issues and policy decisions   Effective managers use citizen groups as a way to confront controversial issues; they attempt to address potential opposition early in the decision-making process, in the hope of reaching consensus. This consensus-building tactic is particularly critical when siting new facilities or transportation corridors where the NIMBY (not in my backyard) syndrome is likely to

---

Rock Island's brainstorming approach   Community development agencies must deliver a wide range of services to diverse population groups. Because funding is limited, the agencies must conduct thorough needs assessments to assist in establishing priorities for selected projects. After completing a needs assessment survey, Rock Island, Illinois, asked its community development housing task force, composed of citizen representatives, to identify options to stabilize or improve neighborhood conditions.

Rock Island's housing task force used a brainstorming approach to complete this task. Several creative ideas were presented and action plans developed for their implementation. Among options considered were a mortgage credit certificate program; a low-interest loan program for improving existing homes; expansion of financial incentives to encourage housing rehabilitation; more effective inspection of rental units; and more borrower education and counseling for first-time home buyers.

Source: Adapted from Harry Hatry, Elaine Morley, George Barbour, Jr., and Steven M. Parjunen, *Excellence in Managing: Practical Experiences from Community Development Agencies* (Washington, DC: The Urban Institute, 1991), 185–186.

appear. On controversial issues, the manager cannot reasonably expect to satisfy everyone, but it is crucial that opponents of a policy have a forum to voice their concerns. John E. Arnold and Barry Selberg, former city manager and assistant city manager, respectively, cautioned that citizens become most upset when they feel that their rights of due process have been denied. They warn, "If your process fails the fairness test, your proposal is dead." They advise managers to seek public input early on controversial issues and ensure full disclosure of all data related to the issue to avoid allegations of misrepresentation.[17]

John C. Thomas, director of the L. B. Cookingham Institute of Public Affairs at the University of Missouri–Kansas City, has conducted extensive research on public involvement in controversial decisions to determine whether successful policy implementation could be explained by adherence to developed decision-making models. He concluded that managers faced with a difficult policy question should resist their instinctive preference to make a tough decision and move ahead rather than draw out an issue through a time-consuming public process. He says that inviting public involvement early rather than later often is best because "a dissatisfied public may resist imposition of a management decision, creating an even messier, perhaps unresolvable impasse."[18]

One of the most troubling questions facing managers, however, is how much public involvement is needed for the long list of important policy issues they confront almost daily. The very high-profile issues (e.g., locating a new landfill, closing parks because of budget cutbacks, rezoning land to allow major commercial development) obviously should have extensive public review and involvement. But other less visible issues, such as changing a policy on prosecution of selected misdemeanor offenses or deferring roadway maintenance, also may have important consequences for the community. When and how should these issues be brought forward for public debate?

There is no clear-cut answer. It will vary tremendously depending on the character of the community. The general public may have limited interest in some policy questions; consequently, these questions will receive little discussion at traditional community forums and public budget hearings. Managers must be careful not to interpret a lack of discussion at these community meetings as carte-blanche approval to initiate policy changes. In these situations, the temptation for the elected official and manager will be to follow the path of least resistance. But the policy decision may not be fair.

Conscientious managers must make sure that those most affected by the decision truly have their views represented. They must identify how policy changes will affect different groups and reach out to those groups in order to involve them in the public decision-making process. They must encourage public policies that are equitable for all citizens.

Adapting to cultural diversity

Many cities today are facing a large influx of immigrants. Traditionally, immigrants have come from European countries. In the early 1990s, the largest number of new arrivals to North America, Australia, and New Zealand were from Asian and Latin American countries. Judith Waldrop, senior editor of *American Demographics* magazine, predicts that by the year 2010, Hispanics will lead African Americans as America's largest minority. By 2020, Waldrop says immigration will outpace natural births in the United States.[19]

For many immigrants, no support systems exist to help them learn the culture, language, and traditions of their new country. The sheer number of immigrant languages and dialects makes the transition more complex. For example, in the Los Angeles city school system, more than 170 different languages and dialects are spoken. Managers who aspire to excellence will be responsive to the needs of *all* the community's residents, including recent immigrants. Ways in which managers

---

European Americans . . . need to step outside their traditional comfort zones . . . and learn about different cultures and ethnic groups, attend cultural festivals, and visit the homes and businesses of the various ethnic groups in the community.

Frank Benest

---

can reach out to and involve immigrants and members of minorities are discussed in Chapter 2.

In addition to using community participation efforts to involve diverse groups, local government managers should help develop solutions to community problems by bringing diverse groups together. City manager Frank Benest notes that it is critical that different ethnic groups interact because "cultural isolation breeds misunderstanding—and worse."[20]

Interactions with elected officials

As discussed in Chapter 3, local government managers must have effective working relationships with elected officials in order to be successful. The principal challenge for the manager is to support elected officials in dealing with the critical issues of concern to the community, without interfering or getting overly involved in the political process. This interaction between the manager and the elected officials determines the manager's leadership capabilities both within and outside the organization. Managers cannot be strong leaders if either the community at large or employees within the organization do not believe that they have strong support for their policies from the elected officials.

A manager must adjust his or her approach to presenting policy issues to the individual interests and needs of the elected officials. On any given policy issue, some elected officials want a detailed explanation of alternative positions, whereas others require only a general briefing. The manager must always ensure, however, that the information provided to the elected officials, whether in detail or summary, has been thoroughly researched and verified for comprehensiveness and accuracy.

Shared responsibility for policy and administration

Traditionally in council-manager cities, the manager has been responsible for administration and the council for policymaking. Yet, it is commonly acknowledged that managers play an important role in policymaking and that the council gets involved in administrative matters. This policy-administration dichotomy has been the subject of much discussion and debate in graduate schools of public administration.

John Nalbandian predicts that "the blurry line between what is political and what is administrative will continue to disintegrate because political values provide the essential legitimacy for administrative practice and administrative experts provide essential information for informed public policymaking." As a result, city managers—who have always played important roles in the policymaking arena—will have to do more than ever before to develop their negotiating, brokering, and consensus-building skills to be successful.[21]

Avoiding conflicts with elected officials

Managers who interact with councils in setting policy often are faced with the question of what behavior is acceptable. The manager must be careful not to become overly political in his or her efforts to persuade the council to develop sound policies for the community. City manager Kevin Duggan suggests that managers first must have a clear understanding of how involved their council wants them to be. Reminding managers that ultimately the council decides the policy direction for the community, Duggan encourages them to focus their efforts on helping the council to develop positions, so that they will "be viewed as supporting, not competing with, the council in the policy area." Providing leadership for the council without appearing political is like walking a tightrope. Duggan says that managers most likely will appear to be too politically involved when they take high-profile positions on issues that are highly sensitive. Duggan warns the manager to know when to withdraw after he or she has "said all that can or should be said appropriately" about an issue.[22]

Some conflict between the local government manager and the council is normal. These conflicts do not necessarily have to lead to confrontation or to the manager's termination or resignation. In their study of turnover among city managers, Whitaker and DeHoog found that "no type of managerial role orientation was particularly associated with a conflict between a council and a manager." They found that conflicts arose primarily because of sharp differences in expectations between the manager and the council. They concluded that managers who maintained a professional posture and avoided being drawn into council conflicts were more likely to succeed. They stressed that managers should work across council factions rather than become linked to any one group and noted that elected officials—particularly during an election campaign—who identified the manager with an opponent "could make it very difficult for a manager to remain neutral."[23] Sources of conflict between local government managers and their governing bodies are discussed in more detail in Chapter 3.

Achieving excellence within the organization

The effect of the manager's personal skills in working with elected officials to help them develop strong policies can be negated completely if the organization cannot implement the council's directives. A successful manager understands that the strength of the organization lies in its rank-and-file employees. The front-line employees must share the vision of the elected officials and the management team if the community is to receive quality services. Employees must be motivated, but the organization also must have the characteristics and tools necessary to operate effectively without bureaucratic logjams.

The achieving organization

What are the characteristics of an organization that is responsive to the needs of the community? What distinguishes an organization that aspires to excellence from others? One useful attempt to define these characteristics is known as "the achieving organization" model. From 1987 to 1989, a group of suburban New Jersey municipalities participated in the Municipal Executive Program (MEP) developed by Deborah Cutchin of Rutgers University. MEP was an intensive organization- and executive-development program in which data about individual behaviors and skills and organizational structures were collected and monitored. The MEP steering committee, made up of New Jersey municipal chief administrators, established four goals for the project. These were

1. *Teambuilding* to increase the effectiveness of municipal management through a high-quality training and development program designed for key administrators
2. *Individual development and skill improvement* to facilitate the professional development of individual executives

3. *Productivity improvement* to increase responsiveness to community needs, create a positive image of the organization, and achieve cost savings
4. *Intercommunity cooperation* to promote cooperation among communities within the state.[24]

The achieving organization model used for the municipalities participating in MEP was designed to be an ideal. The characteristics of this ideal organization are

1. A clear sense of mission: a vision
2. Clearly stated expectations of performance and a sense of individual accountability and responsibility
3. Positive regard for people
4. Performance-based reward system
5. Fairness and honesty in dealing with internal and external clients (including employees)
6. Clear communications—internal and external
7. High levels of performance—measurable results/outcomes
8. Responsiveness to community needs
9. "Can do" attitude—energy in the system (lack of entropy)
10. Environment that encourages creativity and rewards risk-taking.[25]

Part of the evaluation of MEP centered around employees' perceptions of their own organizations compared with the model. This approach elicited quantitative and qualitative data about the managerial strengths and weaknesses of the participating municipalities at the time of implementation of MEP and two years later.

Participants in the program reported that its greatest benefit was improved communication both within their organizations and with citizens. Individual managers stressed that the program was highly beneficial as a self-development and skill-improvement tool. It also reinforced the importance to the management team of working together and focusing on key objectives.

Entrepreneurialism and innovation

As mentioned earlier in this chapter, local government managers increasingly need to be innovative, flexible, and entrepreneurial. Organizations that achieve excellence in serving their citizens also embody these characteristics. David Osborne and Ted A. Gaebler, co-authors of *Reinventing Government: How the Entrepreneurial Spirit Is Transforming the Public Sector*, feel that citizens do not need more government or less government; they need better government. Gaebler was himself a city manager, and together they have spent considerable time studying governments noted for innovation and entrepreneurialism. They were looking for characteristics common to progressive governments but absent in nonresponsive organizations. What they found was "a coherent whole, a new model of government" embodied in ten fundamental principles. They say that most entrepreneurial governments

1. Promote *competition* between service providers
2. *Empower* citizens by pushing control out of the bureaucracy
3. Measure the performance of their agencies, focusing not on input but *output*
4. Are driven by their goals–their *missions*—not by their rules and regulations

---

The key element is a collective vision of a city or state's future—a sense of where it's headed. If you haven't put that together, it's very difficult to make these innovative approaches work.

John Parr

---

5. Redefine their clients as *customers* and offer them choices
6. *Prevent* problems before they emerge, rather than simply offer services afterward
7. Put their energies into *earning* money, not just spending it
8. *Decentralize* authority, embracing participatory management
9. Prefer *market mechanisms* to bureaucratic mechanisms
10. Focus not simply on providing public service, but on *catalyzing* all sectors—public, private, and voluntary—into action to solve community problems.[26]

   Innovative approaches used by local governments include contracting for services traditionally performed in house; creating partnerships with other government agencies and the private sector to spur economic development; empowering citizen groups to play a more active and responsible part in community planning; developing self-help programs such as block watch crime prevention activities to supplement existing services; improving personnel practices in order to involve employees in work design and project implementation; and applying technology to expand service provision and enhance efficiency. The accompanying sidebar provides examples of how various local governments in the United Kingdom have applied innovative concepts for providing services.

Employee involvement efforts

The best organizational systems depend on an informed, involved, and motivated workforce. Without the commitment of its employees, an organization lacks energy and creativity. Effective managers make sure that employees do not feel isolated from management and that they feel that they are part of the programs affecting their work. Even under adverse circumstances, when budget shortfalls may require

---

Examples of service innovations in British local governments

Brent Assisted the Harlesden People's Community Council in converting an abandoned bus garage into a community complex including an information technology center, day-care center, workshop areas, sports halls, and other facilities.

Clywd County With the cooperation of public and private agencies, developed an alleviation program to offset the high unemployment and to address the social and economic problems caused by the closure of Shotton Steelworks.

East Cambridgeshire Turned over the management of its leisure centers to local users on a self-supporting basis.

Thanet Entered into a partnership with the private sector to develop a new ferry terminal that could not be financed through local revenues alone.

Morton-in-Marsh Created a Rural Action Project that implemented improved transportation through the "Villager" minibus service organized and staffed by volunteers.

Islington Created neighborhood offices in decentralized locations to house personnel from several departments working together in a multi-skilled integration team.

Halton Assigned project architectural and design staff for the Stewards Avenue Refurbishment Project to work directly on site to improve communications and gain acceptance from the tenants.

Source: John Stewart, *The New Management of Local Government* (London: Allen & Unwin, 1986), 31, 59–60, 144–45.

cutbacks in services, a strong organization will continue to be supported by employees. But this support requires commitment from management as well. For example, organizations that use layoffs or reductions in force only as a last resort and offer employees severance packages and outplacement services will be seen as caring employers. Barbara S. Romzek states that "managers need to be alert to commitment as a basis for employees to be psychologically tied to their employers; it also has long-term consequences for the retention of high quality employees."[27]

Managers use many different approaches to get employees involved in the organization: quality circles, labor-management committees, employee work teams, and ad hoc task forces are all commonly used in many organizations. Their purpose is to seek a "win-win" environment in which management feels that productivity has been increased and service quality improved, and in which employees feel that they have been involved in decision making and their work environment and career opportunities enhanced.

We . . . think that the most important people in government are the mayor, the city council, the city manager and management. But . . . the really important people . . . are the people who mow the park lawns, stop people from speeding, find housing, issue permits, fight fires. In other words, the most important people are the employees.

Frank Fairbanks

From her study of employee involvement programs in the Pennsylvania Department of Transportation, Susan G. Clark found some success, particularly in improving efficiency. Clark concludes from her study, however, that "employees . . . can provide well-researched suggestions for change. However, if the employee side of the win equation is missing from the program—training opportunities, recognition and reward for their efforts, management support for their ideas—it is unlikely they will want to participate.[28]

While managers concentrate on developing employee involvement programs, they also may have to deal with many frustrated middle managers and staff members. Judith Waldrop says that by the year 2000, one-fifth of the labor force will be forty-five to fifty-four years of age and will expect to move into management positions. But the effects of organizational streamlining and budget cutbacks will significantly reduce the number of executive positions available. A major challenge of the local government manager will be to keep these employees productively employed and motivated to contribute positively to the organization.[29]

Workforce improvement

Ultimately, the success of local governments' ability to provide high-quality services to the community resides with its employees. No amount of strategic planning or operations analysis will compensate for poor morale and disillusioned employees. Any concentrated effort to improve service provision within an organization must evolve as a cultural change. It cannot be mandated by management. Cities with a long history of productivity programs, such as San Diego, California; Phoenix, Arizona; Charlotte, North Carolina; and Dallas, Texas, learned that personnel practices play as important a role in improved organizational performance as service-level standards and effectiveness measurements.

Efforts to motivate and involve employees in order to help make their jobs more rewarding and challenging are often referred to as job enrichment. The following are key elements of job enrichment:

Team effort Work groups are formed to bring together employees working on related assignments so they can function more effectively as a team.

Empowerment   Employees are given expanded opportunities to have input and some decision-making authority in the development of policies and procedures through the use of labor-management committees and special task forces.

Job rotation   Personnel rules are revamped to allow employees more flexibility to rotate assignments within a department or throughout the organization to provide different experiences, both for career advancement and job satisfaction.

Job redesign   Employees are provided more varied and general assignments with more autonomy to make decisions and responsibility for final service delivery. An example is the move to community policing, which gives patrol officers more leeway to do follow-up investigations and interact with the neighborhoods they serve. Job redesign requires that traditional job classifications be revised so that employees can assume more varied roles.[30]

Cultural diversity

As cultural diversity increases, local government organizations can maintain their standards of excellence only by responding creatively to cultural diversity within their community. Managers must not only ensure that the local government workforce reflects the diversity of the community; they must also be sensitive to different cultural values and attitudes in order to ensure maximum productivity and harmony in the workplace. In 1991, former city manager Sylvester Murray reminded managers that managing cultural diversity is not just promoting affirmative action or equal employment opportunities to ensure fair hiring practices. It is also "creating an environment for productive work after a person is hired . . . [it is] a comprehensive management philosophy designed to enable managers to tap the potential of all employees, regardless of how diverse they may be." Murray explained that it is important that managers allow people to be different and that they stress ways for employees to work together effectively while recognizing and respecting their cultural and gender differences.[31]

Many local governments are using awareness workshops and seminars to teach employees from different cultural backgrounds how to work together effectively. The awareness programs focus on how cultural differences influence responses to authority and on the importance of financial and nonfinancial rewards. Local governments vary in the way these awareness sessions are structured. Some use employees within the organization to conduct the sessions and share their cultural experiences. Others use videos followed by discussion groups, or bring in consultants or university personnel who have expertise in facilitating cultural diversity workshops.[32]

Modern technology in local government

Local governments need to stay abreast of new technological developments. Fiscal constraints require that cities and counties ensure that service delivery systems incorporate the most efficient, up-to-date technology possible. It is hard to explain to citizens why antiquated equipment and procedures are still used by a government agency when modern technology is available to reduce costs and streamline bureaucratic processes. Health and safety concerns also create a demand for local governments to use advanced technologies. The general public and employee groups both expect managers to ensure that the latest technology is used to protect against environmental dangers and enhance safety in the workplace.

Although financial limitations may prevent purchase of the more expensive products of technology, many local governments have documented significant savings through minimal expenditures. Simple computer software can be used to create sophisticated route scheduling for meter readers or automated user-fee processing for building permits. Local governments must be creative in finding ways to finance

Workplace diversity Located in Bergen County, in the greater New York City metropolitan area, Teaneck, New Jersey, is a diverse community of about 38,000 residents. According to 1990 census data, approximately 33 percent of Teaneck residents are considered minorities.

The Teaneck Municipal Government is composed of seven departments—fire, police, public works, building, finance, health, and recreation. In 1989, when Jack Hadge became manager of Teaneck, he recognized the lack of minority representation and the absence of programs designed to recruit minorities to key positions in these departments. The municipal government therefore established a work plan aimed at hiring minorities and women in high-level positions throughout town government and created a local government work force that more accurately reflected the town's population.

To recruit minority candidates, the township first created selection committees for the positions of deputy manager, fire chief, engineer, and public works director whose members more closely represented Teaneck's population, providing a balanced system of candidate review. Hadge also appointed minorities to the town's citizen advisory boards and implemented the Progressive Personnel Program, which expanded the civil service eligibility list and the amount of educational assistance available to successful applicants. As a result, a minority deputy fire chief was appointed.

By recruiting and developing a more diverse work force, the municipal government fostered a new attitude within the community of Teaneck.

Source: *Public Management* (October 1992): A-8.

purchases. Savings from technological improvements often can be used to offset initial costs. Joint ventures between jurisdictions can defray total costs.

Managers and administrators have the responsibility to train the workforce to be aware of and adapt to modern technology. It is essential for employees at all levels to be computer literate. In the 1990s, local government employees simply cannot do their jobs properly without modern technological skills. Water service employees must monitor sophisticated equipment to detect water quality problems. Administrative assistants send reports electronically. Planners analyze design options through computer imaging. Engineers revise infrastructure requirements through geographic information systems. Safety specialists develop hazardous materials mitigation plans through computer analysis of chemical compounds.

One way managers can learn about applications of technology that have a proven record of success in local government is through the publications and networking services offered by Public Technology, Inc. (PTI). Annually, PTI publishes hundreds of examples of applied technology in local government (see sidebar on next page).

Quality management

As mentioned, local government managers have used different approaches to encourage employee commitment to the organization's goal of providing high-quality services. Management by objectives (MBO) was popular in the 1950s and 1960s, productivity and industrial engineering approaches were stressed in the early 1970s, and the idea of quality circles gained acceptance in the 1970s. During the 1980s, the quality improvement concepts of total quality management (TQM), which had their roots in the work of W. Edwards Deming, became very popular in private enterprise. TQM was used increasingly in the public sector in the late 1980s and early 1990s.

Successful applications of technology in local governments

City of Dallas Set up a computer-based system to gauge rainfall and stream levels as part of the Dallas Area Flood Warning and Control System. With this system, the entire Dallas floodway area can be monitored to get instantaneous information on potential flooding conditions.

City of Newport News, Virginia Enhanced public recreational opportunities for Huntington Park along the St. James River shoreline by stemming soil erosion and applying a multilayer geotechnical fabric to stabilize the bottom of an unimproved lake.

City of New York Designed laptop computers to link hazardous materials inspectors in the field with the central computer, allowing complete analysis of incidents on site.

City of Quebec Established a multi-agency facility, CECEQ, to provide start-up high-technology firms with business consulting services and training assistance. The program combined the resources of Laval University, Limoilou Community College, Professional Training Commission, Quebec Foundation of Entrepreneurship, Poulin-Dumais, Inc., and the city of Quebec.

City of Phoenix Installed magnetic card readers in all Phoenix Transit buses so employers could provide "credit cards" to employees who wanted to take the bus as part of an air pollution reduction program. Employers receive documentation and cost data on ridership for their trip reduction statistics.

Prince George's County, Maryland Implemented a closed circuit television line between the jail and the courts, allowing bond hearings and arraignments to proceed without transporting 40 to 70 prisoners daily.

Source: *Solutions 91* (Washington, DC: Public Technology, Inc., 1991).

TQM combines productivity and work-improvement evaluations with employee-oriented organizational development techniques and strategic planning to focus attention on quality results and customer satisfaction. TQM represents an evolutionary stage in management theory, bringing together various approaches and concepts that have been successful in the public sector over the last thirty years.[33]

The importance of the quality movement in U.S. business management circles led to the creation of the Malcolm Baldridge National Quality Award in 1987.[34] Named for a former secretary of commerce, the Baldridge Award is given annually to private corporations that demonstrate excellence in service quality. The criteria and point-award system used in the Baldridge award, shown in Figure 4–1, give a good summary of the important components of a quality management program; these components apply equally to quality management in the public sector. However, the structure that quality management ultimately will take in the public sector is still uncertain. James E. Swiss found that the use of TQM in government had problems related to complex quality indicators; difficulties in defining the government "customer"; differences in emphasis on input and output measures; and demand for a degree of top-management involvement that is unrealistic in the public sector. Swiss suggests that TQM still can be effective in the public sector, however, if it is modified and adapted to the special needs of government. According to Swiss, the elements of TQM that are particularly useful to government are

Client feedback Reactions to an agency's immediate customers represent an important consideration for future decision making.

Tracking performance Because TQM stresses both employee participation and quantitative analysis, it often is easier to implement than the traditional efficiency

Figure 4–1 Malcolm
Baldridge National
Quality Award.

Criteria	Points
1. Leadership	100
2. Information and analysis	60
3. Strategic quality planning	90
4. Human resource utilization	150
5. Quality assurance of products and services	150
6. Quality results	150
7. Customer satisfaction	300
Total points	1000

management model. Employees often suggest meaningful changes in statistical information and data collection that more accurately reflect work activity.

Continuous improvement TQM's continuous improvement principle is highly valuable because of its adaptability to innovation and change.

Worker participation Employee empowerment and involvement is a critical component of TQM that applies to both the public and private sector.[35]

Michael E. Milakovich also sees problems in adapting TQM in the public sector. He says that the emphasis most governments place on the annual budget cycle—with its short-term focus and cost-cutting philosophy—inhibits the long-term planning necessary for successful TQM programs. As a result, he says, "The continual improvement of process, the training of employees, and the upgrading of services that would satisfy customers [are] too often ignored." Milakovich believes, however, that as elected officials and public managers see the advantages of TQM as a "nonpartisan and fact-based approach to solving problems in the quality of public service," it will become widely accepted in government.[36]

Customer service

The TQM element that has gained the greatest acceptance among public sector agencies is the concept of customer service. This concept focuses on a change in the organizational culture to incorporate customer service into the job responsibilities of all employees. Customers are defined both inside and outside the organization. For local governments, this would mean citizens who interact with the city or county, either recipients of services or those involved in business transactions. It also applies within the organization to interdepartmental activities.

George Wagenheim and John Reurink have identified the basic elements of a customer service program for the public sector. The first step in this program is to document customers' service needs. They list the following needs as most critical:

1. Information and communication
2. Responsiveness
3. Problem resolution
4. On-time, reliable, consistent service delivery
5. Competence of personnel
6. Accuracy
7. Courteous and friendly service.

Following the identification of customers' service needs, managers must develop revised service delivery systems to respond to those needs. According to Wagenheim and Ruerink, establishing better management processes leads to organizational benefits by eliminating wasteful and unnecessary regulations and procedures.[37]

Volusia's employee teams   Volusia County, Florida, activated 160 employee teams throughout its organization to identify customer service improvement opportunities. Working in nearly every county department, Volusia's employee teams developed many cost-saving ideas. Examples include:

Airport maintenance workers designed a faster and more effective degreaser for oil spills, leading to both cost savings and higher user satisfaction.

Deputy sheriffs shifted non-law-enforcement calls to other appropriate service agencies. This action allowed the deputy sheriffs to devote more time to law enforcement duties and improve response time to citizen calls.

The Development and Code Administration Office simplified and combined residential and commercial zoning permit applications. The forms were computerized and reduced in number from five to three.

Source: Pat Keehley, "TQM for Local Governments," *Public Management 74* (August, 1992): 14.

In the United Kingdom, a similar customer-oriented program has been in effect since the mid 1980s in local governments. Known as "public-service orientation," or PSO, the program stresses customer service, citizen participation, and public accountability.[38]

Critical to the success of TQM and customer service is the complete acceptance of the program by the rank-and-file workers. Some unions see TQM as a threat; they may think that TQM is another word for "productivity," aimed at reducing jobs. Another union fear is that TQM promotes multi-skilled workers. This disrupts the existing labor negotiation groups, which often are composed of employees within narrow job classifications. Experts who design TQM programs both in the private and public sectors strongly urge managers to get unions involved at the earliest possible stage. Managers need to inform unions that the organization is considering a TQM program. They should learn how TQM may affect existing labor negotiation agreements; above all, they should make the unions part of the TQM planning and implementation team.[39]

Joseph Sensenbrenner, former mayor of Madison, Wisconsin, and now a TQM consultant, says that unions initially were lukewarm about installing TQM in Madison; nevertheless, "Some wary union leaders and members turned out to be among

Customer service   The Structuring for Service Program in College Station, Texas, has shifted employee attitudes to a customer focus and also has spurred implementation of other service programs, including neighborhood immunization sites, a one-stop permitting program, and front door garbage collection for handicapped residents.

The Structuring for Service Program is a seven-phase operation. During the first phase, customer service trainers introduce the program, explain what to expect, and discuss the objectives of the program. In addition, employees complete an attitude survey, which is used to measure their customer service orientation. In the subsequent six phases, employees concentrate on service leadership, building customer skills, systems and structures, and feedback.

As a result of the Structuring for Service Program, customer care is now the norm throughout the organization.

Source: *Public Management* (November 1991): 23.

my strongest backers." He credited the turnaround on a change in management behavior from "telling" the employees what to do to "asking" for their advice on the potential for service improvements.[40]

Setting standards of ethical conduct

Standards of ethical conduct that are clearly articulated and understood by all employees are essential to attaining excellence in an organization. Such standards must be so strong that the community recognizes and takes pride in having an honest,

---

Quality improvement efforts in Madison, Wisconsin The Madison quality improvement process began in 1983, when the mayor and other top administrative officials were exposed to the quality management philosophy and methods of W. Edwards Deming. The first team project, implemented in the First Street Garage, resulted in the reduction of the average vehicle turnaround time from nine days to three. There was also a savings of $7.15 in down time and repair for every $1 invested in preventive maintenance. The annual net savings amounted to $700,000. By 1989, the city had 30 quality improvement teams.

The biggest difficulty the city has faced in keeping the quality improvement effort on track, according to the city's organizational development and training officer, has been "the traditional paramilitary systems we have in place [for] compensation, performance evaluation, rewards and recognition, suggestions, etc. . . . Until our employees see that these systems are being changed we will not have real transformation."

The mayor who launched the quality initiative was not reelected in 1989. His replacement initiated an evaluation of the city's quality improvement process. This five-month evaluation determined that direct costs totaled $262,414 and indirect costs—time spent by city employees in training, formal projects and other related activities—amounted to $1,146,587. Agency heads estimated that the 56 improvement projects had a positive cost savings of between $1,100,000—$1,400,000. It was noted that many projects focused on im-

proved customer satisfaction, labor/management relations, scheduling of services and streamlining of procedures, projects whose dollar savings were hard to calculate. In the five agencies that had most completely implemented TQM—police, Madison Metro, public health, data processing, and streets—the following nonquantifiable benefits were noted:

Decrease in grievances

Improvement in staff morale, attitude, cooperation, and interpersonal relations

Better planning and more sensitivity to customer needs

Improved intra-agency and inter-agency cooperation and teamwork

Faster turn-around time and improved customer service.

The TQM effort has continued, but with modifications. It was determined that the process had matured from its primary emphasis on continuous improvement teams. Consequently, it has shifted to a more comprehensive approach that aligns the initiative with the city's goals and strategies. In addition, a comprehensive learning system has been developed within city government that includes workplace education centers and quality improvement training and education initiatives.

Source: Adapted from James J. Kline, "Top Quality Management in Local Government," *Government Finance Review* (August 1992): 9. Copyright Government Finance Officers Association. Reprinted by permission.

---

corruption-free government. Elected officials and the local government should take the lead in establishing ethical standards for the organization but should not simply attempt to impose them from the top. If the rules for ethical conduct are to be taken seriously at all levels, they must be developed in collaboration with local government employees. If employees are consulted as the standards are being formulated, they are likely to be more committed to upholding them.

Managers must be certain to set an example for the organization through their own scrupulous adherence to the standards, as the manager's behavior often becomes the model for the employees. If a manager appears to be more concerned with getting the job done than with considering the ethical issues involved, employees may feel justified in not taking ethical concerns too seriously.

In examining why good managers sometimes make bad ethical choices, Saul W. Gellerman observed that top managers seldom asked subordinates to do things that they both knew were against the law or unethical. However, Gellerman found that managers "sometimes leave things unsaid or give the impression that there are things they don't want to know about . . . implying that rich awards await those who achieve certain results—and that the methods for achieving them will not be examined too closely."[41]

Ethical standards have been promulgated by many national public organizations. Both ICMA and the American Society for Public Administration have well-established ethical standards of conduct for their members. Other professional associations that include public sector employees, such as the American Bar Association and the International Association of Chiefs of Police, also have ethical standards for their members. Local government officials need to be familiar with and adhere to the ethical guidelines of their own professional association in addition to observing the ethical standards of the local government association.

Knowing exactly what is acceptable ethical behavior, however, can be complex even when standard guidelines are followed. Public administration professor York Wilbern identifies six levels of morality of concern to public administrators. These levels vary from personal integrity issues to the very complex questions of the morality of policy decisions that determine government service. Wilbern's six levels of morality are defined as follows:

1. *Basic honesty and conformity to law*   Public administrators must be honest in all of their work activities and personal behavior. Wilbern notes that "there is almost certainly less tolerance of public employees than of private employees who deviate from accepted standards in such personal matters as marital behavior, sexual deviance, and the use of alcohol and drugs, as well as basic honesty."

2. *Conflicts of interest*   Citizens expect government employees to look out for the public interest. Public administrators must make sure that their actions are not guided by their desire for financial gain, or by the demands of special interest groups.

3. *Service orientation and procedural fairness*   According to Wilbern, "procedural due process" is a cornerstone of public morality. Public employees often have tremendous authority—for example, to arrest people, assess property taxes, or approve building plans. Particular attention must be given to avoid any abuse of authority that could damage the rights of individual citizens. Proper safeguards must be established so that citizens who believe that government acted improperly or arbitrarily have an opportunity to appeal an action. Municipalities often address this issue through the use of administrative hearing offices to handle formal complaints or customer-service representatives to resolve minor problems.

4. *Ethic of democratic responsibility*   Public administrators must ensure that citizens have an opportunity to participate in government decision making. A professional delimma can occur when citizens choose to follow a policy that

administrators believe to be incorrect. When citizens make clear their policy choices through their elected officials, public administrators generally should carry them out, even if the action conflicts with their own professional judgment.

5. *Ethic of public policy determination*   Perhaps the most complex moral choices are made in determining public policy as it relates to equity and equality. Wilbern explains: ''The perpetrator of a regressive tax, or a regulation which permits water or air used by thousands to be polluted . . . may do far more harm to far more people than hundreds of common burglars.''

6. *Ethic of compromise and social integration*   Compromise is an essential part of the political process. Both elected officials and managers know that most significant policy decisions are the product of many compromises among dissenting groups. An ethical question arises when a compromise is unacceptable or immoral. The problem is that sincere people may hold strongly divergent views, as the ongoing debate on abortion clearly shows. Administrators must be satisfied that the compromises they make do not violate their ethical standards.[42]

If the local government manager believes a policy decision to be illegal, such as an order not to enforce environmental laws or correct an obvious safety hazard, the elected officials should be told that the manager cannot implement that directive. If the elected officials later insist, then the manager's ethical standards would require notification of federal or state authorities and perhaps, ultimately, resignation.

Managers looking at ways to assess ethical practice within their own organization may want to consider using an ethical assessment survey. City manager Stephen Bonczek used this method to evaluate the effectiveness of his city's formal employee training program on ethics. He advises that a survey on ethical behavior must represent all levels of the organization, from executive management to frontline employees.[43]

One basic conclusion surfaces from this discussion of ethics: ethical behavior is the ultimate standard of excellence in an organization. Without ethical standards, an organization's focus on total quality management, customer service, employee empowerment, or citizen participation means nothing. The highest responsibility for a manager, in his or her quest for excellence, is to set and abide by ethical standards as an example for the community and the organization.

Recap

This chapter examines the conditions that help to create excellence within an organization. After a brief discussion of the changing environment in which local government managers operate, the chapter identified the most critical skills needed by virtually all managers. The importance of citizen participation in the public policy process was stressed, with the recognition that often the community must first be mobilized to get meaningful input and discussion. The manager's interactions with elected officials were also discussed.

The chapter also looked at the characteristics of local governments perceived to be excellent. The conditions that foster entrepreneurship and innovation were analyzed, as well as the importance for employee involvement in establishing the culture of the organization and in enhancing motivation. The necessity for local governments to adapt to state-of-the-art technology was reviewed, as was the need for a computer literate workforce. The emergence in the late 1980s and early 1990s of emphasis on total quality management and customer service was highlighted; adoption of these concepts is likely to gain momentum into the twenty-first century. Finally, the chapter stressed the importance of ethics in the organization, observing that, above all else, ethical behavior is the highest standard of excellence for local government.

Self-appraisal guide for local governments

Although the specific skills of the manager combined with the unique demands of each community determine exactly how each local government achieves excellence, it is possible to set some guidelines to use as benchmarks. The following self-appraisal guide allows local government managers to determine whether their local government creates the conditions for the attainment of excellence. There is no specific measure of how well a local government should score on this self-appraisal. As a general rule, however, a local government with well-established programs to promote excellence will score high on about 80 percent of the criteria. A scoring guide follows the self-appraisal.

Directions: Apply a rating of 1 to 4, as defined below, to indicate how well you think the statement applies to your local government.

Rating scale
(1) *Disagree*   My local government does not do this.
(2) *Disagree somewhat*   My local government does this only on a very limited basis.
(3) *Agree somewhat*   My local government does this partially, or in some areas.
(4) *Agree*   My local government does this.

A. Policy direction
____ 1. My local government has a mission statement that is recognized and understood throughout the organization.
____ 2. Goals and objectives have been established for all departments.
____ 3. Job responsibilities are clearly defined for executives and middle managers in the organization.
____ 4. Reward systems for managers are based on performance results.
____ 5. Council policy decisions are explained and disseminated to all affected personnel throughout the organization.
____ 6. Ethical standards have been set for the organization and communicated to all employees.
____   *Subtotal*

B. Community involvement
____ 1. Citizens have convenient access to elected officials and top managers to provide input on policy decisions.
____ 2. Public forums are routinely held throughout the community to solicit general public comment about city services.
____ 3. Public opinion surveys are conducted on a regular basis to obtain citizen ratings of services.
____ 4. My local government sponsors outreach programs to encourage citizens to be active in public issues.
____ 5. Neighborhoods in my community have been empowered to make some decisions impacting service delivery in their areas.
____ 6. My local government provides assistance to neighborhoods who want to organize and be eligible for special grant programs.
____ 7. My local government makes an effort to promote the cultural diversity of its residents through special events such as festivals, parades, and neighborhood pride parties.
____ 8. A community-needs assessment has been conducted to gauge the effectiveness and responsiveness of current government services.
____   *Subtotal*

C. Employee development

_____ 1. Employees have an opportunity to participate in setting objectives and performance requirements for their work groups.

_____ 2. Effective communications systems are in place to encourage employees to receive and provide feedback to management.

_____ 3. Training programs in my local government have been set up to allow employees to

      _____ a. Refine their skills to keep current on new technologies and procedures to do their jobs better.

      _____ b. Develop new skills to prepare for advancement or other careers within the organization.

      _____ c. Learn how to interrelate more effectively with other employees and co-workers from different cultural backgrounds.

_____ 4. Alternative employment options (e.g., job sharing, flexible work hours) are available in my organization.

_____ 5. Minority employees in my organization are encouraged to pursue advancement opportunities.

_____ 6. Physically challenged employees are provide responsible jobs within my organization.

_____ 7. My local government has a comprehensive safety program for its employees.

_____ 8. Employee suggestion programs are supported, and good ideas are implemented.

_____ 9. Employees in my organization are encouraged to take risks and to be creative and innovative.

_____ 10. My local government sets up labor-management committees to address employee issues of general concern (e.g., health insurance, training programs).

_____ 11. In the event of employee layoffs due to budget cuts, my organization has a plan to assist displaced workers.

_____ *Subtotal*

D. Service delivery

_____ 1. My local government has an established customer service program for all departments and activities.

_____ 2. Total Quality Management, or a similar program, has been implemented in my organization.

_____ 3. My organization has prepared a long-range strategic plan to identify community needs and develop strategies to meet the service demands of the future.

_____ 4. Our existing technological capabilities have been fully evaluated and a program developed to bring new technology into our organization.

_____ 5. My local government adheres to all environmental requirements.

_____ 6. The costs of our government services are compared to competitive alternative private sector services.

_____ 7. My local government's services are supportive of business and economic development activities that are beneficial to the entire community.

_____ 8. My local government's ordinances and regulations are reviewed regularly to eliminate outdated or overly burdensome requirements.

_____ 9. My local government's organizational structure has been analyzed to ensure that unnecessary layers of bureacracy have been eliminated.

_____ 10. My organization's service standards for its departments compare favorably to those of national professional associations such as International Association of Chiefs of Police, National Fire Protection Association, American Library Association, and so forth.

_____ *Subtotal*

E. Budget and financial controls

____ 1. My local government's financial reports meet the requirements set by the Government Finance Officers Association (GFOA).

____ 2. Our budget process allows for timely and meaningful public discussion of proposals and alternatives.

____ 3. My local government's budget document clearly delineates expenditure allocations and sources of revenues for all funds in all programs.

____ 4. My local government has a multiyear capital improvements program.

____ 5. Comprehensive efficiency and effectiveness measurements have been established for all programs.

____ 6. Financial and program audits of departments are performed on both a random and scheduled basis.

____ 7. An outside audit of the local government's overall finances is performed annually.

____ 8. A long-range financial plan has been prepared to ensure the stability of my local government's bond ratings.

____ *Subtotal*

Summary

	Your score	Possible score
A. Policy direction	____	24
B. Community involvement	____	32
C. Employee development	____	52
D. Service delivery	____	40
E. Budget and financial controls	____	32
Total score	____	180

Scoring guide

160–180   Your local government meets most of the criteria for excellence.

140–159   Your local government meets many of the criteria for excellence; some areas need development.

100–139   Your local government meets some of the criteria for excellence; many areas have not been addressed.

Below 100   Your local government needs to work on implementing many of the criteria recommended in the self-appraisal guide.

1 Amy C. Paul, *Future Challenges, Future Opportunities: Final Report of the ICMA FutureVisions Consortium* (Washington, DC: ICMA); quotations from James R. Griesemer, "Introduction," pp. 3 and 2, respectively.

2 Todd Sloane, "States Hemorrage Red Ink," *City & State* 9 (August 10–23, 1992): 1.

3 James Crupi, "Forces Shaping Local Governments in the 1990's," *Public Management* 72 (December, 1990): 3–6.

4 Chester A. Newland, "The Future of Council-Manager Government," in *Managing for Tomorrow: Global Change and Local Futures*, ed. Amy Cohen Paul (Washington, DC: ICMA, 1990), 172.

5 Joseph N. Cayer, "Qualities of Successful Program Managers," in *Managing Public Programs: Balanc-ing Politics, Administration, and Public Needs*, Robert E. Cleary, Nicholas Henry, and Associates (San Francisco: Jossey-Bass, 1989), 121–141.

6 James L. Perry, "The Effective Public Administration," in *Handbook of Public Administration*, ed. James L. Perry (San Francisco: Jossey-Bass, 1989), 619–627.

7 Loretta R. Flanders and Dennis Utterback, "The Management Excellence Inventory: A Tool for Management Development," *Public Administration Review* 45 (May–June 1985): 403–410.

8 Jeffrey S. Luke, "New Leadership Requirements for Public Administration: From Managerial to Policy Ethics," in *Ethical Frontiers in Public Administration*, ed. James S. Bowman (San Francisco: Jossey-Bass, 1991), 158–192.

9   David N. Ammons and Charldean Newell, *City Executives: Leadership Roles, Work Characteristics, and Time Management* (Albany; State University of New York, 1989), 120.

10 David N. Ammons, "Reputational Leaders in Local Government Productivity and Innovation," *Public Productivity & Management Review* 15 (Fall 1991): 19–43.

11 Martin Vanacour, "A Positive Look at Our Profession," *Public Management* 72 (September 1990): 16–17.

12 Jeffrey M. Berry, Kent E. Portney, and Ken Thompson, "Empowering and Involving Citizens," in *Handbook of Public Administration*, ed. James L. Perry (San Francisco: Jossey-Bass, 1989), 217–218.

13 Susan Carpenter, "Solving Community Problems by Consensus," *MIS Report* (October, 1989): 1–4.

14 Joseph N. Cayer and Louis F. Weschler, *Public Administration: Social Change and Adaptive Management* (New York: St. Martin's Press, 1988), 122–141.

15 Harry Hatry, Elaine Morley, George P. Barbour, Jr., and Stephen P. Pojunen, *Excellence in Managing: Practical Experiences from Community Development Agencies* (Washington, DC: The Urban Institute, 1991), 31.

16 Thomas F. Mikulecky, "Neighborhoods: Smaller, More Responsive Local Governments," *Public Management* 72 (August 1990): 9–10.

17 John E. Arnold and Barry Selberg, "Mastering the Practical Politics of Getting Your Ideas Adopted," *Governing* 4 (June 1991): 10.

18 John Clayton Thomas, "Public Involvement in Public Management: Adapting and Testing a Borrowed Thesis," *Public Administration Review* 50 (July-August, 1990): 441.

19 Judith Waldrop, "You'll Know It's the 21st Century When . . ." *Public Management* 73 (January 1991): 2.

20 Frank Benest, "Marketing Multiethnic Communities," *Public Management* 73 (December 1991): 4–14.

21 John Nalbandian, *Professionalism in Local Government: Transformations in the Roles, Responsibilities and Values of City Managers* (San Francisco: Jossey-Bass, 1991), 53, 108.

22 Kevin C. Duggan, "Leadership Without Appearing Political," *Public Management* 73 (February 1991): 12–15.

23 Gordon P. Whitaker and Ruth Hoogland DeHoog, "City Managers Under Fire: How Conflict Leads to Turnover," *Public Administration Review* 51 (May-June, 1991): 156–165.

24 Paul D. Epstein and Deborah A. Cutchin, "The Achieving Organization in Local Government," and Deborah A. Cutchin and Paul D. Epstein, "Make No Small Plans: New Jersey Municipalities Attempt to Become Achieving Organizations," *National Civic Review* 79 (May-June, 1990): 207–243.

25 Cutchin and Epstein, "Make No Small Plans."

26 David Osborne and Ted A. Gaebler, "Bringing Government Back to Life," *Governing* 5 (February, 1992): 46–50.

27 Barbara S. Romzek, "Employee Investment and Commitment: The Ties That Bind," *Public Administration Review* 50 (May-June 1990): 381.

28 Susan G. Clark, "Employee Involvement Programs: Will Win/Win Work?" *National Civic Review* 78 (March-April 1989): 94–102.

29 Judith Waldrop, "You'll Know It's the 21st Century When . . .," *Public Management* 73 (January 1991): 3.

30 John M. Greiner, "Motivating Improved Productivity: Three Promising Approaches," in *Creative Personnel Practices: New Ideas for Local Governments*, ed. John Matzer (Washington, DC: ICMA, 1984), 109–111.

31 Sylvester Murray, "The Challenge Not to Adjust," *APWA Reporter* 58 (October 1991): 19.

32 Cheryl Farr, "Building and Supporting a Multicultural Workforce," *Public Management* 74 (February 1992): 22.

33 See Mary Walton, *The Deming Management Method* (New York: Dodd, Mead, 1986).

34 United States Public Law 100–107, August 20, 1987.

35 James E. Swiss, "Adapting Total Quality Management (TQM) to Government," *Public Administration Review* 52 (July-August 1992): 356–362. See also Philip S. Kronenberg and Reness G. Loeffler, "Quality Management Theory: Historical Context and Future Prospect," *Journal of Management Science & Policy Review* 8 (Spring–Summer 1991): 204–221.

36 Michael E. Milakovich, "Total Quality Management for Public Sector Productivity Improvement," *Public Productivity and Management Review* 15 (Fall 1990): 19–32.

37 George D. Wagenheim and John H. Reurink, "Customer Service in Public Administration," *Public Administration Review* 51 (May-June 1991): 263–270.

38 Christopher Pollitt, *Managerialism and the Public Services: The Anglo-American Experience* (Oxford, England: Basil Blackwell Ltd, 1990), 149–153.

39 David K. Carr and Ian D. Littman, *Excellence in Government: Total Quality Management in the 1990's* (Arlington, VA: Coopers and Lybrand, 1990), 147–150.

40 Joseph Sensenbrenner, "Quality Comes to City Hall," *Harvard Business Review* 65 (March-April 1991): 64–75.

41 Saul W. Gellerman, "Why Good Managers Make Bad Ethical Choices," in *Ethical Insight, Ethical Action: Perspectives for the Local Government Manager*, ed. Elizabeth K. Kellar (Washington, DC: ICMA, 1988), 42–47.

42 York Wilbern, "Types and Levels of Public Morality," in *Ethical Insight, Ethical Action*, 9–21.

43 Stephen Bonczek, "Creating an Ethical Work Environment: Enhancing Ethics Awareness in Local Government," *Public Management* 73 (October 1991): 19–20.

Managing programs and services

Managing in order to get the right things done efficiently and economically is the traditional crux of public administration. In contemporary society, conflicting forces make managing an even greater challenge. Whereas citizens have always expected essential services at acceptable costs, they now seem to demand more services—along with reduced spending and lower taxes. At the same time, national and state governments impose mandates on local governments without providing funds for their implementation. (As mayor Peggy Rubach put it in testimony before the Senate Committee on Banking, Housing, and Urban Affairs, "Stop passing the buck without the bucks."[1]) The resulting resource scarcity presents a real challenge to local government managers. As there appears to be no end to resource scarcity in sight, local government managers must find ways of bringing citizens' expectations of local government in line with resources. This chapter examines five areas affecting the local government manager's efforts to manage services and programs: (1) the context of service-oriented management, (2) developing and managing policy for program and service delivery, (3) implementation, (4) productivity, and (5) evaluation.

The context of service-oriented management

The manager's functions are to help define reasonable policies and oversee their responsible implementation. Success in these demanding tasks requires expertise in internal organizational management. It also requires values consistent with the principles of constitutional self-government and personal qualities of courage, sensitivity, and vision.[2] These qualities are particularly important at a time of rapid social, political, and technological change. Much of the local government manager's time today, for example, is spent in reconciling popular politics and expert administration.

The unstable environment

The contemporary environment of local government managers is highly dynamic. There is a great deal of opportunity to participate in the decision-making process for those who have an interest in the content and outcome of policy. Government managers always have worked in a "fishbowl," allowing interested people to see what is happening and facilitating their participation in decision making. But citizens and groups have become much more aggressive in pressing their interests. They are aided by communications technology that enables freer flow of information and the rapid mobilization of people. Aided by court decisions and other public policies that permit and encourage participation, citizens and groups are able to become involved in virtually any issue. Public managers find that any decision or action is likely to evoke an almost immediate reaction.

Under these circumstances, efforts to plan and maintain stability in policies and programs become complicated. No longer can the manager manage in the traditional sense. Whereas once the local government manager was not actively involved in politics and policymaking, the manager's role has changed dramatically. Although elected officials still have the primary responsibility for shaping community vision and dealing with community responses to policy and programs, the manager is clearly involved in these activities. Elected officials expect the manager to have a finger on the pulse of the community and to anticipate its reactions so that they are kept abreast of new developments. The local government manager therefore becomes more and more a link with the external community and must rely on others to carry on day-to-day internal management activities. Consequently, the local government manager must be able to create a vision for subordinates and delegate responsibilities effectively.

In a political climate that won't allow for tax increases, we have to look at the expenditure side.

Mike Hargett

The changing environment creates continually changing roles for the local government manager. Although intergovernmental relations have always been important to the manager, the emphasis on them has increased, chiefly because the diminished resources of local governments and the increased number of federal and state mandates make intergovernmental cooperation essential. Clearly, the activities of every level of government affect the activities of others. Local government managers are responsible for assuring the coordination of activities with neighboring jurisdictions. In addition, local government managers have to deal with the state and national governments. Much of their effort involves working with national and state officials to ensure that they understand the implications of their policies (see Chapter 7). As state and national mandates increase, the local government manager is likely to be the one who has to make certain that mandates are complied with and funded.

The local government manager's role in economic development has also changed. Increasing resource scarcity has led all levels of government to search for strong, stable bases of revenue without raising taxes. As a result, the local government manager spends much time attempting to promote economic development in a highly competitive environment. Although "smokestack chasing" was the traditional approach to economic development, the new challenge is to find ways of providing a stable economic base while giving attention to quality of life issues, including the provision of amenities, social services, and a clean environment. Thus, efforts now focus on creating a good employment base without changing the characteristics of the community that led people to live there. The local government manager, therefore, must be ready to respond to concerns about any effects of economic development that may harm the community. (The manager's role in economic development is discussed further in Chapter 6.)

The 1980s generated a new round of ethnic conflict across the country. Although others may debate its source, local government managers do not have the luxury of placing blame. They often find themselves in the role of mediator and instead must discover ways to achieve compromise. Most communities have some ethnic neighborhoods, and conflicts often develop over differing levels of services or ways in which services are delivered. In addition, what benefits one neighborhood may have a detrimental effect on another. Neighborhood identity has both positive and negative consequences. Although a sense of neighborhood identity and community can enhance efforts at policing and community improvement, the interests of the community as a whole can get lost in the competition for services or benefits. How to balance the needs of the whole community with the interests of specific areas presents another major challenge to the local government manager.

Finally, world events have given many local government managers an international role. Dramatic changes in the late 1980s and early 1990s propelled local government managers into the international arena in record numbers. Even though managers from the United States and Canada have always acted as role models and mentors, events of the early 1990s placed them more squarely in such roles. The collapse of the Soviet Union in 1991 led to the involvement of many local government managers from North America and Western Europe in efforts to decentralize the governing process in countries that had been part of the Soviet bloc. ICMA participated in many such initiatives, and local governments across the United States and Canada established relationships with Eastern Europe and the new Commonwealth of Independent States (eleven republics of the old USSR). These relationships give local government managers a role in the development of local government around the world.

Values in local government management

Traditionally, managing service delivery required balancing three classic concerns of public administration—getting the right things done (effectiveness), doing them the right way (efficiency), and regulating the use of scarce resources (economy). Today, a fourth concern is social equity, which deals with fair distribution of services to all groups in the community. Balancing these four concerns requires coordinated policy analysis and management systems.

In addition, local government managers are expected to act in an ethical manner in all their activities. In our complex society, determining what ethical behavior is sometimes presents a challenge, but ICMA provides guidelines in its code of ethics. The importance of ethical standards and behavior is discussed more fully in Chapter 1 and Chapter 4.

Harnessing new technologies and information

Unending technological change affects every activity in which managers engage. The computer, of course, has revolutionized information processing, storage, and retrieval. It also assists in many management activities by making data analysis quicker and more accurate. Rapid advances in communications technology, in particular, challenge managers to harness new tools for management, and part of the manager's responsibility is to determine the most appropriate technology for the local government organization given resource constraints. Technical experts are likely to press for the most advanced technology regardless of resources, and the manager must be able to assess their needs compared with those of others in the organization and the resources available. Doing so requires the ability to analyze the costs and benefits of the technology and to maintain the morale of subordinates when the organization cannot afford the sophisticated technology some of their colleagues in other jurisdictions have. Technology is discussed more fully later in the chapter as part of the discussion of productivity improvement.

Accountability

Managers are held accountable for their activities. The governing board of the city or county hold the manager accountable for effectively accomplishing the goals that they establish. Citizens and interest groups hold the manager accountable for the results of the policies that he or she implements. The successful manager establishes a management system that requires accountability of subordinates as well. Administrative procedures, discussed later, provide mechanisms for assuring accountability, which is measured by results as well as by the professionalism of managers' actions.

Developing and managing public policy

The relative emphasis on effectiveness, efficiency, economy, and social equity varies according to the different needs and resources of communities. When local government functions were relatively simple and uncomplicated by intergovernmental and judicial entanglements, efficiency and economy were the chief concerns of professional public management, and the budget was the chief management tool. Following World War II, increased complexities in policy moved effectiveness to the forefront. For example, developing a housing program required consideration not only of costs, but also of number of units to be built, eligibility of applicants for housing, and impact on neighboring property values. During the 1960s, social equity became a major concern that grew in importance until the late 1970s. By the 1980s, managers faced conflicting demands for high levels of service, low costs, and increased responsiveness. Even before the tax limitation and public sector retrenchment movements, many local government managers took the lead in reducing the costs of providing services.

Vision and empowerment

The first step in effective management and delivery of local government services is to establish and communicate a vision for the community. Although elected officials have the major role in establishing a vision for the community, the manager helps to ensure that the vision is realistic and to communicate it to citizens and the management team. Establishing and communicating a vision requires articulation of a set of values that support the mission of the organization and that are compatible with the expectations of citizens. Local government managers are recognized as among the most professional of all public managers and thus enjoy acceptance and respect. Using that advantage to ensure the best in program and service delivery is a major challenge for the local government manager, who must show strong leadership to gain acceptance of the vision among the management team.

Empowering local government employees   The manager who succeeds in gaining the commitment of the management team usually is one who understands the necessity of empowering members of the organization. As former city manager Roy Pederson put it:

I am talking about organizational values important to success—customer responsiveness, treating people right, supporting city policies, being a good source of information, getting and giving "more bang for the buck," and providing anticipative rather than reactive management. I reward those who join in to support these expectations and "unreward" those who do not . . .

   The point of all this is to empower the people in the organization to exert themselves by their own volition, in the right direction. A manager can encourage needed values and can create the climate in which employees will choose to make the organization's success their goal. Managers used to see success as a function of the assertion of their own power. Now they see empowerment of others as a more likely avenue to success.[3]

Empowerment implies more than just participation in the processes of management. For people to be empowered, they must actually have control over their situations. Obviously, the manager cannot provide complete autonomy, but subordinates who understand that they have a real say in how activities are organized and services are provided are more likely to be committed to outcomes. Empowered people also understand that they are accountable for their activities.

Empowering citizens   For the local government manager, it is not enough to empower subordinates. To be effective, he or she must ensure that the citizens receiving services also feel empowered. Empowering citizens presents many challenges, but community-oriented policing, neighborhood watch programs, and community-based recycling projects are examples of successful citizen empowerment.

Delegation Empowerment involves delegation of responsibility; thus, the manager must give up some control. Managers need to recognize that even if things do not turn out as they plan, it is important to allow others to have control; if they have control, they are likely to assist in the development of a stronger community in the long run. Along with delegation goes participation. Of course, everyone concerned must recognize the limits to what can be delegated and what participation means. Effective managers communicate clearly what the constraints are so that participants will not be disillusioned when those constraints come into play. For example, it is imperative that people understand whether they are making a decision, making a recommendation, or just providing relevant information.

Creating public policies

Public policy refers to the actual programs of government. Public policies further define the general goals and mission of government by specifying a particular planned outcome. Usually, policy is in the form of stated goals and objectives, but sometimes policy may be a decision not to do something. Policy may be differentiated by whether it simply takes a stand on an issue or whether it prescribes a course of action. Sometimes policies are symbolic in that they are adopted to give the impression that an issue is being addressed but no resources are applied to make them work. Policies have specific intended results, but the actual results may be very different from those intended. Policies also can be distinguished in terms of outputs (the activities associated with a policy) and outcomes (the consequences of the activities).

In professionally managed local governments, policy formulation, implementation, and evaluation reflect efforts to combine professional expertise with citizen involvement, leadership with representative decision making, and experience-based continuity with deliberate change. Traditionally, the council-manager form of government separated the roles of the governing body and manager into those of policymakers and policy implementer, respectively. Clearly, that distinction is not realistic. Policy formulation and implementation are not distinct phases; they overlap, each informing and affecting the other. Local government managers and political leaders alike recognize this overlap in their roles.[4] The following discussion explains the role of the local government manager in the policymaking process.

Setting the policy agenda

What issues get on a government's policy agenda—and how they get there—is a key concern of elected officials, managers, and citizens. Interest groups and elected officials generally have the greatest say, but policy agendas also are important to less vocal citizens and to many others who remain uninvolved.

Policy agendas generally are set through a process in which the professional manager plays the role of an informed facilitator while the council interacts with other government officials, interest groups, and citizens in different social and political circles. As a professional broker at the junction of policy formulation and implementation, the manager must be familiar with relevant social, economic, political, and governmental forces and institutions and with past and present policies. The manager must also be able to communicate that knowledge to responsible officials and administrators.

Community participation in agenda setting Wise professional managers give serious consideration to all segments of the community in setting the local government policy agenda and depend upon citizens and citizen groups to help identify agenda items. Cities and counties often use citizen surveys for this purpose. The citizen survey may be a fairly informal one in which citizens are asked to give their reactions to a suggested policy or program. More formal survey methods include putting a short questionnaire in a regular mailing such as a water or sewer bill or hiring experts to conduct a survey and analyze the data.

Some communities use a town hall format to involve citizens in decision making. A particular problem or issue is identified and a background document is prepared. A meeting of interested citizens is then conducted, with formal deliberation over the background research. From the town hall meeting come recommendations for action that the decision makers then consider. In many communities, advances in technology have made it easier for citizens to get background information and to give their input through computer terminals located in convenient places, such as shopping malls or strategically placed kiosks.[5]

Citizens' right to withdraw consent   There are many important reasons for involving citizens in the agenda setting process, some of which were discussed in Chapter 2. From a purely practical standpoint, the effective manager recognizes the importance of involving citizens at an early stage, because those who are uninvolved at first may become active later. Usually relatively few citizens are engaged in setting specific policy agendas, but all citizens have the right to withdraw consent from governmental actions of which they disapprove. A controversy over public art in Phoenix in early 1992 illustrates the point. Citizens initially opposed construction of a freeway, but acceded after agreement that funds would be allocated for mitigation of negative effects. Money was set aside for noise abatement and visual enhancement. Although public hearings and council meetings addressed the plans for the public art included in the project, people seemed uninterested. However, when the art began to appear, citizens and politicians alike excoriated the project. Even though those responsible had done what was expected and required, they had to endure the ire of citizens who exercised their right to withdraw consent.

The professional manager is thus expected to anticipate reactions from the community, although it is impossible to predict with certainty what those reactions will be. Effective managers often rely on their professional colleagues for information and guidance in anticipating policy outcomes. They also rely on professional sources to help them identify important issues that would otherwise fail to get on the policy agenda and to help them exercise political leadership in formulating those agenda items.

Gatekeeping   Gatekeeping—the process of including or excluding agenda items—generally involves both long-range and short-range strategic considerations. For that reason, managers commonly are expected to have expertise in strategic planning—to be able to explore probable futures and alternatives for dealing with them. Managers must also know how to reduce present uncertainties in order to limit the necessity for crisis management, and they must be prepared for contingencies. Systematic approaches to policymaking processes are required to meet those expectations.

The manager's role in agenda setting involves many skills and activities. Common items on the public policy agenda include recurring considerations such as employee compensation and the budget allocation for fire services. New agenda items spring from new needs or the demands of citizens or other influential participants—such as interest groups, politicians, or the media—in the agenda setting process. New items might include programs to deal with gang activity in a neighborhood or a policy to respond to citizen fear of AIDS. The success of the local government manager in helping to set the agenda depends—among other traits—on the ability to communicate, to set priorities, and to specify alternatives.

Managing agenda setting   Persuasion and bargaining are major techniques that local government managers use in managing the agenda setting process. Persuasion involves the exchange of information in the hope that it will lead to a preferred decision. Clearly, persuasion techniques depend upon the personality and management style of the manager. Bargaining may take a win-lose or a win-win approach. In the win-lose approach, one party's gain results in loss to the other party. In a win-win approach, all parties gain. If bargaining takes a win-win approach, it has a much greater chance of success; therefore, the manager must try to ensure that win-win situations prevail, even in the most difficult circumstances. In agenda setting and decision making, no one is likely to get everything asked for. However, making trade-offs in which everyone gains may lead to an acceptable compromise.

Generally, bargaining works best if people can be kept from hardening their attachment to a position. Fisher and Ury suggest that successful bargaining depends upon

1. Separating the problem from the persons involved
2. Focusing on interests, not on positions
3. Generating a variety of alternatives before deciding what to do
4. Insisting that the results be measured by some objective standard.[6]

The same principles apply in attempting to persuade. The important point is to depersonalize the situation as much as possible and focus on the issues, with respect for all parties involved.

Of course, there are other means of influencing the public policy agenda and decision-making process. Some managers attempt to influence by retaining control. Although such an approach might work in the short run, in the long term it invariably results in resentment toward the manager and difficulties in dealing with others involved in the process. Once again, the concept of empowering people often works better; thus, the successful manager provides interested parties the opportunity to engage in decision making, recognizing that his or her long-term power will thereby be enhanced.

To engage members of the community in the decision-making process, managers may use a number of techniques. The most important consideration is that whatever technique is used, the process must be clear and some mechanism must exist for ensuring that decisions are made and recorded. An effective manager steers the process so that goals are accomplished. Effective techniques include the following:

1. Writing down all ideas expressed
2. Categorizing the ideas according to whether they identify a problem, a responsible party, or a solution
3. Examining each of the categories through discussion
4. Focusing on reaching consensus on priorities and on what alternative solutions to accept.

Attention to these techniques can facilitate decision-making processes while allowing all concerned to have input.

Maintaining the predictability of services

Although making policy is important, citizens and their elected representatives are most concerned about predictable delivery of established services. For that reason, citizens expect the local government manager to keep uncertainty about routine services to a minimum. However, changes in circumstances (decreased income from taxes or a sudden influx of immigrants, for example) compel responses.

Generally, responses to changed circumstances are deliberate and gradual, made as necessary to maintain stability. But some situations, even predictable ones, require clear breaks with past policy. For relatively unpredictable changes—storms or other disasters, unforeseen economic developments, equipment failure, or a spontaneous public demonstration—the manager must be prepared with contingency responses. Because contingencies themselves are predictable, even if their substance and scope sometimes are not, contingency management techniques should be established in advance. Professional managers need to be proactive, not reactive, in order to help keep political leaders abreast of events. The manager bears most of the burden for translating both incremental and major policy changes into program implementation.

Designing plans for implementation

Developing public policy requires designing strategies for its implementation. Thus, the local government manager must oversee the completion of two sets of activities during policy formulation:

1. Set goals, objectives, and priorities in terms of available resources and results to be accomplished within a given period. (Goals are the expected long-term results of policies or programs. Often, they are couched in five-, ten-, or twenty-five year time frames. Objectives are the expected results in a more immediate time frame, such as the current quarter or fiscal year.)
2. Develop plans for accomplishment of goals and objectives.

Goals and objectives In order to be effective in policy formulation and implementation, all managers, assistant managers, and department heads should have a clear understanding of

Their broad mission, as defined in a mission statement

Key service areas in which particular results are expected

Indicators of accomplishment.

Mission statements describe the purpose of a department or government unit and how it measures accomplishment of its purpose. The mission is accomplished through the attainment of specific expected results or goals. Key service areas are areas in particular services in which time, money, and other resources are invested, and they generally relate directly to missions and goals. For example, in fire departments, these areas might be fire prevention, fire suppression, and emergency rescue. Indicators of accomplishment might be a reduction in the number of fires or an improvement in the fire insurance rating.

Before setting objectives, managers must clarify the outputs (activities) and outcomes (effects) expected from policies. Evaluation approaches and criteria also must be determined and understood before implementation if objectives are to be accomplished. Ideally, feedback from evaluation is considered during policy formulation to assure the most informed policy choices. Unfortunately, this ideal is not always reached.

Guidelines for setting objectives

1. An objective should be consistent with authorized goals (legislative policy, charter provisions, and so on).
2. An objective should be stated in behavioral terms, as a guide to action. That is, it should clearly describe desired, observable results.
3. An objective should have intermediate targets and a specific completion date—in terms of the budget year or other time schedule.
4. An objective should include specific performance criteria, such as how many, what percent, which site, personnel levels, and costs.
5. An objective should be both challenging and attainable.

Setting objectives requires a statement defining expected behavior, desired final results, dates for tracking accomplishment, and necessary resources and their limits. Typically, the manager shares the responsibility for formulating specific objectives with assistants and department heads. Development of the details of the objectives is the responsibility of those charged with accomplishing them. Open communication facilitates formulating objectives as well as determining accountability for achieving them.

Action plans Managers also have responsibility for developing action plans to achieve objectives. These plans typically include specific actions to be taken and define time lines for action. Successful action plans require the participation of line managers, such as assistant department heads and work group supervisors.

Once action plans are made, it is necessary to establish essential administrative rules and procedures, assign formal responsibility and authority, and allocate resources. In results-oriented management, administrative procedures are designed to encourage and facilitate accomplishment of results rather than to provide negative sanctions for not following procedures or not achieving desired results. Results-oriented management emphasizes facilitating rather than policing activities.

Three common failures occur at this stage of policy formulation. First, managers sometimes err in forcing line managers and workers to adopt "one best way," without allowing them situational flexibility. Such rigidity may promote failure. Second, managers may require excessive or overly complex paperwork and documentation, even when situational adaptations are encouraged. Third, managers may violate the purposes of results-oriented management by tying it too closely to individual performance reviews and compensation. What is most needed to achieve excellence in local government management is informed organizational leadership and management systems dedicated to that goal. Management by objectives (MBO) is one of several such systems, but it does not work well as a general management system if it is used primarily for individual performance appraisal and determination of compensation.

The ever-changing policy agenda

Local governments are the general-purpose public service delivery organizations of the American political system. Between the 1930s and 1990s, the size, scope, and complexity of government activities grew dramatically. Growth of local government was especially rapid from the late 1950s through the early 1970s, partly because of federal and state mandates and partly because of a general belief that government could and should tackle many urgent problems that were not being solved in the private sector. The transition from growth to no-growth policies started in local and state governments in the last half of the 1970s, and public sector retrenchment became a national movement by the early 1980s. The attempts at downsizing the national government during the 1980s led to many program costs being shifted to state and local governments. States, in turn, shifted many of the costs to local governments. Thus, local governments found themselves in the 1990s with increasing responsibilities and limited resources with which to meet them.

The era of growth Developments during the public sector growth period need to be recalled to understand later developments. Local governments grew only gradually from the 1930s through the mid 1950s, keeping pace with the federal and state governments. Then, demands for new services produced substantial growth and changed attitudes among professional managers about local government functions. During the twenty-year period starting in 1957, combined state and local government employment grew 131.5 percent, from 5.4 million to 12.5 million. At the end of that period, 72.5 percent of total growth was found in local government, where the largest increase occurred in school systems. During the same period, federal government employment grew only 22.7 percent, and the private sector work force increased 47.7 percent.[7]

Local government growth in the 1960s was in part a response to social problems that led in some cases to rioting and burning in urban areas. Growth was generated issue by issue and program by program, often with little consideration of the larger system. By the mid 1970s, one-third of the U.S. gross national product went to public sector expenditures. During this period, the prevailing attitude was that when services are provided by government, they should be provided equally to all and that all similar units of government should provide essentially the same services. In addition, people expected government to be able to solve virtually all problems and to take responsibility for doing so. The national government developed numerous grant programs that expanded federal government activity, and many local governments became dependent on these programs.

Retrenchment   Retrenchment in the late 1970s and early 1980s brought changed attitudes and consequent changes in policy. Robert Biller, then Dean of the University of Southern California School of Public Administration, discussed the change as follows:

When you can do for some only what you can do for all, and when you are limited to these common service levels, you quickly spend to exhaustion. You satisfy no one, because everyone still looks at any service level and says "Not enough" or "Too much." No matter how hard you try you can't satisfy anyone, much less everyone. We are discovering that when we are limited to doing for some only what we can do for all, we're limited to very low quality in most public service areas.[8]

The retrenchment era altered the prevailing notions of the growth period. For local government officials who advocated changed attitudes and policies, equity no longer meant providing the same services for everyone, but recognizing differences in needs. Thus, while they recognized that some services were absolutely necessary for everyone, they believed that others were necessary only for some and should be provided according to need. They felt that there were alternatives to government provision of services and that fees might be appropriate for some services. In other words, government was no longer seen as the sole solver of problems and provider of services.

The serious questions raised about the scope of government during the 1980s led to cutbacks at the national and state levels, and local government was often left to pick up needed services without having the resource base of the national government.

Many local governments, such as those of Wilmington, North Carolina, and San Antonio, Texas, developed procedures for assigning priorities to services to help in allocating resources (see Figure 5–1). "Two-tier" policy and budget packages

Figure 5–1   Assigning priorities to programs and services.

Wilmington, North Carolina: one city's priority list

Near the top	*Near the bottom*
Police patrols	Affordable multi-family rentals
Fire suppression	Affordable single-family housing
Water treatment	Community development
Investigative services	Landscaping
Waste collection	Golf course clubhouse
Waste disposal	Tree trimming
Property tax collection	Athletic programs
Zoning administration	Senior services
Fire code enforcement	Arts center
Land use planning	Outdoor recreation

are an important development of the retrenchment era. Essential services such as police and fire protection are identified as one policy and budget tier; they consist of what a government absolutely must do. Differentiated services (those that may be offered in varying levels, e.g., recreation and utilities) are a second tier. These services may have alternative funding sources; some funds, such as fees, may be discretionary. Costs and benefits may be calculated in both tiers, but they are particularly tied to citizen demand and willingness to pay in the second tier, compelling individuals, groups, and neighborhoods to choose among options. For example, in the 1970s and 1980s, retrenchment resulted in new or increased fee systems for many public services, such as trash collection, and also in the adoption of some alternative systems for service delivery.

Increased diversity in policies, policymaking processes, and service delivery was one result of retrenchment by the 1980s, along with obvious general cutbacks or slowing of public sector growth. The same trends appeared to be shaping approaches in the early 1990s.

Implementation

Implementation—getting objectives accomplished—is a central concern in policy formulation and a fundamental managerial responsibility. If the objectives are to be accomplished, the policymaking process must include consideration of the problems and processes of implementation. Four managerial activities are basic to accomplishing objectives:

1. Assigning responsibilities, delegating authority, and allocating resources
2. Using functionally oriented management systems to coordinate organizational resources and performance
3. Involving people in productive activity through shared performance targets and work processes and through training and the reinforcement of positive job-related behaviors
4. Tracking progress toward end results through intermediate productivity indicators.

Communication is the essence of these four managerial functions. Taken together, they are designed to maintain an organization-wide exchange of information. Because increasingly many traditional government functions are not performed directly by government, the discussion of implementation concludes with an examination of alternative delivery systems.

Responsibilities, authority, and resources

Assignment of responsibilities, delegation of authority, and allocation of resources are among the most important of the manager's activities. They also present contradictions. Subordinate managers and nonsupervisory personnel need clear job assignments and the authority to carry them out, yet responsibilities often overlap, organizational boundaries blur, and authority is in constant flux. In this complex organizational environment, the manager attempts to create and maintain workable relationships. That effort requires an understanding of organizational structures and processes. It also requires active leadership to balance the requirements of stability and change.

Organizational structure　Organizations can be structured in many ways, but to keep the inevitable contradictions from resulting in chaos, managers need to draw on both hierarchical and open-systems organizational methods. In assigning responsibilities, they can use two concepts from the traditional hierarchical model as generally workable starting points:

1. Specialization and organizational grouping by function (e.g., fire fighting, law enforcement, planning) are the most commonly accepted bases for assignment of responsibilities. For example, crime prevention is generally a matter for the police; wastewater treatment is usually a function of the utility or sanitation department.
2. Authority needs to be function-specific and commensurate with responsibilities.

These commonly accepted structural principles facilitate assignment of responsibility. Continuity and stability are usually possible at the operations level because, in an existing organization, most functions can be assigned on the basis of past practice and experience. The chief administrator does not need to make organizational changes when established routines work reasonably well and new functions readily fit existing patterns.

Often, however, new responsibilities do not fit old patterns. If prevention of crime related to drug use is a priority, for example, that function may well need to be assigned to organizational units other than the police, such as the health and recreation departments and the schools. Wastewater treatment may involve not only several departments of a local government but also relationships among several jurisdictions. Because of such complexities, "matrix forms" of project management may sometimes work better than hierarchical structures. A project structure may be formed for such activities from various parts of the organization on the basis of the skills and expertise needed, regardless of the hierarchy.

There are practical limits to how complex matrix forms can be if the desired outputs and outcomes are to be achieved. Jeffrey Pressman and Aaron Wildavsky, who studied policy implementation in Oakland, California, warned that designers of policy need to use the most direct means possible to accomplish their objectives. They noted that "since each required clearance point adds to the probability of stoppage or delay, the number of these points should be minimized wherever possible." Echoing Woodrow Wilson, they also concluded that policymakers should "pay as much attention to the creation of organizational machinery for executing a program as for launching one."[9] Two practical guides to assigning responsibility and delegating authority, therefore, are these: (1) maximize functional expertise; and (2) minimize organizational and administrative complexity.

Allocation and utilization of resources   Once policy responsibility is assigned, the manager must see that the resources to perform the job are allocated and utilized. Generally, resource allocation relates to four basic administrative service areas: finances, personnel, plant and equipment, and information. One of the manager's hardest tasks is to maintain these service areas both as a service to line management and as a control system for general management. For example, in hiring personnel, management control may be enhanced by having a centralized system that standardizes most recruiting and hiring processes in a central personnel office. The line (department) manager, however, may find such a system dysfunctional because it inhibits the department's ability to gear the processes to the needs of the department. If the system makes it difficult to employ the individuals most suited to doing the department's work, resources are not being allocated effectively, and service delivery and quality suffer. Resource utilization—in this example, how personnel actually are used—rests in the hands of the department manager. Resource utilization is monitored in part by the local government manager's evaluation of service and program delivery, which will be discussed later in this chapter.

Resource utilization is successful if it accomplishes the desired results. Results-oriented management assumes that there is a focus on the outputs and outcomes of management activities. *Operations management* is a term applied to a number of results-oriented approaches to managing organizations. It requires specification, in operational terms, of the activities that fulfill government responsibilities. Thus

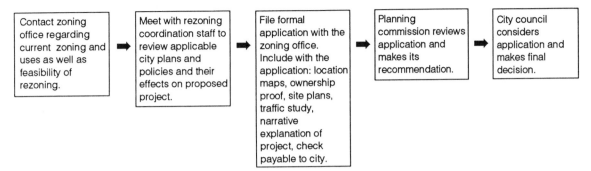

Figure 5–2   Flow chart for a rezoning application.

operations management might focus on the library's circulation of books or responses to requests for information, or the public works department's maintenance of streets. In addition to the specification of outputs and outcomes, operations management involves planning the processes for achieving them. Thus a flow chart or PERT (program evaluation and review technique) chart portrays the methods and resources used to provide the service. These charts help in making the most efficient use of resources by providing a visual depiction of how each step relates to another. They help to avoid overlapping and unneeded steps. Flow charts also help to determine the time and resources needed to achieve the desired results. In addition, they facilitate identification of changes needed in an organization, procedures, or resources. Figure 5–2 depicts a flow chart for processing a rezoning application.

For the local government manager, managing for results should be the overriding goal. In order to ensure that policies are implemented—and results attained—the manager must coordinate organizational resources and performance. This process is often referred to as functional management.

Functional management systems

Functional management means that the manager must keep an eye on the maintenance and development of the whole organization in order to coordinate activities among different units. Otherwise, competition for resources may become destructive to the organization. In short, attention must be focused on management processes, not simply on final results. In addition, while keeping the overall result in mind, the manager must also see that intermediate productivity controls are established for each department so that progress can be monitored and problems identified before they become crises.

Intermediate measures are particularly important in public service delivery. For example, police performance may be measured by the number of arrests made (output). However, if a visible police presence results in reduced criminal activity or an increase in citizens' feelings of well-being, the number of arrests may become less important than these measures. Intermediate measures also may provide time and cost comparisons required for important subfunctions and may reveal activities that should be changed or terminated before final results are in.

The functional management system allows organization-wide coordination and integration of activities. That, in turn, allows the manager to focus on key issues—cost-benefit trade-offs, contingency responses, and organizational procedures—and to make the resulting information available to others. The police department, for example, may want to know the relative cost and effectiveness of foot versus bicycle patrols. In addition, it needs to know how well each would respond to an emergency and what the procedures should be for deploying patrols to emergencies.

The answers to all of these questions are critical to effective coordination and integration of the department's efforts.

Coordination and integration depend on agreed-upon work rules and performance targets. If they are not established through managerial leadership, they emerge through practice and generally become binding in fact. These rules must be related to function and kept up to date. They should be guides to behavior rather than limits on action, and they should be kept to the minimum necessary to achieve desired results. On occasion, explicit rules to establish limits on behavior may be required, generally to meet legal or technical requirements.

Performance targets   Performance targets help supervisors improve service delivery when they are established for work groups. When applied to individuals, they may be useful indicators of the need for training, higher motivation, or disciplinary feedback. Performance targets may also be used as a basis for reward, although they can result in counterproductive employee behavior and limits on managers' discretionary use of authority. Unions generally seek to control performance when quantified work standards are applied to individuals for compensation purposes; unionized workers may then tend to work to the rules, becoming relatively rigid and inclined to contest management's decisions.[10]

Operational reviews   The city of Sudbury in Ontario, Canada, initiated operational reviews of major programs by interdepartmental teams to identify efficiency and productivity improvements. The following are some of the recommendations for significant changes in procedure that resulted from this process:

Utilize high-density garbage packers to reduce number of trips to landfill sites.

Clear snow from sidewalks on only one side of street in residential neighborhoods. (This eliminated twenty-four miles of sidewalk and two sidewalk plows and created a snow storage area, thus avoiding snow removal.)

Eliminate clean-up week and provide year-round collection of all items.

Convert all street lighting to high-pressure sodium. (This resulted in a 20-percent reduction in power consumption.)

Participate in bulk purchase of natural gas. (This resulted in savings of 18 percent.)

Allocate funds to any energy conservation retrofit with a pay-back of five years or less.

Carry out aggressive marketing of surplus lands with proceeds used for land acquisition portion of capital projects.

Increase canine license revenue by door-to-door license sales by students.

Improve scheduling of hours of work for transit drivers to reduce overtime.

Engage in more aggressive marketing of Sudbury Arena (seating capacity 6,000) to produce a bottom-line profit.

Eliminate day shift at one of three swimming pools.

Reduce summer hours of operation at all pools.

Streamline management of facilities (arenas and pools) to reduce number of positions from seven to three.

Decentralize some purchasing functions and utilize blanket orders and direct delivery from stationery contractor.

Decentralize printing and duplicating.

Move computer services from proprietary hardware/software to an open system. (This eliminated three staff positions and reduced servicing costs.)

Source: Ontario Municipal Administrators Association, "Coping in Tough Times," Clearinghouse Report no. 40744 (Washington, DC: ICMA, 1992).

Work processes Work processes in direct public service delivery generally are defined largely by those who perform the work. Routine processes may be designed more uniformly by management, which sees the needs of the whole organization. In either case, three factors must be considered in establishing work processes: (1) governmental functions; (2) the workers and their skills and needs; and (3) the people served or affected by the activity. Here, too, managers generally should focus on work modules and work groups rather than on discrete units of work and individual workers. In short, as with performance targets, work processes need to be considered from the perspective of functional organizational management, not individual employee control.

For results-oriented functional management to succeed, managers need to pay careful attention to how they organize for implementation of policies. Traditional theory assumes that the manager informs subordinates of what needs to be done and that they do it because of the authority that the manager has over them. As evidenced by much of the discussion in this chapter, contemporary managers recognize the need for the participation of those responsible for achieving results in the process of deciding how to achieve them. Ultimately, the local government manager has the responsibility for results, but in reality, local government employees share this responsibility.

Involving people through sharing authority

Since the 1960s, various approaches have been developed to engage members of the work organization in planning for attaining results. Team (or task force) management and project management are common approaches to involve members of the organization in this process. In team management, parameters are established and a team representing all the units involved in the service or program are brought together to work on planning and organization. Typically, the team or task force has a specific objective in mind, and often a time line is established as well. The advantages of the team approach are that multiple perspectives are likely to emerge and the needs of various parts of the organization are considered in working toward objectives. Redundant efforts can be avoided, and steps that are counterproductive can be avoided. It is important that the expectations of the group be clearly defined, or the team may spend a lot of time in meetings that serve no useful purpose.

Project management is similar to the team approach, but it usually focuses on a specific problem or project. Again, it brings representatives from various parts of the organization together to work toward the most effective accomplishment of some task. Project management is particularly effective in cases in which a problem or program involving several units of the organization arises.

Another approach to involving people in planning for the achievement of results is quality management. As described in Chapter 4, the most common approach in the early 1990s was Total Quality Management (TQM). Initially, the public sector, like other service sectors, thought that TQM was inappropriate to the service mission. However, the basic points of this approach apply to service delivery as well as to manufacturing. Local government managers have achieved good results with quality management programs, although—as Chapter 4 pointed out—there are problems in adapting TQM to the public sector.

A major concern of quality management is the process for ensuring quality. Traditionally, evaluation techniques focus on the results or end service or product. In the quality management approach, evaluation is a continuous process, meaning that people throughout the organization must examine their activities to identify problems along the way, rather than waiting until an acitivity is complete. In that way, problems can be detected early and corrections made. This approach saves resources by reducing defects—the goal is zero defects—and time by reducing the need to go back and find out what went wrong.

When corrections are made on the spot, time is not wasted in producing a defective service. An additional benefit of this approach is that the whole organization is brought into the process and employees develop a stronger commitment to producing services of high quality. Productivity is likely to improve, and the people served are likely to perceive more interest in their concerns. Employees of the government are empowered through this process, if it is implemented correctly. Such empowerment requires the local government manager to be willing to give up some control and to accept the full participation of subordinates in decision-making and service delivery processes.

If your goal is to create a quality product or service, you can systematically strive to accomplish it by finding out what quality means to your consumers and then delivering a product or service that meets, or preferably, exceeds their expectations.

Jeff Bradt

Empowerment also requires the manager to provide people the tools to work effectively. The most important of these tools are training and development. In addition, specific skills are often necessary for analyzing the work process and detecting errors or problems. In most quality management approaches, statistical process-control techniques—used to measure and correct variations in service level or quality—are very important. There also must be team training to focus on quality improvement from a group perspective.

Strategic planning, which is often referred to as long-range planning, also is important to quality management. Strategic planning involves identification of long-range goals and objectives for the community and the organization through the participation of citizens, the governing body, and local government employees. Strategic planning for service delivery requires determining who is to be served and how. In addition, environmental scans are conducted so that the organization can identify and readily adapt to changes that are likely to affect the organization.

In contrast to operations, which require focus on day-to-day activities, strategic planning focuses on overall goals and policies. Strategic planning keeps an eye on the ever-changing environment, and thus plans are adapted or extended to accommodate change. The local government manager who practices strategic planning practices strategic management.[11] (Strategic planning and environmental scans are discussed in more detail in Chapter 6.)

Tracking progress

Another important aspect of policy implementation, for the manager and for department heads, is tracking progress by means of intermediate productivity measures that indicate, for example, the level of recreational services in a given neighborhood. Automated information systems can help if they are oriented to the needs of central, departmental, and supervisory management. But relatively simple paper and oral reporting systems may serve just as well. For example, a calendar marked with target dates may serve adequately to track some timetables.

Tracking activities and results must be a sustained managerial activity—regular, but not merely routine. Periodic reports are a classic monitoring device. Some audits may need to be randomly, and others selectively, scheduled. An apparently spontaneous visit by the manager to an operating department can serve a constructive purpose, particularly when it is timed to highlight an important accomplishment, such as a significant increase in productivity.

Monitoring must be visible except in rare instances when security or privacy rights are involved, such as investigations of theft. Whenever possible, the information gained from monitoring should be open to all concerned managers. Monitoring can serve as a positive organizational management mechanism rather than as a negative control, if used to encourage employees by calling attention to their accomplishments and helping them identify areas for improvement.

Alternative delivery systems

Although public services generally are delivered directly by local government, numerous alternative delivery systems have been used for years, ranging from food and recreation service franchises to virtually full-scale government by contract, as in cases in which urban counties provide virtually all services to small communities. During the retrenchment of the late 1970s and early 1980s, interest in alternative delivery systems increased as efforts were made to reduce costs and offer different levels of service based on citizens' willingness to pay.

When choosing alternative service delivery systems, local governments need to develop criteria for evaluating them. The criteria generally include

1. Cost of service
2. Financial cost to citizens
3. Choices available to service users
4. Quality and effectiveness of the service
5. Distribution of services in the community
6. Service continuity
7. Feasibility and ease of implementation
8. Potential overall impact.

Alternative service delivery systems take many forms, as described below.

Privatization   Privatization of services, including contracting out and franchising, has become common in local government. Contracting out is the purchase of services from another government or private firm, for-profit or nonprofit; all or a portion of a service may be involved. Small governments may obtain specialized services and gain advantages of scale by purchasing services. (For similar reasons, a government may choose to sell services to neighboring governments. For example, urban county governments often sell computer, law enforcement, and fire services to local municipalities.) Contracting out also allows the purchaser to take advantage of market competition to gain efficiency and cut costs.

Contracted services are usually those that are easily defined, new, or unique in character. Solid waste collection and water services are relatively easily defined, and both are often contracted for privately. Auburn, Alabama, for example, contracted with a private firm for wastewater treatment in 1985, and since then the city has experienced greatly improved service while it has been relieved of a major financial burden. Law enforcement, however, is more complex and rarely contracted out, except to another general-purpose government. New services, such as

Accounting firm takes over   The South Oxfordshire District Council in the United Kingdom has contracted out the preparation of the jurisdiction's budgets for fiscal year 92 and 93 to Touche Ross, one of the world's leading accounting firms. The move by the Conservative-run council represents the first privatization of municipal financial services in the U.K. Touche Ross was chosen in a competitive bidding process over an in-house offer. In 1982, South Oxfordshire became one of the first local governments in the country to contract out its entire garbage collection service.

Source: *Public Innovation Abroad* (November 1991): 3.

day care or drug treatment, may be purchased more readily than traditional government activities. Unique or occasional services, such as medical care or transportation of disabled people, are commonly provided by specialized contractors.

Like special services contracts, franchises have been used for decades by local government. Typically franchises are awarded to exclusive or nonexclusive providers through competitive or negotiated bidding. Individual citizens usually pay directly for the service, such as the food served at a local-government-owned sports arena or an ambulance ride to the hospital. Governments generally charge a percentage of gross or net income as a franchise fee.

Joint ventures   Local governments can become partners with the private sector or other government units in joint ventures. Public-private ventures have long been common in community endeavors such as revitalization of the business district or local industry. Many local governments have entered into joint ventures in an effort to keep sports franchises or other private enterprises from moving to other cities. Construction or upgrading of airports may also reflect such efforts. Denver and Minneapolis, for example, entered into joint ventures with private interests to construct airports. Similarly, Phoenix entered into a joint venture with its professional basketball team for construction of a new facility and development of the area around it, and Arlington, Texas, agreed to build a new stadium for its baseball franchise by using an increased sales tax approved by voters. In many of these cases, the local government provides incentives and subsidizes the venture through the development of parking facilities and amenities for patrons of the facility.

During the difficult economic times of the early 1990s, local governments were eager to foster economic development and create jobs in their communities. Thus, there was a great deal of competition among local governments to attract employers to their areas. Such competition often leads to bidding wars among communities. For example, airlines can create hubs throughout the country by the alignment of their routes. Communities often engage in bidding wars to entice airlines to use their airport as a hub or to locate their reservations or maintenance centers in their area. The bidding often includes such inducements as tax breaks, facility construction, direct subsidies, and utilities breaks. Professional sports franchises, of course, have mastered the process of creating competition among cities for new or relocated franchises.

Local communities bank on being repaid through taxes on the earnings generated by increased employment and other multiplier effects of the new venture. Sophisticated citizens, however, may question whether growth compensates for the changes in the environment and character of the community. Thus, during the 1970s and through the early 1990s, slow-growth or no-growth groups emerged in many parts of the country. The local government manager is challenged to accommodate these conflicting needs and perspectives; this challenge will be discussed in Chapter 6.

Intergovernmental contracts and agreements   Local governments have a long tradition of engaging in intergovernmental agreements and contracts, although some states traditionally restricted them. In 1988, the city of Corvallis, Oregon, contracted with the county for repairs on its vehicle fleet, expecting to save as much as 20 percent on maintenance. Fire service is frequently provided under contract or agreement by a large jurisdiction to smaller communities, and sometimes several units of government get together to provide a service such as mass transportation when the need is area-wide and requires integration of service. It is not uncommon for the largest jurisdiction to be the prime provider of the service, with other communities subsidizing the service to their communities through agreement with the major provider. Urban counties in California and Florida often provide municipal services to small communities under contract or by agreement.

Volunteer activity   Such citizen roles as hospital aide, school monitor, and fire volunteer were common in early twentieth-century America but declined in importance from the 1940s through the mid 1970s. However, during the late 1980s and early 1990s, volunteer activity received increased attention as George Bush made it a focus of his campaign for the presidency and part of his administration's approach to social problems. Facing budget cutbacks, some local governments also began to turn again to volunteer services in the 1980s as a way of supplementing meager resources, and volunteer and self-help activity emerged as an important alternative to direct public service delivery.

New forms of self-help emerged, such as neighborhood watch programs, neighborhood clean-up activities, and mutual assistance to mentally or physically disabled and elderly residents. In Henrico County, Virginia, for example, a task force was created to study the issue of the aging population. Part of the result of the task force's study was the creation of a volunteer program for seniors in which they helped one another, thereby reducing their dependence on the local government.[12]

Volunteer and self-help programs help to reduce the demand for direct service by local governments, but they have other ramifications as well. For the local government manager, these efforts often bring new actors into the management and policymaking process. Neighborhood groups often have positive impacts on the neighborhood, but they are also interest groups that participate in the policymaking process, and local government managers need to be able to deal with them effectively, as discussed in Chapter 2. In addition, risk-management issues may arise, and the manager should consider local government liability when deciding on the level of official responsibility to be assumed by volunteers.

Conclusion

The policy implementation process is complex, and it involves the participation of many actors. The traditional assumption in public administration was that elected officials make policy and managers implement it, but that assumption no longer holds. If implementation is to be effective, it must be considered as part of the policymaking process. Plans for implementation and its cost as well as benefits must be considered while policy is being made. Otherwise, the policy that is developed may not be at all realistic. Once developed, the policy depends upon the involvement of the whole management team to be effective. Therefore, the effective local government manager must ensure that the management team assumes its responsibility for policy implementation. In addition, it is important to involve citizens and groups affected by the policy.

Productivity

Productivity is defined in economics as the efficiency with which output is produced by the resources used, and it is usually measured as the ratio of output to input. A broader definition is more commonly used in the public sector to focus on effectiveness as well as efficiency: the transformation of inputs into desired outcomes. Productivity improvement efforts in government, then, generally include actions to improve policies and services as well as operating efficiency. A variety of productivity indicators exist: efficiency, effectiveness, responsiveness, quality, timeliness, and cost.

Productivity indicators and the information they yield are useful only if they are employed to provide excellent public services, reduce costs, and make improvements when possible. Three approaches to productivity improvement have been followed successfully in the public and private sectors: (1) investment in capital resources and technology; (2) strengthened management and work redesign; and (3) work force improvement—working smarter and harder. The second and third approaches relate primarily to improving internal management, which was discussed in the previous chapter. This chapter therefore discusses only investment in capital resources and technology; in addition it explores ways of overcoming obstacles to productivity improvement.

Use of technology in productivity improvement

The greatest increases in output generally have resulted from investments in capital resources (e.g., plant and equipment) that utilize state-of-the-art technologies. In fact, in the discipline of economics, the prescription for improved productivity is greater technological efficiency in combining human, natural, and capital resources.

Five interrelated aspects of investment merit the attention of top managers: (1) the relationship of investment to labor costs; (2) changes in services and public expectations resulting from technological advances; (3) technological exchange and its impact on organizations; (4) use of computers in decision making; and (5) cost savings and investment.

Investment and labor costs   Investment in scientific and technological advances and capital resources, along with readily available energy resources, has resulted in large increases in worker productivity. During the forty years prior to the extended decline in improvement of productivity that began in the United States in 1968, output per worker increased an average of 3 percent per year, making possible large increases in worker compensation, even in fields outside those responsible for the increased output. Higher labor costs, in turn, created incentives for further investment in labor-saving technology in fields that were neglected earlier, including local government services. Historically, local governments have been extremely labor intensive, with high work force costs. When cost savings justify it, investment may help change the situation.

Changes in services and citizen demand   Investment typically results in development of new products and services as well as new technologies for more efficient production of old ones. Until recent years, local governments tended to focus only on production of existing services or outputs. But the larger thrust of research and development is technological change that produces new processes and products to displace or add to old ones. In the private sector, such new product development is often preceded by market research designed to identify or change consumer demands. Traditionally, little comparable activity occurred in government. Today, citizen surveys and other instruments help identify citizen demands and facilitate government's response to them. In addition, the greater involvement of citizens and groups in the policymaking process helps educate them to the limits of government's ability to provide services. Thus, citizen demand changes as well.

Technological exchange and its impact on organizations   The usefulness of technology depends on organization size, structure, processes, and external connections. Optimum size for use of some technologies simply is not achievable in some governments. Moreover, it makes no sense to acquire firefighting equipment for high-rise structures in a jurisdiction that has no buildings over three stories high. Prescriptions from other jurisdictions may or may not apply in a particular community; technological exchange must be evaluated case by case. But, as a general rule, experience supports technological exchange and even the shared use of equipment to improve public service and reduce costs. That was a thesis behind the creation of Public Technology, Inc. (PTI) by ICMA, the National League of Cities (NLC), and the National Association of Counties (NACo). The experience of various local governments and PTI has demonstrated the usefulness of such technological development and exchange in local governments.

Use of computers in decision making   The computer has revolutionized information storing and analysis. The ability to retrieve almost unlimited information simplifies policymaking and implementation because it makes it much easier to consider alternatives and analyze their potential impact. The technology involved in geographic information systems (GIS) is just one example of how the computer facilitates management decision-making processes and helps in effective delivery of services. GIS allows analysis of data in a spatial framework (see Figure 5–3). Thus, it allows a local government to view the many different types of data that pertain to a particular location or area. For example, if a building permit is applied for at a given intersection in the community, GIS has the capability of bringing up data about the entire infrastructure of the area, types of buildings and businesses, traffic patterns, and virtually anything else relevant to the decision. Such a system saves an immense amount of time. Once entered into the system, the data are readily available to provide decision makers with a complete picture. There are many benefits to GIS:

1. It allows coordination of data throughout the organization, thus eliminating duplication of data gathering.
2. It aids in map making and in issuing and tracking of permits.
3. It enhances accuracy of data.
4. It makes information more meaningful.
5. It facilitates effective decisions on planning and location of facilities.[13]

Figure 5–3 Database layering concept from Louisville/Jefferson County, Kentucky, GIS.

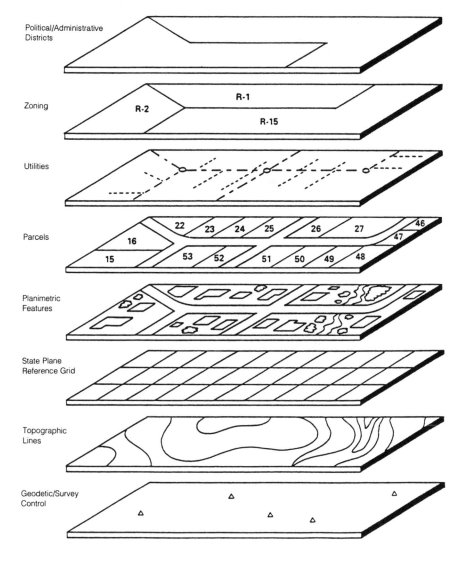

The system also has the benefit of speeding up the process of making decisions and delivering services. To the customer or citizen, that is an important benefit that is likely to result in a positive view of the local government and its management.

Cost savings and investment   Cost savings through investment in equipment and technology are the test of whether the investment should be made. If cost savings cannot be anticipated, investment probably is unwise, although responsiveness to citizen demands must also be considered. Savings resulting from investment in equipment should at the very least amortize outlays by the end of its useful life. For productivity improvement, savings should also yield a net return on the investment (including an amount equal to or exceeding the interest).

Overcoming obstacles to productivity improvement

Local government managers may obtain useful results by periodically looking for and eliminating obstacles to productivity improvement. Generally, rank-and-file workers and managers can identify many barriers to getting their work done and target them for elimination. Common obstacles to improvement in local government are of four types: organizational constraints, resource limits, information deficiencies, and disincentives. Local government managers have varying levels of control over these different obstacles and can take a number of actions to overcome them.

Organizational constraints   Organizational constraints in government may derive from political and legal frameworks that cannot be easily changed. Often, however, the limiting factors are structural and procedural and therefore amenable to management. A manager must strike a balance between the one extreme of centralization and uniform prescription of rules and procedures and the other extreme of dispersion of responsibility and differentiation of processes to suit every individual's wish. The manager can achieve control, especially with current information technology, without resorting to rigid and unchanging procedures. In addition, he or she can identify legal obstacles that are beyond change by management and bring them to the attention of officials for revision.

Resource limits   Resource limits are common obstacles to policy, service, and productivity improvement. Managers need to inform citizens and elected officials of those constraints. Reallocations of money, people, equipment, buildings, or other resources may be justified by cost-benefit assessments to improve productivity.

Information deficiencies   Information is one resource whose deficiencies are most subject to managerial correction. Three practical questions may help identify and eliminate barriers: What data and analyses are needed? How is the information disseminated? How is it used?

Disincentives   Finally, disincentives to production are common in governments. Although great attention is often given to motivation and incentives, often it is easier to correct matters in ways that alienate people, such as across-the-board budget cuts for both productive economizers and unproductive spendthrifts.

Innovative management systems and tools provide a major opportunity for the local government manager to overcome obstacles to productivity improvement. Such approaches as zero-defects management, strategic planning, and quality management are efforts to improve productivity and eliminate nonproductive practices and activities. This process sometimes is called ''rightsizing'' (see accompanying sidebar). As discussed, these approaches are part of efforts to get members of the organization to achieve the results intended.

Seven steps to rightsizing

1. *Downsize* Make across-the-board cuts that shrink the size of government and democratize the pain of an initial round of cuts.
2. *Bank vacancies* Hold for the future any jobs slots freed up through early retirement, hiring freezes, or the like.
3. *Inventory programs* Make a list of all programs in the government's repertoire—how much each one costs, whom it serves, what it does, whether it is mandated.
4. *Set priorities* Legislative bodies assign rankings to programs so that budgets can be crafted accordingly.
5. *Shift funds* Take money out of low-priority programs and put it into high-priority programs.
6. *Establish a training program* Personnel dislocated by restructuring are retrained for openings in programs in which funding is being increased.
7. *Consolidate services or functions* Look for horizontal ways of consolidating or compacting services across agency lines or even across jurisdictional lines.

Source: Penelope Lemov, "Tailoring Local Government to the 1990s," *Governing* 5 (July 1992): 31.

Evaluation

Evaluation is the regular collection and analysis of data and information about the efficiency, economy, and effectiveness of government services and other activities. The purposes of evaluation are (1) to help managers and elected officials improve the implementation of policies and programs, (2) to allocate and limit use of scarce resources, and (3) to decide among programs and policies and levels of various activities. Three principal evaluation activities are common in local government:

1. Internal management evaluation, focusing on resource utilization and operating methods discussed earlier in this chapter as an aspect of implementation
2. Performance measurement, a continuing management responsibility concerned with outputs and outcomes
3. Policy and program evaluation, a general management assessment of implementation, results, and alternatives.

In practice, the distinctions among these kinds of evaluation are not sharp, and they need not be separated except to ensure that each kind of evaluation is performed.

Performance measurement

Performance measurement, like internal management evaluation, is an ongoing, day-to-day responsibility of the local government manager and department heads. Performance measurement is a systematic method of determining whether the local government is doing—with the resources available—what the government needs to do. As Paul D. Epstein puts it: "Performance measurement is government's way of determining whether it is providing a quality product at a reasonable cost."[14] Measuring performance involves individual performance as well as organizational performance.

Evaluation of individual performance   Individual performance management should focus on the relation of an individual employee's performance to the achievement of the desired results of the organization. Although the details of individual performance evaluation are part of personnel management and thus beyond the scope of this book, it is important to remember that the evaluation of individual employees' performance has an impact on how the local government delivers its services. Strategic management and quality management approaches provide a context for individual performance measurement. Within this context, individuals should be involved in the design of the evaluation criteria and process in order to feel committed to achieving desired results. Clearly, the criteria must focus on service if the system is to facilitate quality service delivery. Ongoing evaluation helps establish a focus on quality and the contribution of individual performance to organizational performance.

Evaluation of organizational performance   Organizational performance should be evaluated regularly using uncomplicated procedures: audits of departmental records, ratings by trained observers, and citizen surveys.

Audits of departmental records   Departmental records often contain the information needed to calculate ratios of output to input in order to measure efficiency: for example, the number of employees trained (output) per $1000 spent (input). Sometimes, however, measures of unit cost may be needed, which are expressed as ratios of input to output (dollar cost per employee trained, for example). Unit costs are especially useful in evaluating the cost implications of proposed changes in service levels, and they often are used to justify budgets. In any case, reliable data are needed to serve as output and input indicators.

Output indicators should have several characteristics. First, they should be comprehensive enough to cover all major workloads. Second, they should not mix dissimilar categories. (For example, individual residential and personal property assessments should be separate categories and also should be separated from business property and inventory assessments). Third, they should be quantifiable and related to workload. That is, an output indicator should be a measure of something that is a direct result of an activity, such as miles of street cleaned. (*Outcomes*—cleanliness of streets or citizen perceptions of cleanliness—must generally be determined from sources other than department records.)

Three types of *input indicators* can be used. First, if the activity is labor intensive, the only indicator may be the cost of employee labor. Labor cost is used by the U.S. Bureau of Labor Statistics to measure productivity, and it is the easiest indicator for most governments to use. The drawback of this simple statistic is that it fails to account for investment in capital resources or for technological and managerial inputs, which are often the greatest contributors to improved productivity.

A second input indicator takes account of all direct production costs—labor, equipment, and supplies. It is highly feasible except when allocation of equipment costs is complicated. A third input indicator is total costs, which include direct costs and indirect or overhead costs. Except for externally funded projects, total cost measurement may be unjustifiably complicated.

Efficiency analysis based on output and input information generally involves four types of comparison: (1) over time; (2) among internal organizational units; (3) with external organizations; and (4) with a standard. Comparison of past and present ratios of output to input (or vice versa) is one of the two most common uses of efficiency data. The other is comparison among similar organizational units, such as among work crews, service centers, or projects within a department. Comparison with similar activities in other governments or private business depends on availability of data from the other organizations. Comparison with a standard requires determination of the standard. If available, historical records provide the best standard by which to measure change over time. Engineered standards are the purest, but deriving them requires specially trained personnel. Estimated standards—such as the time that knowledgeable people think necessary to complete the work—can be established with the cooperation of supervisors and workers in the service-providing unit.

Efficiency (as well as effectiveness) can also be measured against two criteria: that of quality in service delivery and that of citizen perceptions of quality. Some objective measures of quality can be based on departmental records for response time, error rates, thoroughness or completeness of outputs, and task complexity. However, measures of citizen perceptions cannot be gleaned from usual government records but must be obtained through other means, such as citizen surveys.

New demands on municipalities call for a more aggressive approach to efficiency through a focus on the quality concept.
Michael Fenn

Ratings by trained observers Most of the performance measures discussed above deal primarily with efficiency, but performance measurement is more concerned with effectiveness, which requires methods that usually go beyond managerial records. One such method is rating by trained observers.

The Urban Institute has reported extensively on the use by trained observers of photographs and rating guides to evaluate effectiveness of such services as solid waste collection and disposal and street and parks maintenance.[15] Physical condition, appearance, and delays in rectifying visible problems are particularly amenable to evaluation by such simple approaches. Also, specialized equipment may be used by technicians to measure such factors as roughness of roads or air or noise pollution.

Citizen surveys Another method that goes beyond managerial records is the use of citizen surveys. These may be used to collect factual information or to determine public perceptions of services. For example, a survey can be directed to a sample of the general population or to a specific group of users. Thus, counts of users can help assess use of a recreation facility or library. Evaluation of such factors as accessibility, usefulness, or general citizen interest in parks or libraries requires other feedback methods. Focus groups or other methods involving knowledgeable citizen groups can be used to secure valuable information.

Figure 5–4 summarizes the characteristics, strengths, and limitations of measures of service based on citizen perceptions compared with relatively more objective ones. Subjective citizen evaluations have become increasingly valued, as such input is evidence of renewed interest in volunteerism and citizen co-production of selected services.[16]

Performance measurement may lead to increased productivity of the employees and the organization, but it is probably more important as an instrument for the examination and improvement of the decision-making process. By focusing on what is to be performed or what service is to be delivered, people delivering that service can consider what the appropriate approach is or what application of resources makes sense. Thus, the decision-making process is improved to the extent that it really considers what is to be accomplished and how that accomplishment is to be measured.

The actual delivery of services also can be improved through identification of specific objectives and monitoring of their achievement. Quality controls can be developed for the steps in the delivery process to identify and correct errors as they take place, resulting in a better service in the end. Citizens and clients also are likely to benefit from performance measurement approaches in that they will receive better service and will be more able to hold the local government accountable. Performance measurement is an essential tool of the effective local government manager.

Figure 5–4　Subjective versus objective measures of service performance.

Dimension	Subjective	Objective
Focus	Citizen-based	Agency-based
Service function	Political	Economic
Urban service goals	Responsiveness Equity	Efficiency Effectiveness
Policy perspective	Impact-oriented	Output-oriented
Strengths	Tap distributional aspects of service performance Outside perspective/evaluation of local government performance Alternative citizen participation mode Commitment to democratic norms	Readily quantifiable Accessible data Based upon recognized technical standards Easily interpretable
Limitations	Tenuous correspondence with service outputs At a more general level than policy decisions Problems with perceptual and evaluative criteria Nature and determinants of citizen service attitudes unclear	Bias in reporting and coding information Changes in definition of measures over time Focus primarily on quantifiable/available information Primary emphasis on agency goals

Policy and program evaluation

Distinctions between ongoing performance measurement and in-depth policy and program evaluations are largely a matter of focus and degree. Whereas line managers share responsibility for performance measurement, the manager's office generally is responsible for in-depth policy and program evaluation.

Differences between policy and program evaluation are also matters of focus and degree. The purpose of policy evaluation is to assess the content, implementation, and effects of particular policies, and it is weighted heavily toward determining whether legislative intent is followed. Policy evaluation particularly seeks to determine the impact of policy on the real-life problems it was designed to solve. It is oriented toward outcomes. The purpose of program evaluation is to appraise specific programs through which policies are implemented, and, although it is oriented somewhat more toward administrative concerns, it also serves legislative needs for assessment of outputs and outcomes of defined programs. Policy outcomes are commonly evaluated in terms of

1. Approximation or achievement of intended effects
2. Unintended impacts
3. Current and projected future impacts
4. Direct and indirect costs.

Ad hoc evaluations are employed particularly to disclose policy failures and their causes. As noted earlier, complexity and excessive clearance requirements in implementation are major causes of policy failures. Other factors that often impede success include confusion, incompatibility, or displacement of goals and an unenthusiastic administration.

Evaluation criteria typically focus on effects, whether they are intended or unintended, long-range or short-range. Often there are specified expectations against which measurement may be made. However, the general concern with efficiency and effectiveness provides a broader measuring stick. The cost-benefit factors mentioned earlier and noted below are important and integral parts of evaluation. However, how well a program or organization accomplishes its goals also is important and is assessed by using some of the methods mentioned previously in the section on performance measurement. Contemporary local government managers must always include the criterion of equity in evaluation of policies and programs, although it may be difficult to apply when different groups and citizens require different services to meet their needs. Local government managers, therefore, must be sensitive to those differences when evaluating programs.

The costs of evaluation also must be examined to ensure that they do not consume more resources than the benefits justify. Performance measurement, as a day-to-day management approach, may be particularly subject to cost-benefit analysis because it regularly involves managers, whose time is both valuable and limited. A balance must be struck between the time they spend on evaluation and their many other responsibilities.

The uses made of evaluation information largely determine its benefits. Departmental managers may regularly use evaluation processes and information. However, the manager's office and elected officials also must make constructive use of evaluation for it to fulfill its primary purpose—providing information for the improvement of policies, services, and productivity.

Recap

Traditionally, local government managers have had to balance three major concerns in administering public policies: efficiency, effectiveness, and economy. Today, however, equity and ethics are receiving increased emphasis. This chapter examined five broad dimensions of local government program and service management to identify ways to address these concerns: the context of service-oriented management; developing and managing public policy; implementation; productivity; and evaluation.

The contemporary manager works in an environment characterized by rapid social, political, economic, and technological change that has altered the nature of the community and its government and has had a dramatic effect on the manager's role. Today the manager is closely involved in community affairs, intergovernmental relations, economic development efforts, and conflict resolution. Some managers have also played an important part in the development of local governments around the world.

The chapter stressed that the first step in developing and managing public policy is to establish a shared vision of the community that is compatible with citizens' expectations and to incorporate that vision into the mission of the organization. Various aspects of the manager's role in the policymaking process were described: setting the agenda; gatekeeping; bargaining; and designing plans for implementation that define goals, objectives, and priorities. Guidelines for setting objectives were outlined, which noted, among other criteria, that objectives should be both challenging and attainable.

Communication is essential to the success of managerial efforts to implement policy, which fall into four main categories: assigning responsibilities and allocating resources; using functional management to coordinate resources and performance throughout the organization; encouraging productivity through performance targets and reinforcement of positive job-related behaviors; and tracking progress toward desired results. Quality management, employee empowerment, strategic planning, and productivity measures were examined. Because today local governments themselves often do not directly perform many traditional government functions, alternative service delivery systems were examined, among them privatization, joint ventures, intergovernmental agreements, and volunteer activities.

Successful approaches to the improvement of productivity were explored, such as investment in capital resources and state-of-the-art technologies. The chapter observed that rank-and-file workers and supervisors can identify and eliminate many obstacles to efficient operations, but noted four more general barriers: organizational constraints; resource limits; information deficiencies; and disincentives.

Finally, the role of evaluation in program and service management was discussed. Several measures of organizational and employee performance were described, including citizen surveys. The chapter concluded by emphasizing that the ultimate purpose of evaluation is to improve the decision-making process, public policy, local government services, and the productivity of the organization.

Exercise

Assume you are the manager of a medium-sized municipality with its own fire department.

1. Specify the criteria you would use for measuring the performance of the department.
2. What processes would you use for actually conducting the assessment?

Now assume you are the manager of a similar city that contracts for fire service.

1. What are the criteria you would use in evaluating bids to provide the service?
2. Are there differences between the criteria used in evaluating this service and those used for the service in the city with its own fire department? If so, explain what they are and why different criteria would be applied.

1 "Rubach Tells Congress Cities Need Cash Now," *Mesa Tribune*, January 31, 1992, sec. B.

2 Wayne F. Anderson, "Meeting the Needs for Better Managers and Management Practices," in *New Dimensions in Public Administration: The Federal View*, ed. N. Beckman and H. Handerson (Washington, DC: The Bureacrat, Inc., 1975), 157–164.

3 Roy R. Pederson, "Empowering an Organization," *Public Management* 71 (August 1989): 3.

4 David N. Ammons and Charldean Newell, "City Managers Don't Make Policy: A Lie, Let's Face It," *National Civic Review* (March/April 1988): 124–132.

5 Rich Lovett, "City Hall in the Mall," *Public Management* 71 (August 1989): 2–3.

6 R. Fisher and W. Ury, *Getting to Yes: Negotiating Agreement Without Giving In* (New York: Penguin Books, 1981), 11.

7 Council of Economic Advisors, *Economic Report of the President* (Washington, DC: Government Printing Office, 1978).

8 Robert P. Biller, "Turning Conflicts into Challenges," *Public Management* 64 (January 1982): 143.

9 Jeffrey L. Pressman and Aaron Wildavsky, *Implementation*, 2d ed. (Berkeley: University of California Press, 1979), 143.

10 Chester A. Newland, "Labor Relations," in *Productivity Improvement Handbook for State and Local Government*, ed. George J. Washnis (New York: John Wiley, 1980), 503–529.

11 Jerry L. McCaffery, "Making the Most of Strategic Planning and Management," in *Managing Public Programs: Balancing Politics, Administration and Public Needs*, Robert E. Cleary, Nicholas L. Henry, and Associates, (San Francisco: Jossey-Bass, 1989), ch. 8.

12 George Drumwright, "The Graying of Suburbia— One County's Perspective," *Public Management* (July 1989): 10–12.

13 Tony Leno, "Is GIS Good for Local Government?" *Public Management* (June 1989): 15–16.

14 Paul D. Epstein, *Using Performance Measurement in Local Government: A Guide to Improving Decisions, Performance, and Accountability* (New York: Van Nostrand Reinhold Company, 1984), 3.

15 Harry P. Hatry et al., *How Effective Are Your Community Services?* (Washington, DC: The Urban Institute and ICMA, 1992).

16 Jeffrey L. Brudney and Robert E. England, "Urban Policy Making and Subjective Service Evaluation: Are They Compatible?" *Public Administration Review* (March/April 1982): 127–135.

Promoting the community's future

The future of communities is becoming increasingly less certain. Because of rapid economic, social, demographic, and technological change, contemporary local government managers have been forced to recognize the need for cities and counties to deliberately chart their futures, not just in terms of the physical use of land, as has often been the case in the past, but in regard to a complex host of factors that affect the quality of life in the community and the ability of the local government to carry out its mission effectively.

Planning the community's future has become a broad-based activity that encompasses land use and other considerations such as tax base stability and expansion, economic development goals and strategies, social needs and problems, and environmental protection and enhancement—all of which affect the community's overall quality of life. The planning now necessary to ensure a successful future for the community goes far beyond the traditional activities of the planning department.

In the United States, community land-use and development plans, a mainstay of local government planning since the 1920s, now represent only the tip of the iceberg. In large jurisdictions, service-specific plans are often prepared by individual departments such as parks and recreation, emergency services, and public works. In addition, jurisdictions of various sizes are involved in economic development planning, growth management planning, transportation planning, and environmental planning.

Regardless of the type of planning, communities want the process and product to be technically correct. The expansion of planning activity at the local level of government has increased the need for individuals who possess the technical competency to develop plans for the areas in question. For example, as late as the early 1980s, economic development planners were not likely to be found on city staffs; now they are commonplace.

As the number of staff trained in specialized areas of planning increases, where does that leave the manager? As managerial generalists, city and county managers cannot be expected to be planners. Managers can be expected, however, to have an understanding of the various forms of planning, the ability to integrate planning and decision making, and a willingness to educate the organization and the community about the importance and promise of planning.

The meaning and context of planning

Public sector planning occurs in cities, counties, councils of governments, and state and federal agencies. In the private sector, planning activities are found in businesses that range from small partnerships to multinational corporations. Planning is a pervasive activity for which experts and practitioners have developed myriad definitions. Nevertheless, the many types of planning that are practiced in the United States and throughout the world have a common focus: "All have in common a conscious effort to define systematically and think through a problem to improve the quality of decision making."[1] Planning is differentiated from other managerial activities primarily by its focus on the future.

Local public managers are ideally positioned to affect the future by virtue of their central role in the community. Working with the governing body, they help shape public events by deciding what to do and how to do it. If that sounds like simply being a good manager—it is. Good management, like good planning, involves anticipating the future as well as affecting it by doing the right things today and making the right decisions for tomorrow.

However, although local government managers are in a prime position to affect the future of their communities and local jurisdictions are increasingly the units of government that deal with the most important issues facing citizens, a paradox of action/inaction exists:

In a world where success stems from responsiveness and organizational flexibility, local government presents a special challenge. Slow to change by design and often rigid in structure, traditional governmental organizations are less than ideally suited to an environment of rapid change. Yet no organization in society performs more important work, deals with more important issues, or affects more lives than local government.[2]

To succeed in a rapidly changing environment, organizations—both public and private—must anticipate, react, and adapt quickly. In the United States, local governments, particularly those operating without political consensus, often find quick action difficult.

How then does a manager reconcile the necessity of actively promoting the community's future with the reality of a traditional organization that may be slow to respond and willing to accept short-term gains at the expense of long-term benefits? In this common situation, managers act primarily to promote the community's future through leadership that creates organizational and community-based acceptance of and support for various types of planning activities. The local government manager, then, is a key agent in the jurisdiction's effort to chart a future that takes physical, economic, social, and environmental factors into account in maintaining a desirable community.

The planning process has added certainty to public and private decision making.

Steven G. Gordon

Without question, significantly more planning is done in the United States today than at any other time during the country's history. Unfortunately, planning efforts between levels of government and even within a single county or city remain disjointed and fragmented. One of the major tasks of the future will be to coordinate, at least loosely, the many diverse local planning activities and direct them toward a common end. Coordinated local planning that receives adequate funding, that expands comprehensive planning to include social and environmental issues, and that unites economic development and managed growth with other planning activities will be a tremendous asset as managers attempt to promote the future of their communities.

Critical trends facing local government

The issues and trends facing local government today are critical to the survival of the community as a stable entity. An increasingly diverse population, global economic competition, serious social concerns, infrastructure decay, and persistent environmental problems are issues that, if left unattended, will present insurmountable challenges to local governments. For this reason, the planning process has broadened to encompass many more participants. Unlike their historical counterparts, who often viewed the future as a simple linear extension of the past, local government professionals, elected officials, and community residents are beginning to accept the necessity of developing plans and strategies that include all citizens and guide the community as a whole through today's changing environment toward an acceptable future.

Demographic change and cultural diversity

Local government managers across the country are beginning to feel the effects of an increasingly diverse population. Many U.S. cities will follow the path of Miami and Los Angeles as their populations become a "majority of minorities." The aging of America will continue—17 percent of the U.S. population will be more than 65 years old by the year 2020 and 21 percent will be more than 65 by the year 2030.[3] In order to accommodate the differing needs of a greater variety of people, local governments will have to offer more flexibility in the mix and types of service they deliver.

Economic globalization and competition

The ability of governments—national, state, and local—to control their economies will continue to erode as the world economy continues to develop. A city's efforts to attract a new or retain an existing manufacturing plant may be foiled, not by a neighboring city, but by one in Korea, Japan, Mexico, or Germany. Developing and maintaining a stable tax and resource base will become a much more challenging and complex task that requires careful advance planning.

With only 4.5 percent of the world's population and a shrinking share of world economic production, the United States will not have the same degree of influence and ability to determine its own fate as it once did.
R. Scott Fosler

Social issues

An analysis of the 1991 State of the Profession survey of ICMA's membership suggests that although traditional managerial concerns remain top priorities among most managers, social issues are receiving increased attention. Approximately 51 percent of the respondents cited drug abuse and its prevention as a priority in their communities; approximately 48 percent cited education, and 30 percent cited demographic changes.[4] Local government agendas will include social issues in greater numbers in the future; these issues must be addressed if communities are to provide opportunities to all citizens to attain a satisfactory standard of living.

Decatur has redefined its public infrastructure to include housing, children, and drug reduction. That change has been recent but swift, and it has been accomplished consciously and publicly.
James Bacon, Jr.

Infrastructure concerns

A strong, well-maintained infrastructure is necessary both to provide services to citizens and to sustain, retain, and attract economic development. The ability of a community to successfully promote its future is linked directly to the existing and future quality and capacity of such infrastructure components as streets, roadways, bridges, parks and recreational facilities, civic centers, sports stadiums, and water and sewer systems. Combining capital facilities planning, programming, and budgeting with other community planning efforts increases the probability of attaining desired goals.

Environmental problems

Concern for the environment has finally reached the agendas of local governments. Air and water pollution, erosion of natural resources, depletion of open space, and rapidly filling landfills are now common considerations of city and county officials. The capacity of the environment to withstand detrimental action is limited. In order to preserve and protect both the environment and the quality of community life, the environmental impact of today's decisions and programs must be taken into account.

Responding to critical trends

As has been the case for years, many of the problems faced by local governments today are not neatly confined to the boundaries of existing cities and counties; transportation, water supply and quality, air quality, solid waste disposal, land use, and economic development are among the issues with regional ramifications. A manager cannot be successful in promoting a city's future if that future is seen as isolated from the future of surrounding communities. Since the formal consolidation of local governments continues to be politically unacceptable, the regional council of governments model, although seriously damaged as a result of federal budget cuts throughout the early 1980s, remains in place and may be able to serve as the vehicle for continued regional cooperation and coordination. Local government managers therefore need to be familiar with, and when appropriate, participate in, the activities of relevant councils of governments. (Regional cooperation is discussed further in Chapter 7.)

The goal is to combine total resources to meet regional challenges that may transcend individual capabilities while retaining and strengthening local autonomy in all other governmental matters.
Alison D. Winter

In addition to cooperating with other jurisdictions as they respond to the critical issues confronting their communities, local government managers must also work closely with citizens. The implications that these problems and issues have for the future make it imperative that citizens be involved in planning and decision making from the outset. The professional expertise of the staff must be blended with the values, perceptions, and desires of local residents in order to identify the direction the community ought to pursue in regard to its population size, development patterns, land-use configuration, public services, and facilities. Put simply, what do residents want the community to be like in ten years?

Community strategic planning

The growing importance of incorporating concerns about the future into planning and decision making today has made strategic planning attractive to local governments. Community-wide strategic planning does not replace traditional planning; rather, it is a dynamic new tool that is useful in identifying the critical issues facing a community as it moves into the future.

Although private corporations have been practicing strategic planning to increase organizational effectiveness since the late 1950s, it did not become widespread in the public sector until the 1980s. Once government agencies began to use strategic planning, it was heralded by many as a technique that would improve decision

Figure 6–1
Comprehensive and
strategic planning.

Comprehensive planning	Strategic planning
1. Long-range	1. Short-range
2. Land use/physical orientation	2. Orientation determined by critical issues
3. Not tied to available resources	3. Tied to available resources
4. Rational model base	4. Rational and intuitional elements
5. Strategies omitted from plan	5. Strategies as part of plan
6. Elected officials and citizens only recently added as participants	6. Widespread participation
7. Planner driven	7. Executive driven

making, thus improving performance.[5] However, by the late 1980s, questions similar to those that were raised about other decision-enhancement processes (systems analysis; planning, programming, and budgeting; zero-based budgeting) were being directed at strategic planning. Opponents debated the claims of effectiveness and efficiency, arguing instead that strategic planning failed to improve decisions and that it was too complex for many local government to implement effectively.[6]

The intent here is not to offer strategic planning as a panacea or to defend its implementation in its current form. As it is now practiced, strategic planning has weaknesses and limitations as well as strengths. If managers recognize the weaknesses and limitations inherent in the process and do not expect miraculous results, strategic planning can be an effective organizational management tool. More important, strategic planning may provide managers with the cornerstone they need to develop an effective process to promote the future of their communities. The importance of effective strategic planning lies in its ability to identify the critical current issues that an organization—in this case a community—must confront in order to adequately address and accommodate future issues. Community-wide strategic planning often serves best as a supplement to and not as a replacement for comprehensive planning.

Figure 6–1 compares the characteristics of comprehensive and strategic planning; it is clear from the figure that the two processes differ significantly. Comprehensive planning tends to be long-range (covering twenty to thirty years), oriented toward the community's physical development, idealistic, and dominated by professional planners. Strategic planning, on the other hand, has a much shorter time horizon (usually about three to five years), focuses on whatever issues are critical to the community, and advocates realistic change. It is designed as a management as well as a planning tool.

The strategic planning process

The distinctive character of strategic planning becomes evident when the steps in the process are identified further, as in Figure 6–2.[7] Conducting an environmental

Figure 6–2 Strategic
planning process.

1. Conduct environmental scan.
2. Identify critical issues.
3. Define mission and identify goals.
4. Conduct internal and external audits in terms of Strengths, Weaknesses, Opportunities, and Threats (SWOT).
5. Develop goals, objectives, and strategies for each critical issue.
6. Develop implementation plan for strategies.
7. Monitor effectiveness of strategies and update as needed.
8. Employ continuous scanning.

scan may seem similar to the information-gathering efforts that take place in the first phase of comprehensive planning; however, it is quite different. The first step in comprehensive planning is simply an effort to gather information in designated areas that is then used to formulate plans. The environmental scan attempts to identify those issues and problems that might have a significant impact on the community. Strategic planning recognizes that the organization does not exist in a vacuum. Both the organization's objectives and the steps it takes to achieve them are seen in the context of the organization's environment.

Unlike traditional planning, in which the basic elements of the plan—land use, housing, transportation, and open space—essentially are predetermined, the focus of a community's strategic plan is dependent upon what issues emerge from the initial environmental scan; as a result, they vary significantly from city to city and county to county. A community whose tax base has eroded because of a decline in population or the loss of a key industry may identify economic development as critical to community survival. On the other hand, a community that is close to a growing metropolitan area, has land available for development, and has maintained a balance between resources and demand for services may see controlling growth as one of its critical concerns.

Local planners often have taken community goals as given, framing them in terms of improved housing, transportation, land use, and general quality of life with little involvement of the community in the goal identification process. In strategic planning, the development of a mission and goal statement is crucial. The key is to involve all affected parties (or more likely some representative form of the parties) when the mission statement is being developed. The resulting statement, although general, charts the direction of the community. The following statement from Denton, Texas, is a typical example:

Through our combined strengths, it is our mission to create jobs, strengthen and expand the tax base by attracting new industry, as well as nurture small business and encourage retention and expansion of existing business.[8]

The essential features of local government strategic planning are captured in the acronym SWOT, which refers to strengths, weaknesses, opportunities, and threats. Once the critical issues facing the community are identified and a mission statement is developed, the local government begins to assess its strengths, weaknesses, opportunities, and threats in relation to the critical issues; strategies are then devised to address those issues.

Figure 6–3 presents a simplified SWOT analysis in which economic development has been selected as one of the key issues facing a community that has a declining population and tax and industrial base. In developing action strategies, the city will have to consider basing its economic development effort on the high-technology industrial base that already exists and utilizing the city's existing economic development office. Community-wide efforts should focus on upgrading the school system, and city officials, perhaps working through the economic development office, will have to improve relations with the chamber of commerce. If its economic development program is successful, the city should experience expansion of its economic and tax bases. Individuals involved in the strategic planning process will have to take intercity competition and the divided council into consideration.

Figure 6–3 SWOT analysis.

Critical issue: Economic development		
SWOT	*External analysis*	*Internal analysis*
Strengths	High-tech concentration	Economic development office
Weaknesses	Education system	No city-chamber cooperation
Opportunities	Economic expansion	Expanded tax base
Threats	Intercity competition	Split city council

Once the SWOT analysis is complete, the next task is to develop an action plan that includes goals, objectives, and strategies for each critical issue. Implementation of action plans may be assigned to existing governmental units, such as the economic development office, or new organizational mechanisms may be created. For example, an economic development committee consisting of representatives from different city departments, the council, the business community, and the general citizenry could be established to oversee the city's economic development activities.

Continual monitoring and updating complete the strategic planning cycle. The desired outcome is that substantial progress will have been made toward addressing the critical issues identified within a two- to five-year period. Strategies and programs designed to address most critical issues are not likely to be terminated after two or three years. However, if significant progress has been made, those programs can continue as regular local government activities, while other issues assume critical status.

The specificity and direct-action orientation of the strategic planning process make it distinct from it comprehensive counterpart. Managers have at their disposal action strategies tailored to address the critical issues as they attempt to guide the community toward identified goals.

The participants

Public sector strategic planning begins with the recognition that a high level of participation from a wide spectrum of players is essential. Open participation is grounded in basic democratic principles; moreover, widespread participation in the strategic planning effort results in greater understanding and acceptance of the process and the plan, which, in turn, increases the probability of successful implementation. From the manager's perspective, the increased chance of success is reason enough to promote a process open to all who have a stake in the results—unions, neighborhood organizations, chambers of commerce, civic organizations, and so forth.

Community-wide strategic planning as a management tool

The role of the local government in strategic planning is to act as organizer, coordinator, and facilitator of a process that will benefit the entire community. The local government manager most often provides the initial impetus for the strategic planning effort and later continues to provide leadership and support. In return, the manager receives information that has a direct bearing on the future of the community—information that can be used to take advantage of strengths, correct weaknesses, maximize opportunities, and respond to threats as the community moves toward a less uncertain future.

Economic development

In 1987, Lester Thurow, an internationally known economist, gave the keynote address at ICMA's annual conference in Montreal. Thurow's presence underlined the importance that is now given to economic development by modern managers.

The extensive involvement of local governments in economic development efforts is a result of economic conditions that are significantly different from those of the past. The traditional view of the federal government as the primary economic actor changed in the 1980s. Local governments can no longer rely on federal attempts to control the economy. Local and state governments now must act in their own best interests.

Communities must put themselves in a position to market their resources intelligently and gain competitive advantage to create new firms and maintain their existing economic base.

That is, communities must use their current human, social, institutional, and physical resources to build a self-sustaining economic system.[9]

The new economic playing field

Most state and local government practitioners continue to define economic development in terms of economic growth that results in job creation and retention. The evolution of economic development as an activity and the significant changes that have occurred in local and state as well as national and international economies may have rendered such simplistic definitions obsolete. It is important for both public and private actors involved in economic development to realize that underlying the basic definition is a complex set of factors that must be understood in order to establish and implement an effective economic development program.

Four significant transformations have occurred in the United States that bear directly on state and local economic development: economic globalization, service-based employment, technology-intensive manufacturing, and the new economic federalism. These transformations have spawned new strategies and approaches to economic development on the part of state and local governments.

Globalization   Modeling the U.S. economy on the basis of factors that exist solely within the country's geographic boundaries is no longer viable. Foreign trade, trade deficits, multinational corporations, and international finance have to be understood if an accurate picture of the national, state, and local economies is to be drawn. Economists, government officials, and business representatives no longer refer to a national economy, but rather to a global economy that rests on "an interdependent system of worldwide production, trade, and financing ... [in which] nearly 80 percent of all new manufacturing jobs in the United States are related to exports."[10]

Two consequences of the development of a global economy are of primary importance. First, the task of arriving at an understanding of the factors affecting state and local economic conditions has become more difficult. As the number and complexity of external forces that might affect their economies increase, state and local officials must include additional variables—variables they may not understand very well—in their economic development programs.

The second consequence of globalization is more direct and easily observable: foreign competition. A global economy now exists as a result of the development of various national economies—particularly those of the United States' two primary capitalist competitors, Germany and Japan, and those of many third world nations. American industries thus have been challenged from all sides since the early 1970s.

The new global economy is fast-paced, turbulent, and uncertain. It will not treat kindly those who cling to passive, reactive, and narrow economic perspectives.

R. Scott Fosler

The impact of foreign competition normally is discussed in terms of aggregate statistics such as trade deficits, increases or decreases in the gross national product, and world market shares of product groups such as aircraft, computers, and automobiles. However, the immediate effects of foreign competition are felt first at the state and local levels of government when a plant closes or an attempt to attract an industry fails as a result of foreign competition, resulting in lost jobs and a reduced tax base. Increased foreign competition has forced many local governments to adopt new economic development strategies designed to allow them to compete directly in the international arena.

Information, knowledge, and service-based employment Once an industrial and manufacturing giant, the United States has experienced a shift in employment patterns as a result of international competition, technological change, and an increased demand for knowledge and information. In 1987, of the 111 million people employed in the United States, approximately 82 million (74 percent) worked in the service sector; 26 million (23 percent) worked in goods-producing jobs; and the remaining 3 million (3 percent) worked in agriculture.[11] The distribution and skills of workers in the labor force have obvious implications for economic development programs.

Technology-intensive manufacturing The change in employment patterns did not result from a decrease in the production of or demand for manufactured products. The manufacturing systems used to produce the products, however, have undergone remarkable changes. The labor-intensive assembly line pioneered by Henry Ford is, or soon will be, a thing of the past, as technological advances such as robotics, miniaturization, and computer-controlled operations continue to revolutionize the manufacturing industry.

Technological innovations allow manufacturing plants to produce more goods of higher quality with far fewer workers. In addition to the reduction in employment opportunities that results from these innovations in traditional manufacturing industries, there is a continuing "shift from industries that [are] primarily labor-intensive to industries that, from the beginning, are knowledge-intensive.[12] Consequently, in order to design and implement a competitive economic development program, local governments have to offer a highly skilled work force that is able to meet the demands of the technical jobs that have replaced the low- to semi-skilled manufacturing jobs of the past.

The new economic federalism The retrenchment and decentralization of the federal system that began in the late 1970s is not likely to be reversed. In the 1980s, President Ronald Reagan succeeded in altering the course of a federal system that had been broadening its scope since the Great Depression, by returning power and responsibility—but not necessarily revenues—to the state and local governments. Decentralization of federal programs has resulted in federal mandates that place the responsibility for clean air, water quality, access for the disabled, and landfill safeguards directly in the hands of local government, along with a greater degree of decision-making authority—but without the necessary funding.

The financial buck-passing has not stopped with the federal government. In Michigan, the already financially strapped city of Detroit now must provide emer-

Innovation in New Zealand New Zealand has made significant changes in its government structure and operating philosophy in order to be more competitive in the world economy and to maintain its quality of life. Three strategic approaches were used in the restructuring effort:

1. To make sure that all appropriate government activities were transferred to the private sector
2. To inject an enterprise orientation, with market discipline, in as much of the government as possible
3. To structure the remaining parts of the government in such a way as to provide managers the freedom to maximize the use of resources, with appropriate accountability.

Source: Frank P. Sherwood, "The New Zealand Message," in *Thinking Differently About Government Reform in Florida* (Tallahassee: Center for Public Management, 1992): 6.

gency housing and food for recipients of general assistance in order to replace a program axed by the governor and state legislature.[13]

The financial restructuring of the federal system is evident particularly in the area of economic development. From 1980 to 1990, funds for the Small Business Administration and community development block grants were reduced and funds for the Economic Development Administration and urban development action grants were eliminated. The new economic federalism that has emerged has resulted in increased responsibilities with lower levels of federal financial support for local governments. In the field of economic development, as in other areas, local governments must seek innovative approaches to finance and implement activities that once were at least partially supported by federal dollars.

Approaches to economic development

There are two well-defined approaches and one emerging approach to economic development: industrial relocation, demand-side entrepreneurialism, and shared responsibility, respectively. Of the three, industrial relocation has been in existence the longest and perhaps is the approach most often associated with state and local economic development.

Industrial relocation (the supply-side approach)   Since its beginnings in the 1930s, modern economic development policy has been dominated by one approach: industrial relocation, commonly referred to as "smokestack chasing." When the Great Depression exacerbated the long-standing need of Southern states for a solid manufacturing base to bolster their agriculturally dominated economy, officials in these states initiated efforts to attract industries from the North. They used various incentives, including the promise of low employee wages and tax breaks, to persuade many industries, particularly textile plants, to move south. The efforts of the Southern states during the 1930s proved to be only a forerunner of an economic development strategy that would spread nationwide to all state governments and many municipal ones as well.

Industrial relocation is also known as the supply-side approach to economic development: those industries that are available for relocation constitute the supply that cities then compete for as they seek to expand their economic base.

Armed with the belief that one of the primary methods to create jobs and expand the economy is to attract new business and industry, state and local officials continue to place industrial relocation strategies at the heart of their economic development programs. Advertising campaigns in the best Madison Avenue style are developed to tout the virtues of their states and cities. However, as economic development activities have become common, the competition among suitors for new businesses and industries has become more intense. The advertising campaign has been replaced with more aggressive techniques. Comprehensive promotional packages are designed to promote the special attributes a community might have, such as a pleasant climate, proximity to a major airport, a well-developed mass transit system, cultural attractions, and entertainment opportunities. Television spots attempt to lure visitors; government representatives attend trade shows and business conventions across the country and throughout the world; and local governments send trade missions to foreign countries.

As competition for existing industry intensified, cities and counties developed the incentive package. Today, through a combination of tax, financial, and special-service incentives, state and local governments attempt to create an environment in which business can be conducted at lower costs and thus earn higher profits. The alleged relationship is simple and direct: incentives attract economic development, and in order to compete successfully, local governments must include them in their economic development packages. Originally, the emphasis was on tax-reduction packages; currently, all three types of incentives are used extensively.

Although the specifics of a package would be discussd with and designed for an individual industry, especially if the business is a large one, a standard menu of incentives is offered by most local governments as a result of state actions and legislation (see Figure 6–4).

The role of incentive packages   Extensive debate has occurred over the use of incentive packages to attract or, in recent cases, to retain business. Research findings on the impact of incentive packages on decisions to locate are contradictory, with some claiming that incentives have no effect and others suggesting that incentives play some role in a very complex decision.[14]

Given the contradictory research findings, what should the local government manager do? The emerging consensus appears to be that incentive packages have relatively little impact when the site selection process is still at the national level and the competition is among a number of states. Incentives become more important as the list of prospective sites narrows and comparisons begin among different metropolitan areas and then among specific cities.[15]

Regardless of the impact of incentives at the local level, many other factors combine to influence a site selection decision. For example, in a survey of corporate planners, 45 percent said that quality-of-life factors were very important in business site selection decisions, suggesting that quality-of-life factors may begin to dominate the entire site selection process in many cases.[16]

Quality of life and relocation decisions   A 1989 survey of corporate executives asked what quality-of-life factors were important in making business relocation or expansion decisions. The executives mentioned such things as a good educational system, affordable housing, reasonable cost of living, an attractive physical environment, and recreational opportunities.[17] Although local governments can influence many quality-of-life elements to some extent, providing such things as a good educational system, affordable housing, and a reasonable cost of living depends on the ability of the city or county to coordinate its activities with other government and private sector entities. Chapter 7 discusses in more detail the importance of intergovernmental relations to today's manager.

The increasing importance of quality-of-life factors to business executives does not mean that state and local governments will dismantle the incentive packages they have created. In the minds of many managers and economic development

Figure 6–4   Examples of development incentives used by state and local government.

Growth management incentives	Number of states
Tax incentives	
Corporate income tax exemption	34
Personal income tax exemption	32
Tax exemption on land or capital improvements	35
Inventory tax exemption on goods in transit (freeport)	49
Financial incentives	
State-sponsored industrial development authority	40
Privately sponsored development credit corporation	36
City or county revenue bond financing	49
City or county general bond financing	37
Special services	
City or county provides free land for industry	32
City- or county-owned industrial park sites	49
State funds public works projects	48
State funds recreational projects	44

officers, the use of incentive packages in all fifty states and many local governments means that termination of such programs is unlikely. Because incentives do offer definite advantages to business, even if they are not a primary consideration in location decisions, no state or local government is likely to be willing to assume the risks associated with unilaterally eliminating incentives as long as they are offered by their competitors.

The demand-side entrepreneurial approach   The second approach to economic development is summarized by Peter Eisinger, who explains that state and local economic development policy has shifted "from an almost exclusive reliance on supply-side location incentives to stimulate [growth] to an approach that increasingly emphasizes demand factors in the market as a guide to the design or the invention of policy."[18] The underlying premise of the demand-side approach is that to be effective in the 1990s, economic development policies must be based on the creation of new businesses and new capital. Jurisdictions that rely solely on the traditional industrial relocation approach to economic development reduce the probability of their success.[19]

The primary difference in the two approaches is the demand side's emphasis on new business, new capital, market development and expansion, resource protection, and entrepreneurialism. Instead of seeking low-risk industries that are possible candidates for relocation, demand-side practitioners approach economic development from an entirely new perspective. They look for growth opportunities primarily in the creation of new businesses and in the retention and expansion of existing businesses, many of which can be classified as high-risk, entrepreneurial enterprises. Local government managers should be cautious when considering government involvement in a high-risk entrepreneurial venture. Although such ventures can benefit the community, they can also result in losses to the community and the local government.

The shared-responsibility approach   According to John Herbers, a third wave of economic development strategies began to break across the United States in the late 1980s. Unlike industrial relocation and demand-side approaches, in which state and local governments assumed the leading role, the newest approach places a much greater emphasis on shared public and private responsibility for economic development. However, again initiative seems to be taken by state and local governments. Herbers summarizes the shared-responsibility approach as follows: governmental subsidies for a single firm or small group of firms are replaced by private corporations created by government to attract private capital and to reach many different businesses.[20]

The new approach is in its nascent stage, and it is not yet well defined, but its early forms embody three principles:

Interlocal cooperation in economic development   Canada's Technology Triangle is composed of the business development departments of the cities of Kitchener, Waterloo, Cambridge, and Guelph, in Ontario (combined population 400,000). The development interests of these four competing cities were combined into one economic unit without increasing the size of staff or budgets. The cities have learned to share ideas, contacts, opportunities, and staff in a highly competitive environment and have found they operate more efficiently and more effectively together than alone.

Source: *ICMA Newsletter* (June 17, 1991).

1. Financial responsibility is shared between the public and private sectors, the intent being to leverage initial capitalization with private contributions.
2. Competition among various economic development providers—some private but created with public sponsorship, some private, and some still public—replaces the monopoly in existence when the public sector is the sole provider.
3. Decision making is decentralized through the creation of organizational structures that serve clients at the "grass-roots" level, avoiding sole reliance on public bureaucracies.[21]

It is too early to tell whether the newest economic development technique is a viable alternative or just another example of an innovative technique that causes a ripple but is not successful enough to warrant widespread adoption. Regardless of the outcome, the shared-responsibility approach provides evidence that state and local governments continue to seek new ways to invigorate their economies.

A local government that pursues a multifaceted strategy of business attraction, retention, and development increases the probability of the success of its economic development program. Smokestack chasing is an outmoded approach only if it is the sole component of a jurisdiction's economic development plan. Industries, both foreign and domestic, still relocate, and local governments continue to compete for their favors. It is equally foolhardy to concentrate all of a jurisdiction's economic development efforts in demand-side strategies or in the yet-to-be-proven shared-responsibility approach. A local government is not obligated to choose one of the three approaches. All three are legitimate, and all three—or parts of all three—can be carefully coordinated to create an effective economic development program.

Managing economic development

Prior to launching or, in some cases, to continuing an economic development program, local government managers must ask two key questions. Is economic development always in the long-term interest of the community? Is there always a "community profit" when the economic development ledger is balanced? For many years the answer to both questions was a resounding "yes." The consensus was that an effective economic development program would produce a strong and expanded tax base that in turn

Creates new jobs, provides resources to solve existing social problems, meets the housing needs caused by natural population growth, and allows the market to serve public tastes in housing, neighborhoods and commercial development.[22]

By the early 1990s, after more than a decade of experience with economic development programs and a continuing increase in the number of local governments actively involved in economic development, a growing contingent of managers realized that there are definite costs associated with development and that, in some cases, those costs may outweigh the benefits. The costs associated with economic development fall into two categories: (1) problems or negative consequences of development activities that result in indirect costs, and (2) the direct expenditures necessary to support the development program.

Indirect costs Indirect costs are by-products of economic development and growth. Problems or negative consequences may result from job creation, increased demand for services, inadequate infrastructure, and quality-of-life and environmental concerns. Indirect costs must be calculated in order to determine the net benefit to be derived from new development.

Unemployment Economic development creates jobs—or does it? The number of jobs available in a community should increase if economic development efforts have been successful in attracting, retaining, and developing businesses. However, an increase in jobs may result in two negative consequences. First, an increase in jobs in the community that attracts the industrial client is offset by a decline in the number of jobs in the community that loses the industry. Second, it is probable that a rapidly growing community will attract unemployed workers from other parts of the state and nation. These workers not only will fill the new job vacancies, but—because demand for the jobs will soon exceed supply—they also will form a work-force sector that is continuously unemployed.[23] An increase in jobs, then, may provide only short-lived benefits to the community.

Increased demand for services   Industrial and population growth results in an increased demand for local government services. The capacities of municipal, educational, and human-service delivery systems have to be expanded to accommodate the increase in demand. Although advocates of development claim that new growth will pay for the increased demand, financing increased service levels may prove difficult and serve to negate some of the benefits of development.

The ability of a city or county to respond to a growth-induced increase in service demand may be curtailed by the same program that produced the growth. If, as so often is the case, a package of tax abatements and other incentives was a part of the development deal, growth will take place and increase the demand for services, while collection of revenues that could be used to help finance service expansion will be deferred as a condition of the development agreement. Local officials then have two less than desirable options: (1) increase revenues, probably by raising taxes on current residents, or (2) increase the capacity of the service delivery system, not by augmenting departmental budgets, but by spreading services thinner to serve more people through such measures as reduced frequency of garbage collection, fewer police patrols per neighborhood, and higher child/instructor ratios in recreation programs. Neither option is likely to be popular with current residents who were led to believe that economic development was going to solve problems, not create them.

Overburdened infrastructure   Industrial development and population growth can also place a significant burden on a jurisdiction's infrastructure. Public buildings, park and recreation facilities, water supply and sewage disposal systems, and, most certainly, the transportation system have to accommodate growth and development. Expansion of an infrastructure system is particularly difficult in many communities where the existing infrastructure may be in need of improvement simply to handle pre-growth demand. As with service delivery expansion, the idea is that growth will produce the additional revenues needed to improve and expand the infrastructure.

Unless a community is experiencing slow, gradual growth, it is far from certain that sufficient revenues will be generated to finance infrastructure-related costs that result from development. The state of Florida offers an extreme example. Despite continual, rapid population growth that began to strain the state's infrastructure, state and local officials continued to operate under the erroneous assumption that growth and development would ultimately generate sufficient revenues to maintain and expand the infrastructure. In reality, the future-payment method resulted throughout the state in enormous infrastructure debt and a threatened environment. To rectify the situation, Florida reverted to a strict pay-as-you-go system that was framed in the state's 1985 Growth Management Act.

Since this act was passed, the concept of concurrency has been the key to growth management in Florida. This concept stipulates that before growth can occur, it must be demonstrated ''that public facilities (infrastructure) needed to support new development shall be available concurrent with the impact of that development.''[24] Although most states may be reluctant to adopt Florida's strict concurrency requirements, the issue of infrastructure capacity and the ability to finance infrastructure improvement are important considerations in developing an economic development program.

Impact on quality of life   Another claim is that development will produce sufficient revenue to help the community deal with some of the problems it currently faces. The additional revenue generated supposedly will help support programs that are presently either unfunded or underfunded. Proponents suggest that the revenues generated from new economic growth could be used to address the problems of the homeless, improve public housing projects, enhance funding for children's recreational programs, provide public day-care services, or offer improved programs for the elderly. Newly generated funds also could be used to strengthen and improve existing basic services such as solid waste collection, emergency street maintenance, recreation programs, and general customer service.

The local government manager and the governing body must consider whether economic development will in fact enable their community to deal effectively with many of its current problems. Some contend that although economic development does not, in most cases, cause specific problems, it may actually exacerbate those that already exist. For example, Logan and Molotch argue that growth makes dealing with such social problems as integration and inequality more difficult.[25]

Local officials also need to consider whether their community would allocate funds to social programs that had not previously been on the agenda. History tells us that past spending priorities are an excellent predictor of future choices, and it is unlikely that extensive funding of new social programs would take place if a jurisdiction did not have a history of funding such programs.

Finally, as local government managers consider whether economic development will help address any of a community's current problems, they must focus on the amount of new revenues to be generated by economic development. In situations in which revenue generation lags behind growth, the total available resources will have to be stretched to accommodate a higher level of demand. Furthermore, if growth and revenue generation attain a balance and funds are available to meet the increased demand, it is unlikely that there will be additional funds to address previously existing problems.

Environmental impact   Environmental concerns as they evolved in the 1950s and 1960s were rooted in the belief that the degradation of the nation's land, air, and water resources was so serious that it constituted a major public policy problem. Environmentalists were the first to speak out in opposition to economic development. When they began their efforts to save us from ourselves, environmentalists had few listeners and even fewer supporters. Today, the situation has changed dramatically. The American public is now very concerned about the environment, and many officials are beginning to question the overall benefits of growth, particularly if it is uncontrolled. One need only to look at Florida or Southern California to realize the negative impact of uncontrolled growth on natural resources and the environment. In Florida, the Everglades are in serious trouble as a result of developments at the swamp's boundaries that threaten the water supply and endanger much of the wildlife population. Only a concentrated effort will save this valuable Florida resource.

An increase in the number of industries and the size of the population can result in serious detrimental effects. Air and water pollution increases, congestion of people and traffic moves from being inconvenient to being intolerable, and the overall quality of life declines.

As they plan their community's economic development, local government officials therefore need to consider such issues as the possible increase in air and water pollution and soil erosion and the loss of open space.

Direct costs   In addition to considering all the possible indirect costs of economic development, local government officials must consider the question of who will pay the direct costs associated with growth. Is government—or more precisely taxpayers—the responsible party because citizens are the supposed beneficiaries of more jobs and income and an enhanced tax base? Or are economic development investors, developers, banks, venture capitalists, and their associates to be assigned the responsibility because it is they, as individuals or institutions, who will profit from growth? Perhaps the answer, as it so often does, lies somewhere between the two extremes.

Publicly financed economic development occurs when people who do not necessarily benefit from a public facility in proportion to their share of the cost contribute to its financing through general and special taxes. Conversely, private financing of growth attempts to shift some of the cost burden to developers and new residents through implementing fees, assessments, and exactions requiring developers to set aside land for facilities such as parks and schools.

Public financing: general taxes   Property, income, and sales taxes all may be used to finance the costs created by growth. The revenues generated from these tax sources go into the general fund of the state or municipality and, therefore, may be used as the elected decision makers deem appropriate. Identifying the proportion of these tax revenues that is allocated to finance growth is difficult. However, it may be assumed that in high-growth jurisdictions, if tax rates are increased, at least part of the increase will be directed toward financing the area's growth.

It is also possible in some states to add a specified percentage to the local sales tax to finance the development of a particular project. In 1992 taxpayers in Grand Prairie, Texas, approved a half-cent sales tax add-on to help attract and then finance a horse racetrack. The tax hike was to fund a bond package of approximately $60 million.

Public financing: special taxes   Special taxes are those that are levied on specific products or services, such as alcoholic beverages, tobacco products, gasoline, and hotel or motel accommodations. Revenue produced by these taxes also goes primarily into the general revenue fund, but there are exceptions. In Cleveland, Ohio, the financing of a new sports complex including a baseball stadium and basketball arena is being provided by a voter-approved 15-year half-cent increase in the sales tax on alcoholic beverages and tobacco.

Public financing: service charges   Perhaps the most obvious method of using public money to finance the costs of growth is the application of service charges, commonly referred to as user fees. User fees are charged in many local government service areas: parks and recreation, refuse and sewage disposal, transportation, utilities, health, and community development. Because they are tied directly to the use of a service or facility, user charges not only help finance growth, they distribute the financial burden more fairly among users.

There is an obvious limit to the extent to which user fees will finance the costs of growth, however. First, there are services that are not fee-based and thus cannot be financed by the application of user charges. Street maintenance, traffic signs and signals, and police and fire protection are examples of non-fee-based services. Second, those fee-based services that are tied to components of the infrastructure may only partially recover the costs of growth. For example, refuse collection rates and tipping fees may not pay for the costs of operation and maintenance of the municipal landfill, although states are now moving to require that landfills be self-supporting.

Private financing: special assessment districts   In order to finance infrastructure in a new residential development, a local government might create a special district encompassing the development and then levy a special assessment on the property owners in the district. Special assessments are used for street improvement, drainage, street lighting, water and sewer lines, and recreational facilities. In some states, the use of special assessment districts has been broadened beyond its traditional association with new housing developments and the infrastructure needs of those developments. In Washington, special assessment districts have been created to finance libraries; in Colorado and Texas, to finance utilities.[26]

Private financing: exactions   Many local governments use exactions to finance on-site improvements on newly developed land. The most common exaction requires that the developer dedicate land for such public purposes as a park, recreational facility, or school. Many local governments also require that the developer provide the facility as well as the land. For example, the developer may be obligated to landscape and provide equipment for a neighborhood park.

Private financing: development impact fees   The use of development impact fees is perhaps the most popular technique for passing infrastructure costs on to the in-dustrial or residential developer. Unlike exactions, which finance on-site improve-ments, impact fees are used to finance off-site infrastructure developments such as streets, water supply systems, landfills, emergency medical facilities, parks, and schools. Courts have upheld the use of development fees as long as the fee assessed represents an equitable share of the cost.[27]

In reality, however, developers do not bear the full cost of impact fees. The initial outlay by the developer is passed on to the industrial or residential client who buys or rents the property. In this case it is the new occupant and not the current residents who will be helping to finance the costs of growth, and the bill can be quite high. For example, in Florida, where multiple impact fees are assessed, the cost per unit may increase as much as $10,000.[28]

Who pays the bill?   In the final analysis, the established and new residents of a community, not its developers, pay for the majority of the costs associated with growth. Established residents pay their portion through general and special taxes, as well as user fees. Despite their claims that they should not be held financially responsible for the costs of growth, established residents do use the city's infra-structure and it does need to be maintained and periodically upgraded. Using tax revenue and user fees to help defray costs in cases such as these is a legitimate means of financing growth.

New residents, however, face a double-edged sword. They face the same package of taxes and service fees that confronts established residents; nevertheless, they also pay an additional share of the costs of growth, either directly through special assessments or indirectly through the higher price they pay for property because of the passed-on costs of exactions and development fees.

Growth management and economic development

As mentioned in the preceding section, economic development and growth can have serious environmental consequences. Is the argument then to stop all growth to protect natural resources, the environment, and possible future land uses? In the minds of those who take a no-growth position, the answer is an unqualified "yes." However, to a growing number of state and local officials, members of the business community, and citizens, the answer is not found in stopping growth, but rather in managing growth.

Proponents of managed growth suggest that many of the disadvantages and prob-lems associated with development are alleviated through growth management, which, according to Vogel and Swanson, is

A rational process to arrive at community decisions regarding growth rates, the mix of residential, industrial, and commercial development, the trade-offs between "use" and "exchange" values, the provision of public services, and the protection of the environment.[29]

Extremists who voice opposition to all forms of growth remain. Yet, the number of growth management advocates is increasing. They propose managed development as a method to identify and incorporate growth objectives into state or municipal planning in order to maximize the benefits and minimize costs.

Growth is a healthy and necessary process for any community.
O. Paul Shew

Growth management can enhance economic development by establishing a framework for development, fostering a positive business climate, and reducing the negative consequences of development. First, a systematic approach to growth management includes an annual plan that sets forth a framework containing goals, objectives, and criteria for making decisions. Such a plan enhances economic development possibilities.

Second, corporations and industries seeking to relocate, firms reassessing their current location, and entrepreneurs considering the establishment of a new venture are all interested in the business climate of potential sites for their operations. Business executives recognize that an area's business climate consists of far more than the local government's willingness to grant concessions and incentive packages in order to attract new industries and expand existing operations. A free-for-all approach to growth in which anything goes and any industry is considered fair game detracts from the local business climate in the minds of many private sector executives.

On the other hand, a growth management system that sets forth an orderly plan and reasonable criteria for development, while recognizing the importance of preserving the quality of life of residents and corporate clients, sends a positive message to business executives. Certainly, market access, labor costs, raw materials, and transportation availability remain critical components of location and expansion decisions. However, various quality-of-life factors, ranging from the educational system to recreational opportunities to the capacity of the social service system, are becoming increasingly important to businesses seeking to relocate, expand, or develop.

The growth management plan reflects the philosophy of a community that wants to grow, and quite frankly needs to grow, but one that is committed to growth only within the city's ability to serve.
William Christopher

Third, growth management enhances economic development by reducing the negative effects that may result from business development and population growth. In the previous section, some of the disadvantages of economic development were described. They may be summed up as follows:

Economic development is by no means a pure blessing. Rapid development can bring temporary shortages of classrooms and other public facilities, pollute the air and water, cause local housing prices to increase, turn beautiful natural lands into subdivisions, and increase labor costs for businesses already operating in the area.[30]

By balancing the capacity of service delivery systems and basic infrastructure with the demands of development, a growth management system can help establish equilibrium among the often conflicting concerns of development, environment, and quality of life.

As a result of the increasing importance that is being accorded to quality-of-life factors by the business community, jurisdictions that offer growth management as a means to preserve and enhance living conditions will be more competitive than those that simply pursue development without concern for its potential impact.

Growth management objectives and techniques

On the surface, the objectives of growth management (see sidebar) do not differ drastically from the traditional objectives of community development that were concerned primarily with land-use control and density. However, growth management—while also seeking to control land use and density—is primarily concerned with the timing and impact of development.[31] Growth management, therefore, assumes a much broader perspective and attempts to link land use and the density of development with community services, environmental concerns, infrastructure, and a plan for timed development. The objectives of growth management are quite compatible with economic development, if the overall goal is to combine development with the preservation or improvement of the community's quality of life. Most, if not all, of the objectives listed would be welcomed by business leaders seeking to relocate, expand, or begin a business.

Despite claims that growth management is new to cities and counties, local governments have been involved in limited growth management endeavors since the development of zoning, building, and subdivision regulations. These regulations have been used primarily to facilitate the implementation of land-use and community development plans, and in a limited fashion, they may have been used to control growth. Contemporary growth management techniques are a product of the various measures and regulations used in the past. The wide array of growth control measures currently in use is described by Elizabeth A. Deakin:

Limitations on the level of intensity of development permitted (subdivision control, zoning)

Stringent design and performance standards for lots and buildings (subdivision control, zoning)

Shifting of costs from the public to the development project (adequate public facilities ordinances, exactions and impact fees, administrative fees for application review and processing)

Reductions in supply of developable land and/or restrictions on the locations where development is permitted (zoning, urban limit lines, greenbelt, agricultural reserves)

Twelve major objectives of growth management

1. Preserve the character of the community and provide community identity.
2. Conserve agricultural land and preserve open space.
3. Encourage full utilization of existing facilities.
4. Control development of new areas to ensure coordination with existing and proposed facilities.
5. Maintain or improve the level of community services.
6. Improve housing opportunities, increase diversity, and promote better housing development.
7. Avoid environmental problems.
8. Prevent sprawl.
9. Promote aesthetics and preserve historic and cultural features.
10. Reduce traffic congestion and improve the road system.
11. Promote public safety.
12. Provide flexibility to meet future needs.

Source: Katherine E. Stone and Robert H. Freilich, "Writing a Defensible Growth Ordinance," in *Balanced Growth: A Planning Guide for Local Government*, ed. John M. DeGrove (Washington, DC: ICMA, 1991): 106.

Reductions in the amount of growth permitted, overall or per time unit (population caps, square footage or housing unit caps, annual permit caps)[32]

Even the specific techniques used in current growth management programs bear a striking resemblance to their traditional counterparts: land acquisition, zoning, exactions, annexation, capital improvements planning, and quotas on new development. The techniques themselves, then, are not what makes growth management different. Instead, the context and objectives of growth management distinguish it from traditional land-use control. Incorporating the techniques into a broader plan for the community's future, while at the same time emphasizing the timing and impact of development and land use, defines the approach of growth management.

Political concerns

The roots of growth management lie in the political maneuverings of early environmentalists whose primary objective was to stop growth. As concerns about growth became more widespread and began to appear on the mainstream political agenda, the no-growth concept was modified to permit managed growth. The primary obstacles that any growth management system is likely to encounter come from the political arena. Pragmatic and realistic managers and political leaders interested in a system of managed growth find that linking growth management with the politically more acceptable issue of economic development is one way to gain greater acceptance for managed growth.

Over the past several years, initial moves toward growth management have been described in terms of economic development in Georgia, Texas, Arizona, and South Carolina.[33] Explaining the virtues of growth management in terms of what it can accomplish for economic development establishes its legitimacy, particularly in politically conservative states where opposition to land-use controls and regulation of private development traditionally has been strong.

When growth management is offered as a system that can achieve the multiple goals of development, infrastructure improvement, environmental protection, and quality-of-life enhancement, the basis for a coalition of diverse interests is created. Politicians can adopt a middle-ground position, avoiding the extremes of the growth/no-growth debate. Developers and business executives see a favorable attitude toward growth that is supported by a diverse constituency. Environmentalists, once considered radical extremists, are associated with a more politically acceptable coalition and can see at least some progress being made in environmental protection. Professional planners, long advocates of land-use control, support the increased stature and authority that planning acquires in a more centralized growth management system that is endorsed by key elected officials. Finally, citizens see a movement that can protect their investment in their community as well as preserve or improve the quality of life and the environment.

When growth management and economic development are integrated into one

---

Growth management in Florida   Key West's 1986 growth management ordinance established the number of dwelling units that still can be constructed before the island is completely built out. Before the enactment of the ordinance, the city approved an average of 400 to 500 dwelling units annually. Under the ordinance, the city can allow either seven percent of the total units permitted or 300 units per year.

Source: American Planning Association, "Taming The Exclusionary Effects of Growth Controls," in *Balanced Growth: A Planning Guide for Local Government*, ed. John M. DeGrove (Washington, DC: ICMA, 1991).

system, the potential exists to establish a broad base of support and perhaps even to attain consensus. A growth management system that is designed to promote planned, desirable development can provide significant benefits for everyone. When such a system is presented objectively to the many diverse interests in a state or municipality, most can see that it increases the resources available through an increase in the number of jobs and promotes retention of industries, protection of natural resources and the environment, and enhancement of services and infrastructure.

Despite the potential for widespread support, ensuring the adoption of a growth management system remains a difficult political task. Acceptance of growth management will not be immediate and will necessitate a significant educational campaign on the part of local officials and private sector supporters. In most cases, it is doubtful that a comprehensive growth management system will be adopted in those jurisdictions with little growth management experience. Adoption of a first generation of laws that initiate a limited system of growth management, followed by adoption of a second generation of laws that expand the system, is a common pattern and the most likely to succeed. Regardless of the strategy pursued, local officials should seriously consider a growth management system for their jurisdictions if they have not already done so. Those jurisdictions that have instituted a growth management program should be encouraged to retain it; the program should yield economic, environmental, physical, and social benefits to the local government, businesses, and citizens.

Three promotion and planning roles for the manager

Two questions are fundamental to this chapter: How can local public managers effectively promote the future of the community? What roles should they play given the increasing complexity and uncertainty of the future? The emergence of critical issues that can have a major impact on local communities and their governments requires managers to become much more involved in promotional and planning activities than they were in the past. The inability of traditional, comprehensive planning to accomplish the task of dealing with these issues has forced local managers to consider new options, such as strategic planning, economic development, and growth management, as they seek ways to guide their communities toward the future.

Many of the activities associated with strategic planning, economic development, and growth management are not foreign to local government. However, the consequences of unsuccessful planning and promotional activities have become so serious that managers cannot delegate all responsibility for planning to the planning department. Local public managers who hope to play a prominent role in securing a positive future for their communities must understand and be able to deal with all the factors that affect that future.

Managers must learn the importance of forming a vision of the community of tomorrow, the importance of initiating processes that promote that vision, and the importance of implementing plans and processes that link vision to action. These three activities fit logically together from both planning and management perspectives. In past organizational settings, however, they were often performed by several players: vision (planning), initiation (managers), and implementation (staff). Now, local managers are asked to assume a proactive position in each activity.

The three activities discussed here blend well with the important skills and attributes identified in *Future Challenges, Future Opportunities* as needed by local government managers (see Chapter 1). Managers who are effective in integrating and performing the activities and who master some or all of the skills identified are in a good position to promote the future of their community.

Vision

The local administrator, whether in a large or small city or in a rural or urban county, sits at the center of a complex set of public and private institutions that explicitly or implicitly, through action or inaction, have an impact on the community's future. On the broadest scale, the manager's role involves facilitating complex interactions among all elements in the community. This means, in the phrase of Paul Appleby, the late public administration scholar, "learning to make a mesh of things." Elements of this managerial "meshing" process include finding planning expertise, creating a purposeful agenda for future civic actions, involving the local government and other public bodies in future-oriented processes, and leadership.

Finding expertise   Individuals with promotional and planning expertise may be located in independent planning commissions; operational planning or economic development units that report to a local public manager or chief administrative officer; or in staff support units in the mayor's office or in another agency, such as community development. Wherever the necessary expertise is located, most managers recognize that including expert opinion in a community's promotion and planning processes is important.

Despite the prominent role they play, managers cannot single-handedly plan the future of the community. Diligent care is required to develop a competent professional staff that can assist in the preparation of plans and programs designed to achieve the future desired. Finding experienced, able individuals is by no means easy, but unless they are found, managers can be severely handicapped by inadequate staff support. Circuit-riding planners or managers sometimes share their expertise among many small towns unable to afford full-time planners. Some governments use short-term consultants to assist in planning and economic development. In medium-sized and large jurisdictions, building a full-time professional staff requires finding individuals with formal academic training in the appropriate fields who have a record of innovative work with and particular knowledge of the issues and problems of the community (such as historic preservation, low-cost public housing, or economic development).

Creating a purposeful agenda for future civic actions   Community agendas for action are known by many names—general plans, master plans, community development guides, and economic development strategies. Agendas are also designed with many purposes in mind—to control land-use patterns, to renew downtown industrial development, to preserve a historical heritage, or to protect critical environmental areas. Whatever its name, content, and focus, the community agenda is fundamentally a purposeful document for action—a call for the community to do something. Helping to shape the community's agenda for action requires a manager to be something of a visionary who can act as catalyst. The manager's role is

1. To codify the community's desires and aims in terms of a vision of the future
2. To provide the general direction and procedures for guiding approaches to creating and promoting the action plan and programs
3. To ensure that the legal requirements—local, state, and federal—are met
4. To be certain that action strategies, above all, address the central current and future problems facing the community by offering a logical, realistic sequence of attack on these issues.

Before the strategic planning approach was adopted by local governments, Alan Jacobs put his finger on the crux of what any effective local public manager must do to ensure that he or she is successful in promoting the community's future—

make certain that the strategies address, as openly, realistically, and thoroughly as possible, the "pressing current issues" of the community. If these issues are not addressed effectively, the planning effort is likely to fail.[34]

Involving the local government and other public bodies Another important task for the manager is to involve all components of the local government in promotion and planning for the future. In the past, despite exhortations by planners and public administrators, planning often proceeded apart from the daily operations of the government. As Harvey Perloff notes, "A major reason for the distance of urban planning from other municipal operations is the failure of the central planning activity to translate all of its plans and program proposals into terms that are operationally meaningful for other municipal agencies."[35]

Local government managers are the critical link in making certain that this translation takes place and that plans and programs are indeed developed in relation to the people, resources, and operational requirements of line agencies. In turn, managers need to curb the often myopic preoccupation of their line departments with immediate, ad hoc, project-by-project approaches. Bringing line decision making into the broader context of the community's future is a difficult, continuous problem but nevertheless a very important managerial responsibility.

Leadership Managers stand in the midst of many contending interests involved in promoting some version of the community's future. Moving the community forward and responding to critical issues within a consensual framework means that managers must mediate the often conflicting views of the various groups and interests involved.

Managerial leadership is essential through all phases of the community's attempt to plan and promote its future. Leadership is important in facilitating the creation of community goals and priorities, in assuring council or commission involvement, in directing staff analysis, and in relating promotion and planning to other activities of the jurisdiction. Also important is solicitation of and responsiveness to ideas—by observation and by structured processes that involve the public, elected officials, community interests, staff, and departmental personnel.

In all this, the manager needs to realize that promoting the future of the community involves people. Accordingly, the manager thinks politically and continues to exercise leadership by assuming the role of broker or negotiator—remaining aware of competing and conflicting interests and ever-watchful for opportunities to tap resources or foster coalitions to promote overall community goals.

Initiation

If the first hat worn by the local manager in promoting the community's future is that of a visionary, the second is that of initiator. This managerial role includes three components that create a framework for effective promotion of the future: education, citizen involvement, and process oversight. The role of initiator relates directly to the processes—comprehensive planning, strategic planning, economic development, and growth management—employed to achieve community goals and objectives.

Education The manager as educator is really an extension of the manager as leader. The general public, community leaders, organized interests, staff, and elected officials need to be informed about the importance of promoting and planning the community's future and about the processes and techniques used to chart its course. They will be much more likely to support and participate in the jurisdiction's efforts if they understand what is at stake and the nature of their role in the promotion and planning process. Widespread community participation and support are essential to success.

Educational efforts must take place before the actual promotion and planning processes begin. Education of the community, then, is a preparatory step to establish a foundation for the successful completion of the processes that follow.

Council and staff education can be achieved through a combination of work sessions and retreats that explore and explain what is involved in promoting and planning the community's future. Experts in strategic planning, economic development, and managed growth can be brought in to speak to council and staff about specific methods and techniques used as well as about the general nature of the process.

Organized meetings of business leaders, civic groups, educational organizations, neighborhood associations, and the like can be held to inform the community about upcoming promotion and planning activities. Even though these sessions are likely to be less technical than those held with the staff and council, the purpose is the same—to develop an understanding of why planning is critical, what goals the jurisdiction hopes to achieve, and how it plans to achieve them.

Extensive media campaigns involving ads in local papers, inserts with utility bills, articles in the city or county newsletter, direct mailings to residents, and town hall meetings can be used to provide information about and encourage participation in the community promotion and planning process. Media campaigns are the least technical of the educational activities, providing information at a level that can be readily understood by the public.

Managers have some direct involvement in the educational campaign with respect to staff and council instruction and occasional speaking engagements in the community. However, the manager's primary role is that of catalyst; many of the direct tasks are performed by other staff members.

Involvement of citizens   It is essential that citizens be involved in all activities that relate to promoting and planning the future of the community. The reasons for involving citizens in the visioning process were summed up in ICMA's *Future Challenges, Future Opportunities*:

Involving community members in a visioning process offers a number of advantages and opportunities. First, individuals and groups within the community bring experiences and expertise beyond that which exists within the organization. Second, by involving them throughout the process, you will generate support for the implementation phase. Finally, you will help develop an extended group of leaders and knowledgeable citizens within the community—a critical element in the democratic process.[36]

Communities are abundant sources of ideas about where they should head in the future and how they should get there. It is up to the manager to tap into as many of these sources of advice as possible. Not only is this often an avenue for coming up with innovative ideas, it is also an excellent way of getting people committed to the planning process and to particular ideas about future courses of action. After all, a plan created in a vacuum undoubtedly will remain in a vacuum.

In 1992, under the guidance of mayor Kay Granger, Fort Worth, Texas, launched Fort Worth Vision Coalition: Committee of 450,000. This project was explicitly designed to seek out and pull together many varieties of citizen input in order to frame the city's long-range agenda. Input was sought in several ways:

1. At a city-wide town hall meeting citizens identified—orally or in writing— the issues they thought important to the city.
2. A telephone survey based on the input provided by the town hall meeting was conducted and generated a database representative of the city's adult population.
3. Focus groups organized by citizen volunteers were formed to react to the findings of the telephone survey.
4. Updates were aired on the community-access channel to keep residents informed of the progress of the project.
5. Citizen committees, which focused on particular elements of the process such as council district meetings, youth involvement, a newspaper survey,

the telephone survey, and citizen issues and concerns, continued to refine and monitor the participation effort.

6. Special council district-based town meetings were held to set further priorities and amplify the agenda for community action.

Although there is no single best way to achieve effective citizen participation, the Fort Worth project is an excellent example of a multifaceted participatory model that incorporates several citizen participation techniques. By the early 1990s, citizen involvement had become an expected and necessary element of all community promotion and planning endeavors. Today's managers must integrate some combination of participatory techniques into their efforts to chart the community's future.

Process oversight   Because promotion of the community's future involves a number of different planning processes that cut across departmental lines and involve private as well as public players, responsibility for oversight of all processes resides in the manager's office. Unlike comprehensive planning, which carries with it a defined and accepted series of steps, the processes developed to promote a community's future vary from jurisdiction to jurisdiction. A rural county may be able to use strategic planning alone to monitor critical issues and design action programs. A large city may combine strategic planning, economic development, and growth management to promote the community's future.

Whether the task involves bringing together a planning team with different areas of expertise to engage in strategic planning or integrating the work of many professionals working in different areas, once again managerial leadership is necessary to keep the planning effort on track.

Implementation

Planning without paying attention to implementation is similar to the behavior of a football coach who designs a detailed and intricate strategy for the championship game and then, on game day, throws the plan out the window in favor of the make-it-up-as-you-go approach. The players may prefer the flexibility of the latter, and the game may still be won, but uncertainty and lack of organization increase the risk of a less than desirable outcome—for the football team and for the community.

The final promotion and planning role of the manager concerns linking planning and action strategies through implementation. Today, the stakes are too high to allow plans to sit on the shelf, as so many plans have done in the past. In order to deal effectively with the critical issues facing the community—issues that have the potential to dramatically alter the future—plans must be implemented through their associated strategies.

There is no guarantee that the strategies selected will be correct. It is quite likely that, as a result of new information or an unanticipated event, some alterations will be necessary and, in the extreme case, that new strategies will have to be developed. Regardless of the possibility of change in direction, success cannot be attained without implementation. Although actual implementation occurs in various departments, managers can provide the impetus for implementation through the budget process, public-private relationships, and plan review and revision.

Linking promotion, planning, and budgeting   The typical twenty- to thirty-year time frame of traditional comprehensive planning made it difficult for managers to relate the general plan to the yearly budget cycle. The much shorter time horizon of strategic planning makes the link between planning and budgeting much easier to attain. Managers can demonstrate to the council the necessity of funding improvements to the municipal water supply and sewage treatment systems if the functioning of these public works has been identified as a critical problem by a strategic plan.

Full support is even more likely if the public works improvements can be tied to the community's economic development program to attract and retain industry.

Capital improvements budgeting has been a major instrument of planning since the 1920s. Annual operating budgets are separate from capital budgets, which fund the long-term, large-scale capital projects financed largely through public borrowing and amortized over a number of years. Capital improvements programs (CIPs) allow for multiyear systematic scheduling of local physical improvements based on (1) public demand for the improvements; (2) the local government's ability to pay for the improvements; and (3) priorities for their completion in relation to various socioeconomic and physical developments. Effective CIP planning is essential if community infrastructure is to be maintained both for use by residents and as a part of the community's economic development efforts. Deterioration of the infrastructure may deter new business from locating in a city or county, discourage expansion of existing businesses, and contribute to business and industry leaving for a more attractive location.

The local public manager should take the lead in linking the CIP with both the general and strategic plans and with economic development efforts. Forging this link is critical to effective implementation of short- and long-range plans and economic development objectives. Successful achievements in downtown development, such as Baltimore's Inner Harbor, Cleveland's Gateway, and Fort Lauderdale's New River, link planning with CIPs.

Linking the public and private sector With the growth of public-private partnerships and privatization, lines between government and business are becoming increasingly blurred. As discussed earlier in this chapter, economic development activities offer an excellent opportunity for an ongoing relationship between the public and private sectors, through which they may provide joint funding for programs of benefit to the community and its business interests.

If economic development continues to unite public and private sectors, it is likely that the days of economic development programs that are funded solely with public funds will disappear. A 1987 survey commissioned by Lakeland, Florida, of several hundred cities found that two-thirds of local economic development campaigns were run by some form of independent agency that received funding from both the public and private sectors.[37]

The manager—often in conjunction with elected officials—will be a key player in establishing and maintaining whatever public-private relationships that develop, regardless of the form they take. The city or county must retain sufficient involvement in the organizational structure so that community goals do not become subservient to the goals of the business community, especially when the jurisdiction has developed a growth management system as the guiding framework for economic development.

Reviewing and revising plans Although much of a local manager's role involves gaining a broad and deep commitment to the community planning process, it is equally important to avoid being overcommitted to outdated plans. As Bertram Gross writes: "When a plan is thoroughly 'sold' to all who are involved in its operations, it tends to take on 'a life of its own.' The sunk costs invested in the development of purposefulness may make its scrapping, or even any major change, seem inordinately expensive—as in the case of a battleship which is half constructed.[38]

There is less chance of following outdated plans today if the jurisdiction uses strategic planning, alone or in conjunction with comprehensive planning. The strategic planning process, as well as the plans developed for economic development and growth management, forces communities to continually examine their plans and action strategies. Corrections, or in some cases substitutions, are possible because the investments of both time and money are much less. For example, planned marketplace projects proved disastrous in Toledo, Ohio, and Flint, Michigan. Rather than simply forsaking the idea of development, these cities replaced the original concept with mixed-use developments that emphasize retail space, housing, and offices.[39]

The manager plays an important role in monitoring and review by prodding the community into an ongoing reassessment of plans and projects. Too often in the past, oversight of planning has been left totally in the hands of the planners. Placing responsibility for review in the hands of the manager assures that oversight becomes a component of the mainstream managerial decision-making process. Managers are often in a much better position than traditional planners to make certain that monitoring and review are used to update and revise plans and strategies when necessary.

Conclusion

None of the three promotion and planning roles or the activities associated with them convert the manager into a planner. Despite the integration of various promotion and planning activities into the manager's duties, he or she will still rely on others with appropriate expertise to carry out the primary planning functions. The common ingredient in all three promotion and planning roles is leadership. Effective performance of the three roles by the manager creates a positive framework that results in the manager becoming a key actor and primary facilitator in the successful effort to promote and plan the community's future.

Recap

This chapter stresses that rapid economic, social, demographic, and technological change make the future difficult to predict and plan for. Yet the complexity and uncertainty that make the task of planning difficult make effective planning a necessity. Local government managers are increasingly recognizing that planning and promoting a community's future must go beyond the traditional activities of the planning department; communities today must chart their future through a range of planning activities that take into account a number of complex factors that may affect the community's quality of life.

The chapter touched on some of the critical trends that make planning for the future essential: an increasingly diverse population; global economic competition; serious social issues such as quality of education and drug abuse; infrastructure decay; and environmental problems.

In planning for a future made uncertain by these trends, local government managers are increasingly using community-wide strategic planning as a tool with which to supplement traditional comprehensive planning. The chapter therefore explained the strategic planning process and the necessity for widespread community participation in it.

The first step in strategic planning is to scan the environment to identify critical issues and problems that could affect the community's future. For many communities, economic development emerges as a crucial issue for community survival. A substantial part of the chapter was devoted to the discussion of changed local economic conditions, the three main approaches to economic development, and the costs (both direct and indirect) of economic development and the question of who should pay for these costs.

Many local government officials now recognize that rapid economic development often has disadvantages as well as benefits. A community that is concerned with improving the quality of life for all its residents will find that a system for managed growth is the most effective way of avoiding some of the negative consequences of economic growth. Growth management objectives and techniques were discussed, as were the political obstacles that a growth management program may encounter.

Planning has become so vital to safeguarding the community's future quality of life that responsibility for it cannot rest with the planning department alone; overall responsibility for promoting and planning the community's future must lie with the local government manager.

The last section of the chapter pointed out that managers wear three hats in promoting the future:

First, the manager must play a visionary role in thinking about the future of the community and pull together people and processes to make that future vision a reality.

Second, the manager must be the key initiator in promotion and planning activities, achieving an effective process through education, citizen involvement, and process oversight.

Third, the manager must integrate planning and action through implementation that links planning activities with budgeting, integrates public and private resources, and incorporates plan review and revision into managerial decision making.

Checklist for strategic planning

The following outline of steps in the strategic planning process may be useful to local government managers as they embark upon strategic planning for their community.

I. Identify the need for strategic planning
    A. Explain the benefits of the strategic planning process
    B. Explain the strategic planning process
    C. Solicit support for the strategic planning process from
       1. Elected officials
       2. Senior appointed officials
       3. Department heads and key staff
       4. Citizens

II. Announce the decision to use the process and the expected benefits to
    A. Employees
    B. Key appointed members of boards, commissions, etc.
    C. The press, newsletters, etc.
    D. Citizens and other users of public services

III. Determine the structure of the process
    A. Decision-making approach (top-down, bottom-up, or combination)
    B. Review process
    C. Approval process
    D. Schedule

IV. Select the participants
    A. Elected officials
    B. Senior appointed officials
    C. Employees
    D. Public school officials
    E. External representatives
       1. Citizens at-large or citizen groups
       2. Board and commission members
       3. The business community
       4. Interest groups

V. Empanel the group
    A. Convene the first meeting
    B. Announce, appoint, or select a chairman
    C. Issue the charge to the group

      D. Review the schedule
         1. Meetings
         2. Products
         3. First draft
         4. Final draft
         5. Reporting requirements and the review process
         6. The approval process
         7. Timing of the implementation
      E. Announce support and incentives for the planning group
         1. Rewards of success
         2. Support of the local leadership
         3. Guidance available
      F. Develop committee structure, membership, and operating principles

VI. Lay the groundwork
      A. Identify the mission for the local charter, state law, or other source
      B. Develop a mission statement if none exists
      C. Through interviews and other means, identify key local decision-makers and their inherent beliefs

VII. Conduct the environmental scan
      A. Structure the scanning matrix
         1. Identify the environments to be scanned
         2. Identify the environmental factors to be observed in each environment
      B. Using an environmental scanning matrix, assign the review process for each cell (each factor within each environment) to a person or persons
      C. Ensure that participants develop a full understanding of each cell
      D. Reconvene the planning group or assemble the intelligence it has gathered
      E. Describe possible scenarios for the future
      F. Detail the single description which most accurately depicts the future
      G. Ensure that participants discuss the description of the future for concurrence and understanding
      H. Review the scenario of the future and extract from it:
         1. Internal weaknesses
         2. Internal strengths
         3. External opportunities
         4. External threats

VIII. Review the scan and its conclusions
      A. Achieve the maximum consensus on goals
      B. Develop objectives for each goal
      C. Achieve the maximum consensus on objectives
      D. Develop strategies for each objective
      E. Achieve the maximum consensus on strategies
      F. Develop initial implementation plans
      G. Develop as many contingency situations as possible
      H. Develop plans for each contingency situation
      I. Develop control mechanisms and incorporate into the plan

IX. Prepare a written plan
      A. Assign writers to prepare a draft
      B. Review draft internally
      C. Revise draft as needed
      D. Submit revised draft for external review to elected officials, civic groups, and other stakeholders
      E. Revise draft again as needed

X. Submit the plan to the governing body for official adoption

XI. Publicize the plan to
   A. Constituents
   B. Media
   C. Others

XII. Implement the plan
   A. Implement strategies
   B. Design and institute controls
   C. Monitor and assess ongoing performance
   D. Assess feedback and revise implementation plans as needed

XIII. Prepare for next planning cycle
   A. Ensure that feedback is captured for future planning cycles
   B. Outline and schedule next planning cycle

Source: Gerald L. Gordon, *Strategic Planning for Local Government* (Washington, DC: ICMA, 1993), 81–83.

1 John M. Levy, *Contemporary Urban Planning* (Englewood Cliffs, NJ: Prentice Hall), xvii.

2 Amy Cohen Paul, *Future Challenges, Future Opportunities: The Final Report of the ICMA FutureVisions Consortium* (Washington, DC: ICMA), 1.

3 Ibid.

4 Victor DeSantis, "State, Local, and Council Relations: Managers' Perceptions," *Baseline Data Report* 23 (March/April 1991): 11–13.

5 Barry Bozeman, "Strategic Public Management and Productivity: A Firehouse Theory," *State Government* 56 (1983): 2–77; John M. Bryson and William D. Roering, "Applying Private-Sector Strategic Planning in the Public Sector," *American Planning Journal* 53 (Winter 1987): 9–22; Robert B. Denhardt, "Strategic Planning in State and Local Government," *State and Local Government Review* 17 (1985): 174–179; and Douglas C. Eadie, "Putting a Powerful Tool to Practical Use: The Application of Strategic Planning in the Public Sector," *Public Administration Review* 43 (September/October 1983): 447–452.

6 See Gregory Streib, "Applying Strategic Decision Making in Local Government: Does the Promise Justify the Challenge?," *Public Productivity Review* 15 (Spring 1992) for a review of the literature detailing the pros and cons of strategic planning.

7 The process is based on material in Donna L. Sorkin, Nancy B. Ferris, and James Hudak, *Strategies for Cities and Counties: A Strategic Planning Guide* (Washington, DC: Public Technology Inc., 1984) and Jerome L. Kaufman and Harvey M. Jacobs, "A Planning Perspective on Strategic Planning," *American Planning Association Journal* 50 (Winter 1987): 23–33.

8 Quote from "Joint Statement on Economic Development," Chamber of Commerce and City of Denton, Texas, 1991.

9 Edward J. Blakely, *Planning Local Economic Development: Theory and Practice* (Newbury Park, CA: Sage, 1989), 57.

10 Jeffrey S. Luke, Curtis Reed Ventriss, B.J. Reed, and Christine M. Reed, *Managing Economic Development: A Guide to State & Local Leadership Strategies* (San Francisco: Jossey Bass, 1988), 9.

11 Luke et al., *Managing Economic Development*, 7.

12 Peter F. Drucker, "The Changed World Economy," in *Local Economic Development: Strategies for a Changing Economy*, ed. R. Scott Fosler (Washington, DC: ICMA, 1991), 8–10.

13 Todd Sloane, "Cities Confront Gloomy Scenarios," *City and State* (November 8, 1991): 9.

14 Peter K. Eisinger, *The Rise of the Entrepreneurial State*, (Madison: University of Wisconsin Press, 1988), 202.

15 See, for example, Robert L. Bland, *A Revenue Guide for Local Government* (Washington, DC: ICMA, 1989); Alberta Charney, "Intraurban Manufacturing Location Decisions and Local Tax Differentials," *Journal of Urban Economics* 18 (September 1983): 184–205; and Eisinger, *The Rise of the Entrepreneurial State*, 200–224.

16 Jack Lyne, "Quality-of-Life Factors Dominate Many Facility Location Decisions," *Site Selection Handbook* 33 (August 1988): 870.

17 Jack Lyne, "Education Ranked as Key Element in Quality of Life Equation," *Site Selection* 34 (August 1989): 946.

18 Eisinger, *The Rise of the Entrepreneurial State*, 10.

19 A number of authors share Eisinger's view on demand-side entrepreneurial development. See Blakely, *Planning Local Economic Development*; Luke et al., *Managing Economic Development*; and R. Scott Fosler, *The New Economic Role of the American States: Strategies in a Cooperative World Economy* (New York: Oxford University Press, 1988).

20 John Herbers, "The Third Wave of Economic Development," *Governing* (June 1990): 43–50.

21 Ibid.

22 John R. Logan and Harvey S. Molotch, *Urban Fortunes: The Political Economy of Place* (Los Angeles: University of California Press, 1987), 85.

23 Harvey Mototch, "The City as a Growth Machine," *American Journal of Sociology* 82 (July 1976): 320–321.

24 John DeGrove, "Forging Ahead in Growth Management," *Growth Management Innovations in Florida*, ed. Westi Jo de Haven Smith (Fort Lauderdale, FL: Center for Environmental and Urban Problems, 1988), 4.

25 Logan and Molotch, *Urban Fortunes*, 94.

26 Thomas P. Snyder and Michael A. Stegman, *Paying for Growth: Using Development Fees for Finance Infrastructure* (Washington, DC: The Urban Institute, 1987), 9.

27 Nancy Stroud, "Legal Considerations of Development Impact Fees," in *Development Impact Fees*, ed. Arthur C. Nelson (Chicago: American Planning Association, 1988), 83–94.

28 James E. Frank and Paul B. Downing, "Patterns of Impact Fee Use," in *Development Impact Fees*, ed. Arthur C. Nelson (Chicago: American Planning Association, 1988), 20.

29 Ronald K. Vogel and Bert E. Swanson, "The Growth Machine Versus the Antigrowth Coalition," *Urban Affairs Quarterly* 25 (September 1989): 66.

30 Enid F. Beaumont and Harold A. Hovey, "State, Local and Federal Development Policies," *Public Administration Review* 45 (March/April 1985): 327.

31 Katherine E. Stone and Robert H. Freilich, "Writing a Defensible Growth Ordinance," in *Balanced Growth: A Planning Guide for Local Government*, ed. John M. DeGrove (Washington, DC: ICMA, 1991), 106.

32 Elizabeth A. Deakin, "Growth Management: Past, Present, and Future," in *Balanced Growth*, 5.

33 William Fulton, "In Land-Use Planning: A Second Revolution Shifts Control to the States," *Governing* (March 1989): 42.

34 Alan Jacobs, *Making City Planning Work* (Chicago: American Society of Planning Officials, 1978), 307.

35 Harvey Perloff, *Planning the Post-Industrial City* (Washington, DC: Planners Press, 1965), 258.

36 Paul, *Future Challenges, Future Opportunities*, 9.

37 Todd Sloane, "Public-Private Ventures Help States Sell Themselves," *City and State* (October 7, 1991): 5.

38 Bertram Gross, *Organizations and Their Managing* (New York: Free Press, 1968), 577.

39 "Interest Runs Deep in Waterfront Projects," *City and State* (October 21, 1002): 21.

Relating to other governments

This book has focused so far on the local government manager's role within a single community and a single organization. However, no local government exists in a vacuum. Actions by other governments—in nearby communities, in the state capital, in Washington, indeed, in foreign countries—influence the conduct of daily business and require the manager to assume a role in intergovernmental relations. Few managers need proof that outside governments influence the major decisions that affect their community's economy, social climate, transportation system, revenue powers, air and water quality, and often even the water supply.

Local government managers recognize the importance of intergovernmental relations and are increasingly beginning to heed advice that they clearly define their relations with other governmental units and deal with them in an organized, systematic manner rather than wait until a crisis forces an intergovernmental confrontation. Local managers need, in effect, a well-thought-out "foreign policy" in dealing with other governmental units.

Intergovernmental relations take place largely on two planes—horizontal and vertical. Relations among local governments are conducted on the horizontal plane. Local government interactions with state governments and the federal government, both of which have a higher level of authority, take place on the vertical plane. In addition, local officials have become increasingly aware of the actual and potential effects of developments in other countries on the welfare of their communities.

This chapter first looks at what local government managers should know about the various sets of intergovernmental relationships and then gives some observations and practical advice about working in the intergovernmental environment.

Relations with neighboring local governments

"To put the matter bluntly, government in the United States is chaotic." Thus wrote political scientist Morton Grodzins nearly thirty years ago.[1] Grodzins had in mind both the large number of governments in the United States and the complicated set of relationships among them.

Most governments in the United States are at the local level. The total count is nearly 87,000 separate units, including 3,043 counties, 19,296 municipalities, 16,666 townships, 14,556 districts, and 33,131 special districts.[2] Over the years, the most dramatic drop has been in the number of school districts, and the most dramatic increase has been in the number of special districts. Special districts are commonly created to deal with such matters as irrigation, flood control, and soil and water conservation.

Metropolitan areas may contain hundreds of separate local government units. What is the significance of having so many? The answer depends on who is asked. Looking at metropolitan areas, some see an unhealthy fragmentation of governmental authority; others see a dynamic system of local interaction.

Those who take the first perspective argue that a large number of separate governments creates problems such as the duplication of services, taxing and service inequities, ruinous competition resulting in giveaways to large businesses, public confusion over which government is responsible for what, and the inability to focus effectively on area-wide problems.

Defenders of fragmentation argue that a large number of local governments is desirable because it allows citizens to choose the lifestyle and level of services they want and keeps government more accessible and accountable to the people. Those who take this viewpoint also often emphasize the value of competition among local units, for example, in keeping taxes down and encouraging more efficiency.[3]

Both perspectives contain elements of truth. Throughout the United States one finds both interlocal competition, which often has positive as well as negative effects, and interlocal cooperation. Having a large number of separate local governments within a metropolitan area or region, moreover, does not necessarily mean functional fragmentation or the inability to deliver services (see accompanying sidebar).

Governing a metropolitan county

The jurisdictional fragmentation of Allegheny County, Pennsylvania, is both extraordinary and long-standing—most of the county's 130 municipalities have existed since World War I. For a time, the city of Pittsburgh was able to expand unilaterally, and it absorbed the community of Allegheny over the objections of residents. Eventually, however, the rules governing consolidation of municipalities prohibited further expansion without the consent of the citizens affected.

According to the Bureau of the Census, Allegheny is the most fragmented of the counties in the United States with populations of more than a million. Allegheny County has 4 cities, 84 boroughs, 42 townships, 43 school districts plus 2 intermediate education units, and 149 municipal authorities. This number does not include the county's 250 volunteer fire companies, 8 councils of governments, or 9 education "jointures" that provide for special and vocational-technical education. If a high density of governmental units creates a jurisdictional "jungle" through which citizens wander in a vain search for local services, Allegheny County should be marked with signs warning away unsuspecting visitors—and potential residents.

Jurisdictional fragmentation, however, does not necessarily lead to functional fragmentation. Jurisdictional fragmentation means that a metropolitan area contains many independent political jurisdictions. Functional fragmentation means the lack of coordination in performing functions and services. Newcomers to Allegheny County need not fear that they are entering a land where local government has spun out of control. On the contrary, there is a wide range of options among diversely governed local communities, knit together in various ways that form discernible patterns of metropolitan organization.

A major reason that jurisdictional fragmentation does not create insuperable barriers to coordination and problem solving in Allegheny County is the contribution of the county government. Because the county is fully incorporated, the jurisdiction of the county government is complementary rather than competitive. County officials are free to concentrate their energies on providing and producing a limited number of services and otherwise relating in productive ways to municipal governments. They have given considerable attention to problems that spill over municipal borders and to assisting distressed communities.

Source: Adapted from United States Advisory Commission on Intergovernmental Relations, *Metropolitan Organization: The Allegheny County Case* (Washington, DC: GPO, 1992), 81, 87.

Over the years there has been considerable discussion over the desirability of vesting authority in a single government in metropolitan areas—either by using an existing jurisdiction such as a county as the base or creating an entirely new entity. However, reform of this nature has been rare. A more common approach has been a federated or two-tier system, in which various area-wide functions are assigned to area-wide governments and local functions remain with local governments.

Area-wide services may be provided by special district governments or authorities concerned with only a single service such as sewage disposal, mass transit, libraries, or water supply. General purpose governments such as counties and councils of governments have increasingly assumed responsibility for area-wide services.

To a certain extent, relations among local units of government in metropolitan areas or regions resemble those between nations. Each local government pursues its self-interest, as it sees that interest. Each government seeks to maintain its legal autonomy and territorial integrity and competes with other units for scarce resources, such as profitable economic enterprises. Thus, relations between local governments may be characterized by conflict. On the other hand, enlightened self-interest may encourage otherwise competing local governments to open diplomatic relations with each other and produce agreements in order to avoid conflict or to solve common problems.

Interlocal cooperative activities

Interlocal arrangements are entered into by all types and sizes of local governments in the United States for a wide variety of purposes.[4] Among the broader regional cooperative efforts, for example, is the arrangement forged by Montgomery County, Ohio, with Dayton and twenty-two other municipalities to bring about economic development. The county sets aside revenues from its sales tax to fund selected projects proposed by participating cities and townships. Elsewhere, smaller jurisdictions engage in a variety of activities. For example, in the early 1990s, the village of Nyack, New York, dissolved its police force and began contracting for police services with neighboring jurisdictions in order to hold down costs. Other small municipalities in the state of New York pool their garbage to make better use of recycling plants. To improve their administrative capabilities, some small municipalities in Pennsylvania share the services of a circuit-riding professional manager.

Nationally, the cooperative pattern includes special-purpose governments as well as multipurpose governments such as cities and counties. School districts, for example, are involved in cooperative activities with each other and with other units of government. In Bergen County, New Jersey, two school boards joined together to hire a private food-service company, saving $40,000 for each community. In Westchester County, New York, a two-way video monitor brought instruction in Latin to classrooms in different communities.[5]

City governments have taken a new interest in local public education and have initiated several types of partnerships with independent school districts. This interest reflects in part the feeling that "cities are increasingly being judged—by both the business community and the citizenry—on the reputation of their public education."[6] Cities thus have become advocates for education and its improvement (see the sidebar on p. 170).

In many parts of the United States, not only intergovernmental agreements but broader intercommunity partnerships exist in which nonprofit, academic, civic, and private organizations work with local government officials in addressing regional issues (see the sidebar on p. 171). It is not unusual to find a private firm contracting with several cities to provide services such as tax billing and refuse collection. Local managers have also found that private firms have research and development capacities that can be tapped to resolve regional problems such as solid waste

Initiatives in education: Phoenix

In the 1980s, Phoenix, Arizona, focused much of its economic development efforts on sharpening its competitive edge. To help define the role of the municipal government in economic development, the mayor and city council commissioned a study by an outside consulting group. The group's report reflected the concern of local business and industry about the perceived lack of preparedness of students entering the workforce.

The report noted that a key element in any economic development agenda is an excellent education system, and it strongly recommended that Phoenix become involved in education even though the city had no statutory authority to do so. In Phoenix, as in Arizona generally, there is a strong tradition of local control of school districts. The city was therefore cautious about what role to take with the 28 separate school districts within its 435 square miles.

The mayor and city council appointed an ad hoc citizens' committee to study the issue and recommend action. The committee, recognizing that the economic viability of the community was inextricably entwined with the quality of public education, proposed a role for the city that encompassed supporting the efforts of the schools, promoting excellence in education, celebrating diversity, and where appropriate, developing city programs and policies that would enhance the quality of education in Phoenix. The committee also recommended hiring an education coordinator and establishing a permanent education commission. All recommendations were unanimously accepted.

Although historically a number of city departments had been involved with the schools, the commitment of the mayor and city council strengthened the association. Existing activities—such as Head Start, job training, drug-education classes, school safety promotions, and recreation and arts programs—were given higher priority.

In addition, Phoenix developed a number of formal and informal collaborations with schools and colleges. The CARE Center (Clearinghouse for Advisement, Referral, and Education) was established by bringing together staff from several agencies, schools, colleges, and city departments to examine the overwhelming need of the students of South Mountain High School for social services. The Urban Teachers Corps Partnership was formed to address the need for more minority and bilingual teachers. The establishment of such programs reflects the community's awareness of the special requirements of the city's schoolchildren and their families—an awareness clearly heightened by the city's educational initiative.

Source: Adapted from a working paper by Deborah Dillion, Education Program Director, City of Phoenix, and Nancy Jordan, Maricopa Community College.

management. Broader based business associations sometimes take leadership on community issues. An example is the Greater Cleveland Growth Association, which has participated in a capital investment strategy for the Cleveland area.[7]

Types of agreement

Local intergovernmental agreements range from the highly informal, "handshake" variety to highly formal and legally complex types. Informal agreements—such as one that allows a jurisdiction to temporarily use a streetsweeper belonging to another—are easily arranged. Among the formal means by which local governments cooperate are (1) contracts and agreements, (2) the transfer of functions, and (3) the use of interjurisdictional agencies.

Homelessness: overcoming jurisdictional disputes in Portland   The city of Portland and Multnomah County in Oregon recognized that jurisdictional disputes can inhibit overall planning, create duplication of effort, and perpetuate gaps in homeless services. In 1984, they reached an intergovernmental agreement to resolve disputes related to meeting emergency needs. When Mayor J. E. Bud Clark took office in 1985, he further enhanced intergovernmental cooperation by appointing a task force to examine ways to improve methods for meeting emergency needs within the city and county.

The task force led to the formation of an Emergency Basic Needs Committee (EBNC) to investigate client needs and develop the best service delivery model in seven basic areas: shelter, food, case management, health services, energy assistance, transportation, and employment. Representatives from the city, the county, United Way, the Housing Authority of Portland, and citizen groups worked through EBNC to address jurisdictional disputes, as well as overlaps and gaps in services within the city and county. The EBNC was responsible for developing policy and for recommending budgeting and planning procedures for homeless issues to the city council and board of county commissioners.

On the basis of EBNC's assessment of basic needs, a consultant created a service delivery model to meet those needs. After the model was approved by the participating organizations, the city and county service providers voluntarily reorganized in accordance with the model and created a community action agency (CAA). The EBNC completed its work and disbanded on July 1, 1988.

The CAA now has the responsibility for comprehensive planning. It coordinates the independent service providers that make up Portland/Multnomah's system for delivering services to the homeless and pursues federal, state, and local funding sources. Success can be claimed on many fronts:

The emergency shelter system has the capacity to provide for all those who need shelter.

A comprehensive housing program, which would provide for affordable permanent housing, is being developed.

Employment opportunities for homeless people are now available through several programs including employment counseling, high school equivalency classes, and job placement.

City and county services have been reorganized to eliminate overlaps and gaps in service and to end jurisdictional disputes.

Private organizations have an opportunity to better target their efforts.

Coordinating requests for funding through the EBNC has yielded an additional $6 million from the Stewart B. McKinney Homeless Assistance Act.

The success of the EBNC serves as a model for cooperation that can be applied to long-term homeless issues as they become evident.

Source: Adapted from Catherine Zudak, "Fragmented Approach to Homelessness," *Public Management* (March 1992): 10, 13.

Contracts and agreements   Under the system of local contracting, one unit of local government purchases a service from another. Counties and municipalities in metropolitan areas in particular have found contracting beneficial. Through service agreements, two or more entities jointly plan, finance, or deliver services. Intergovernmental service agreements are commonly used to provide detention facilities, police training, street lighting, refuse collection, libraries, solid waste disposal, water, and police crime-laboratory services. Agreements often lower costs through economies of scale and enable local governments to do what they cannot do by themselves.

Transfer of functions   Localities commonly transfer service responsibilities from one local government to another—for example, from cities to counties—as allowed by state law. To avoid overlap and fragmentation, counties in various parts of the country have assumed responsibility from municipal governments for jails, libraries, and street repairs, for example. Also increasingly shifted to the county are water and sewer services, which require considerable capital investment, and police and fire department radio systems.

Interjurisdictional agencies   In any given state, various types of regional or metropolitan entities exist. Some, such as councils of governments (COGs) are general, multipurpose bodies; others deal only with specific issues, such as air pollution or mass transportation. (COGs are discussed in more detail later in this chapter.)

Increase in regional cooperation

The late 1980s and early 1990s brought an increased emphasis on cooperative endeavors and improved regional problem solving. Interlocal contracting has been driven principally by cost considerations. Joint ventures have increased, in part, as a way of coping with reductions in federal aid and the financial constraints caused by general economic difficulties. Joint actions are also more popular because localities need to share the expense of costly technological innovations in service areas such as solid waste management. Improved regional problem solving has also been encouraged by public awareness of transportation needs and other such problems that transcend local boundaries.[8]

Much intergovernmental cooperation is voluntary. In many places, local officials and leaders agree that the well-being of their communities is directly related to the success of regional problem-solving efforts. To some extent, however, what passes for "voluntary" cooperation among local officials reflects the fear that if local units do not cooperate, the state will mandate solutions to area-wide problems. As the ICMA FutureVisions Consortium warned: "Increasingly, local governments face problems that cannot be addressed by single jurisdictions. Our future depends on comprehensive solutions to issues that range from transportation, solid waste management, and air quality control to drugs, homelessness, and poverty . . . If local governments do not willingly collaborate to address regional issues, solutions are likely to be mandated by the state."[9]

Local governments are unlike autonomous nations in that they are subject to the control of their state government. A growing number of states, for example, require local governments to work together in preparing regional plans to meet the interrelated goals of controlling growth, combating environmental problems such as air and water pollution, and providing an adequate infrastructure. Some observers label this approach "top down" regionalism.[10] There is already a considerable amount of top down regionalism that emanates from the states rather than "bottoms up" regionalism that emanates from the voluntary efforts of local units. Some of the problems involved in these types of arrangements are discussed later in this chapter, in the section concerning local government relations with the states.

New income for UK communities

The Metropolitan Consortium, which currently counts among its members some 140 metropolitan, county, and district councils in the United Kingdom, seeks to maximize income-generating opportunities for its members. It engages in collective negotiation with service providers on behalf of its members, brokers national and regional sponsorships that produce advertising revenues, and operates an information exchange that provides members with new income ideas. There is no membership charge for local authorities since the consortium's operating costs are met by private industry fees and commissions paid to the consortium for recommending income-generating projects to members for their consideration. Members are not obligated to join any one scheme. Decisions to participate are left entirely up to each member.

In its first year of operations, the consortium achieved the equivalent of about half a million dollars in income for its membership. Income of nearly $5 million was projected for 1993, and the organizers aim for project income in the $80-million annual range by the end of the decade.

Income has been generated for member authorities by poster and ticket advertising as well as by the launch of a new line of street furniture sponsored by commercial suppliers without cost to local authorities. Future plans include income from municipal golf courses, revenue from products sold from vending machines on public premises, sponsorship income from sports events organized under local government auspices, and revenue from sponsored street signs and bus shelters. A marketing team fielded by the consortium is looking into new possibilities to generate income from shopping centers and municipal markets, local authority mailings, transport systems, libraries, and museums.

The consortium's advisory teams are staffed by senior executive officers from local jurisdictions; the board, which decides whether to recommend new projects to members, is made up of elected officials. When an income-generating scheme is recommended to member authorities, the consortium negotiates the most favorable terms for participating members.

Source: *Public Innovation Abroad* (January 1992): 4.

Changing the system

Many students of intergovernmental cooperation have concluded that the relationships among local units of government could be improved in several respects. The need for actual change, of course, varies from area to area and, as noted, may be a matter of considerable disagreement.

One commonly prescribed reform is to reduce the number of special districts and authorities—including those operating at the regional level—in favor of multipurpose and politically accountable units of government. Special districts and authorities play positive roles in providing needed environmental, transportation, housing, water, sewage, and other services. They make it possible for government to target costs to specific groups of people, thus avoiding general increases in property taxes. At the same time, however, they add to the fragmentation of government and to problems of political accountability. Moreover, functions provided by special districts or authorities may be equally well provided by multipurpose governments such as cities or counties.

Another set of recommendations focuses on minimizing potential problems caused by the emergence of numerous independent municipal governments. To guard against this type of fragmentation, reformers have sought state laws that make annexation easier and incorporation more difficult. Easier annexation laws encour-

Interlocal cooperation

The best policy alternative to the problem of building administrative capacity among local governments is the expansion of local intergovernmental cooperation. Most municipal managers and many political leaders support increased cooperation, and they tend to realize that significant improvements in services, more professional administration, and reductions in total costs can be achieved through such cooperation.

Source: Jim Seroka, "Community Growth and Administrative Capacity," *National Civic Review* (January/February 1988): 42–46.

age cities to expand their boundaries into unincorporated territory, thus preventing the growth of new municipal governments. More difficult incorporation laws have the same effect. Another reform, proposed to minimize problems caused by population growth in unincorporated areas, is state legislation strengthening the extraterritorial authority of cities to control land use in areas beyond their boundaries.

Perhaps all that is needed in terms of reform in many jurisdictions is to strengthen cooperation by making local contracting and service agreements easier to enter into and by making the transfer of functions less difficult. Reformers, however, have generally maintained that attention should also be given to shifting greater responsibilities to multipurpose, politically accountable entities with broad metropolitan or regional jurisdictions. For this reason, much consideration has been given to county governments and to councils of governments.

County governments   County governments serve about 90 percent of the United States population; with the exception of Connecticut and Rhode Island, they exist in all states. Counties, in contrast to municipalities, have traditionally functioned as administrative units for the states in providing such services as welfare, health care, road construction and maintenance, education, and the administration of justice. The state controls the major decisions regarding the level and quality of these services. Laws affecting the traditional county vest authority in a board of commissioners or supervisors and further disperse authority among a large number of elected officials—the sheriff, county attorney, country treasurer, county assessor, and so forth—who are often known as "row" officers. County governments, however, have undergone considerable change in services offered, structure, and operation since the 1950s.

Changes in services offered   In addition to the traditional services required by the state, many counties now provide services to people in unincorporated areas comparable to those provided in cities by municipalities. In some places, counties are the sole direct provider of services. In other places, they provide services through some type of arrangement with other governments—often, but not exclusively, with other local governments.

The direct provision of municipal services is a relatively recent addition to the responsibilities of county governments necessitated by the rapid growth of "noncities" in the unincorporated areas of metropolitan counties. In states such as Florida, where more than half of the population resides in such areas, counties provide water and sewer utilities, police and fire protection, waste collection and disposal, mass transit, law enforcement, and other services.

Changes in structure   Several states give counties generally or certain categories of counties home-rule charters that allow them to provide many of the services once performed only by municipalities. As counties have assumed new responsibilities, many have changed their governmental structures from the traditional com-

Alamosa: successful intergovernmental relations   The relationship between a municipality and its county can be intricate, and the process of turning around a relationship mired in distrust can be difficult. But the city and county of Alamosa have shown that it can be done. Here is how they worked to improve their relationship.

Relations between the city of Alamosa and Alamosa County, Colorado, had reached a low point in the mid 1980s for the same reasons that relations between many cities and counties deteriorate: mistrust, an "us vs. them" attitude, and misunderstanding of the level of each other's legal authority and responsibility.

After the completion of a study that recommended consolidation of the city and county governments, these problems worsened. Although the recommendations were intended to break down barriers and create the means to merge the functions of the city and county, they drove a spike between the two governments.

In 1988, when both the city and the county hired new managers, the problem had reached the point that the city was on the verge of cutting off services to residents of unincorporated areas and the county was preparing to cut off services to city residents in retaliation. Discussions between the two governments were always attended by their legal staffs. There were frequent

threats of lawsuits, and working through arbitrators seemed to be the only way to make progress.

There were two main issues: First, elected officials from both the city and county felt that their positions were threatened by the recommendations. Second, then-current intergovernmental agreements had been in effect in some cases for forty years. The only updates had been arranged through "gentlemen's agreements" and back-room politics.

The process used in Alamosa to improve city-county relations is not new. Officials simply applied good management techniques, dealing with one another in an open, communicative manner. Educational meetings for members of the city council and board of county commissioners were held, in addition to other formal and informal meetings. Officials worked together to remove obstacles that in the past had prevented them from achieving solutions to problems in city-county relations. In the end, this team-building, cooperative approach transcended city and county politics and benefited all the residents of the city of Alamosa and Alamosa County.

Source: Abridged and adapted from Michael Hackett and James Malloy, "Alamosa: A Successful Approach to Intergovernmental Relations," *Colorado Municipalities* 68 (January–February 1992).

mission form to a more centralized model headed by an appointed administrator or an elected executive. Nevertheless, most have retained a long list of independently elected row officers.

Those concerned with shifting responsibilities to multipurpose, politically accountable entities with broad metropolitan or regional jurisdiction naturally think first of the county government. An improved role for the county is particularly feasible in the more than 100 single-county metropolitan areas. The larger jurisdiction of counties, compared to municipal governments, makes them potentially better able to effectively deal with problems such as environmental protection and transportation. Compared to special authorities, counties offer well-established general purpose governments directly accountable to the voters. Shifting responsibilities to the county also may provide economies of scale and a broader and more stable tax base.

One approach to making greater use of the county's capabilities is simply to transfer functions to it on a piecemeal basis, as has been done in various parts of the country over the last several decades. Alternatively, the county role could be increased by reorganizing the county's charter to give it general responsibility for the provision of area-wide functions, and leaving local matters to municipal governments. Exactly which services should be provided on an area-wide basis and which on a local basis—and who should pay for them—may be a matter of considerable dispute. This type of two-tier government or metropolitan federation has been experimented with in Dade County, Florida, since 1957. Experiments of this nature have been inspired by the use of federated governments for some metropolitan areas in Canada, beginning with Toronto in 1953. (See accompanying sidebar.)

A federated system may be easier to adopt than a complete consolidation of city and county governments because it reduces the amount of change involved. Only

---

Toronto: a federative government

In contrast to Miami, Toronto represents a true federative government. Whereas Dade County has unincorporated areas in which the two-tier system does not operate, Toronto's two levels of government operate throughout the entire metropolitan area. A second difference lies in the nature of representation: in Miami, the city governments are not represented in the county government, while in Toronto, the city governments have been represented on the Metropolitan Council from the very beginning.

By the 1950s, Toronto was plagued with the same metropolitan growth problems that plagued United States metropolises. Because of governmental fragmentation, there was an inability to plan regionally. The metropolis was without adequate water and sewer facilities and a modern, coordinated public transit system, and individual jurisdictions were unable to finance major projects and programs.

In 1953 the Ontario Province Municipal Board studied various plans for coping with these metropolitan problems and recommended a federal system that would guarantee the continued existence of the thirteen existing municipalities in the Toronto area. Based on these recommendations, the Ontario Province legislature created a 24-member Metropolitan Council for the Toronto area. Half of the members were municipal officials from the city of Toronto, and the other twelve were municipal officials from each of the twelve suburbs.

The Metropolitan Council was made responsible for providing services that transcended local boundaries. These primarily included property assessment, construction and maintenance of freeways, and development of regional parks. Other functions such as street lights, provision of public health services, fire protection, and marriage licenses were left to the individual municipalities.

The early years of metropolitan government in Toronto were a time of unmitigated success in providing services that had been neglected. The water and sewer systems were greatly expanded. More schools were built. An extensive program of expressway construction was undertaken. Subway and bus lines were extended. A regional park was created. Because of the very high financial rating given the Metropolitan Council, it was estimated that having metro handle all the capital financing costs saved over $50 million in interest charges during the first ten years of its existence.

Source: Adapted from John J. Harrigan, *Political Change in the Metropolis*, 3d ed. (Little Brown, Co., 1985), 326–327. Reprinted by permission of HarperCollins College Publishers.

a few city-county consolidations have taken place in the last forty years. Examples are those of Davidson County and Nashville, Tennessee, in 1962; Duval County and Jacksonville, Florida, in 1967; and Marion County and Indianapolis, Indiana, in 1969. The last example was brought about by an act of the state legislature; no vote was taken in the local jurisdictions affected. Legislatures generally, however, have required that consolidation proposals be approved by voters in each of the jurisdictions involved.

Securing voter approval for city-county consolidations requires enlisting the active support of local citizens and holding numerous public hearings. Perhaps more important, successful efforts appear to depend on the existence of a crisis in public-service provision or a scandal that has generated public support for reform. Consolidation attempts are apt to be opposed by incumbent office-holders, both elected and appointed, who see the prospect of losing their jobs. Opposition is also likely to come from those who champion retaining home rule and the identity of their local units or who fear an increase in taxation because of consolidation. Smaller units of government, if given the opportunity, may well refuse to become part of the consolidation. Minorities in large cities also may see a loss of political power through consolidation with suburban governments.

Given all these obstacles, it comes as no surprise that proposals for city-county consolidation are likely to be rejected by the voters—five of six recent attempts have failed at the polls.[11] For this reason, consolidation has fallen from favor as a remedy for improving metropolitan government. Reformers have turned instead to less drastic restructuring and to various types of cooperative activities.

Changes in operation   Increasing the responsibilities of counties has often been made contingent on making them more streamlined, professional, and creditable entities. Progress has been made toward these goals, especially in metropolitan areas, through structural changes designed to centralize authority and through the hiring of professionally trained personnel.[12] The increased professionalism of administrators has made it easier for counties to cooperate with neighboring jurisdictions. Indeed, Vincent L. Marando and Mavis Mann Reeves have concluded: "Differentials between the professional competence of counties and cities need no longer stand in the way of effective partnerships. Professional parity between county and city administrators fosters communication, increased interaction, and the search for joint approaches to problem solving.[13] Survey data indicate that county officials generally think their units are willing and able, both politically and administratively, to undertake new responsibilities. They do, however, think that the lack of state financial support severely limits their ability to perform their functions.[14]

Councils of governments   Counties are the natural building blocks for metropolitan or regional governments in many parts of the country. In sprawling areas extending into two or more counties, however, councils of governments, of which counties are a part, could be more suitable units of multipurpose regional government.

COGs are voluntary or state-mandated associations of governments. A majority of the approximately 500 regional councils in the United States serve governments in specific metropolitan areas or groups of metropolitan areas. Membership varies greatly. The Association of Bay Area Governments in Oakland, California, has 84 member cities and 8 member counties. The Washington Metropolitan Council of Governments has 19 city and county members representing the District of Columbia and jurisdictions in suburban Maryland and Virginia. The governing board of the council represents each local government and members of the Virginia and Maryland state legislatures.

Federal requirements that applications for federal grants be compatible with metropolitan or regional plans stimulated the development of COGs in the 1960s and 1970s. COGs assumed a "review and comment" role in the development of grant applications, and they received substantial funding from the federal government. Federal encouragement and support for COGs, however, was withdrawn during the Reagan administration.

Most councils survived by assuming some state functions and receiving greater state support. Some also sought and received more local fiscal contributions, and some became regional service agencies—providing, for example, planning services to constituent local units. In short, during the 1980s COGs were driven by state and local agendas rather than by a national agenda. More recently, the federal government has given COGs considerable decisional and allocational responsibilities under the Intermodal Surface Transportation Efficiency Act passed in 1991.

The role played by COGs in regard to intergovernmental planning and the coordination of federally aided projects varies from state to state. Most councils continue to perform some type of clearinghouse function and to be catalysts for regional problem solving. In many cases, they are the only organization that generates information for metropolitan-wide planning. In addition to their roles in long-range intergovernmental planning, COGs provide various types of technical assistance under contract to member governments.

Councils of governments historically have been the principal instruments for addressing regional problems; however, they typically play only an advisory role in regional policymaking, and their decisions have little binding authority over member units. They also tend "to be committed to the preservation of home rule, reflecting the composition of their governing boards."[15]

At the same time, COGs have considerable potential as a means by which regional problem solving can be undertaken in a comprehensive fashion. At times, this has meant the involvement not only of local government, but also of other actors and institutions in the community critical to the resolution of conflict. The Mid-America Regional Council in the Kansas City metropolitan area, for example, has frequently used regional task forces composed of business, civic, and government leaders to address problems such as transportation and air quality.

Some COGs have evolved into regional entities that amount to multipurpose special districts with real powers. Portland, Oregon's Metropolitan Service District, a multipurpose government run by officials directly elected by voters, is a prototype. Metro extends into three counties and is active in area planning, environmental protection, and operating such enterprises as the zoo and convention facilities.

The full development of councils as viable units of regional government awaits large-scale efforts to increase citizen participation in the governing system. In order for COGs to be vested with more authority, they need the political legitimacy provided by a public constituency. Several COGs have taken steps away from reliance on elected officials toward more direct citizen involvement through, for example, the creation of short-term task forces and the use of advisory committees.[16]

Other regional approaches   As states increase in population and confront new problems, pressures may prompt legislatures to consider establishing a new frontier for local government at the regional rather than county level. In 1991, for example, leaders in the California legislature called for a tier of thirteen regional governments superior to the state's fifty-eight counties to cope with the transportation, pollution, housing, and other problems created by population growth. Reasons advanced for the change centered on the need for greater area-wide planning and regulation, a broader and fairer tax base, and improved economies of scale—the same arguments often used for making the county a metropolitan government.[17]

Along with reforms designed to strengthen the cooperative approach to provision of regional services, the reform agenda includes programs to pool the financial resources of neighboring governmental units. An example is the Minneapolis-St.

Paul Regional Tax Base Sharing Program, through which each jurisdiction in the area can draw upon a portion of increases in the area's industrial tax base for revenues. As noted earlier, a related approach—that of pooling resources on a county-wide basis for economic development—is being experimented with in Montgomery County, Ohio.

Relations with state and federal governments

A number of years ago William Anderson published a book entitled *The Nation and the States, Rivals or Partners?*[18] The question of whether the essential relationship between the national government and states in the United States should be one of rivalry or partnership has long divided scholars and politicians. Federal systems, unlike unitary ones, allow for a great deal of debate over ultimate authority (see the accompanying sidebar). Although some observers have stressed the cooperative, fluid, political, and pragmatic aspects of the federal system, others have emphasized its static and layered characteristics.

In the debate over authority in the U.S. federal system, scholars often contrast the views of dual federalists and cooperative federalists. Those who favor the dual federalist approach, or what Michael Reagan calls "old style federalism," place emphasis on a constitutional division of authority and functions between a national government and state governments.[19] Each has its own separate sphere of authority, and each is supreme in its own sphere. The sphere of state authority is protected by the Tenth Amendment to the U.S. Constitution. Because all governmental authority is distributed among the national and state governments, the expansion of the authority of one diminishes the authority of the other. Dual federalism essentially is a legal concept and a static notion of federal-state relations. Local governments exist, from this perspective, simply as political subdivisions of the states.

Cooperative or "new style federalism," on the other hand, is a political and pragmatic concept, stressing the actual interdependence and sharing of functions among the federal, state, and local governments. Under cooperative federalism, the focus is on what needs to be done rather than on which level of government has

Unitary and federal systems

Most national governments have been and still are unitary. That is, there is a single source of authority in the nation. If there is a constitutional basis for the government, there is a single constitution. Subordinate units of government in a unitary nation are just that—subordinate. Provincial and local officials often are appointed by the central government, and they are responsible directly to the central government rather than to their own populations. When a unitary government decentralizes, it makes the rules, and it can modify those rules any time it pleases.

Federal governments like the United States are relatively new in historical terms, having been around for only about 200 years. Their distinctive char-acteristic is that they consist of multiple sources of governing authority—that is, multiple constitutions. The component governments—the states in the United States—have their own realms of authority and sources of revenue under their own constitutions. Their leaders are separately elected by their own citizens, and are answerable to their citizens rather than to the central government. Thus, federal governments are not so much decentralized as they are constructed of independent components.

Source: Adapted from Bruce D. Mc-Dowell, "Governing Diversity: The International Experience," *Intergovernmental Perspective* (Winter 1992): 43–45, 47.

authority.[20] Functions are not divided among levels of government but are performed through a partnership of various levels of government.

Shared functions

Morton Grodzins has noted that "the history of the American governments is a history of shared functions. All nostalgic references to the days of state and local independence are based upon mythical views of the past. There has in fact never been a time when federal, state, and local functions were separate and distinct."[21] To Grodzins, the federal system resembles a marble cake in which federal, state, and local activities run together, rather than a layer cake in which these activities are separated.[22]

Another scholar, Thomas Anton, notes that one consequence of power sharing by federal, state, and local governments is that relations among governments are unstable. The fact that governments share authority for a variety of services means that governmental organizations frequently bump into one another. "With each bump," Anton writes, "an opportunity is provided to challenge or affirm existing understandings regarding who should do what, on whose budget."[23]

Officials representing local, state, and federal governments in the vertical system may be somewhat suspicious of each other. John J. DeBolske, the executive director of the League of Arizona Cities and Towns, has summarized these sentiments in three axioms: (1) the level of government I am with is good, (2) any level of government above me is putting it to me, (3) any level of government below mine cannot be trusted and needs watching.

In addition, officials at one level often find it convenient to blame their problems on officials at another level. As one author notes, mayors and governors "are alike in finding the principal causes of their official woes not in the inadequacies of their own governments, but in the level of government just above them."[24] It is also true, of course, that federal officials blame state and local officials for program failures. In either case, how one views the other actors in the intergovernmental arena is, in part, an application of Miles' Law: "Where you stand depends on where you sit."[25]

Basic problems

Recent years have demonstrated that local governments cannot rely on federal and state assistance. Federal aid to local governments has steadily declined since the late 1970s. During the early 1980s, states generally attempted to fill in for the decline in federal revenues. The state response, however, has been spotty and, as evidenced in recent times of economic stress, unreliable.

One mayor's view of intergovernmental relations By mandating, preempting, and placing conditions on the spending of our own money, the Congress has effectively reduced state and local governments to mere agents of the federal government. Where does it get that power? It just takes it. Federalism today is an intergovernmental arrangement in which Congress declares everything to be of national interest, and then requires the states and local governments to raise the money and perform the mandates under threat of civil and, often, criminal sanctions.

Source: Robert M. Issac, Mayor, City of Colorado Springs, "A View from the Commission," *Intergovernmental Perspective* (Fall 1991): 2.

Unfunded mandates   Both the federal and state governments, moreover, have responded to their own financial problems by shifting the costs of implementing their mandates to local officials. One observer estimates that localities dedicate over 40 percent of their expenditures to implementing federal and state mandates.[26] Mandates are popular in Congress because they allow members to take credit for popular programs while the costs of providing these programs are borne by state officials. State legislators find mandates on local officials to have the same beneficial effects. As the U.S. Advisory Commission on Intergovernmental Relations noted: ''In the absence of sufficient funds—whether by legislative choice or economic constraint—there is a strong temptation to satisfy policy demands by mandating that functions be performed by other governments.''[27]

Difficulties in securing local policy objectives   Influencing federal and state policies to maximize local authority and the ability of local governments to meet citizen demands for services is a recurring problem for local officials. Nevertheless, local officials have had considerable success, working both directly and through various organizations, in influencing state and federal policies in past years.[28] Securing policy objectives at the federal and state level has been particularly difficult for local officials in recent years, however, due in part to a general economic downturn. Needless to say, convincing federal and state lawmakers to assume responsibility for problems, rather than dismiss them as being local in nature, is a difficult task even in the best of times.

Further compounding the problem is the growth of interest groups in Washington and most states in recent years that has made it more difficult for local officials to make themselves heard. Being one among several voices has also meant that state and local officials frequently appear to national decision makers to be just another group of special pleaders. Local officials do not look upon themselves as special pleaders, but as ''spokesmen for semi-sovereign subnational governments rendering the bulk of the nation's domestic services and functions.''[29] They prefer the designation ''governmental partner'' rather than ''another special interest.''

Judicial decisions   In assessing the overall impact of state government and the federal government on localities, one must also consider the effect of judicial activity. Over the years, state courts have built up an enormous body of case law regarding what local governments can and cannot do. State courts have had an increasingly important impact on matters related to local budgeting, development, planning, housing, and other policies. State courts in some places have prodded state and local units into reexamining housing policies. New Jersey courts led the way by requiring each municipality in the state to assume its share of responsibility for providing low-income housing.

Within the intergovernmental system, federal courts also strongly influence the policies of local governments. An illustration is the U.S. Supreme Court's decision in *Missouri* v. *Jenkins* [485 U.S. 495 (1990)]. In this case, a divided court (5 to 4) held that federal judges may order local governments to increase taxes to remedy constitutional violations even when raising taxes conflicts with state laws limiting local taxing authority.

In 1985, in the case of *Garcia* v. *San Antonio Metropolitan Transit Authority* [469 U.S. 528 (1983)], the Supreme Court reversed an earlier decision by holding that the question of whether the federal Fair Labor Standards Act applied to state and local employees was to be answered by Congress rather than the courts. As the result of such rulings, Congress has been free to impose costly mandates on state and local governments. In effect, the High Court has also told state and local governments that their only protection against restrictions on their use of tax-exempt financing is through the congressional political process (*South Carolina* v. *Baker* [486 U.S. 1062 (1988)]).

State-local relations

Federal and state courts commonly view local governments as the "legal creatures" of their states. As such, local governments may exercise only those specific powers given to them. In practice, the amount of discretion varies by region, type of unit, and type of function performed. The tradition of local self-government is, for example, stronger in New England than in the South. Municipalities, on the whole, enjoy greater self-government than do counties and other units of local government. Generally, local units enjoy more discretion regarding their structure and organization than they do regarding the functions they perform or the ways they raise and spend revenues. As Christopher Hamilton and Donald Wells have noted, "One of the factors in understanding the actions of local governments is to see how the 'legal cards' are stacked against them inside the states."[30]

As mentioned earlier, the attitudes of state and local officials toward state-local relations tend to reflect Miles' law. From where they sit, local officials usually see more local autonomy to be a good thing. From where they sit, state legislators—regardless of the nature of their constituencies, ideologies, or party identification—are generally reluctant to relinquish control over local governments and often see more local autonomy as something that might bring undesirable results.[31] Businesses and various other groups also worry about the effects of giving local governments more discretion. They find it easier and more comfortable to deal with a single state legislative body than with a multitude of local government authorities.

Finance and mandates   On the average, 20 percent of the hundreds of measures introduced in state legislatures significantly affect local governments.[32] Because of the inferior legal status of local governments, states have virtually unlimited ability to intervene in local affairs by stipulating rules and requirements and by mandating the performance of certain functions. States have increasingly relied on their legislative and regulatory authority to compel local units to assume responsibilities for services and to absorb the resulting costs. They have also issued directives that prohibit local officials from becoming involved in certain areas, performing certain functions, or taking certain actions such as raising revenues.

In financial terms, local governments are heavily dependent on state assistance. State aid accounts for approximately 30 percent of all city and county revenue.[33] States also greatly affect local financial problems by their policies regarding the distribution of state-local responsibilities, mandates, and local revenue authority.

Types of mandate   Local managers have little difficulty with the goals of many state mandates. They find that state intervention may have valuable results—for example, in setting minimum standards for jails. In some cases, local managers also welcome the political "cover" that mandates give them when they try to implement programs that are unpopular with segments of their communities (for example, low-income housing). Yet, although the goals of some mandates may be desirable, mandates may also distort local priorities, impair managerial flexibility, and impose costs that have to be met by local revenues. In some states, mandates account for 60 percent or more of all municipal spending.[34] Many of the most expensive mandates are federal requirements in areas such as environmental protection, which are often passed on to localities by the states.

State mandates in such areas as land-use planning and solid waste management are often of particular concern to local officials. Several states now require municipalities and counties to develop growth management plans that are consistent with state comprehensive plans. One prominent example is the Florida Comprehensive Plan Act of 1985. One problem with such legislation is that it sometimes ignores the limitations on the ability of local governments to do the job. The ability to plan land use and to implement plans requires a level of professional expertise and organization that is very often lacking in local governmental units, especially smaller ones in nonmetropolitan areas. Capacity building may require increased state technical assistance.[35]

State laws also commonly mandate local action regarding the disposition of solid wastes. Under the landmark California Integrated Waste Management Act of 1989, local officials must plan and coordinate their efforts toward the goals of diverting 25 percent of the waste stream from landfills by 1995 and 50 percent by the year 2000. Yet, as in the case of comprehensive planning, achievement of waste-reduction goals in California and elsewhere requires state support. In this area, support includes not only technical assistance but assistance in developing markets for materials and action to change packaging standards.[36]

Also of some concern to local officials are state mandates of a preemptory, or "thou-shalt-not," nature. Prohibitions of this type frequently reflect the desire of a particular group to avoid local authority in order to minimize—if not escape completely—governmental taxation or regulation. Local officials, for example, continually guard against state legislation that would exempt certain businesses from local sales taxes. In recent years, efforts to circumvent local authority have been especially intense in regard to controls over such matters as public smoking, rents, and guns.

Funding for mandates   Local officials constantly seek funding and various types of state assistance for new mandates. With luck, they may be successful in securing partial funding. At other times, legislatures give local governments increased authority to raise revenues needed to meet various mandates. In this case, local officials rather than the state legislature run the risk of incurring the wrath of taxpayers.

Over forty states require the formulation of statements called fiscal notes, which contain estimates of the costs imposed on localities by state laws or regulations. These are prepared by various state agencies, such as local advisory commissions on intergovernmental relations. Fiscal note requirements, however, have limited effects. Even assuming that the process makes legislators more aware of the cost problem, this knowledge does not mean that they will vote against legislation imposing costs. After all, the costs imposed are not assumed by the state, but by the local governments that have to comply with the mandates. Fiscal notes appear to be of primary value in providing local governments with lobbying ammunition.[37]

About one-third of the states require (either by statute or voter-approved constitutional amendment) the state government to reimburse, either fully or partially, the costs of mandates imposed on local governments. Mandate reimbursement is more efficient than simple cost estimation in deterring unfunded mandates. In some states, however, legislatures ignore the requirements or get around them by simply earmarking part of the funding already allocated for state aid to localities as mandate reimbursement. Mandate reimbursement costs are, in effect, deducted from what would have gone into local-aid programs.[38]

States could generally help financially strapped localities by increasing aid, assuming the costs of programs now financed out of local revenues (as often has been done in the areas of courts and corrections), easing the burden of costly mandates, and allowing localities greater discretion in raising revenues.

Working with state agencies and organizations   Local government managers have expressed considerable concern over the status of state-local relations. They have been troubled by the loss of local government authority, the lack of sufficient discretion to generate revenues, the lack of state technical assistance and, perhaps most of all, the growth of unfunded mandates.

Local managers are often concerned also about the lack of state executive and legislative staff with appropriate expertise to serve as a contact with local governments and to help develop and implement intergovernmental policies. One study concluded that a major reason that many states have lagged in fostering cooperation is the lack of professional staff in the governor's office and legislature who are charged with responsibility for state-local relations.[39]

On the administrative side, various state agencies interact with local officials on a function-by-function basis. State departments of transportation, welfare, and public safety are examples of such agencies. Local officials have to be constantly on guard against agencies changing rules and regulations unilaterally. On the other hand, state administrators often rely on the cooperation of local administrators in securing support for their programs in the legislature. Local officials need not hesitate to contact state officials about activities in which they have a common interest.[40]

In addition to specialized state agencies, most states have a single agency such as an office of community or local affairs with more general responsibilities related to local governments. These agencies function as clearinghouses for information and provide technical assistance to local governments in such matters as planning and local finance. Such services are particularly useful to smaller jurisdictions lacking well-developed professional staffs.

Community or local-affairs agencies are important means of communication between state and local governments. One study suggests that officials in these agen-

---

Electronic purchasing in New South Wales   Twenty-five local governments in New South Wales (NSW), Australia's largest state, have joined with the state government in electronic purchasing and supply management. Pioneered by NSW in 1991, the statewide system streamlines purchasing practices and achieves substantial savings for participants because of negotiated quantity discounts. It is operated on a contract for the state by a private firm that has replaced cumbersome and costly paper-based purchasing procedures with an inexpensive computerized database and electronic purchasing software.

SUPPLYLINE, as the system's software is known, links the database with authorized personal computers in the purchasing and supply departments of public agencies throughout the state and participating local governments. At present more than 400 organizations are on-line at a fraction of the cost of paper-based methods. The basic monthly charge for participating groups is just A$11.50, and the NSW government expects that it will save in the range of A$100 million a year on the

A$4 billion statewide public purchasing tab.

The SUPPLYLINE system consists of a central database in the Sydney suburb of Ashfield, accessed electronically by purchasers on the system. After logging on, using their individual control codes, purchasers search for suppliers and items, and put in their orders by electronic mail. Suppliers take the orders from their electronic mail boxes and arrange for delivery.

Under the terms of its contract, the private contractor, National Electronic Interchange Services (NEIC), manages the system for the state government and performs the required marketing tasks among public agencies, who are not compelled to use the system but are expected to find it convenient and cost-effective to do so. With 25 signed up, the state government's hope that local governments will discover the advantages of electronic interchange services for their own recurrent purchases seems to have been realized.

Source: *Public Innovation Abroad* (August 1992): 1–2.

Intergovernmental cooperation in Central Illinois The project began with a phone call in 1984 to Mayor Richard Godfrey of Normal, Illinois, from Dan Rutherford, director of international regulations for the Illinois Department of Commerce and Community Affairs (DCCA). Rutherford informed Godfrey that he was leaving shortly for Japan to discuss the possibility of locating a new, state-of-the-art automobile assembly facility in Illinois. He wanted to know whether Normal had any sites that could accommodate this type of facility.

In response to Rutherford's call, officials in Normal—as well as those in the neighboring city of Bloomington and in McLean County—made the quick decision to work with DCCA to bring the facility to their area. The group realized the tremendous economic benefits the facility could bring to the region and began to prepare information on potential sites within the county.

This effort was the beginning of what became a rather lengthy process of negotiation involving all of the affected government agencies and the site selection committee organized by the Mitsubishi Motor Corporation and Chrysler Corporation. Mitsubishi and Chrysler had joined forces to build an automobile assembly plan in the United States to produce automobiles for both corporations and later formed what is known as Diamond-Star Motors.

In preparation for their formal presentation to the site selection committee, the town of Normal, the city of Bloomington, McLean County, the Normal Unit 5 School District, Dry Grove Township, the Bloomington-Normal Water Reclamation District, the Bloomington-Normal Airport Authority, and the state of Illinois had held discussions to determine how to attract this major industrial development project to the area. In an unprecedented display of intergovernmental cooperation, these diverse public agencies entered into a total of thirty-nine intergovernmental agreements to create the Normal-Bloomington-McLean County Enterprise Zone and to offer an incentive package to the site selection committee that ultimately resulted in the construction of the Diamond-Star Motors plant in Normal.

Source: Adapted from "Regional Strategies for Local Government Management," *MIS Report*, March 1992 (Washington, DC: ICMA), 7–9.

---

cies "usually consider themselves as intermediaries between state and local governments, the advocates of the state point of view in dealing with local officials, and the advocates of the local point of view in dealing with state officials."[41]

On the whole, the emphasis in state-local administrative relations has been as much or more on assisting local units as on supervising them. State agencies not only offer general assistance but may play an important role in assisting localities in forging cooperative arrangements for various projects (see the sidebars on pages 184 and 185).

About half of the states have small advisory commissions on intergovernmental relations (ACIRs) or comparable organizations to provide a forum for discussing intergovernmental issues and devising solutions. Such bodies may also conduct research, analyze problems, and make recommendations to the legislature and governor on intergovernmental matters. The range of their activities depends on the size of their budgets and staff. Membership is typically open to various state as well as local officials. The voluntary Colorado Advisory Committee on Intergovernmental Relations, for example, has twenty-four members representing the Colorado Municipal League, Colorado Counties Inc., the state senate and house, and the state executive branch.[42]

University-based institutes of government may also be of considerable help to local government managers in undertaking a variety of tasks in research, training, technical assistance, economic development, and other areas of community interest.

On the political level, local officials can often rely on the tendency of state legislators to safeguard the interests of the local areas they represent. At other times, local officials may want to take matters into their own hands. For example, mayors might form regional coalitions to maximize their influence in the legislature. Such a coalition was put together in Connecticut in 1990. The mayors came away with a $6-million program to combat crime. A similar coalition among California mayors produced legislative support for homeless and other programs.[43]

Various organizations also protect and advance the interests of local units. State municipal leagues or leagues of cities are found in nearly every state, usually located in or close to the state capital. So too, are county associations. Local government managers and their elected officials usually are knowledgeable about the organization and workings of their leagues and associations. They also know that they have to be active in them and support them financially if local government is to fare well in the competition with other interests for state resources.

Federal-local relations

Though courts view local governments as the legal creatures, or political subdivisions, of their states, this legal condition has not prevented the establishment of direct ties between local government and the federal government. In fact, the practice of giving local governments substantial responsibilities for implementing national policy has been a part of American federalist practices from the start.[44]

Even in the best of times, the federal-local partnership has been less than ideal in terms of finances and discretionary authority. Nevertheless, at various times in history local governments have found the federal government willing to help address problems facing local officials and willing to involve local officials in the shaping of national policies directed at these problems.

Growth of federal aid (1932–1978)
The New Deal, born in the 1930s out of the devastation of the Great Depression, dramatically increased the scope of the federal-local partnership. Local officials from all over the country, but especially from large cities, clamored for federal assistance to meet the problems of unemployment, relief, housing, public works, and slum clearance. The federal government stepped in when it became clear that the states were not going to be of much help in providing relief or administering programs. Direct national-city relations were founded on a mutual dependence: the cities' need for national finances and the national government's need for local administrative support and leadership in swiftly implementing the emergency programs.[45] The political affinity of Franklin Roosevelt's administration and the Democratic party organizations in large cities strengthened these ties.

Following the depression years, direct city-national programs emerged in such areas as housing and urban development. These programs called for only the minimal involvement of state governments. School districts, counties, and other units of local government also enjoyed relatively free access to federal funds. This access meant that, although state legislatures provided a large portion of local revenues, they had only fragmentary information about how much money was coming to local units from federal sources and how that money was being spent. Those who favored bypassing the state governments argued that they were unable or unwilling to cope with local problems. They also contended that states should be excluded because they had nothing to add (for example, funds or technical expertise) to the provision of a particular program.

It is no exaggeration to say that dramatic developments from the 1960s to the late 1970s transformed the intergovernmental system. In a process described as the "galloping intergovernmentalization" of nearly all governmental functions, the number of federal aid programs rose from 132 in 1960 to over 540 in 1980.[46] The dollars involved grew from $7 billion to over $90 billion in the same period. All this growth came with little change in the number of federal employees. As it has since the New Deal, the federal government relied on state and local governments to deliver new services, even for national programs that might advantageously have been administered by federal agencies.

This explosive growth in federal aid was made possible by the large amount of money flowing into the federal treasury. With ample funds on hand, members of Congress felt free to respond to the demands of their constituents and of state and local officials for new programs.

Reductions in federal aid (1978–1993)   The intergovernmental facts of life began to change drastically in the late 1970s and particularly after the election of President Ronald Reagan in 1980. The federal government's fiscal strength seriously deteriorated. The shift in spending from defense to social programs ended, and the pendulum began to swing back.

Federal aid to state and local governments peaked in 1978 and began to decline in real dollars in 1982. Funds from the national government fell from 18.7 cents per dollar of state and local government revenue in 1978 to 13.6 cents per dollar in 1987. Over the 1980s, the percentage of the average local government budget composed of federal funds fell from around 16 percent to 8 percent.[47] Municipal programs—including low-income housing, wastewater treatment, public transit, and job training—were particularly hard hit in the 1980s and early 1990s.[48]

Continued reductions in federal spending have led to increases in state and local spending. As John P. Thomas, former executive director of the National Association of Counties, pointed out, "Congress has been unwilling to abolish the established programs or to reduce public expectations regarding their continuation." Thus, "each time the federal government withdraws its financial participation in a locally provided service, one of two things happens to assure continuation of the program: either federal rules and regulations are created to force state and local governments to bear the financial burden, or a local political constituency develops around that service to demand its continuation, again at the expense of state and local government."[49]

Making matters even more difficult for state and local officials has been the growth of costly federal mandates in areas such as education, environmental protection, labor management, and transportation. The change in federal policy from using subsidies to using regulatory mandates to encourage states and localities to take various courses of action began in the mid 1970s. One repercussion of the change has been increased costs. Mandates cost state and local governments approximately $100 billion a year.[50]

Local governments—at the end of the path of "one-way federalism"—wind up paying many of these costs. Thus, when Congress decides to increase Medicaid coverage, the states must pay more for their share of the increased costs (or risk losing the program), but state governments do so by passing the increased costs on to their local governments.[51] Many of the environmental mandates local governments must deal with are federal mandates passed on by the states.

The future   Local officials have not given up altogether on the idea of a restored federal-local partnership. Yet, few observers expect drastic changes in federal aid policies in the immediate future. Many are prepared to face the future with fewer federal dollars. Faced with resistance to increased taxes and a massive debt problem, it is unlikely that the federal government will find it feasible, either economically or politically, to return to an active role in financing state and local programs.

Patrick Glisson, director of finance for Atlanta and former president of the Government Finance Officers Association, noted a few years ago: "One of the things we've got to do as a profession is to reorient ourselves to a state level. The federal government is not ever going to get back into the business of giving us major aid, even if they wanted to. The deficit is a major part of that."[52]

Relations with foreign governments

Local governments increasingly find themselves involved in foreign affairs. During the 1980s, for example, a number of cities adopted selective or principled purchasing programs restricting their purchase of goods and services from companies doing business in South Africa. Nearly 1,000 communities in the United States participate in sister-city programs, through which they are paired with communities in other countries. Sister cities share a number of activities such as athletic events, exhibitions, trade fairs, and the exchange of people and ideas. They foster cross-cultural friendships and help create business opportunities.[53]

Local officials are well aware of the importance of global economic conditions on local economies. As Chapter 6 points out, a number of counties solicit foreign business. Others try to develop export markets for the products of firms vital to the local economy. To achieve these ends, local businesses advertise in the international media and send trade missions of local government and business leaders to foreign countries. As one observer noted: "Ten years ago, it would not have been important for mayors to go on foreign trade missions. Today it is not only important that they do so, but essential."[54]

Working in the intergovernmental environment

How should the local government manager approach his or her role in intergovernmental relations? What the manager probably knows best are the formidable barriers and difficulties that hinder the achievement of many intergovernmental goals. Citizens focus inwardly on community affairs and often fail to appreciate the community's stake in cooperation with other governments. They are suspicious of elected officials or managers who "spend too much time" in Washington, at the state capital, at the council of governments, hosting foreign dignitaries, or going on foreign junkets. Traveling too often is perceived as vacationing at taxpayers' expense. The difficulty of conducting intergovernmental relations is increased because the system is vast. Most local government managers must relate not only to the federal and state governments but to a dozen or more other local governments in the region and, increasingly, to foreign governments. The list of potential contacts is virtually unlimited.

The effective local government manager understands the most important aspects of the intergovernmental system, is able to identify what the community needs and realistically can get from and through other governments, selects which intergovernmental actions and proposals to advance and which to oppose, and develops relationships and skills that promote effectiveness in achieving intergovernmental goals. Throughout this process, the manager assumes a leadership role in the policy arena, though not conspicuously. As participants in the policymaking process, managers build the agenda as a primary source of information for policy makers. Moreover, as Deil Wright has noted, "Managers gain intergovernmental influence chiefly through expertise, formal control over budget and personnel, and a reputation for achievement or implementation—getting done what a community deems desirable."[55] To accomplish their intergovernmental duties, managers need to think extraterritorially, monitor relationships, and know when it is time to take action (see the sidebar on p. 189).

Intergovernmental leadership   It is not natural for leaders in any community to think extraterritorially. One tends to think of addressing issues internally or not at all. It takes a special sensitivity to explore the implications of an issue for other communities and to initiate conversations with the leaders of these communities.

It takes even greater sensitivity to determine whether it is timely to address an issue, especially in cooperation with other communities. Is it timely to consider a joint police force with a neighboring community when the chief retires? It is timely to stop depending on landfills for solid waste disposal and begin recycling and resource recovery programs with neighboring communities? It is timely to take advantage of a new technology, such as automated computer networks to share information, emergency medical service dispatching, or tax billing with neighboring communities? It is all too easy to "cry wolf" too early and jeopardize future cooperative efforts or too late and lose an opportunity to design a workable partnership before an issue evolves into a crisis.

Fortunately, enlightened government leaders exist and with training and encouragement can see opportunities for cooperation and select timely ones.

Source: Adapted from William R. Dodge, "The Emergence of Intercommunity Partnerships in the 1980s," *Public Management* (July 1988): 4.

Effectiveness in intergovernmental relations requires that local managers be selective and "street-wise," often working through others. Because typical managers have little time for intergovernmental relations—and could not keep abreast of the whole scene even if they had time—they need to determine what they must know personally, and what they can delegate or neglect. A useful practice is to assign day-to-day intergovernmental responsibilities to a particular individual or office. This approach provides coordination and a single point of contact for other governments.

Roles of the manager and elected officials

A particular manager's role and areas of operation in intergovernmental relations depend upon the division of labor with the politically elected officials in the community. The effective local government manager urges elected officials to take on as much of role as they are willing to assume and those negotiating tasks in which their political and elected status is an advantage. If a mayor (or other elected official) is willing to take the lead and exploit political ties to members of Congress, governors, state legislators, and locally elected officials, aspects of intergovernmental relations become that official's rightful territory. Managers in these situations typically play supporting roles, calling on their technical and administrative expertise to do whatever is necessary to enhance elected officials' effectiveness.

In numerous communities, however, much or all of the intergovernmental work is left to managers and administrators. Managers in many communities are also involved in supervising program specialists who are engaged in intergovernmental management or day-to-day transactions with their counterparts in other governments. Intergovernmental management involves the interrelated activities of problem solving, conflict management, and bargaining.

In many jurisdictions managers have a leading, though not highly visible, role in intergovernmental negotiations. Often the most difficult intergovernmental tasks are thrown into the manager's lap. As Walter Scheiber once noted: "Here in the Washington area . . . on some of the tough intergovernmental issues the elected officials quietly say to the managers, negotiate the problem with those other three governments. When you get a solution bring it back to me. If I like it—and I probably will—then we'll have a ceremony and a press conference, and I'll sign a document. It will be mine, but we'll all know that you did it.''[56]

Managers may increasingly be called upon to assume the role of intergovernmental negotiator, interacting with their peers in other jurisdictions, while elected officials deal with other types of policy issues. Yet, it is important to secure the support of elected officials for a general policy of intergovernmental cooperation and to involve them in the development of cooperative programs (see the accompanying sidebar).

Interlocal agreements

Managers should evaluate the nature and scale of the city, county, and other local government activities in their areas and look for ways to improve them through contracting, service agreements, transfers of functions, and participation in interjurisdictional agencies such as councils of governments. Local officials may find it easy to make informal, handshake agreements. Yet, the absence of a written agreement may lead to misunderstandings and conflict; problems also may arise concerning such matters as liability and workers' compensation. Projects that involve

---

The local legislature and intergovernmental policy development   One way to get the full support of the legislative body is to involve it in the development and approval of a public policy statement or goal. Formal action by the governing body is desirable. In a small municipality it could be as simple as the following ordinance in a hypothetical small town in the Midwest:

The Mayor and City Council of Lake Pleasant recognize the interest and potential support of other governments, the business community, civic groups, and other voluntary organizations in the provision of cost-effective services for the citizens of Lake Pleasant. The City will seek to take full advantage of opportunities for effective collaboration with such groups in order to meet citizens' needs effectively and at the lowest practicable cost.

The City Manager is directed to develop cooperative relationships with other governments and the nonprofit and business sectors that are able to contribute to the quality of life in Lake Pleasant. This includes preparing cooperative programs and projects that are advantageous to the

city and taking such other initiatives as will further the objectives set forth above. Proposals that affect the City's budget or require formal contractual relationships with other jurisdictions and organizations shall be submitted to the City Council for approval. The City Manager is requested by the Council to keep it informed of progress under this ordinance.

In a larger jurisdiction a more definitive statement may be desirable, including a formalized goal-setting, work-programming, and budgeting process based on consultations with other jurisdictions and organizations that have existing or potential partnership roles. Participation in a COG is an example of an action that requires formal approval by a jurisdiction's legislative body.

Source: Adapted from Coalition to Improve Management in State and Local Governments, *Improving Local Services Through Intergovernmental and Intersectoral Cooperation*, Special Report no. 5, January 1992 (Pittsburgh, PA: School of Urban and Public Affairs, Carnegie Mellon University), 16–17.

borrowing funds, joint ownership of property, and other legal responsibilities require carefully drawn documents.

The following are among the most important questions local officials should ask themselves before entering into an agreement:

1. Do the jurisdictions have legal authority to enter into a cooperative agreement?
2. How are costs determined?
3. What is the level of trust and cooperation between the jurisdictions?
4. Can the quality and quantity of the service be achieved with current resources?[57]

Interlocal contracting and joint endeavors may be desirable but, given the disinclination of elected officials to relinquish control over the level and quality of services, managers must build a strong case based on cost in order to secure approval. In putting together the specifics of an agreement, managers should anticipate bad times as well as good times. Managers should proceed slowly, despite the pressures for prompt action, especially when coping with an agreement involving matters such as a major sewage plant or the consolidation of police programs. A cooperative program generally takes longer to organize than a municipal program for the same service simply because more people are involved and more approvals are required.

Managers should also work toward creating new regional solutions to problems, exploring the possibility of regional tax sharing and various means of improving service delivery. Possible structural changes such as the consolidation of local governments or the creation of new ones should not be ignored, but such changes do not constitute the whole of reform, nor are they the first step to be taken. In building broader intercommunity partnerships, local managers should first draw upon the expertise of local businesses, explore the possibility of bringing in research institutes associated with universities in their area to analyze regional issues, and examine the feasibility of using citizen leagues to examine controversial regional issues and build the agenda for reform.

Dealing with the state government

Local government managers should explore ways of encouraging the state to (1) ease the financial burden on local governments (e.g., by getting the state to fund mandates, assume certain costs, and reexamine the system of grants and shared revenues), (2) enhance local home rule, particularly in regard to revenue diversification, and (3) facilitate the ability of local governments to engage in creative partnerships with other local governments.

Managers should get to know the principal actors in the state government, including not only legislators from their area and legislative leaders, but also elected and appointed agency heads and their deputies and division heads. Effective local government managers work with and within associations of city and county governments, state departments of community affairs, and university research and training institutes that provide long-range political, educational, and administrative benefits. They find ways that they and other community officials can become members of or participants in the deliberations of state bodies and study commissions whose decisions affect local government.

The local government manager probably is not the principal actor on state policy matters, but he or she should constantly encourage those with leading and supporting roles—mayors, county board chairpersons, city and county department heads, planning directors, state highway professionals, and others—to keep on top of legislation, policy changes, and other elements in the ebb and flow of day-to-day government.

Starting off on the right foot

Many intergovernmental cooperation efforts promptly fail because well-intentioned local officials do not lay a sound foundation for their cooperative efforts. A good start is essential. If a program starts off on the wrong foot, local officials spend most of their time trying to get back in step rather than proceeding with the program.

Be inclusive Most ideas for cooperation start with a small core group. It is often the tendency of such groups to keep the effort to themselves until they fully develop their plans. This closed effort may have the unintended appearance of excluding municipalities and officials who are not part of the core group, which can create animosity and resistance toward an idea that may have considerable merit.

It is better to be inclusive from the start. Let all potential participating municipalities and municipal officials have an opportunity to participate in the development of the idea or at least in the selection of a core working group. Those who are not included are suspicious of a self-selected group. A program developed with the presumption that certain municipalities will participate and others might participate later if they are interested in effect excludes the latter group.

Involve elected officials Often the impetus for a cooperative program comes from a planning commission, a recreation board, a community group, or a county official. It is very important that the initiating group secure the involvement and support of the municipal elected officials early in the process, even if the initiating group is to do all the work to develop the program. Otherwise, they may waste a great amount of effort developing a program that may not get final approval for funding from the key decision-makers, the locally elected officials.

Involve local staff Local government employees often view cooperative programs as a threat to their position, or "turf." In some cases these threats are real: a cooperative program may mean that jobs are lost or that responsibilities are transferred elsewhere. In such cases, the local managers must deal with the affected employees fairly and forthrightly. Otherwise, the employees may organize an effective opposition campaign that generates emotionally charged negative publicity and causes the demise of the cooperative program. Frequently, the employees' view of the threat is more a matter of false perception than fact. Local staff who are not brought in, however, respond on the basis of their perceptions. Negative publicity may defeat a program they

Dealing with the federal government

In dealing with the federal government, local officials rely on congressional delegations, public interest groups, and, sometimes, lobbyists in their own Washington offices. It may be useful to form local delegations, including prominent citizens as well as public officials, to make the rounds of Washington seeking high-level political and administrative contacts in order to influence decisions regarding such matters as funding programs, awarding grants and contracts, and interpreting rules and regulations.

Local officials also may make use of national organizations that in one way or another represent the views of local officials on matters of federal policy. Lobbying organizations include the National League of Cities, the United States Conference of Mayors, the National Association of Counties, and the National Association of Towns and Townships (NATaT). These groups also provide information and other types of assistance to local governments. NATaT, for example, through its Environmental Resource Center, provides low-cost information to local officials in smaller jurisdictions to help them comply with complex state and federal mandates.

would have supported had they been accurately informed.

Start with an easy project   In an area where there is potential for several co-operative programs or a council of governments, it is best to start with an easy project. An easy project facilitates consensus among the participating municipalities, involves limited financial risk, and has a high potential for success. The municipal official can savor first hand a successful effort and build future cooperative efforts on this solid foundation.

Communicate effectively   More good ideas for intergovernmental cooperation fail because of poor communications than for any other reason. Without effective communications, decisions about a cooperative program are made on the basis of assumptions and perceptions rather than facts. Newsletters, annual reports, well-documented budgets, minutes of meetings, and regular reports by municipal representatives on cooperative programs are all good ways to communicate. Reliance on a single approach is unwise; it is best to reinforce messages by using more than one method of communication. For example, an oral report by a local government delegate to a regional program board may suffer if the delegate is inarticulate or unenthusiastic. Incom-

plete or distorted information can result from such a report. At the same time, the personal observations and support of a delegate can be crucial to a cooperative program's success. In sum, regular reports from municipal representatives are very important, but other means of communication are also valuable.

Communication to the public through the press and electronic media is also important. If the public has a perception that officials are hiding something, the reaction is swift and negative regardless of the merits of the program. Openness is crucial to the success of intergovernmental programs and provides an opportunity to explain the benefits of programs to the citizens. In general, the media favor cooperative programs in principle, as evidence of good government. Therefore, they usually give positive coverage to cooperative activities unless there is an effort to maintain secrecy—an easy way to get negative coverage.

Source: Adapted from Thomas S. Kurtz, *Intergovernmental Cooperation Handbook* (Harrisburg: Pennsylvania Department of Community Affairs, Bureau of Local Government Services, 1990), 39–43.

Also providing information are the International City/County Management Association and the United States Advisory Commission on Intergovernmental Relations.

National associations representing local officials have generally encouraged the growth of the federal role in funding domestic programs. They also provide structures through which local officials can network, exchange ideas and information, and both shape and respond to changes in federal policy. Another of their functions is to help educate people in Washington about the roles and activities of local governments in the federal system.

Federal and state grants

Since the late 1970s, the importance of grantsmanship in intergovernmental activities has declined considerably. Federal grants-in-aid and, in many parts of the country, state grants-in-aid have been cut back. Yet, in a period of revenue scarcity, it is important to turn to what remains of the grant program as well as to other possible bases of support. Pursuit of grants is also necessary to assure a skeptical public that an effort is being made to exhaust outside sources of revenue before turning to local taxpayers. Local government managers who directly participate in obtaining grants must, like full-time grant specialists, master the fine points and skills involved in writing applications, negotiating and building relationships with grantor agencies, administering grant programs within federal regulations, coping with audit exceptions, and participating in the incremental improvement of grant programs and regulations.

Recap

The web of intergovernmental relations is complex, involving federal, state, and local governments in the United States and, increasingly, governments in other countries. This chapter describes these relations, discusses some of their advantages and disadvantages from a local government perspective, and suggests ways in which local government managers can work effectively with other governments to benefit their own communities.

The chapter points out that interlocal cooperation, though sometimes difficult to achieve, can bring a number of benefits. For example, it is an important way of building the administrative capacity of local governments, especially smaller ones. It may also lead to significant improvements in services and reductions in total costs.

Different types of interlocal agreement were discussed, and examples of successful cooperation were described. These examples include both agreements between local jurisdictions and broader intercommunity partnerships involving nonprofit, civic, and private organizations.

In addition, the chapter discussed suggestions for governmental reform, focusing in particular on greater responsibilities for county governments and councils of governments.

The U.S. federal, state, and local governments have always shared functions. The chapter described the legal relations between state and local governments, discussed the importance of state financial aid and the costs of state mandates, and described the role of state agencies in state-local relations. It also emphasized the problems caused by unfunded federal mandates and reductions in federal aid and suggested ways in which local government managers can work to represent the concerns of local governments at the federal level.

Intergovernmental relations at all levels require the manager to assume a leadership role, though he or she often works behind the scenes, leaving the limelight to elected officials. The last section of the chapter provided practical suggestions for managers as they exercise their negotiating, brokering, and consensus-building skills in developing and implementing collaborative arrangements with other governments.

Interlocal contract checklist

The following checklist is a useful tool for managers who are considering entering into an interlocal agreement.

Identification of parties and purposes

Describe the nature of the service or function to be performed.

Explain the desirability of the undertaking.

Cite the legal authority.

Define terms, as necessary.

Description of work to be performed

Explain in detail the service that will be provided, or the activity or project to be jointly undertaken.

Identify any boards, administrative agencies, or third-party contractors and detail their powers and duties.

Explanation of contract limitations

Clarify any quality or quantity standards to be observed by the parties.

Indicate the need to comply with federal or state regulations or other requirements.

Spell out priorities for using space or equipment as necessary.

Include language that protects the right of one or both parties to perform for other parties not named in the agreement.

Financing

Outline procedures for financing the services that will be undertaken jointly by the parties.

Stipulate the amount and/or basis on which payments will be made (e.g., population served, services received, capacity required, assessed valuations, actual expenses incurred).

Indicate the authority for acceptance of any grants or contributions.

If long-term financing is involved, explain the need for bond counsel, the types of bonds to be issued, and allocation of debt among the parties.

Administration

Clearly identify the administrators responsible for supervising the contract.

Describe how notices will be given and which persons representing each party will receive the notices.

Stipulate who will exercise control over those who will supply the service.

Fiscal procedures

Stipulate how and when payments are to be made and procedures for record keeping and reporting.

Provide for periodic review and for adjustment of rates and charges.

Provide methods for preparing, submitting, and approving a budget, and the duties of those responsible for receiving or paying out funds.

Personnel matters

Indicate who will hire employees to be engaged in a joint endeavor.

Specify the rights, privileges, immunities, and benefits of employees working away from home.

Specify the professional qualifications of personnel that will be hired under a joint venture.

Property arrangements

Indicate how to handle matters such as acquisition of property, conveyance of title to real estate and allocation of expenses.

Provide procedures to dispose of property after the contract expires.

Include language that waives a party's liability for damage to property for specified causes that are beyond a party's control and/or are not the sole result of a party's negligence.

Duration, termination, and amendment

State the contract's term, which may be either a period of time specified in the contract or indefinite.

Provide for amendments in writing before signing the contract so that the amendments will not adversely affect existing contractual obligations.

Provide a procedure for changing consideration and notifying parties.

Provide for termination by either party after a specified period of time following written notice of intent to end the contract.

List occurrences that would be sufficient justification for ending the contract.

Miscellaneous provisions

To permit suspending contractual obligations because of circumstances beyond a party's control, include a "force majeure" clause.

Include an indemnity or "hold harmless" clause as necessary to transfer the ultimate financial responsibility for a given contingency from one of the parties to another.

Include a section that dictates required insurance coverages and limits, and that names the other party by the insurer as an additional insured.

To prevent transferring any interest in the contract to a third party without the written consent of all parties to the contract, include a "non-assignment" provision.

Include a nondiscrimination clause to ensure affirmative action in employment and employee solicitation, and to ensure compliance with federal civil rights legislation, such as the Civil Rights Act of 1991, the Americans With Disabilities Act of 1990, etc.

Include a severability clause that protects the validity of the rest of the contract if a provision is held to be invalid.

If the parties want any attached materials to be considered as part of the contract, provide for an "incorporation by reference" clause.

Source: *City & County Financial Management* (newsletter of the office of the Texas Comptroller of Public Accounts, Austin), May–June 1992.

---

1   Morton Grodzins, "Centralization and Decentralization in the American Federal System," in *A Nation of States* (Chicago: Public Affairs Conference Center, 1964). Reprinted in Marilyn Gittell, *State Politics and the New Federalism: Readings and Commentary* (New York: Longman, 1986), 18.

2   U.S. Department of Commerce, Bureau of the Census, *Preliminary Report: 1992 Census of Governments* (Washington, DC: GPO, 1992).

3   On marketplace analogies, see Charles M. Tiebout, "A Pure Theory of Local Expenditures," *Journal of Political Economy* 64 (October 1956): 416–424. See also John Kincaid, "Metropolitan Governance: Reviving International Market Analogies," *Intergovernmental Perspectives* (Spring 1989): 24. Among the recent studies on the value of competition are Mark Schneider, "Intermunicipal Competition, Budget-Maximizing Bureaucrats, and Levels of Sub-

urban Competition," *American Journal of Political Science 33* (August 1989):612–628, and U.S. Advisory Commission on Intergovernmental Relations, *The Organization of Local Public Economies* (Washington, DC: GPO, 1987).

4 Examples of cooperative activity are found in "Regional Strategies for Local Government Management," *MIS Report*, March 1992 (Washington, DC: ICMA), and in Coalition to Improve Management in State and Local Government, *Improving Local Services Through Intergovernmental and Intersectoral Cooperation*, Special Report no. 5, January 1992 (Pittsburgh, PA: Carnegie Mellon University). See also Joy McIlwain, "Regional Approaches Gaining Ground," *American City & County* (August 1991): 38–40; Eileen Shanahan, "Going It Jointly: Regional Solutions for Local Problems," *Governing* (August 1991):70–75; and *Government Finance Review* (October 1991):4.

5 For further examples, see Edward C. Sembor, Jr., "A Partnership for Citizenship Education," *Public Management* (August 1991):10–12.

6 Quote from *Creating Excellence in Education: The Role of Phoenix City Government* (Arizona State University, School of Public Affairs, Morrison Institute for Public Policy, December 1988), ii.

7 William R. Dodge, "The Emergence of Intercommunity Partnerships in the 1980s," *Public Management* (July 1988): 2–7.

8 McIlwain, "Regional Approaches Gaining Ground."

9 Amy Cohen Paul, *Future Challenges, Future Opportunities: The Final Report of the ICMA FutureVisions Consortium* (Washington, DC: ICMA, 1991).

10 See, for example, Shanahan, "Going It Jointly."

11 Ibid.

12 See generally David R. Berman, ed., *County Government in an Era of Change* (Westport, CT: Greenwood Press, 1993).

13 Vincent L. Marando and Mavis Mann Reeves, "Counties: Evolving Local Governments, Reform, and Responsiveness," *National Civic Review* 80 (Spring 1991): 224.

14 See Gregory Streib and William L. Waugh, Jr., "Administrative Capacity and the Barriers to Effective County Management," *Public Productivity and Management Review* 15 (Fall 1991): 61–70; Waugh and Streib, "County Officials' Perceptions of Local Capacity and State Responsiveness After the First Reagan Term," *Southeastern Political Review* 18: 27–50; and Waugh, "States, Counties, and the Questions of Trust and Capacity," *Publius: The Journal of Federalism* 18 (Winter 1988): 189–198.

15 Doris M. Ward, "Regional Governance Issues in California: Citizen and Policy Implications," *National Civic Review* 79 (March–April 1990): 133.

16 Lenneal J. Henderson, "Metropolitan Governance: Citizen Participation in the Urban Federation," *National Civic Review* 79 (March–April 1990): 105–117. See also "Regional Strategies for Local Government Management," *MIS Report* (March 1992).

17 "Counties Are Out of Date in California," *State Legislatures* (March 1991): 9.

18 William Anderson, *The Nation and the States, Rivals or Partners?* (Minneapolis: University of Minnesota Press, 1955).

19 Michael D. Reagan, *The New Federalism* (New York: Oxford University Press, 1972).

20 David R. Berman, *State and Local Politics* (Dubuque, IA: William C. Brown, 1991), 28–30.

21 Grodzins, "Centralization and Decentralization in the American Federal System," in Gittell, *State Politics* and the New Federalism, 22–23.

22 Morton Grodzins, *The American System: A New View of Governments in the United States* (Chicago: Rand McNally, 1966).

23 Thomas J. Anton, *American Federalism and Public Policy: How the System Works* (New York: Random House, 1989), 102.

24 Anderson, *The Nation and the States*, 17.

25 Rufus E. Miles, "The Origin and Meaning of Miles' Law," *Public Administration Review* 38 (September–October 1978): 399–403.

26 This estimate comes from Barbara P. Greene, "Counties and the Fiscal Challenges of the 1980s," *Intergovernmental Perspective* (Winter 1987): 16.

27 U.S. Advisory Commission on Intergovernmental Relations, *Mandates: Cases in State-Local Relations* (Washington, DC: GPO, 1990), 2.

28 Donald H. Haider, *When Governments Come to Washington* (New York: Free Press, 1974). See also Jonathan Walters, "Lobbying for the Good Old Days," *Governing* (June 1991): 33–37.

29 David B. Walker, "Intergovernmental Relations and the Well-Governed City: Cooperation, Confrontation, Clarification," *National Civic Review* 75 (March–April 1986): 83.

30 Christopher Hamilton and Donald T. Wells, *Federalism, Power, and Political Economy: A New Theory of Federalism's Impact on American Life* (Englewood Cliffs, NJ: Prentice-Hall, 1990), 131. See also Joseph F. Zimmerman, *State-Local Relations: A Partnership Approach* (New York: Praeger, 1983), and David R. Berman and Lawrence L. Martin, "State-Local Relations: An Examination of Local Discretion," *Public Administration Review* 48 (March–April 1988): 637–641.

31 David R. Berman, Lawrence L. Martin, and Laura Kajfez, "County Home Rule: Does Where You Stand Depend on Where You Sit?", *State and Local Review* (Spring 1985): 232–234. See also Miles, "The Origin and Meaning of Miles' Law."

32 See David R. Berman, "State Actions Affecting Local Governments," *The Municipal Yearbook 1990* (Washington, DC: ICMA, 1990), 56.

33 U.S. Department of Commerce, Bureau of the Census, *City Government Finances in 1988–89* (GF89-4) and *County Government Finances in 1988–89* (GF89-8). For assessments of the performance of the states, see Helen F. Ladd and John Yinger, *America's Ailing Cities* (Baltimore: Johns Hopkins University Press, 1989), and Steven D. Gold, "A Better Scoreboard: States Are Helping Local Governments," *State Legislatures* (April 1990): 27–28.

34 David R. Berman, "States and Their Local Governments: Mandates, Finances, Problems," *The Municipal Yearbook 1991* (Washington, DC: ICMA, 1991), 77.

35 See generally Jane Elizabeth Decker, "Management and Organizational Capacities for Responding to Growth in Florida's Nonmetropolitan Counties," *Journal of Urban Affairs* 9 (1987): 47–61, and Robyne S. Turner, "Intergovernmental Growth Management: A Partnership Framework for State-Local Relations," *Publius* (Summer 1990): 79–85.

36 Linda Morse, "California—How Can We Get to 50 Percent?", *Public Management* (October 1991): 4–10.

37 See generally Ann Calvaresi Barr, "Cost Estimation as an Anti-Mandate Strategy," in *Coping With Mandates: What Are the Alternatives?*, ed. Michael Fix and Daphne Kenyon (Washington, DC: The Urban Institute, 1990), 57–61. See also *Legislative Man-*

dates: State Experiences Offer Insights for Federal Action (Washington, DC: General Accounting Office, 1988).

38 See Richard H. Horte, "State Experiences With Mandate Reimbursement," in Fix and Kenyon, *Coping With Mandates*, 57–61.

39 Coalition to Improve Management in State and Local Government, *Improving Local Services*, 11.

40 See Glenn Abney and Thomas A. Henderson, "An Exchange Model of Intergovernmental Relations: State Legislators and Local Officials," *Social Science Quarterly* 59 (March 1979): 720–731.

41 *State Planning: New Roles in Hard Times* (Lexington, KY: Council of State Governments, 1976), 9–10.

42 Corina Eckl, "Spotlight on Colorado's Advisory Committee on Intergovernmental Relations," *Intergovernmental Perspective* (Spring 1991): 5–6. See generally U.S. Advisory Commission on Intergovernmental Relations, *State-Local Relations Organizations: The ACIR Counterparts* (Washington, DC: GPO, 1991); Deborah D. Roberts, "Carving Out Their Niche: State Advisory Commissions on Intergovernmental Relations," *Public Administration Review* 49 (November-December 1989): 576–580; and Andree E. Reeves, "State ACIRs: Elements of Success," *Intergovernmental Perspective* (Summer 1991): 12–13, 24.

43 Jamie Cooper and Linda Tarr-Whelan, "Turning Urban Nightmares to Dreams," *State Government News* (October 1991): 14–15.

44 Hamilton and Wells, *Federalism, Power, and Political Economy*, 174.

45 Raymond S. Short, "Municipalities and the Federal Government," *The Annals of the American Academy of Political and Social Science* 207 (January 1940): 44–53.

46 Mavis Mann Reeves, "Galloping Intergovernmentalization as a Factor in State Management," *State Government* 54 (1981): 103–108.

47 William R. Dodge, "The Emergence of Intercommunity Partnerships in the 1980s."

48 Randy Arndt, "NLC Fiscal Survey: Budget Gap on Rise," *Nation's Cities Weekly* (July 8, 1991): 1, 8.

49 John P. Thomas, "Financing County Government: An Overview," *Intergovernmental Perspective* (Winter 1991): 11.

50 Jacqueline Calmes, "Bricks Without Straw: The Complaints Go on but Congress Keeps Mandating," *Governing* (September 1988): 21–25.

51 Barbara Todd, "Counties in the Federal System: The State Connection," *Intergovernmental Perspective* (Winter 1991): 21–25.

52 Interviewed in "Glisson: State/Local Partnership Is Needed," *American City & County* (May 1988): 64.

53 Wilbur Zelinsky, "Sister City Alliances," *American Demographics 12* (June 1990): 43–45.

54 James Crupi, "Forces Shaping Local Government in the 90s," *Texas Town & City* (September 1991): 18.

55 Deil S. Wright, *Understanding Intergovernmental Relations*, 2d ed. (Monterey, CA: Brooks/Cole), 397.

56 Walter Scheiber, quoted in John Nalbandian, "Tenets of Contemporary Professionalism in Local Government," *Public Administration Review* 50 (November/December, 1990): 656.

57 Questions adapted from *Interlocal Service Delivery* (Washington, DC: National Association of Counties Research Foundation, 1982), 1.

Leading a manager's life

In 1973, ICMA published a collection of cartoons by Douglas Harman, entitled *On the Joys of Being Manager.*[1] Harman, who was deputy county executive of Fairfax County, Virginia, at the time and later became city manager of Alexandria, Virginia, and Fort Worth, Texas, poked fun at the travails of his own profession: impatient elected officials and citizens; relentless scrutiny and second-guessing; excruciating pressure; long hours that intrude on the manager's personal life; and constant scarcity of resources. But barely hidden in Harman's lighthearted satire are unmistakable clues to what makes the manager's life worth leading: the work of local government is important, otherwise community groups and the media would not care so much; the manager's role is crucial, otherwise the pressures from elected officials, citizens, and employees would not be so great; and the manager's job can provide a sense of accomplishment, satisfaction, and enjoyment, otherwise far fewer talented individuals would be attracted to the ranks of local government managers and fewer still could so comfortably poke fun at themselves.

The life of a local government manager is demanding and stressful; yet for many managers, it is highly stimulating. This chapter discusses the appeal of a career in local government management. It reviews some of the attractions and sources of satisfaction reported by managers themselves, and offers guidance to assist managers in developing a satisfying career. Also included is a discussion of the personal demands placed on managers, as well as a recapitulation of job-related demands, many of which have been addressed in previous chapters. The ability of managers to cope with stressful situations affects not only their effectiveness but also the level of enjoyment and satisfaction they are likely to derive from a career in local government management. For that reason, several techniques for stress management are introduced. Finally, the chapter emphasizes the importance of assessing not only one's own desires, values, personality, and preferred management style but also the characteristics of a given community before accepting a position as its local government manager.

Why be a local government manager?

It is doubtful that any local government manager has escaped altogether the incredulous look of a sympathetic friend who has become aware of the tremendous pressure the manager faces or has just witnessed the manager serve as a community scapegoat. "Why," the friend asks, "would anyone want this job?" A simple response begins with the caveat that the job of city or county manager—or a multitude of other local government management positions of various titles—is not for everyone. But among those committed to a career in public service, the response typically ends on a decidedly positive note. Practicing managers offer a variety of reasons for their attraction to local government and their decision to remain; the most common may be summarized as follows:

The opportunity to perform work that is important
The opportunity, even at a young age, to influence crucial community decisions
The opportunity to see the product of one's work
The high-profile nature of local government issues and activities

The challenge to succeed where success is not guaranteed
The opportunity to take charge of a complex operation
The opportunity to have a positive impact on a community and on individual citizens.

There is an awesome power in public service: the power to do good; the power to fight for what is right and proper; the power to help shape a community's future in some small way.

G. Curtis Branscome

Most local government managers are satisfied with their career choice. In the 1991 State of the Profession survey of ICMA's members, 89 percent of the responding managers described themselves as at least "moderately satisfied" with their jobs. The principal reasons given by managers for choosing a local government career were commitment to public service, the challenge of solving problems, and the opportunity to see tangible results of managerial efforts.[2] Reasons for choosing a career in local government and sources of eventual satisfaction coincide in some respects. Two years earlier, responding local government managers had reported as their greatest sources of satisfaction their relationships with department heads, the opportunity to see the results of their efforts, the quality of their staff, policy implementation, and their relationships with citizens.[3]

Career development

Careers in local government management are shaped in a variety of ways. Individuals from different backgrounds, with different occupational experiences and varying degrees of formal education in assorted disciplines, may become managers. Some highly successful managerial careers have been built on unusual foundations. Nevertheless, common patterns of preparation may be identified.

In the early years of council-manager government, many local government managers were trained as engineers. Over time, however, patterns of preparation and career paths changed considerably, leading to the observation that "the ideal training for a city manager today seems to consist of an undergraduate degree in the liberal arts, graduate work in public administration, and on-the-job training as interns or assistants in city management."[4]

Education

Preparation for a successful career in local government management typically includes advanced education. In 1971, seven of every ten local government managers possessed at least a bachelor's degree. Less than two decades later, the number had soared to nine of every ten.[5] Even more striking, the percentage with graduate degrees had more than doubled from 27 percent to 64 percent. The predominance during the first half of the twentieth century of city managers with training in an engineering specialty has long since passed. Although the college degrees possessed by local government managers reflect study in a variety of fields, today the preference is for a master's degree in public administration or a closely related field (e.g., government administration, city management, city planning, urban affairs, or public affairs).

The tendency for local government managers to possess graduate degrees and for a substantial proportion of them to be in the field of public administration is likely to increase as managers possessing these degrees demonstrate their effectiveness as public administrators. In a study of local government officials with reputations for productivity and innovation, the formal education of those officials was compared with that of local government managers in general. Whereas 64 percent of all managers possessed graduate degrees, 97 percent of those with reputations for productivity or innovation did so. Among those, 61 percent possessed a master's degree in public administration (MPA) or a closely related degree.[6]

Challenges are available in the private sector, but we in the public sector up the ante. Our challenges, our successes, and our failures are public and that adds to the risk, the excitement, and the euphoria if everything comes out okay.
Edward P. Everett

Career paths

A common career path takes a prospective local government manager from an entry-level position as an intern or administrative assistant through the ranks to the position of department head or assistant manager prior to appointment as local government manager. Among the positions often considered conducive to rapid advancement are that of administrative assistant in the office of the city or county manager or in a major department and that of budget analyst, in which an individual can gain broad exposure to governmental operations and simultaneously refine analytical skills. A common second step in large local governments is to the position of senior administrative assistant or budget analyst, perhaps with some supervisory responsibilities, or to the position of assistant to the manager (typically a position with less authority and fewer responsibilities than that of assistant manager). Among smaller local governments, this intermediate step often is skipped in the progression to the next level—assistant manager or department head.

From entry level to manager Although most people serve as assistant managers or department heads before becoming managers, some skip this step, jumping directly to the post of local government manager from an entry-level position. Skipping all of the steps in the normal progression can be a harrowing experience, but it is not altogether uncommon. Governments that hire their manager from the ranks of administrative assistants or ''right out of school'' usually serve small populations.

Previous experience in other jurisdictions The route to the top appointed administrative posts in local government rarely consists of a climb from the bottom rung of the career ladder to the top within a single organization. Although governing bodies tend to prefer managerial candidates with local government experience, they often select managers who acquired that experience elsewhere. A study of city managers appointed in one year revealed that 75 percent were previously employed by another city or town, 10 percent by a public sector employer other than a municipality, and 5 percent by a private sector organization. Only 10 percent were promoted from within.[7] However, it is possible to build an entire career in a single local government, climbing steadily from an entry-level position to the post of manager, although the cases in which this has been done are the exceptions.

A common variation is the manager whose entry-level and perhaps mid-level organizational experience were acquired elsewhere, but whose career as a city or county manager has been confined to a single jurisdiction over a long period of time. Among 1,559 respondents to ICMA's 1990 State of the Profession survey, 12 percent had served in their current managerial position for more that 10 years and more than 5 percent had served beyond 15 years.[8] Such lengthy tenures undoubtedly require many managerial attributes, not the least of which is the flexibility to adapt to the shifting styles and expectations of changing governing bodies that were discussed in Chapter 2.

The assistant manager Common elements may be found in various positions along the career path. Each step up, however, customarily entails additional challenges and broader responsibilities. For this reason, being a manager is very different from being an assistant manager or a department head. One of the major differences is that, to some extent, the attention of most managers is diverted from internal operations to relationships beyond the administrative apparatus of local government—relationships with the governing body, the chamber of commerce and various civic groups, other local governments, the state government, and federal agencies.

For many, the position of assistant manager or department head is a springboard to a position as local government manager. Others, however, remain assistant managers or department heads, often as a matter of preference, and enjoy satisfying careers. Some who choose this path (occasionally after a stint as local government manager) decide that they prefer the role and responsibilities associated with being second in command—concerned mainly with the local government's internal operations—or being in charge of a single department. They choose to build a career in a supporting role, sometimes moving to a larger jurisdiction in a capacity that allows them to broaden their professional skills while retaining a primary focus on internal management or perhaps a particular specialty.

Women and members of minorities For the growing ranks of women and minority aspirants to the post of local government manager, the sequence of steps in the career path is generally one of those previously described. However, the nature of assignments and the rate of advancement often differ from those of their white male counterparts. Greater percentages of women may be found among the ranks of personnel and library directors, for example, than among public works directors and police chiefs, though some may also be found there. Perhaps more significant, the rate of advancement from the position of administrative assistant to that of department head or assistant manager and onward to appointment to local government manager has often been slower for women and members of minorities.

A study of upper- and intermediate-level women managers in Canada's public and private sectors suggested that career advancement of women is hindered not only by the fact that female administrators are outnumbered in most organizations, but also by the persistence of stereotypes. The perceptions and expectations of some colleagues and of society in general continue to form barriers to women's career development.[9]

Members of racial and ethnic minorities may encounter a different set of perceptual hurdles along the career path. However, as more senior managers become aware of the contributions talented women and minority administrators can make and sensitive to the obstacles they confront, as more women and members of minorities are elected to local governing bodies, and as more achieve high-level managerial positions, many of the barriers to advancement will begin to fall. In little more than a decade, the percentage of municipal chief administrative officer/ manager positions in the United States occupied by women grew from 5.9 percent (1980) to 13.2 percent (1991). In comparison, minorities held 4 percent of such positions in 1991, up from 2.3 percent in 1980. At a key intermediate level in municipalities, 34 percent of all assistant manager positions in 1991 were held by women and 9 percent by minorities.[10]

In the 1980s and early 1990s, schools of public administration and members of the local government profession in the United States intensified their efforts to attract women and minorities to the profession. For example, in 1991 the Hispanic Network became a formal affiliate of ICMA after more than ten years of close work between the two organizations to promote the advancement of Hispanics in the local government profession. ICMA also established a formal relationship with the National Forum for Black Public Administrators (NFBPA), with the goal of promoting, strengthening, and expanding the role of African Americans in all aspects of public administration.

Career advancement

Men and women who aspire to a successful and satisfying career in positions of increasing managerial responsibility would be wise to consider each step in their career carefully.

Assessing early opportunities   Even with limited experience, prospective local government managers often are eager—and sometimes overeager—to land a prestigious job with an impressive title and extensive executive responsibilities. Nevertheless, less glamorous choices may better serve their long-term career interests. The following facets of an early job opportunity are often more important than title and starting salary: the nature of the job; the opportunity to test and develop skills; the possibilities for advancement; the opportunity to learn from a respected mentor; the reputation of the employing government; and the job's potential to enhance one's competitiveness for the next step in the career path.

Building a record of accomplishments   Persons intent on reaching the upper echelons of management make a mistake when they define their career objectives only in terms of position title, number of employees supervised, and size of budget. Although such factors are not inconsequential, their significance pales in comparison with a competitor's record of tangible accomplishments. The resume of an administrative assistant who designed and implemented a revised procedure that saved thousands of dollars while improving services is much more impressive than that of a counterpart who "was responsible for supervising three employees while providing assistance to the city manager on a variety of special projects." In most cases, a record of tangible accomplishments is more valuable to a prospective employer than is a background of general experience.

Mobility   Most local government managers build their careers in a series of steps from one local government to another. Ideally, each step marks a greater level of responsibility, either through movement to a higher rung on the career ladder or to a larger or otherwise more challenging or prestigious organization. However, moving too often—"job hopping"—can jeopardize further progress, especially if the moves are not to positions of increased responsibility or if frequent moves persist beyond the early stages of a career. Moreover, ICMA members who job hop violate their code of ethics, which states that a minimum of two years generally is considered necessary in order to render professional service to a community and that a short tenure should be an exception rather than a recurring experience.

Once an individual has achieved appointment to the position of local government manager, the normal career pattern typically entails movement to a similar post in a new city or county every five or six years. There are exceptions. Some managers serve at the head of an organization for more than a decade; others, perhaps because of council turnover or because they may have somehow displeased the council, have a stint or two measured in months rather than years. Aspiring managers who welcome the prospect of at least moderate mobility over the course of a career preserve their options and enhance their opportunities for career development.

Competing in the job market   Local government managers interested in moving to another local government discover quickly that competition for the most desirable positions is fierce. Long before initiating their pursuit, the strongest contenders for such positions establish the foundation for their candidacy by securing the advanced education, gaining the experience, and building the record of accomplishments noted previously. That foundation, coupled with a reasonably keen knowledge of the recruitment process and the ability to present oneself effectively, enhances the odds of a competitive standing in the job market; candidates who meet these criteria enjoy an advantage over their counterparts who do not.

Knowing the ropes in the competition for managerial positions in local government involves not only an awareness of the steps in the standard recruitment process conducted by governing bodies and personnel departments, but also increasingly includes familiarity with the practices of executive search firms. Although most small local governments continue to select their top appointed administrator by screening resumes of candidates and making a choice based on reference checks and interviews with finalists, more and more jurisdictions—especially those with large and medium populations—are enlisting the services of search firms in an effort to enrich the candidate pool and strengthen the screening process. A study of recruitments of city and town managers in 1986 revealed that one in five jurisdictions used the services of a "professional headhunter."[11] All six of the largest cities recruiting a manager that year did so.

Career development is an important matter, deserving the same care and consideration that an executive devotes to major projects on the job. Steady progression through an organization or from one organization to another in increasingly responsible positions rarely just happens. Normally, a candidate must take steps to become qualified for a desired position, develop contacts, make other necessary preparations, and approach professional opportunities knowledgeably and with confidence (see the sidebar on p. 205). Making proper preparations and presenting oneself effectively will not guarantee appointment to a desired position, but failure to do so makes the likelihood of appointment extremely remote.

Employment agreement   Because city and county managers serve at the pleasure of elected officials, they are vulnerable to removal from office with little or no notice. As a result, many have requested and received employment agreements—in the form of a contract, a letter of agreement, or an ordinance or resolution—that clarify and formalize terms of employment. Among the items typically addressed in an employment agreement are duties of the manager, termination procedures, severance pay, periodic performance evaluation, salary, and fringe benefits.

Approximately four of every ten local government managers who responded to a survey on executive compensation reported having an employment agreement,[12] and their ranks are likely to grow as prospective employers vie for desired managerial candidates who already have such agreements in force. Under the tenets of council-manager government, a local government manager cannot be guaranteed a fixed term in office or protected from removal by the governing body. However, an employment agreement may establish clear procedures to be followed in the event of termination and in calculating severance pay. ICMA's model employment agreement recommends a provision for severance pay equal to six months' aggregate salary, benefits, and deferred compensation.

Tackling a new job   Steps taken early in a new manager's tenure—or even prior to the official starting date—can be important to long-term success. A new appointee who invests the time to become knowledgeable about a community and its local government by reading the local newspaper, reviewing the local government charter and organization charts, and examining budgets, financial statements, and major reports before arriving on the job not only benefits from the knowledge gained, but is also likely to make a favorable first impression on new associates. Once on the job, a new manager who attends to the expectations and needs of the governing body, takes advantage of public relations opportunities, promotes staff development and participation, responds to employee input, and willingly gives the

(*continued on page 206*)

Advice to job candidates

Prepare to compete in the future for desired jobs:

Build skills, experience, and accomplishments

Avoid excessive job-hopping, especially later in career

Develop contacts:

Job references

Influential individuals within the profession

Search firms

Consider carefully your choice of references.

Be discreet; but when it is time to move, let the right people know.

Be selective about considering a new position—but only as selective as your circumstances will allow.

Be candid about your strengths, weaknesses, accomplishments, and failures. Make it clear that you have learned from your experiences—good and bad.

Avoid excessive credit-taking and blame-laying.

Be prepared for a comprehensive interviewing process; be prepared to substantiate accomplishments and skills.

Consider your need for confidentiality; do not apply for jobs indiscriminately.

Do not be surprised to encounter an industrial psychologist, simulation exercises, or videotaping in the screening process.

Do not assume that you have to convince a search firm that you are the number one candidate; there will probably be no ranking among the finalists prior to consideration by the hiring body.

Being named as a finalist is complimentary, but do not let up; you must work at establishing a favorable relationship with the hiring body.

Avoid the pitfalls that prevent some candidates from ever making the finalist list:

Applying for positions that you are not qualified to hold; allowing delusions of grandeur to prevent application for and steady progression through the next logical job

Scattershot applications

Poorly prepared resumes and letters

Do not be reluctant to apply for a job that interests you even if you do not match the specified qualifications exactly, especially if the qualifications are unusual and you think you are particularly strong in at least one of the specified areas.

If an executive search firm is involved, use it as a source of information about the position, the community, the organization, and the desires of the hiring body.

A candidate's presence, image, appearance, demeanor, courtesy, and impressions conveyed are all subjective—and also very important.

Do your homework on the jurisdiction.

Approach each stage of the selection process seriously. Do not wait until the final stage to begin considering factors that should have been contemplated much earlier and might result in withdrawal from candidacy.

Source: Adapted from David N. Ammons and James J. Glass, *Recruiting Local Government Executives: Practical Insights for Hiring Authorities and Candidates* (San Francisco: Jossey-Bass, 1989), 189.

(*continued from page 204*)
credit for accomplishments to the governing body or to subordinates is more likely to get off to a good start.[13]

Knowing when to move on　The excitement that a new manager feels upon being hired, the energy that is generated by new challenges, and the honeymoon relationship with a supportive governing body may begin to fade after the first year or two on the job. Saying "no" to enough special interests may gradually gain the new manager a group of detractors. Eventually, new governing body members are elected, perhaps after campaigning on the need for change, and some of them may express privately—or perhaps even publicly—a desire for "their own manager." Alternatively, community satisfaction and the confidence of the governing body may remain firmly intact, but the manager's enthusiasm may have begun to wane after several years with the growing feeling that the major challenges associated with the job have been met. In either case, it may be time to look for new challenges and new opportunities.

In the absence of pressure from the governing body or other, sometimes subtle, signs of growing displeasure,[14] the decision of whether to remain with a particular local government can be difficult. Nevertheless, the decision to remain or leave an organization is made over and over again by many people in various occupations, not just local government managers. According to career consultants Barry and Linda Gale, "above-average" persons typically decide to change jobs approximately eight times during their career.[15] Before one makes such a decision, the Gales suggest careful consideration of important aspects of one's current job as well as personal attributes (see the sidebar on p. 207). Their advice, adapted to apply to local government managers, suggests consideration of the following factors:

Interpersonal relationships with the governing body, the chief elected official, department heads, and other influential individuals

Office politics

Personal values and skills, and the degree to which they are compatible with one's current job

The direction in which the local government is headed and the likelihood that one's contributions will be rewarded in a fashion that is personally meaningful

The stressfulness of one's current situation

One's willingness to take risks or try something new, perhaps an entrepreneurial endeavor

One's willingness to undergo the inconvenience and disruption—both personal and professional—of making a move.

Sometimes the manager decides to stay. Persons well suited to and challenged by their current position and appreciated by their employer need not feel pressured by some rule of thumb that says local government managers should change their jobs every six or seven years.[16]

Pressures on local government managers

A career in local government is demanding and often stressful. The demands on managers take many forms. Some relate to aspects of the job itself and to associated interpersonal relationships. Others, though influenced by the job, are more personal in nature.

Personal values of relevance to career choice

From the following list of job-related values, select the six that hold the most attraction for you.

Above-average income
Adventure
Appreciating beauty
Artistic impression
Change
Community involvement
Competition
Contact with people
Creativity
Excitement
Expanding knowledge
Fast pace
Feelings of belonging
Flexibility of schedule
Helping others
Helping society
Independence from supervision
Influencing people

Location
Making decisions
Mental challenge
Moral fulfillment
Physical challenge
Power
Precision
Recognition
Security
Stability
Supervisory responsibility
Working alone
Working under pressure
Working with others

How many of the six values you selected does your present job satisfy?

Source: Adapted from Barry and Linda Gale, *Stay or Leave* (New York: Harper and Row, 1989), 39–41. Copyright 1989 by Barry and Linda Gale. Reprinted with permission of HarperCollins.

Job demands

Three factors often associated with stressful occupations are role ambiguity, role conflict, and role overload. The management of local government is characterized by all three.

Role ambiguity   The manager is expected to be an expert administrator, carrying out the policy directives of the governing body—even when those directives are imprecise or contradictory, even when resources are insufficient, and even when sufficient authority to perform the task has not been granted. The manager is expected to render sound policy advice; yet many managers believe it wise to refrain from public acknowledgment of a substantial role in the policy process. In some cases, local government managers are denied the authority to appoint and remove department heads and may even possess few realistic options for preventing subordinates from going over their heads to the governing body; nevertheless, managers are expected to maintain control over the entire administrative operation.

Role conflict   Under conditions of ambiguity, role conflict may be extensive. Council members have expectations regarding the manager's role that may differ from those of the manager, professional colleagues, subordinates, and citizens, or that may deviate from professional norms or even charter prescriptions. For instance, the assumption that the manager has full authority over operating departments occasionally collides with council expectations that the manager will assume a more subservient or ''responsive''role on sensitive matters, deferring to the council in such cases. Failed attempts by city managers to remove police chiefs—their nominal subordinates in most council-manager governments—are legendary. Such occurrences dramatically depict the commonplace disparity between the role formally assigned to the post of manager (in this case, management of all municipal operations, including the authority to appoint or remove the chief of police) and the role that the city council may expect the manager to play.

Role overload   Role overload is apparent in the hectic pace and long workweek typical of the local government manager's job. (Surveys have found the typical workweek to average 53 to 57 hours.[17]) Like chief executives in other fields, local government managers rush from task to task throughout the day: a breakfast meeting with community leaders, a staff meeting back at the office, a half hour to dictate responses to letters or answer a few phone calls, a quick visit with a department head to discuss the concerns of a commissioner, lunch at a civic club, an afternoon that proceeds at much the same pace, an evening meeting, and a briefcase full of memos and reports to read at home. Such schedules create a pressure-packed formula for overload; yet, there is considerable evidence to suggest that persons attracted to the role of chief executive may actually thrive on the frantic pace—right up to the point of burnout.

In his seminal study of executive roles and work activities, Henry Mintzberg concluded that executives not only tolerate a work situation characterized by fragmented tasks, brevity in nearly everything they do, and almost constant interruptions, but many actually prefer that mode of operation for at least four reasons. First, they fear any other pattern would deny them the constantly updated information vital to their effectiveness. Second, they become accustomed to great variety in their work and grow to enjoy it. Third, most of their activities are related to problems or opportunities they consider important. Accordingly, they are reluctant to abandon personal involvement in any of them. And fourth, they recognize that some duties can be performed only by the chief executive and may not be delegated.[18]

City manager Arlene Loble confirmed the paradoxical appeal of the pressure-packed pace of local government management: ''The work offers the kind of variety that challenges a creative mind. I love the pressure of the rapid pace. At the same time, I'm always working to relieve that pressure.''[19] Despite the heavy demands placed on local government managers, most continue to report moderate to high levels of satisfaction with their job. Nevertheless, surveys have indicated that 5 to 7 percent may be actively seeking employment outside local government at any given time.[20] Many sources of frustration undoubtedly contribute to this modest, though not inconsequential, evidence of interest in leaving the profession. The frustrations cited most frequently in surveys are inadequate resources, inadequate time for the manager's family and for managers themselves, general job pressures, negative feelings of citizens toward government, and government's inability to take advantage of its opportunities.[21]

Personal demands

As implied in the second most frequently cited frustration for local government managers—lack of time for their family and themselves—some job demands spill over into managers' personal lives. For example, local government managers have less privacy and must relocate more often than members of many other occupations. Some demands, however, work the other way around. A personal crisis can compound job pressures not only on the manager but also on the manager's associates.

Family relations   Nine of ten local government managers are married, and most of them regard their spouse as an important source of emotional support.[22] However, a manager's family can also be a source of pressure. Possible causes include all the common family crises, plus some related to the manager's position: the behavior of a teenaged child that reflects poorly on the manager; a spouse who unintentionally becomes involved in an activity or discussion having local political ramifications; resentment from a family member whose employment options are narrowed by the manager's concern over potential conflict of interest; and even self-inflicted pressure emanating from the manager's sense of guilt at spending too little time with the family.

City managers must be able to patiently and expertly respond to all criticism involving city activities, suffer the consequences of city decisions or indecisions not necessarily under their control, work extraordinarily long hours, and subject their families to some of the same pressures.
David R. Mora

Lack of privacy Privacy is a scarce commodity for local government managers and their families; that, too, places pressure on the manager that may be carried back to the professional arena. Life in the proverbial goldfish bowl can become tiresome. For women and minority managers, the additional burden of being a role model can be especially great and the spotlight of almost constant scrutiny, especially glaring.

Mobility and job security As noted earlier, local government management tends to be a mobile profession. The act of intermittently uprooting a family, as well as the constant realization that the impetus for the move may come suddenly, can be stressful to a family, especially when members have become attached to the community.

The single manager Single managers have many of the same concerns as married managers, but the demands on them can be even greater or more complex. If a single manager is divorced, family relationships can be a source of pressure; if the manager lives in the same community as his or her children and ex-spouse, the pressure may be intensified. Life in the goldfish bowl can be particularly difficult for single managers in small communities; their social life is so public that in order to avoid becoming the subject of gossip, they may feel it necessary to go to other communities to form social relationships. And for single managers, life can be especially "lonely at the top." These managers may need to make a special effort to develop a support network of colleagues and friends (perhaps from other communities) with whom they can discuss both job-related and personal problems.

Psychological factors

Life stages Familiarity with the stages of human psychological development may help managers better understand the pressures that they and their associates sometimes feel.[23] As people move through these stages, their attitudes and behavior are thought to change in fairly predictable ways. In the United States, for example, adolescence is considered a stage in which young people characteristically challenge adult authority in an attempt to establish their own identities. Similarly, middle age is seen as a stage in which adults commonly face what is called mid-life crisis. Although research on women is not extensive, Michael McGill concluded from his studies that as many as one-third of all men experience a significant challenge to their self-concept during this stage.[24] Men and women alike may feel that their identity and the way of life they struggled to establish are threatened by events over which they have no control: their children grow up; they themselves grow older; other people's perceptions of them sometimes change as they begin to age. As a result, adults who find themselves in the throes of mid-life crisis may form a new self-image.

Many managers have entered or are approaching their middle years. Some may find that their achievements have fallen short of their expectations, or consider themselves physically less attractive, or have increased concerns for their health. Some middle-aged and older managers may feel that they can no longer compete with younger, more energetic colleagues for promotions or desirable assignments. If such concerns become preoccupations, they almost inevitably affect job performance. Those most vulnerable to mid-life crisis, according to Michael McGill, are people who have invested themselves primarily in a single aspect of their lives rather than those who draw their sense of self from a variety of sources. These individuals may exhibit significant changes in their attitudes, priorities, and behavior, on and off the job.

Managers who understand the nature of these and similar changes and who are aware of the interaction between people's private and personal lives are better equipped to cope with their own behavior and that of their associates. Without such an awareness, a childless manager or one at an early stage in the family cycle who is being pressured for tougher enforcement of drug laws, for example, may fail to understand the mixed emotions and behavior of a mayor or a police chief who is in what pyschologists call the "full-house plateau" stage and who fears that a rebellious teenager in his or her own household is experimenting with illegal drugs and may suffer the full penalty of those laws. The manager may similarly misinterpret a middle-aged department head's desire to refocus on his family as a sign of waning interest in his work, when in fact it may reflect a more complex, but quite common, life cycle change.

Psychological type   Finally, an individual's personality or psychological type can influence perceptions of, and reactions to, job-related and personal demands. For example, research suggests that three characteristics identify stress-prone individuals: (1) an urgent manner, (2) a tendency toward hostility and aggressiveness, and (3) an excessive need to control.[25] The similarity of those characteristics and the personality traits commonly associated with Type A or "workaholic" behavior is unmistakable.[26]

Local government management is a highly demanding occupation. Many of the job-related demands have ramifications for a manager's family and personal life. In turn, family and personal pressures, the life stage an individual occupies, and his or her pyschological type influence the manager's work experience, relations with work associates, and—inevitably—job performance.

Stress management

Stress induces physical and mental tension. A moderate dose of stress can be beneficial, because it may focus an individual's attention and promote top performance; a great deal of stress, however, can be bad, because it may reduce an individual's ability to perform effectively and, in extreme cases, may be debilitating. Prime sources of stress include not only occupational factors such as role ambiguity, conflict, and overload, but also stressful life events. Prime symptoms of stress include job dissatisfaction, job tension, and emotional and pyschosomatic distress.[27]

The variety and intensity of demands placed on local government managers make theirs a stressful occupation. Coupled with the major job-related and personal demands noted in the previous section are a few other stressors worthy of special mention. Salary is an example. In the interest of personal financial security, managers are advised to enroll in a portable retirement program and to maintain a financial cushion of at least six months' salary against sudden loss of employment or other emergencies. For those straining to build such a cushion or struggling to save for college or retirement while meeting current obligations, it often seems that personal income simply will not stretch far enough. Although the salary of local government managers typically exceeds civil service scales, it remains comparatively modest executive compensation, often much less than that of the private

(*continued on page 212*)

Symptoms of burnout

Physical symptoms

Fatigue, physical depletion, exhaustion

Sleep difficulties (e.g., insomnia, nightmares)

Back pain

Gastro-intestinal problems (e.g., stomachaches, appetite loss, bowel difficulties)

Headaches

Colds and flu

Behavioral symptoms

Job turnover

Poor job performance (e.g., neglectful, mistake-prone, requiring supervisory discipline more often)

Absenteeism/tardiness

Overeating or oversmoking

Extended work breaks

Workplace theft

Prone to workplace injury

Use of alcohol or drugs (e.g., tranquilizers)

Attitudinal symptoms

Cynicism

Callousness

Pessimism

Defensiveness

Intolerance of clients

Lack of confidence regarding personal effectiveness or accomplishments

Lack of commitment to profession

Desire to escape from people or avoid going to work

Reduced expectations

Negative attitudes toward self or life in general

Reduced satisfaction with role and daily activities (personal and professional)

Low job satisfaction

Emotional symptoms

Depression

Guilt

Anxiety

Nervousness

Emotional depletion

Anger

Irritability

Tearfulness

Hopelessness

Loneliness

Interpersonal symptoms

Work interferes with family life

Defensive escape or avoidance of clients (e.g., refusal to answer phone, hanging up on callers)

Verbal attacks or even physical violence toward others

Increased tendency to complain of work problems to family and co-workers ("staff gripes")

Fewer friends

Preference for solitary activities

Lower level of marital satisfaction

Lower quality of personal relations with friends and family

Tendency to display negative emotions and withdraw from spouse or family

More likely to disagree with spouse about children's discipline

Spouse more likely to feel depressed and shut out

Tendency to feel less involved in family matters, more distant from children, and to feel spouse does not understand pressures of job

Note: The relationship of burnout to general physical health and job satisfaction has been explored extensively. All other symptoms listed, though supported by initial research, should be regarded as probable symptoms.

Source: Adapted from Sophia Kahill, "Symptoms of Professional Burnout: A Review of the Empirical Evidence," *Canadian Psychology* 29 (July 1988): 284–297. Copyright 1988 Canadian Psychological Association. Reprinted with permission.

(*continued from page 210*)
sector counterparts with whom managers are expected to interact professionally and socially. This discrepancy may add financial stress to the manager's life, especially if it prevents the accumulation of a personal reserve and thereby induces feelings of guilt over the financial vulnerability of the manager's family.

It appears to be the way of the world that those jobs with high psychic income do not compensate very well with hard cash.
G. Curtis Branscome

A local government manager's susceptibility to termination is another obvious stressor. Superior performance on the job may reduce that vulnerability but does not eliminate it. Changes in the political fortunes of those persons with the authority to retain or replace the manager may result in the manager's dismissal. Personality conflicts with top elected officials or squabbles among those officials themselves may produce the same result. Vulnerability to termination is an occupational hazard that managers learn to live with, but even under the best of circumstances and with the most favorable relations it remains a source of latent stress.

In order to avoid the negative effects of stress, managers are well advised to assess their own stress levels and then to develop stress and time management techniques appropriate to their personality, interests, and needs.

Personal stress level

Several instruments have been developed to measure stress levels. Some focus on individual perceptions and attitudes regarding possible stressors; some focus on life events that could contribute to stress; and others assess pyschosomatic distress, probing, for example, the frequency of headaches, stomach ailments, back pain, chest pain, sleep disorders, and fatigue. Still others combine various elements. Some assessment instruments are relatively sophisticated.[28] Others, such as the two in the exercise at the end of this chapter, are fairly simple. The first, Breakwell's stress checklist, combines elements of individual behavior and attitudes and a few indicators of psychosomatic distress. The second instrument, Holmes and Rahe's social readjustment rating scale, is perhaps the most frequently cited gauge for assessing stress attributable to life events.[29]

Coping with stress

Among the most important factors in successful stress management are an individual's coping strategies, health habits, and support networks.

Coping strategies   Three common strategies, adopted singly or in combination, are often used to cope with the problems associated with stress:

Coping through control

Coping through escape

Coping through symptom management.[29]

Approaches within the first two strategies may focus on action or on a revised mental outlook (''cognitive reappraisal''). Characteristics of the three strategies (not all of which are truly effective or beneficial) are outlined in the sidebar on pages 214–215.

Control   Control strategies tend to involve an active approach. A manager attempts to identify the cause of stress and initiates changes to reduce stress to a tolerable level. If the stress emanates from a relationship, steps are taken to resolve possible misunderstandings and to improve the relationship. If the source of stress is a rule or regulation, steps are taken to bring about its modification. It is also possible, of course, that managers are the source of their own stress—for example, if they are always too eager to accept more work, if they make unrealistic promises to superiors or subordinates, or if their own perception of events exaggerates stress. When a manager's perception of a relationship or situation distorts its stressfulness, reflecting on that perception more realistically or more optimistically (cognitive reappraisal) may be beneficial. Looking for the "bright side" or the "silver lining" in a difficult situation may allow the manager to recognize a previously undetected opportunity that can be tackled enthusiastically.

Escape   The various escape strategies for coping with stress involve problem avoidance. Among the possible active approaches to this strategy are avoidance of difficult issues through delegation to subordinates or "passing the buck" to superiors, waltzing around difficult problems, and even escape through resignation. Among the cognitive reappraisal options of the escape strategy are denial of an issue's existence and insistence that a crucial issue is actually unimportant.

Symptom management   Symptom management strategies are perhaps those most commonly found in formal stress management programs. Even preventive programs designed to increase resistance to, or tolerance of, stress often are geared more toward eliminating the consequences of stress—its symptoms—rather than its causes. Some of the common symptom management techniques are biofeedback, muscle relaxation, transcendental meditation, cognitive restructuring/behavioral skills training, deep-breathing exercises, self-hypnosis, and yoga. Several of these techniques have been found to be generally effective in increasing stress tolerance and reducing the physical and psychological symptoms of stress, thereby producing benefits for both individuals (for example, reductions in anxiety, sleep difficulties, and muscle tension) and their employers. Some analyses claim a benefits-to-cost ratio in excess of 5 to 1 and reduced performance errors among participants in stress reduction programs.[31] Such programs, and those emphasizing exercise, diet, and nutrition, have also been linked to reductions in obesity and heart disease, fewer back problems, and improvements in emotional well-being. Despite evidence of favorable results from these techniques, once the formal program of instruction ends, many participants gradually discontinue their use. To combat that tendency, individuals may find it helpful to reinforce their own commitment by teaching someone else the technique or by securing the participation of a friend or family member.[32]

Of the three coping strategies, control strategies have most often been associated with preferred results.[33] For example, a recent study linked control strategies to decreased burnout, while escape strategies were associated with increased burnout.[34] The third strategy, symptom management, treats the victims and potential victims of stress rather than its causes. Because control strategies cannot be expected to rid a job of stressors altogether, the ideal approach to stress management may be a blend of control and symptom management strategies.

Health habits and lifestyle   Less formal approaches to combating the symptoms of stress include the establishment and maintenance of good health habits and a moderate lifestyle. Limiting consumption of alcohol, caffeine, and tobacco and ensuring proper exercise, nutrition, sleep, and regular physical check-ups are important measures that seldom require formal programs. Although many managers undoubtedly get too little exercise, consume too much coffee, get too little sleep, and otherwise depart from optimal health habits, many others guard their personal health jealously. For many, hobbies and activities outside local government serve as important means of physical and emotional release from occupational stress.[35]

Coping strategies

Coping through control

When facing problems of role ambiguity, conflict, or overload, I . . .

Get together with my city council/supervisor to discuss this.

Try to be very organized so that I can keep on top of things.

Try to think of myself as a winner—as someone who always comes through.

Tell myself that I can probably work things out to my advantage.

Think about the challenges I can find in this situation.

Decide what I think should be done and explain this to the people who are affected.

Request help from people who have the power to do something for me.

Work on changing policies that caused this situation.

Throw myself into my work and work harder, longer hours.

Anticipate the negative consequences so that I'm prepared for the worst.[a]

Delegate work to others.[a]

Coping through escape

When facing problems of role ambiguity, conflict, or overload, I . . .

Avoid being in this situation if I can.

Tell myself that time takes care of situations like this.

Remind myself that work isn't everything.

Separate myself as much as possible from the people who created this situation.

Do my best to get out of the situation gracefully.[b]

Accept this situation because there is nothing I can do to change it.

Set my own priorities based on what I like to do.

Taking time out regularly to do something unrelated to the job that is truly enjoyable may be one of the simplest and most practical methods of diversion and stress therapy. As city manager Linda Barton remarked:

How can I devote time to enjoyment and pleasure when I have such heavy work, family, and community responsibilities? My response to this is: How can we *not* devote some time to relaxing, reducing stress, and smelling the roses? After all, our health and attitudes are the most important elements of our ability to energetically and enthusiastically approach the problems, challenges, and long hours associated with management-related work.

Support networks   Support networks made up of family, friends, or professional associates may provide crucial reinforcement to other stress management strategies. Close confidants who can help a manager assess a stressful situation and design a control strategy to deal with the source, who can provide honest and trusted advice to a manager tempted by escape strategies, or who can encourage and perhaps participate with the manager in an exercise or health maintenance program can be of major benefit.

Few people other than local government managers themselves fully grasp the problems and pressures in their environment. Their job is the only one of its kind in their jurisdiction; no one else shares precisely the same perspective. Nevertheless, a support network can be formed that includes persons who understand at least part of the pressures and who have the manager's interest at heart. The crucial

Coping through symptom management

When feeling tense because of my job, I . . .

Get extra sleep or nap.

Drink a moderate amount (i.e., 2 drinks) of liquor, beer, or wine.

Take tranquilizers, sedatives, or other drugs.

Do physical exercise.

Practice transcendental meditation, biofeedback, or relaxation training.

Seek company of friends or family.

Eat or snack.

Watch TV.

Attend sporting, cultural, or community events.

Take it out on family or friends.

Pursue other hobbies or leisure time activities.

Go buy something; spend money.

Take time off from work.

Change physical state (hairstyle, massage, sauna, sexual activity).

Take a trip to another city.

Daydream.

Seek professional help or counseling.

Turn to prayer or spiritual thoughts.

Complain to others.

Smoke cigarettes, cigars, or pipe.

[a] May be considered an escape strategy in conditions of role ambiguity.
[b] May be considered a control strategy in conditions of role overload.

Source: Adapted from Janina C. Latack, "Coping with Job Stress: Measures and Future Directions for Scale Development," *Journal of Applied Psychology* 71 (August 1986): 377–385. Copyright 1986 The American Psychological Association. Adapted by permission.

element of a support network is someone, often a spouse, who offers unconditional support, a sympathetic ear, and, ideally, an unshakeable emotional foundation.

Trusted department heads or other work associates—especially those whose mutual interests and personality bind them to the manager in a friendship extending beyond their occupational ties—may form part of the support network. They, more than most others, understand the problems and pressures of the work environment they share. Colleagues who hold similar positions in other communities may be another important element of the network. They can offer camaraderie at professional association events and expert advice on difficult or sensitive issues. Whether they offer serious advice or simply swap "war stories," professional colleagues can help a manager to view matters philosophically and keep them in perspective. Finally, personal friends who have no occupational ties whatsoever to the manager may offer diversion, relief from daily pressures, or a welcome outside view on troublesome matters, even if their grasp of the manager's professional world is limited. Personal friends who share a common spiritual faith may be especially comforting in particularly trying times, as when managers face unfair public criticism or the emotional upheaval of a serious family crisis or sudden job loss.[36]

I have come to know a host of other managers, particularly in the two years on the ICMA Board. With that many friends and acquaintances in the same predicament, there is no reason ever to feel "lonely at the top."
Fritz M. Bowers

Time management

The pressures of managing in local government put a premium on the ability to handle multiple functions without creating a bottleneck that slows progress on important projects of the organization. Deriving full value from the time available in a day contributes to effective operations, whereas ineffective time management limits the amount and quality of work the manager can perform and increases the stress at the top of the organization and throughout its ranks.

Potential time thieves are everywhere in city hall and county offices. Incessant, poorly planned, or meaningless meetings, drop-in visitors, telephone interruptions, and erratic crisis management are obvious examples. The manager's own tendencies to handle work personally that could be delegated to others, to procrastinate, and to say ''yes'' when the answer should be ''no'' may also rob the manager of valuable time.[37]

A great deal of time management advice has been offered to busy executives from many different sources. Several such tips are presented in the sidebar on page 217. Time management techniques will not solve all the manager's problems or eliminate stress. Some techniques may not suit a particular individual. Others, however, are likely to have some appeal and deserve a try. Several will prove helpful in relieving part of the pressure on executive time, and for most managers will be more than worth the effort required to use them.

Career suitability

A career in local government management demands long hours, hard work, and the ability to tolerate a great deal of pressure. In return, it offers an opportunity to engage in meaningful work, to influence the direction of a community, to touch the lives of citizens, and to see the tangible results of one's efforts. On most days, managers well suited to their work consider that to be a good deal.

This career offers enormous opportunities for positive contributions to . . . people and communities. I have little doubt but that local government administration today is one of the most challenging and fulfilling careers available.
Douglas Harman

Local government management offers opportunities for public service and challenges to personal strength and professional skill unmatched by most other fields. But it would be inaccurate and inappropriate to imply that anyone who has personal fortitude and managerial expertise is well suited to a career in local government. The career-suitability calculation is a bit more complex than that. In considering a choice of career or a particular opportunity within that career, failure to be perfectly honest with oneself about personal aspirations, needs, likes, and dislikes may have serious, lifelong ramifications. Introspection is especially important when considering whether to embark upon or to remain in a career as potentially stressful as local government management.

A good match

Successful managers are not all cut from the same cloth. They reflect considerable diversity in background and personality, which suggests that individuals need not conform to a particular pattern to consider themselves city or county manager stock. Nevertheless, some general tendencies among managers may be detected. As noted previously, managers increasingly pursue and secure advanced degrees, typically a master's degree in public administration. Most earn their spurs, so to speak, by working their way up through entry- and mid-level administrative positions in local

Tips for gaining control of your time

Control the telephone.

Keep calls short and relevant—guide the caller to the point by asking pleasantly, "What may I do for you?"

Let a secretary intercept calls.

Establish a block of time for returning most calls, ideally at a time of day when others are less likely to want to chat.

Try to limit the scope of the call: "Hi, Sam; I need brief answers to two questions."

Decide what tasks are most important.

Plan. Dedicate time for high-priority items and try to work other things in.

Use spare time wisely—travel time, waiting for a meeting to begin, etc.

Except for highest priority tasks, settle for results that are satisfactory or "good enough"" (i.e., "satisfice").

Set personal objectives with deadlines.

Avoid procrastination.

Break tasks into manageable components.

Attack the most important problems or tasks on your agenda at your best time of the day.

Announce your goals to others.

Gain control of drop-in visitors.

Stand during information exchanges.

Shield some time against intrusions.

Go to the other person's office, so that you can leave when necessary.

Meet meetings head-on.

Discourage unnecessary meetings.

Organize the meeting, including an agenda, a fixed time for convening and adjourning, and a format for follow-up.

Do not allow committees to outlive their usefulness.

Invite persons whose input is needed; exclude those whose time would be wasted.

Schedule meetings with adequate time but close enough to lunch or quitting time to discourage dawdling.

Discourage rambling, off-target speeches or discussions.

Avoid outside interruptions (e.g., telephone, visitors).

Manage your paperwork.

Clear your desk and establish a system for handling paper work.

Handle each item (letter, memo, etc.) only once.

Try speed reading or skimming, especially of lower priority materials.

Use modern technology, such as dictation equipment.

Take legitimate shortcuts—jot your response on the bottom of a letter or memo and return it.

Insist that subordinates provide information succinctly (e.g., one-page summary).

Delegate to the lowest level capable of handling a task competently.

Source: Adapted from David N. Ammons and Charldean Newell, *City Executives: Leadership Roles, Work Characteristics, and Time Management* (Albany, NY: State University of New York Press, 1989).

---

government. A promising potential match for the manager's position would therefore be a person with a strong public service orientation, the intelligence to perform at the graduate level of study, and an eagerness to learn the ropes through a period of apprenticeship.

Efforts to identify the personality types of local government managers have revealed several tendencies or characteristics that distinguish them from their private sector counterparts. Local government managers in one study were reported to be more inclined than private sector executives "to see things in terms of facts, details, the here-and-now"; to base their decisions on logic; to make judgments; and to take actions. They were also found to be less extroverted and perhaps less innovative than their corporate counterparts.[38] Persons of a psychological type similar to that of the majority of managers in the study may find themselves well suited to a local government management career; yet those who differ may be pleased to know that many other personality types were also found in the sample and that different types may thrive in different communities.

As important as an individual's suitability for a career in local government management may be, community characteristics must also be carefully considered prior to any career move. As described in Chapter 2, variations in at least four dimensions of leadership style (internal versus external orientation, innovativeness, technical orientation, and flexibility) produce managerial types ranging from "community leaders" to "caretaker" managers. Each managerial type may be a good match for a community whose character, orientation, political configuration, and needs are most complemented by that type and by the personal characteristics of a given manager. An honest, pre-employment assessment of one's personality and management type—coupled with careful consideration of community characteristics and the prospects of a good fit in a given locale—may make the difference between a managerial stint that is enjoyable and successful, and one that is not.

Know thyself

Personality tests and other instruments to gauge attributes, aptitudes, and preferences may be helpful in weighing career choices and specific job opportunities, but in the final analysis it is the individual who must decide whether he or she desires and is well suited to a career in local government management. The opportunities for meaningful and rewarding public service are great, but so are the pressures. A realistic assessment of the pros and cons is most likely to lead to a satisfactory decision. For those who choose to pursue the life of a local government manager, adopting appropriate coping strategies for dealing with the inevitable occupational and personal stresses is likely to lead to a more enjoyable and rewarding career.

Would I do it all over again? Sure I would. Maybe not *all* of it over again, but most of it . . . Quite simply, I've spent a long time doing something I enjoy.
Donald F. McIntyre

Recap

Local government management is a career that offers immense opportunities for meaningful public service. It continues to draw capable men and women who are attracted by the chance to use their skills for community good and by the opportunity to see the tangible products of their efforts. Most report moderate to high satisfaction from their work.

The career path in local government typically takes the prospective manager from an entry-level administrative position through one or more intermediate steps before appointment to the top position, often in a local government other than the one in which the journey began. Increasingly well-educated, managers usually encounter formidable competition in pursuit of the most desirable positions. Once selected, a manager is well advised to take deliberate steps to get off to a good start in the new job and to establish solid relations. Later, it may be important that the manager be sensitive to signs that it is time to move on.

The work of local government managers entails multiple demands that place considerable pressure on them and their families. Their ability to meet those demands and cope with job-related and personal stress can be the difference between effective and ineffective performance. Coping successfully with stress, both in oneself and in work associates, entails recognizing the symptoms of stress, identifying its source, and devising an effective strategy for dealing with it. Coping through control, coping through escape, and coping through symptom management are three common strategies. Of those three, control strategies have been found to be most effective and escape strategies least effective.

An examination of individual attributes and personality traits offers a revealing glimpse of different types who may be more or less suited for dealing with the difficulties inherent in local government management. It also provides evidence on the prevalence of various types within the field. Despite some common problems and common characteristics, however, differences do exist in the needs and expectations of local governments. A manager who is suitable for one may be less satisfactory for another. In the final analysis, the individual must decide whether he or she desires and is well suited to a career in local government management—whether he or she can tolerate the pressures or perhaps even find them stimulating, and whether the many sources of satisfaction in local government management provide sufficient reward.

Stress assessment instruments

The following stress assessment instruments may be used by managers to assess their personal stress levels. Managers may find it useful to discuss and compare their results with colleagues. Given your stress assessment scores or those of your colleagues, what health maintenance or stress reduction practices would you recommend?

Breakwell's Stress Checklist

The stress checklist was designed to give you some idea of how stressed you are at work. Check the column that best reflects what is true for you. Go through the list quickly; your first response is normally the most revealing. Be honest: after all, only you will see the results.

	Always	Sometimes	Rarely	Never
1. I finish the working day feeling satisfied with what I've done.	—	—	—	—
2. I feel in control of my life.	—	—	—	—
3. I experience dizzy spells or palpitations.	—	—	—	—
4. I feel fatigue or lack of energy.	—	—	—	—
5. I have difficulty getting to sleep.	—	—	—	—
6. I am confident about the future.	—	—	—	—
7. I have a poor appetite.	—	—	—	—
8. I lose my temper over minor things.	—	—	—	—
9. I can rely on my family or friends to support me if I need help.	—	—	—	—
10. I find the amount of work I have exceeds the amount of time available for it.	—	—	—	—
11. I feel I'm as good as anyone else at the job I do.	—	—	—	—
12. I find [the governing body/management] supportive.	—	—	—	—
13. I look forward to going to work.	—	—	—	—

14. I do not know what I'm working for.	—	—	—	—
15. I am unable to unwind in the evening.	—	—	—	—
16. I have more responsibility than I can handle.	—	—	—	—
17. I drink too much alcohol.	—	—	—	—
18. I can switch off thinking about problems.	—	—	—	—
19. I think I manage my time well.	—	—	—	—
20. I know how to refuse to take on additional work if I need to.	—	—	—	—

How to add up your score

Questions 1, 2, 6, 9, 11, 12, 13, 18, 19, 20: Score 1 for *always*, 2 for *sometimes*, 3 for *rarely*, and 4 for *never*.

Questions 3, 4, 5, 7, 8, 10, 14, 15, 16, 17: Score 4 for *always*, 3 for *sometimes*, 2 for *rarely*, and 1 for *never*.

(Minimum score 20; maximum score 80)

How to interpret your score

Interpret your score with some caution. Two people with the same overall score may react differently to stress for a number of reasons: each one's sources of stress differ, as may the strategies each adopts to cope with stress. These interpretations are meant as guidelines to help you compare yourself with others.

Score

70–80 Very few people experience so high a level of stress. Take some action to remove yourself from the sources of your stress.

60–70 About 20 percent of the working population experience this level of stress. Take some remedial action. The longer you bear this level of stress, the more difficult things will become.

40–60 Scores in this range represent a moderate, normal level of stress for a busy professional. Monitor yourself for any drift toward higher levels and watch especially for periods or events that heighten your stress sharply.

20–40 Enviably low level of stress. (Did you answer all the questions honestly?)

It is worth noting your score and rechecking your stress level at regular intervals or after significant changes in your life or in your job. Changes can go unnoticed until the effects are serious because the psychological and physical consequences of stress are gradual and cumulative.

Once you have determined your stress score, you might wish to compare it with the scores of colleagues. This can be instructive because you might be able to pinpoint common sources of stress; you could then consider together what changes need to be introduced.

Source: Adapted from Glynis M. Breakwell, "Are You Stressed Out?" *American Journal of Nursing* 90 (August 1990): 32. Copyright 1990 The American Journal of Nursing Co. Used with permission. All rights reserved.

Holmes and Rahe's Social Readjustment Rating Scale

Life event	Mean value
1. Death of spouse	100
2. Divorce	73
3. Marital separation	65
4. Jail term	63

5. Death of close family member	63
6. Personal injury or illness	53
7. Marriage	50
8. Fired at work	47
9. Marital reconciliation	45
10. Retirement	45
11. Change in health of family member	44
12. Pregnancy	40
13. Sex difficulties	39
14. Gain of new family member	39
15. Business readjustment	39
16. Change in financial state	38
17. Death of close friend	37
18. Change to different line of work	36
19. Change in number of arguments with spouse	35
20. Mortgage or loan for major purchase (home, etc.)	31
21. Foreclosure of mortgage or loan	30
22. Change in responsibilities at work	29
23. Son or daughter leaving home	29
24. Trouble with in-laws	29
25. Outstanding personal achievement	28
26. Spouse beginning or stopping work	26
27. Begin or end school	26
28. Change in living conditions	25
29. Revision of personal habits	24
30. Trouble with boss	23
31. Change in work hours or conditions	20
32. Change in residence	20
33. Change in schools	20
34. Change in recreation	19
35. Change in church activities	19
36. Change in social activities	18
37. Mortgage or loan for lesser purchase (car, TV, etc.)	17
38. Change in sleeping habits	16
39. Change in number of family get-togethers	15
40. Change in eating habits	15
41. Vacation	13
42. Christmas	12
43. Minor violations of the law	11

Add up the values for the events that have happened to you over the past year. A score of 150–199 indicates a small chance that you will have some kind of illness in the next year; 200–299 suggests a moderate risk; 300 or more warns that you are very likely to incur serious physical or emotional illness.

Source: Reprinted with permission from *Journal of Psychosomatic Research*, vol. 11, pp. 213–18, T.H. Holmes and R.H. Rahe, "The Social Readjustment Rating Scale," Copyright 1967, Pergamon Press, Ltd.

---

1 Douglas Harman, *On the Joys of Being Manager* (Washington, DC: ICMA, 1973).

2 *1991 State of the Profession Survey*, unpublished results available upon request from ICMA.

3 Tari Renner, "Appointed Local Government Managers: Stability and Change," *The Municipal Year Book 1990* (Washington, DC: ICMA, 1990), 41–52.

4 Richard J. Stillman II, "Local Public Management in Transition: A Report on the Current State of the Profession," *The Municipal Year Book 1982*, 163.

5 Renner, "Appointed Local Government Managers."

6 David N. Ammons, "Reputational Leaders in Local Government Productivity and Innovation," *Public Productivity and Management Review* 15 (Fall 1991): 19–43.

7 Daniel M. Barber, "Newly Promoted City Managers," *Public Administration Review* 48 (May/June 1988): 694–699.

8 "State of the Profession Survey Results," *ICMA Newsletter* (November 5, 1990), supplement no. 3.

9 Caroline Andrew, Cecile Coderre, and Ann Denis, "Stop or Go: Reflections of Women Managers on Factors Influencing Their Career Development," *Journal of Business Ethics* 9 (April/May 1990): 361–367.

10 *The Municipal Year Book 1981*, 222; *The Municipal Year Book 1992*, 201.

11 David N. Ammons and James J. Glass, "Headhunters in Local Government: Use of Executive Search Firms in Managerial Selection," *Public Administration Review* 48 (May/June 1988): 687–693.

12 *Compensation 92: An Annual Report on Local Government Executive Salaries and Fringe Benefits* (Washington, DC: ICMA, 1992). For a sample employment agreement, see *Employment Agreements for Managers: Guidelines for Local Government Managers* (Washington, DC: ICMA, 1992).

13 For further advice from practicing managers, see the symposium entitled, "A Manager's Opening Move," *Public Management* (August 1989): 2–18.

14 See, for example, Anne Armoury, "The 7 Symptoms of a Manager in Trouble—or How to Spot/Stop a Pink Slip Before It Hits Your Desk," *Public Management* (December 1990): 7–9.

15 Barry and Linda Gale, *Stay or Leave* (New York: Harper and Row, 1989).

16 Arlene Loble, "Becoming a Risk Taker—and Then a City Manager," *Public Management* (March 1988): 19.

17 Respondents to a 1985 survey reported average workweeks of 56.6 hours for city managers and 52.7 hours for assistant managers. See David N. Ammons and Charldean Newell, *City Executives: Leadership Roles, Work Characteristics, and Time Management* (Albany: State University of New York Press, 1989). Local government managers reported an average workweek of 53 hours in 1980. See Stillman, "Local Public Management in Transition."

18 Henry Mintzberg, *The Nature of Managerial Work* (Englewood Cliffs, NJ: Prentice-Hall, 1980).

19 Loble, "Becoming a Risk Taker."

20 See State of the Profession surveys conducted by ICMA in 1988 (*ICMA Newsletter* 69 [November 21, 1988], supplement no. 1); and in 1990 (*ICMA Newsletter* 71 [November 5, 1990], supplement no. 3). The unpublished results of the 1991 survey are available upon request from ICMA.

21 Roy E. Green, "Local Government Managers: Styles and Challenges," *Baseline Data Report* 19, no. 2 (Washington, DC: ICMA); Tari Renner, "Appointed Local Government Managers."

22 Renner, "Appointed Local Government Managers," and Barber, "Newly Promoted City Managers."

23 See, for example, Daniel J. Levinson, "A Conception of Adult Development," *American Psychologist* 41 (January 1986): 7; Michael E. McGill, *The Forty to Sixty-Year-Old Male* (New York: Simon & Schuster, 1980); Suzyn Ornstein, William L. Cron, and John W. Slocum, Jr., "Life Stage Versus Career Stage: A Comparative Test of the Theories of Levinson and Super," *Journal of Organizational Behavior* 10 (April 1989): 117–133; and Donald E. Super, "A Life-Span, Life-Space Approach to Career Development," in *Career Choice and Development*, ed. Duane Brown and Linda Brooks (San Francisco: Jossey-Bass, 1990).

24 McGill, *The Forty to Sixty-Year-Old Male*.

25 R. Bailey, "Keeping Key Players Productive: How to Identify and Manage Stress," *International Journal of Manpower* 9 (1988): 3–87.

26 M. Friedman and R.H. Rosenman, *Type A Behavior and Your Heart* (New York: Knopf, 1974). Also see Daniel C. Ganster, "Type A Behavior and Occupational Stress," in *Job Stress: From Theory to Suggestion*, ed. John M. Ivancevich and Daniel C. Ganster (New York: Haworth Press, 1987), and Gary Helfand, "Work-Related Stress and Productivity," in *Public Productivity Handbook*, ed. Marc Holzer (New York: Marcel Dekker, 1992).

27 Brian D. Steffy, John W. Jones, and Ann Wiggins Noe, "The Impact of Health Habits and Life-Style on the Stressor-Strain Relationship: An Evaluation of Three Industries," *Journal of Occupational Psychology* 63 (September 1990): 217–229.

28 See, for example, Nancy Arthur, "The Assessment of Burnout: A Review of Three Inventories Useful for Research and Counseling," *Journal of Counseling and Development* 69 (November/December 1990): 186–189, and Steffy et al., "The Impact of Health Habits and Life-style on the Stressor-Strain Relationship."

29 Glynis M. Breakwell, "Are You Stressed Out?" *American Journal of Nursing* 90 (August 1990): 31–33; and T.H. Holmes and R.H. Rahe, "The Social Readjustment Rating Scale," *Journal of Psychosomatic Research* 11 (August 1967): 213–218.

30 Janina C. Latack, "Coping with Job Stress: Measures and Future Directions for Scale Development," *Journal of Applied Psychology* 71 (August 1986): 377–385.

31 Lawrence R. Murphy, "Occupational Stress Management: A Review and Appraisal," *Journal of Occupational Psychology* 57 (March 1984): 1–15.

32 Helfand, "Work-Related Stress and Productivity"; Murphy, "Occupational Stress Management."

33 Latack, "Coping with Job Stress."

34 Michael P. Leiter, "Coping Patterns as Predictors of Burnout: The Function of Control and Escapist Coping Patterns," *Journal of Organizational Behavior* 12 (March 1991): 123–144.

35 See, for example, the symposium entitled "Work and Leisure: The Essential Balance," *Public Management* (March 1989): 3–15. A view more skeptical of the actual stress-reduction benefits of exercise, sleep, hobbies, and other popular approaches may be found in Samuel H. Klarreich, *Work Without Stress* (New York: Brunner/Mazel Publishers, 1990), 43–50.

36 For a review of other suggestions for managers dealing with job loss, see the symposium devoted to that topic in *Public Management* (January 1992): 4–32.

37 For a review of time allocation patterns of municipal executives and time management strategies, see Ammons and Newell, *City Executives*.

38 Charles K. Coe, "The MBTI: A Tool for Understanding and Improving Public Management," *State and Local Government Review* 23 (Winter 1991): 37–46.

Afterword

The nature of management, *public* management, and *effective* public management as reflected in the work of the local government manager was considered in the opening chapter of this book. The subsequent chapters covered seven areas of managerial responsibility: relating to the community; facilitating the work of the governing body; defining procedures that help to promote excellence in the organization; managing services and programs in order to achieve efficiency, effectiveness, economy, equity, and accountability; planning strategically for the future of the community and managing economic development; dealing with other governments and the private sector; and establishing a realistic career path and handling the pressures of the manager's job.

Four traditional themes in public administration were shown to cut across these areas of managerial responsibility: (1) managing people; (2) managing change; (3) building and maintaining relationships; and (4) managing publicly. These themes are reiterated directly and indirectly in each chapter.

In addition to the four traditional themes of public management, this book also incorporates four newer themes that are facts of life in contemporary local government management: (1) the expanded definition of local government, (2) complexity, (3) leadership, and (4) the delegation of various governmental functions by the federal government to state and local governments.

Local government management can no longer be narrowly defined as city management. Today's broader definition includes not only counties, special districts and authorities, regional governments, and even nonprofit agencies, but also parallel governments outside the United States. Furthermore, local government management embraces not only the local chief executive, but also all of the managers and directors in the organization.

With each passing decade, local government has become more professional, and this increased emphasis on professionalism can be seen in diverse settings. For example, in the United States, many counties whose governments were once branded as archaic now have sophisticated, representative governmental arrangements. In Russia, cities whose governmental affairs were once dominated by the Communist party are now striving to develop representative systems of self-government to help address their significant economic problems while delivering basic services such as water and transportation services. Now, as the twentieth century ends and the next century begins, the job of the local government manager is considerably more complex than it was when the original concept of a professional local government manager was devised. This book has discussed some of the functional aspects of this complexity, that is, the broad range of tasks that the modern manager must perform. However, in its broadest sense, this notion of complexity is reflected in the local political system. Far more citizens are interested in what local government does, and these citizens no longer represent only traditional business interests.

Now the involved citizenry includes people of diverse ages, ethnic groups, and political ideologies whose politics focus—far more often than a manager might wish—on a single issue. As a consequence, the modern manager spends considerable time managing conflict and trying to resolve disagreements, including those that arise in the governing body itself. He or she also spends considerably more time than was once the case working with members of the governing body and helping them to develop effective public policy.

A local government manager must be an effective leader. In this book, leadership is seen as far more than the ability to motivate employees. Indeed, leadership is seen as the combination of behaviors that results not only in ensuring that things are done right but also in seeing that the right things are done. The successful local government manager is able to move beyond the operational level—getting things done right—to the more value-laden area of helping to determine the future of the community and determining what government *ought* to be doing.

The services and programs demanded by citizens have changed with the passage of time and with the delegation of some federal functions by the national government to the state and local governments. Issues of homelessness, drug trafficking, and public health arise far more frequently now than even in the 1960s, when the national government tended to raise these concerns and to be more directly involved in providing programs to address social problems. The reduction in federal aid in the 1980s and the economic instability of the early 1990s have resulted in greater competition among local governments for new companies and for corporate relocations—and sometimes in a lack of appreciation for small business as the backbone of economic expansion.

In short, the issues confronting the modern local government manager are highly diverse. Not only does he or she have to deal with traditional concerns such as street maintenance, solid waste disposal, and protective services, but also with national and state mandates on everything from clean air to the rights of citizens with disabilities; with competition from the private sector for

the provision of basic services such as fire protection and solid waste collection; and even with social issues such as homelessness and AIDS.

To deal with these complex and diverse challenges, effective local government managers need all the human relations skills identified by the ICMA FutureVisions Consortium and discussed in Chapter 1. Local government managers have always had to manage people and be sensitive to relationships. But managers today need to recognize the importance of their role in helping other individuals participate in local government—that is, in empowering both employees and citizens—and of their role in building an effective local team that can identify and accomplish community goals. These roles, and the task of achieving consensus, are not easy, because of the diversification of society—increasingly reflected in the local government workforce and the governing body—and the broad range of policy issues facing communities.

However, most individuals are attracted to a career in local government precisely because of the challenges it offers and the opportunities it provides to make a worthwhile contribution to the community. They are not surprised that the profession grows more complicated and that it changes as society changes.

As Chapter 1 pointed out, the skills need by public managers and managers in the private sector are similar, but the settings in which these managers work are different. Public managers work in and for the public interest. They serve at the pleasure of a governing body elected by the citizens and are accountable to those citizens as they execute council policy. Their mission is public service, not private profit.

The "publicness" of the job has implications for the organization, for the manager as an individual, and for the manager as a family member. Both the organization and the manager are subject to scrutiny by citizens and by the media. This scrutiny is so intense that the manager knows that he or she not only must always act responsibly and ethically but also must always be *perceived* as acting responsibly and ethically. Members of the manager's family find that their behavior also is on public view. This visibility can strain personal and family relationships, adding to the normal stress of a challenging executive position.

However, the public aspect of the profession is what makes the local government manager's job interesting and meaningful and what links his or her life and work to important events in the community, the nation, and the world. "Publicness" is at the heart of the local government manager's job. He or she has a direct role in the democratic process, reconciling popular government and effective professional management—which is what this book is all about.

Annotated bibliography

1 On being an effective local government manager

Allison, Graham T., Jr. "Public and Private Management: Are They Fundamentally Alike in All Unimportant Respects?" Paper presented at the Public Management Research Conference, Brookings Institution, Washington, D.C., November 1979. An edited version of this paper appears in *Public Management: Public and Private Perspectives*, ed. James L. Perry and Kenneth L. Kraemer, Palo Alto, CA: Mayfield, 1983, 72–92. The case for regarding public and private management as considerably different processes.

Autry, James A. *Love and Profit*. New York: Morrow, 1991. Autobiographical, readable, and provocative, an admonition for a management style that is concerned and caring.

Belasco, James A. *Teaching the Elephant to Dance: The Manager's Guide to Empowering Change*. New York: Penguin, 1990. Based on the private sector, a guidebook for devising new organizational vision and strategies; full of examples.

Bennis, Warren. *Why Leaders Can't Lead: The Unconscious Conspiracy Continues*. San Francisco: Jossey-Bass, 1990. Isolation, cynicism, routine, inertia, and turmoil as barriers to effective leadership; suggests creating conditions for subordinate development (a "transitive" organization), viewing conflict as opportunity, and anticipating and articulating everyone's dreams as possible solutions to the problem.

Bennis, Warren, and Nanus, Bert. *Leaders: The Strategies for Taking Charge*. New York: Harper & Row, 1985. Distinctions between management and leadership; emphasis on managing attention, meaning, trust, and self through vision, communication, reliability, and self-understanding.

Blanchard, Kenneth, and Peale, Norman Vincent. *The Power of Ethical Management*. New York: William Morrow, 1988. Five P's of ethical power (purpose, pride, patience, persistence, perspective) and the three-step ethics check: Is it legal? Is it balanced? How will it make me feel about myself? Fast read.

Boynton, Robert P., and DeSantis, Victor S. "Form and Adaptation: A Study of the Formal and Informal Functions of Mayors, Managers, and Chief Administrative Officers." *Baseline Data Report* 22 (January–February 1990), Washington, DC: International City/County Management Association. Structural changes such as district elections and direct election of the mayor and their effect on municipal executives.

Britton, Paul R., and Stallings, John W. *Leadership Is Empowering People*. Lanham, MD: University Press of America, 1986. Pithy advice on how to move from traditional management to people-centered management. Concludes with a helpful comparison of "power with people" versus traditional management.

Burns, James McGregor. *Leadership*. New York: Harper & Row, 1978. A widely recognized examination of national leadership that distinguishes transformational (deciding what needs to be done) from transactional (doing it) leadership.

Coursey, David, and Bozeman, Barry. "Decision Making in Public and Private Organizations: A Test of Alternative Concepts of 'Publicness.'" *Public Administration Review* 50 (September–October 1990): 525–35. A look at traditional notions of the differences in public and private organizations through the relationship between publicness and strategic decision making.

Daniel, Christopher, and Rose, Bruce J. "Blending Professionalism and Political Acuity: Empirical Support for an Emerging Ideal." *Public Administration Review* 51 (September–October 1991): 438–40. A study of Kentucky managers to test the compatibility of professionalism and political savvy.

Doig, Jameson W., and Hargrove, Erwin C. *Leadership and Innovation: A Biographical Perspective on Entrepreneurs in Government*. Baltimore: Johns Hopkins Press, 1987. Thirteen biographies, mainly of national government executives, that identify key factors that have been used to effect and implement innovative policies.

Drucker, Peter E. *Managing in Turbulent*

Times. New York: Harper & Row, 1980. A review of business fundamentals through an examination of areas of change—population structure and dynamics, production sharing and market control, consumer products, and the labor force. Turbulence seen as a key factor in making planning virtually impossible; strategies for converting change into opportunity. See also *The Effective Executive*, New York: Harper & Row, 1966. A classic work on getting the right things done.

Frederickson, George W., ed. *Ideal and Practice in Council-Manager Government*. Washington, DC: International City/County Management Association, 1989. An anthology of papers and responses from a 1989 conference on council-management government held at the University of Kansas. A good overview of the state of the profession.

Hargrove, Erwin C., and Glidewell, John C. *Impossible Jobs in Public Management*. Lawrence: University of Kansas Press, 1990. Pitfalls that can confront a manager, including an admonition that the manager find ways to facilitate all tasks.

Innovating America. New York and Cambridge, MA: Ford Foundation and John F. Kennedy School of Government, Harvard University, 1991. A two-part videotape about how to create and manage innovation in government, with emphasis both on conceptualization and service delivery.

Kaufman, Herbert. *Time, Chance, and Organizations: Natural Selection in a Perilous Environment*. Chatham, NJ: Chatham House, 1985. An argument that success depends on a combination of the factors of time and chance much more than on any actions by an organization's leadership.

Linden, Russell M. *From Vision to Reality: Strategies of Successful Innovators in Government*. Charlottesville, VA: LEL Enterprises, 1991. Strategies and traits of seven national, state, and local government innovators who have visions of a better tomorrow; intended for use in training.

Mintzberg, Henry. *The Nature of Managerial Work*. New York: Harper & Row, 1973. A classic study of managerial roles based on observation; five case studies used to define what managers actually do.

Morgan, David R. *Managing Urban America*, 3d ed. Pacific Grove, CA: Brooks/Cole, 1989. A local government text that is particularly useful to the practicing manager because of its many case studies.

Nalbandian, John. *Professionalism in Local Government: Transformation in the Roles,* *Responsibilities, and Values of City Managers*. San Francisco: Jossey-Bass, 1991. Transformations in the roles of managers due to political developments and the simultaneous demands for professionalism and political acumen. Roles, responsibilities, and values as the base for managerial professionalism.

National Civic League. *Model City Charter*, 7th ed. Denver: National Civic Leader, 1989. The latest revision of the city charter model first published in 1915; this edition acknowledges that cities have become more political in the ways in which mayors and council members are selected and that legitimate differences exist among communities.

_____. *Model County Charter*, rev. ed. Denver: National Civic League, 1990. The first revision of the 1956 document, incorporating—like its municipal counterpart—greater flexibility and an acknowledgement of the heightened role of the elected executive, particularly in larger jurisdictions.

Newland, Chester A. *Professional Public Executives*. Washington, DC: American Society for Public Administration, 1980. A collection of notable essays on public management that focus on national and local government executives, written by several prominent scholars.

Paul, Amy Cohen. *Future Challenges, Future Opportunities: The Final Report of the ICMA FutureVisions Consortium*. Washington, DC: International City/County Management Association, 1991. Areas of change, implications, and strategies for coping; future managerial skills needed; and advice on structuring a community visioning process. See also *Managing for Tomorrow: Global Change and Local Futures*. Washington, DC: International City Management Association, 1990. A look at trends in futures studies with the message that anticipation of future events makes for a smoother administration in the present.

Rainey, Hal G., Backoff, Robert W., and Levin, Charles H. "Comparing Public and Private Organizations." *Public Administration Review* 36 (March–April 1976): 223-34. A cogent argument against the view that public and private management are fundamentally different; based on an empirical study.

Rehfuss, John. *The Job of the City Manager*. Chicago: Dorsey Press, 1989. A view of the roles of the modern city manager illustrated by anecdotes, cases, and quotations by practicing managers.

Rutter, Laurence. *The Essential Community: Local Government in the Year 2000*.

Washington, DC: International City Management Association, 1980. The book-length version of the report of the ICMA Committee on Future Horizons of the Profession, published in pamphlet form as … *New Worlds of Service*, in 1979.

Stillman, Richard J. II. *The Rise of the City Manager: A Public Professional in Local Government.* Albuquerque: University of New Mexico Press, 1974. A modern history of council-manager government, including discussion of the special problems of urban administrators in highly diverse environments.

Tannenbaum, Robert, and Schmidt, Warren H. "How to Choose a Leadership Pattern." *Harvard Business Review* 36 (March–April 1958): 95-101. A classic conceptual article that shows how the people- and task-orientations of an executive result in a leadership style; raises the question of which style is best.

White, Leonard D. *The City Manager.* Chicago: University of Chicago Press, 1927. The first comprehensive study of the city manager profession; though almost seventy years old, many of the ideas presented are still germane.

Whitaker, Gordon P., and DeHoog, Ruth Hoogland. "City Managers Under Fire: How Conflict Leads to Turnover." *Public Administration Review* 51 (March/April 1991): 156-65. Policy and style differences as the most likely causes of managerial turnover in Florida cities.

Wright, Deil S. "The City Manager as a Developmental Administrator," in *Comparative Urban Research*, ed. Robert T. Daland. Beverly Hills, CA: Sage, 1969. An important and relatively early study of managerial roles in cities of 100,000 or greater population.

2 Achieving effective community leadership

Abney, Glenn, and Lauth, Thomas O. *The Politics of State and City Administration.* Albany: State University of New York Press, 1986. Part II: evidence concerning the differences between mayor-council and council-manager government with regard to relating to constituents and interest groups.

Bachrach, Peter, and Baratz, Morton S. "Decisions and Nondecisions." *American Political Science Review* 57 (September 1963): 632–642. An important contribution to the community power literature, which argues the need for revision of the pluralist

position that influence is widely dispersed.

Banfield, Edward C. *Political Influence.* New York: The Free Press, 1965. One of the classic pluralist studies of influence in community affairs, focusing on Chicago.

Banfield, Edward C., and Wilson, James Q. *City Politics.* New York: Vintage Books, 1963. A textbook on urban politics that had a major influence on academic views of social and political cleavages in the community and of the nature of political alignments in the city.

Boyte, Harry C. *The Backyard Revolution.* Philadelphia: Temple University Press, 1980. Examines the development and purposes of neighborhood associations in order to understand the new citizen movement in American cities.

Browning, Rufus P., Marshall, Dale Rogers, and Tabb, David H. *Protest Is Not Enough.* Berkely: University of California Press, 1984. A study of the forces that produced a shift in the political orientation from conservative to liberal in selected city councils in California; analyzes how minorities are incorporated into city government.

Browning, Rufus P., Marshall, Dale Rogers, and Tabb, David H., eds. *Racial Politics in American Cities.* New York: Longman, 1990. The editors and other contributors examine the participation of African-Americans and Hispanics in eleven cities: Los Angeles, Philadelphia, New York, Chicago, Boston, Atlanta, Birmingham, New Orleans, Miami, San Antonio, and Denver.

Dahl, Robert. *Who Governs?* New Haven, CT: Yale University Press, 1961. The most important statement of the pluralist perspective on community power, based on a study of New Haven, Connecticut.

Dutton, William H., and Northrop, Alana. "Municipal Reform and the Changing Pattern of Urban Party Politics." *American Politics Quarterly* 6 (October 1978): 429–452. Rare empirical study that compares the relative influence of interest groups in mayor-council and council-manager governments. See also Northrop, Alana, and Dutton, William H. "Municipal Reform and Group Influence," *American Journal of Political Science* 22 (August 1978): 691–711.

Ehrenhalt, Alan. *The United States of Ambition.* New York: Times Books, 1992. An examination of the "new breed" of elected official in local and state government; argues that elected officials are increasingly activist, professional politicians for whom reelection rather than governing is the primary goal.

Herson, Lawrence J. R., and Bolland, John

M. *The Urban Web.* Chicago: Nelson-Hall, 1990. A modern textbook with an extensive discussion of interest groups and community power.

Jones, Bryan D., and Batchelor, Lynn W. *The Sustaining Hand.* Lawrence: University Press of Kansas, 1986. A study of how city officials responded to the decisions of business leaders in Detroit, Flint, and Pontiac, Michigan, regarding plant location.

Lipsky, Michael. *Street Level Bureaucracy.* New York: Russell Sage Foundation, 1980. In-depth analysis of the relationship between administrators and clients, particularly those administrators who have close contact with clients and who exercise discretion in the conduct of their jobs (e.g., police officers); identifies factors that can impede administrative responsiveness to citizens.

Prewitt, Kenneth. *The Recruitment of Political Leaders.* Indianapolis, IN: Bobbs-Merrill, 1970. One of a series of books based on surveys of cities in the Bay Area in California; provides evidence of a community-service orientation on the part of most council members.

Stone, Clarence N. *Regime Politics: Governing Atlanta, 1946-1988.* Lawrence: University Press of Kansas, 1989. A study of the shifting coalitions and political influences on government in Atlanta; contributes to the understanding of community power by analyzing how public office holders come to terms with business interests.

Svara, James H. "The Responsible Manager: Building on the Code and the Declaration." *Public Management* 69 (August 1987): 14–19. An argument that community leadership is an ethical obligation of city managers.

_____. *Official Leadership in the City.* New York: Oxford, 1990. A comparison of the roles of mayors, council members, and administrators in mayor-council and council-manager cities; includes an examination of the nature of community leadership provided by each type of official.

_____. *A Survey of American City Councils: Continuity and Change.* Washington: National League of Cities, 1991. Analysis of responses from a national survey of city council members; provides information about those whom council members represent, the relative influence of groups, and the extent to which council members engage in "ombudsman" activities.

Thomas, J. Clayton. *Between Citizen and City.* Lawrence: University of Kansas Press, 1986. A study of the incorporation of neigh-

borhood organizations and the citizen participation initiatives of city government in Cincinnati, Ohio.

Trounstine, Phillip J., and Christensen, Terry. *Movers and Shakers.* New York: St. Martin's Press, 1982. Community power in San Jose studied through multiple methods.

Welch, Susan, and Bledsoe, Timothy. Urban Reform and Its Consequences. Chicago: University of Chicago Press, 1988. An examination of the effect of differing electoral institutions on city government; extensive discussion of the attitudes of council members regarding which groups in the community they represent.

Zisk, Betty H. *Local Interest Politics: A One-Way Street.* Indianapolis, IN: Bobbs-Merrill, 1973. Another in the series based on surveys of cities in the Bay Area in California; examines the citizen groups that are active in urban politics.

3 Enhancing the governing body's effectiveness

Ammons, David N., and Newell, Charldean. "'City Managers Don't Make Policy': A Lie, Let's Face It." *Public Management* 70 (December 1988): 14–17. Rejection of the popular politics/administration dichotomy based on the results of a survey of city managers and mayors that found managers reporting a higher percentage of their time spend on politics than expected and mayors indicating a higher percentage of their time spent on management than expected.

Barbour, George P., Jr., and Sipel, George A. "Excellence in Leadership: Public Sector Model." *Public Management* 68 (August 1986): 3–5. A reiteration of Warren Bennis and Bert Nanus' *Leaders* (see Chapter 1). Leadership model based on visioning, communicating the vision, acting on the vision, and finally, caring about people (citizens, employees, fellow managers, community leaders) and the organization.

Blubaugh, Donald. "The Changing Role of the Public Administrator." *Public Management* 69 (June 1987): 7–10. New roles for managers due to changing political climate. Where elected officials take a more active role in administration and citizens demand more access to the decision-making process, managers must spend most of their time developing policy, encouraging cooperation among policymakers, and coordinating intergovernmental efforts.

Chase, Gordon, and Reveal, Elizabeth C. *How to Manage in the Public Sector.* New

York: McGraw-Hill, 1983. A conceptualization based on the experiences and teachings of Gordon Chase of the tasks of the manager in relation to bosses, elected officials, governing bodies, the bureaucracy, the community, special interests, and the media. Emphasis on the political dimensions of the manager's job.

Gilmore, Thomas N. *Making a Leadership Change: How Organizations and Leaders Can Handle Leadership Transitions Successfully.* San Francisco: Jossey-Bass, 1988. Vulnerability of good leaders to stakeholders resulting in decrease in the average tenure of leaders. Offers organizations an integrated approach for strategically managing leadership transitions.

Johnson, Carl F. and Hein, C. J. "Assessment of the Council-Manager Form of Government Today: Managers Meet the Challenge Through Balance." *Public Management* 67 (July 1985): 4–6. Criticism of professional government including lack of managerial fiscal responsibility, lack of responsiveness to the city council, and lack of responsiveness to citizen needs. Provocative reforms suggested include returning to mayor-council form of government, making neighborhood associations integral parts of the governmental system.

Kunde, James. "Leadership Skills for the Future." *Public Management* 66 (January 1984): 16–19. A conference room, computers, and groups with purpose and expectations as tools for the manager of the future.

Neustadt, Richard E., and May, Ernest R. *Thinking in Time: The Uses of History for Decision Makers.* New York: Free Press, 1988. Focus on using experience—the manager's own and that of others—as a basis for decision making; written for those who govern and manage.

Pfeffer, Jeffery. *Managing With Power: Politics and Influence in Organizations.* Boston: Harvard Business School Press, 1992. Power and its use in organizations; organizations as fundamentally political entities; social processes related to power and influence and the manager's ability to cope with them.

Pisciotte, Joe P. *Community Decision Making.* Wichita, KS: Wichita State University, 1991. Background papers, speeches, and findings of the Wichita Assembly, a gathering of citizens who conducted a practical evaluation of the community's decision-making skills and processes; illustrative chapters on risk-taking by the manager; characteristics of cities that work;

and an adaptation of the National Civic League's "Civic Index."

Ross, Joyce D. and Richard B., Azzaretto, John F., and Blanchard, Kenneth. "Integrating Management and Leadership." *Public Management* 68 (August 1986): 14–15. A new role for managers based on leadership qualities: creating and communicating a shared vision of the future; empowering people to do the best that they can do; and designing organizational structures that focus people's efforts on reaching the desired vision.

Schlesinger, Arthur M. *The Cycles of American History.* Boston: Houghton Mifflin, 1986. Central theme that American government and politics are defined by continuing thirty-year cycles, alternating between emphasis on public purpose and private interest. Projection that 1990s will be the beginning of a shift away from private, individual interests.

Svara, James H. "Dichotomy and Duality: Reconceptualizing the Relationship Between Policy and Administration in Council-Manager Cities." *Public Administration Review* 45 (January-February 1985): 221–232. Definitions of the responsibilities of elected officials and managers: elected officials should be responsible for defining the mission and managers should maintain the management of programs; however, policy and administrative functions should be shared.

Svara, James H. "Sharing the Load of Governance: The Manager's Responsibilities." *Public Management* 67 (July 1985): 16–19. Discussion of model of policy and administrative responsibilities; professional and personal advantages for elected officials and managers of the model and likely outcome of better governance.

4 Promoting excellence in management

Benest, Frank. "Marketing Multiethnic Communities." *Public Management* 73 (December 1991): 4–14. Cities' use of cultural diversity as a positive marketing influence for the community; numerous examples showing how cities have promoted cultural events as a source of community pride.

Berry, Jeffrey M., Portnoy, Kent E., and Thompson, Ken. "Empowering and Involving Citizens." In *Handbook of Public Administration*, James L. Perry, ed. San Francisco: Jossey-Bass, 1989, 208–224. Problems and opportunities for administrators in getting citizens involved in the public policy process, with case studies and guidelines for effective citizen participation programs.

Carpenter, Susan. "Solving Community Problems by Consensus," *MIS Report* 21 (October 1989), Washington, DC: ICMA. Decision-making strategies used to assist community groups in reaching consensus on solutions to complex problems; step-by-step procedures for organizing a consensus-building process; and approaches for different types of problem solving.

Duggan, Kevin C. "Leadership Without Appearing Political." *Public Management* 73 (February 1991): 12–15. Practical advice for city managers on dealing effectively with elected officials; suggestions on when to bring policy issues forward for consideration, how to give advice to elected officials, and when to step aside.

Epstein, Paul D., and Cutchin, Deborah A., "The Achieving Organization in Local Government"; and Cutchin, Deborah A., and Epstein, Paul D., "Make No Small Plans: New Jersey Municipalities Attempt to Become Achieving Organizations." *National Civic Review* 79 (May–June 1990): 207–243. Examination of "the achieving organization" model used as part of the Municipal Executive Program in several New Jersey municipalities.

Hatry, Harry, Morley, Elaine, Barbour, George P., Jr., and Pojunen, Stephen P. *Excellence in Managing: Practical Experiences from Community Development Agencies.* Washington, DC: The Urban Institute, 1991. Reference workbook for practical applications of various community development program activities; provides insight into successful citizen participation efforts in local governments with numerous examples.

Paul, Amy Cohen, ed. *Managing for tomorrow: global change and local futures.* See Chapter 1.

Pollitt, Christopher. *Managerialism and the Public Services: The Anglo-American Experiences.* Oxford, England: Basil Blackwell Ltd, 1990. Various managerial approaches and their influences on both American and British national and local governments during the 1980s; a unique perspective on the inner workings of the British civil service system.

Svara, James H. "Dichotomy and Duality: Reconceptualizing the Relationship Between Policy and Administration in Council-Manager Cities." See Chapter 3.

Swiss, James E. "Adapting Total Quality Management (TQM) to Government." *Public Administration Review* 52 (July–August 1992): 356–362. Suggests that many key elements of total quality management (TQM) are designed for the private sector, not the public sector. Some elements of TQM seen as useful in public sector.

Wagenheim, George D., and Reurink, John H. "Customer Service in Public Administration." *Public Administration Review* 51 (May–June 1991): 263–270. Review of customer-service concept and how it is applied in the public sector. Management skills necessary to implement a customer-service approach.

Wilbern, York. "Types and Levels of Public Morality," in *Ethical Insight, Ethical Action: Perspectives for the Local Government Manager,* ed. Elizabeth K. Kellar. Washington, DC: ICMA, 1988. Examination of morality in the public sector through administrative actions and inactions; questions of equity; the difficulty of making decisions when there are competing values.

5 Managing programs and services

Ammons, David N., and Glass, James J. *Recruiting Local Government Executives: Practical Insights for Hiring Authorities and Candidates.* San Francisco: Jossey-Bass, 1989. Primary focus on how to recruit the top-level manager and how top manager candidates can prepare; elements of what makes an effective local manager; some attention to roles of managers.

Ammons, David N., and Newell, Charldean. *City Executives: Leadership Roles, Work Characteristics, and Time Management.* Albany: State University of New York Press, 1989. In-depth analysis of the roles local government managers play based on a survey of chief executives and principal assistants in United States cities. Context in which managers work and exploration of their roles in local government.

Anderson, James E. *Public Policy-Making.* 2d ed. New York: Holt, Rinehart & Winston, 1979. A leading basic textbook on policy formulation, implementation, and evaluation with a U.S. national government orientation.

Brudney, Jeffrey L. *Fostering Volunteer Programs in the Public Sector: Planning, Initiating, and Managing Voluntary Activities.* San Francisco: Jossey-Bass, 1990. Voluntary activities and how they contribute to delivering public services; emphasis on how local government managers can encourage such activities and what to look for in monitoring them.

Bryson, John M. *Strategic Planning for Public and Nonprofit Organizations: A*

Guide to Strengthening and Sustaining Organizational Achievement. San Francisco: Jossey-Bass, 1988. A guide on how to apply the principles of strategic planning to the public and nonprofit sectors. Examination of each element in strategic planning relative to implications in public and nonprofit organizations. Excellent figures, charts, and procedures.

Cleary, Robert E., Henry, Nicholas, and Associates. *Managing Public Programs: Balancing Politics, Administration, and Public Needs.* San Francisco: Jossey-Bass, 1989. An examination of the complex forces public managers have to face and suggestions for strategies to meet them effectively. A collection of original chapters by noted experts in the field.

Cochran, Clarke E., Carr, T. R., Mayer, Lawrence C., and Cayer, N. Joseph. *American Public Policy: An Introduction.* 4th ed. New York: St. Martin's Press, 1992. A basic text on public policymaking, implementation, and evaluation with an introductory chapter on policy analysis. Other chapters apply the policy analysis framework to specific substantive policy areas.

Epstein, Paul D. *Using Performance Measurement in Local Government: A Guide to Improving Decisions, Performance, and Accountability.* New York: Van Nostrand Reinhold, 1984. A thorough examination of the concept of performance measurement and how it is applied in local government. Cases from across the United States; resource guide of organizations with experience in performance measurement provided.

Green, Roy E. *The Profession of Local Government Management: Management Expertise and the American Community.* New York: Praeger, 1989. Primary focus on the profession of local government and what professionalism involves, with chapters that focus on the roles of top-level local government managers and the environment in which those roles are played out.

Harney, Donald F. *Service Contracting: A Local Government Guide.* Washington, DC: ICMA, 1992. Detailed steps for service contracting provided for the practitioner. Includes guidelines and tips for preparing bid documents, negotiating with providers, and monitoring the contract. Spells out ways of returning to in-house service should the contract not work out as anticipated.

Hatry, Harry P. *Alternative Service Delivery Approaches Involving Increased Use of the Private Sector.* Washington, DC: The Urban Institute, 1982. A report for the Greater Washington Research Center on contracting out, franchises, voucher systems, volunteerism, and other alternative local government service delivery approaches.

Hatry, Harry P., et al. *How Effective Are Your Community Services?* Washington, DC: The Urban Institute and ICMA, 1992. A practical management study of efficiency measurement in water supply operations, criminal apprehension, central purchasing, and group residential care of children.

Hayes, Frederick O. *Productivity in Local Government.* Lexington, MA: Lexington Books, 1977. A major analysis and a collection of case studies of Dallas, Detroit, Milwaukee, Nassau County, New York, Palo Alto, Phoenix, Tacoma, and some collective bargaining experiences.

Honadle, Beth Walter, and Howitt, Arnold M., eds. *Perspectives on Management Capacity Building.* Albany: State University of New York Press, 1986. A collection of original essays on the concept of capacity building, the local government setting, and strategies for building capacity in local governments of all types. Internal and external aspects of capacity building and implications for effective government service delivery.

Jordan, Fred, with Lawson, Simpson. *Innovating America: Innovations in State and Local Government: An Awards Program of the Ford Foundation and the John F. Kennedy School of Government, Harvard University.* New York: The Ford Foundation, 1990. Describes programs receiving Ford Foundation awards for innovation in state and local levels of government. Primary focus on innovations in service delivery.

Kellar, Elizabeth K., ed. *Ethical Insight, Ethical Action: Perspectives for the Local Government Manager.* Washington, DC: ICMA, 1988. Examines tensions faced by managers in attempting to act ethically; considers the individual in the organization and the nature of responsibility in public organizations. Practical suggestions for managers to examine their own ethical standards and practices and to make ethical values an ongoing part of delivering public services. ASPA and ICMA code of ethics reprinted.

Knowles, Raymond S. B. *Effective Management in Local Government: An Introduction to Current Practice.* Cambridge, England: ISCA Publishing, 1988. An examination of local government management in the United Kingdom focused on the system of government and the relationship of the professional manager to the elected government official in the British system.

Levitan, Karen B., ed. *Government Infostructures: A Guide to the Networks of Information Resources and Technologies at Federal, State, and Local Levels.* New York: Greenwood Press, 1987. A collection of original essays on information technology and management. Case studies on selected policy areas that include library services, waste management, education, and nutrition programs.

Matzer, John Jr., ed. *Productivity Improvement Techniques: Creative Techniques for Local Government.* Washington, DC: ICMA, 1986. A collection of original essays dealing with all aspects of productivity improvement including measurement of productivity, techniques for improving productivity, and examples of creative approaches. Case studies provide examples of productivity improvement in law enforcement, streets, sanitation, and purchasing.

Miller, Thomas I. and Michelle A. *Citizen Surveys: How to Do Them, How to Use Them, What They Mean.* Washington, DC: ICMA, 1991. Comprehensive look at citizen surveys. Describes purposes of surveys, offers guidance on designing and conducting surveys, and provides average service ratings to be used in evaluating survey results.

Moore, Barbara H., ed. *The Entrepreneur in Local Government.* Washington, DC: ICMA, 1983. Examples of how local government managers are becoming entrepreneurial in the face of rising costs and resource constraints and how some services are paying for themselves. Original essays and case studies.

Nalbandian, John. *Professionalism in Local Government: Transformations in the Roles, Responsibilities, and Values of City Managers.* See Chapter 1.

Pressman, Jeffrey L., and Wildavsky, Aaron. *Implementation.* 2d ed. Berkeley: University of California Press, 1979. A case study that discloses causes of discrepancies between policy objectives, outputs, and outcomes and suggests practical management approaches to policy formulation and implementation.

Public Technology, Inc., International City/County Management Association, and the Urban Consortium. *The Local Government Guide to Geographic Information Systems.* Washington, DC: Public Technology, Inc., 1991. A guide for the local government manager on the uses of geographic information systems; questions and issues that need to be considered

before choosing a system. Explanation of the development and implementation process with pitfalls the manager should watch for.

Rich, Richard C. *The Politics of Urban Public Services.* Lexington, MA: Lexington Books, 1982. Analyzes the distribution of urban public services in terms of political activities. Impacts of interjurisdictional inequalities on the quality of urban life and on policies for relieving fiscal stress in cities.

Savas, E. S. *Privatizing the Public Sector.* Chatham, NJ: Chatham Publishers, 1982. A book advocating retrenchment in the public sector and replacement of many services through private provision.

Stewart, John. *The New Management of Local Government.* London: Allen & Unwin, 1986. Reviews the changing environment of local government in Great Britain and how local government managers must adjust. Heavy focus on the policymaking role of local government managers and the need for managers to work with the citizens for gaining acceptance of policy.

Svara, James H. *Official Leadership in the City: Patterns of Conflict and Cooperation.* New York: Oxford University Press, 1990. Mayors, councils, and administrators in city government focus on strategies for improving local government. Different roles each official has to perform, the changing nature of those roles, and the overlap among officials.

Walton, Mary. *Deming Management at Work.* New York: Putnam, 1991. A series of examples of efforts to utilize the Deming approach in varied organizations. Difficulties encountered in attempting to implement quality management in both public and private sector organizations.

6 Promoting the community's future

Black, Harry. *Achieving Economic Development Success: Tools That Work.* Washington, DC: ICMA, 1991. Reviews traditional and new techniques that local governments have used in economic development programs. Techniques discussed and illustrated with many local government examples.

Blakely, Edward J. *Planning Local Economic Development: Theory and Practice.* Newbury Park, CA: Sage Publications, 1989. Conceptual base for local government economic development followed by assessment of a number of different economic development techniques.

Bryson, John M. *Strategic Planning for Public and Nonprofit Organizations.* San

Francisco: Jossey-Bass, 1991. Excellent overview of public sector strategic planning that includes the dynamics of the process, key steps in thinking and acting strategically, and implementation strategies.

DeGrove, John. *Land and Growth Politics.* Chicago: American Planning Association, 1984. Comprehensive examination of the development of land and growth management in seven states: Hawaii, Vermont, Florida, California, Oregon, Colorado, and North Carolina. An excellent foundation for understanding current attempts at growth management.

DeGrove, John, ed. *Balanced Growth: A Planning Guide for Local Government.* Washington, DC: ICMA, 1991. Anthology that includes major areas of growth management: policy, finance, local and state roles, and politics. Managers offered a range of techniques for preserving open space, protecting environmentally sensitive areas, and controlling sprawl.

Denhardt, Robert B. "Strategic Planning in State and Local Government." *State and Local Government Review* 17 (Winter 1985): 174–179. Brief discussion of the development of strategic planning and its application in state and local government.

Eisenger, Peter K. *The Rise of the Entrepreneurial State.* Madison: University of Wisconsin Press, 1988. An in-depth discussion of entrepreneurial economic development from both conceptual and practical perspectives.

Faludi, Andreas. *A Reader in Planning Theory.* New York: Pergamon Press, 1973. A reader including many of the classics in planning theory. Application primarily to comprehensive planning, but many implications for strategic planning and growth management.

Fosler, R. Scott. *The New Economic Role of the American States: Strategies in a Cooperative World Economy.* New York: Oxford University Press, 1988. An important book for local managers that outlines various roles states can play in economic development both from a statewide and local perspective.

Gordon, Gerald L. *Strategic Planning for Local Government.* Washington, DC: ICMA, 1993. Step-by-step guidance on preparing a local strategic plan; examines economic, demographic, environmental, and regulatory factors that affect a community's future.

Logan, John R., and Molotch, Harvey L. *Urban Fortunes: The Political Economy of*

Place. Los Angeles: University of California Press, 1987. Detailed discussion of the relationship between economic development and growth control; an excellent foundation for the development of growth management as a compromise.

Molotch, Harvey L. "The City as a Growth Machine." *American Journal of Sociology* (July 1976): 320–21. Early predecessor to *Urban Fortunes*; a framework for understanding the factors that put economic development in the forefront of local government politics and decision making.

Nelson, Arthur C., ed. *Development Impact Fees.* Chicago: American Planning Association, 1988. An overview of the types and application of various development impact fees.

Peterson, Paul E. *City Limits.* Chicago: University of Chicago Press, 1981. An alternative view of urban politics based on the idea that cities are limited in their policy choices by their place in the larger political economy of the nation.

Slater, David C. *Management of Local Planning.* Washington, DC: ICMA, 1984. A treatment of local government planning from the manager's point of view: context of planning, comprehensive planning, project planning, personnel management, financial planning, working with boards and commissions, and values and ethics.

Snyder, Thomas P., and Stegman, Michael A. *Paying for Growth: Using Development Fees to Finance Infrastructure.* Washington, DC: The Urban Institute, 1987. A technical discussion of the various types of development fees that may be used to help offset the costs of growth.

So, Frank S., and Getzels, Judith. *The Practice of Local Government Planning.* 2d ed. Washington, DC: ICMA, 1988. Basic, comprehensive text on local government planning that takes the reader from the origins and development of local government planning to the issues and techniques that are important today.

7 Relating to other governments

Anton, Thomas J. *American Federalism and Public Policy: How the System Works.* New York: Random House, 1989. Looks at the system as a shifting coalition of interests in pursuit of benefits.

Bender, Lewis G., and Stever, James A., eds. *Administering the New Federalism.* Boulder, CO: Westview Press, 1986. Essays on management changes in the federal system brought on by Ronald Reagan's new federalism.

Dye, Thomas R. *American Federalism: Competition Among Governments.* Lexington, MA: Lexington Books, 1990. Treatise on the value of competition between the national government and the states, among states, and among local governments, using market place analogies.

Fix, Michael, and Kenyon, Daphne, eds. *Coping with Mandates: What Are the Alternatives?* Washington, DC: The Urban Institute, 1990. A look by several contributors at the mandate problem and at such reforms as mandate reimbursement.

Gold, Steven D. *Reforming State-Local Relations: A Practical Guide.* Denver, CO: National Conference of State Legislatures, 1989. General recommendations stemming from NCSL Task Force on State-Local Relations.

Grodzins, Morton. *The American System: A New View of Governments in the United States.* Chicago: Rand McNally, 1966. Classic statement of the marble cake thesis.

Hamilton, Christopher, and Wells, Donald T. *Federalism, Power, and Political Economy: A New Theory of Federalism's Impact on American Life.* Englewood Cliffs, NJ: Prentice Hall, 1990. Innovative text on American intergovernmental relations dedicated to showing that federalism has an incredible range of effects.

Kaplan, Marshall, and James, Franklin, eds. *The Future of National Urban Policy.* Durham, NC: Duke University Press, 1990. Chapters on urban needs and federal policies related to these needs.

Ladd, Helen F., and Yinger, John. *America's Ailing Cities.* Baltimore: Johns Hopkins University Press, 1989. Analysis of various types of state assistance to localities.

Nathan, Richard P., and Doolittle, Fred C., and associates. *Reagan and the States.* Princeton, NJ: Princeton University Press, 1987. Examination of immediate effects of Reagan administration policies in states and localities.

Nice, David C. Federalism: *The Politics of Intergovernmental Relations.* New York: St. Martin's press, 1987. Text covering the basic sets of intergovernmental relationships including national-local, state-local, and local-local patterns.

Reagan, Michael D., and Sanzone, John. *The New Federalism.* 2d ed. New York: Oxford University Press, 1982. Essay favor-

ing cooperative federalism to older version of federal-state independence.

United States Advisory Commission on Intergovernmental Relations. *Changing Public Attitudes on Governments and Taxes.* Washington, DC: GPO, annual. Citizen survey information on taxes and performance of various levels of government.

_____.*Mandates: Cases in State-Local Relations.* Washington, DC: GPO, 1990. General discussion of mandates along with case studies from seven states.

_____.*Significant Features of Fiscal Federalism.* Washington, DC: GPO, annual. Detailed information on governmental revenues and expenditures.

_____.*State-Local Relations Organizations: The ACIR Counterparts.* Washington, DC: GPO, 1990. Examination of intergovernmental relations found in 26 states.

_____. The *Organization of Local Public Economies.* Washington, DC: GPO, 1987.

Wright, Deil S. *Understanding Intergovernmental Relations.* 2d ed. Monterey, CA: Brooks/Cole, 1982. Insightful text and examination of fundamental intergovernmental relations.

Zimmerman, Joseph F. *State-Local Relations: A Partnership Approach.* New York: Praeger, 1983. Explores variations in local discretionary power.

8 Leading a manager's life

Ammons, David N., and Glass, James H. *Recruiting Local Government Executives: Practical Insights for Hiring Authorities and Candidates.* See Chapter 5.

Ammons, David N., and Newell, Charldean. *City Executives: Leadership Roles, Work Characteristics, and Time Management.* See Chapter 5.

Gale, Barry and Linda. *Stay or Leave.* New York: Harper & Row, 1989. Includes a series of tests for a self-assessment of the advisability of remaining in or departing from one's current job.

Klarreich, Samuel H. *Work Without Stress: A Practical Guide to Emotional and Physical Well-Being on the Job.* New York: Brunner/Mazel, 1990. Highly readable book on coping with stress, written largely from a psychological perspective. Emphasis on overcoming stress derived from irrational thinking by developing an ability to "counterthink."

Levinson, Daniel J. "A Conception of Adult Development." *American Psychologist* 41 (January 1986): 3–13. Summarizes the formulations of the author, a noted expert in the field, regarding life course, life cycle, and the adult development of the life structure in early and middle adulthood.

Maslach, Christina. *Burnout: The Cost of Caring.* Englewood Cliffs, NJ: Prentice-Hall, 1982. A social psychologist's detailed examination of the burnout syndrome and suggestions for coping with and preventing burnout.

Matteson, Michael T., and Ivancevich, John M. *Managing Job Stress and Health: The Intelligent Person's Guide.* New York: The Free Press, 1982. A detailed yet practical book on stress, its primary sources, prescriptions for dealing with stress, and the development of personal action plans for maintaining physical and mental health.

Mills, James Willard. *Coping With Stress: A Guide to Living.* New York: John Wiley & Sons, 1982. A series of simple suggestions and exercises for managing life's stresses.

Mintzberg, Henry. *The Nature of Managerial Work.* See Chapter 1.

Page, Clint. *Employment Agreements for Managers: Guidelines for Local Government Managers.* Washington, DC: ICMA, 1984. Includes a sample employment agreement.

About the authors

David N. Ammons is an associate at the Carl Vinson Institute of Government at the University of Georgia. He previously served in various administrative capacities in four municipalities—Fort Worth, Texas; Hurst, Texas; Phoenix, Arizona; and Oak Ridge, Tennessee—and taught in the public administration program at the University of North Texas. Dr. Ammons is the author of *Administrative Analysis for Local Government* and co-author of *Municipal Productivity, City Executives* and *Recruiting Local Government Executives*. He received a bachelor of arts degree in government at Texas Tech University, a master of public administration degree from Texas Christian University, and a Ph.D. in political science from the University of Oklahoma.

David R. Berman is a professor of political science at Arizona State University where he specializes in state and local government, politics, and public policy. He has published several books, book chapters, and journal articles in these areas and has been a regular contributor to the *Municipal Year Book*. Prior to assuming his position at Arizona State, he was a research associate with the National League of Cities. Dr. Berman holds a Ph.D. and a master of arts degree from American University, Washington, D.C., and a bachelor's degree from Rockford College, Rockford, Illinois.

N. Joseph Cayer is director of the School of Public Affairs, Arizona State University. He is the author of various books on public personnel management, labor relations, general public administration, and public policy. He is also the author of numerous journal articles dealing with public affairs issues, with an emphasis on public personnel management. A graduate of the University of Colorado at Boulder, he also received his master's degree there; he earned his Ph.D. at the University of Massachusetts. Dr. Cayer previously held faculty appointments at Texas Tech University; the University of Maine, Orono; and Lamar University, Beaumont, Texas.

E. H. Denton is the administrator of Johnson County, Kansas. Previously he was city manager in Wichita, Kansas, and worked as assistant city manager in Dallas and Fort Worth, Texas. He served on the ICMA Committee on Future Horizons of the Profession and was vice-chairman of the ICMA Retirement Corporation. An adjunct professor at the Center for Urban Studies, Wichita State University, and at the Graduate School of Public Affairs, Park College, he holds a bachelor of arts degree from the University of Missouri and a master of public administration degree from the University of Kansas. He was also a Fulbright Scholar at the University of Cologne in Germany.

James J. Glass is a professor of public administration and director of the Center for Public Management at the University of North Texas. He is the co-author of *Recruiting Local Government Executives* and has published numerous articles on local government management. He conducts research in the areas of city management, growth management, and economic development and consults with local governments, particularly in the administration of citizen surveys. He holds a bachelor's degree in government from Denison University, a master of public administration degree from Kent State University, and a Ph.D. in political science from the University of Tennessee, Knoxville.

Patrick Manion is a deputy city manager for the city of Phoenix, Arizona. Before being appointed to this position, he served as executive assistant to the mayor and held various other management positions. He has been involved in public sector productivity research and training projects with several national organizations including the International City/County Management Association, American Society for Public Administration, National Civic League, Urban Consortium, and others. He received a bachelor of arts degree and a master of public administration degree from Arizona State University. He also is an associate professor at the School of Public Affairs, Arizona State University.

Charldean Newell is regents professor of public administration at the University of North Texas where she also served for eighteen years as a departmental and executive-level administrator. This volume is her fourth co-authored book on state and local government; she also frequently serves as a trainer for local government managers. Her public service includes chairing the Denton (Texas) Civil Service Commission, membership on the board of directors of the Municipal Clerks Education Foundation, and chairing a city charter revision committee. She holds a bachelor's degree and a master's degree from the University of North Texas, a Ph.D. from the University of Texas-Austin, and a certificate in educational management from Harvard University.

Joe P. Pisciotte is a professor of government and director of the Hugo Wall Center for Urban Studies at Wichita State University, Wichita, Kansas. Previously he served as executive director of the Sixth Illinois Constitutional Convention and as director of the Illinois Department of Business and Economic Development. He holds a bachelor's degree in government from the University of Hawaii and a Ph.D. in govern-

ment from the University of Colorado. His professional career has included extensive involvement in teaching, research, and service with state and local government; recently, he staffed a Partnerships 21 Task Force working toward the consolidation of the city of Wichita and Sedgwick County, Kansas.

James H. Svara is director of the Public Administration Program and professor of political science and public administration at North Carolina State University in Raleigh. Previously, he was on the faculty at the University of North Carolina-Greensboro. He received a bachelor of arts degree from the University of Kentucky and a Ph.D. in political science from Yale University. His teaching and research deal with local government management and urban politics and focus on the roles of and relationships among appointed and elected city government officials. He is a member of the NASPAA/ICMA Task Force on Local Government Management Education.

Sources of quotations

The following list gives the sources of the boldface quotations that appear throughout the book and the affiliation—or past affiliation—of the person quoted, at the time of the quote. It also gives the then-current or past affiliation of those individuals quoted and identified in the text as practitioners (e.g., city manager, county administrator); sources of quotations for these individuals can be found in the chapter endnotes. Entries followed by asterisks are the names of participants in discussions based on the report *Futures Visions, Future Opportunities* at the Hugo Wall Center for Urban Studies, Wichita State University, Kansas, 1992.

John E. Arnold   Former city manager, Fort Collins, Colorado.

James Bacon, Jr.   City manager, Decatur, Illinois. Quote on p. 137/*Public Management* (May 1990):14-17.

Michael Ball   Chief Executive and Town Clerk, Worthing, West Sussex, United Kingdom. Quote on p. 20/*Public Management* (May 1991):14.

Camille Cates Barnett   City manager, Austin, Texas.

Linda Barton   City manager, Burnsville, Minnesota.

Frank Benest   City manager, Brea, California. Quote on p. 26/*Public Management* (August 1990):6-8. Quote on p. 89/*Public Management* (December 1991):5.

Leonard Biggs   City administrator, Park City, Kansas. *

Carol Bloodworth   City administrator, Cheney, Kansas. *

Stephen Bonczek   City manager, Largo, Florida.

Fritz M. Bowers   City manager, Vancouver, British Columbia, Canada. Quote on p. 215/*Public Management* (March 1988):14.

Jeff Bradt   Assistant personnel director, Minnesota Pollution Control Agency, St. Paul. Quote on p. 122/*Public Management* (April 1992): 9.

G. Curtis Branscome   City manager, Decatur, Georgia. Quote on p. 44/ Professionalism in Local Government (San Francisco: Jossey-Bass, 1991), 94. Quotes on p. 200 and p. 212/*Public Management* (March 1988):8-9.

Melinda Carlton   County administrator, Warren County, New Jersey. Quote on p. 8/*Public Management* (September 1990):18.

William Christopher   City manager,

Westminster, Colorado. Quote on p. 152/*Public Management* (August 1988):19.

Yvonne E. Coon   City administrator, Clearwater, Kansas. *

James Crupi   President, Strategic Leadership Solutions, Inc., Dallas, Texas. Quote on p. 11/ *Public Management* (December 1990):6.

Janet M. Dolan   City manager, Menlo Park, California. Quote on p. 37/*Public Management* (June 1991):18.

Kevin C. Duggan   City manager, Mountain View, California. Quote on p. 9/*Public Management* (February 1991):12.

Meryl Dye   Director of human resources, Hutchinson, Kansas. *

Edward P. Everett   City manager, Belmont, California. Quote on p. 200/*Public Management* (March 1988):16–18.

Frank Fairbanks   City manager, Phoenix, Arizona. Quote on p. 93/*Champions* (newsletter of the City of Phoenix), June 5, 1992: 1.

Michael Fenn   City manager, Burlington, Ontario, Canada. Quote on p. 131/ *Municipal Monitor* (journal of the Association of Municipal Clerks and Treasurers of Ontario), April–May 1992: 22.

R. Scott Fosler   Vice-president and director of government studies for the Committee for Economic Development. Quotes on p. 137 and p. 142/*Public Management* (April 1988):3-10.

Steven G. Gordon   Lane Council of Governments, Eugene, Oregon. Quote on p. 136/*Public Management* (August 1988).

Mike Hargett   Budget officer, Wilmington, North Carolina. Quote on p. 108/*Governing* (July 1992):30.

Douglas Harman   City manager, Fort Worth, Texas. Quote on p. 216/*Public Management* (March 1988):4–6.

C. A. Harrell   City manager, Norfolk, Virginia. ICMA presidential address, 1948.

Mary Jane Kuffner Hirt   Township manager, O'Hara Township, Pennsylvania. Letter to Charldean Newell, ed., November 1991.

Arlene Loble   City manager, Park City, Utah.

Donald F. McIntyre   City manager, Pasadena, California. Quote on p. 218/*Public Management* (March 1988):12.

Arthur A. Mendonsa   City manager, Savannah, Georgia. Quote on p. 14/*The Effective Local Government Manager* (ICMA, 1983), 10.

Thomas Mikulecky   City manager, Peoria, Illinois.

David R. Mora   City manager, Oxnard, California. Quote on p. 209/*Public Management* (March 1988):10–11.

E. A. Mosher   Executive director, retired, League of Kansas Municipalities.*

Sylvester Murray   Former city manager, Cincinnati, Ohio, and San Diego, California.

Don Osenbaugh   City administrator, Halstead, Kansas. *

Joe J. Palacioz   City manager, Hutchinson, Kansas. *

John Parr   Executive director, National Civic League. Quote on p. 91/*Reinventing Government* (Reading, MA: Addison-Wesley, 1992), 327.

Paschal, Don   City manager, McKinney, Texas.

Roy Pederson   Former city manager, Colorado Springs, Colorado.

Jan Perkins   City manager, Morgan Hill, California. Quote on p. 7/Letter to Charldean Newell, ed., April 1992.

George W. Pyle   City manager, retired, Hutchinson, Kansas. *

Peggy Rubach   Mayor, Mesa, Arizona.

Jewel Scott   City manager, Delaware, Ohio. Quote on p. 25/*Reflections of Local Government Professionals* (University of Kansas, Department of Public Administration), 208.

Barry Selberg   Former assistant city manager, Fort Collins, Colorado.

O. Paul Shew   Town administrator, Franklin, Maine. Quote on p. 152/*Public Management* (August 1988):15.

Stan Stewart   City manager, El Dorado, Kansas. *

Howard Tipton   City manager, Daytona Beach, Florida.

Martin Vanacour   City manager, Glendale, Arizona. Quote on p.5/*Public Management* (May 1991):19.

Alison D. Winter   Township manager, Lower Moreland, Pennsylvania. Quote on p. 138/*Public Management* (July 1988):10–12.

Jan Winters   Administrator, Palm Beach County, Florida.

Illustration credits

Chapter 1   Figure 1–1: Adapted from Henry Mintzberg, "The Manager's Job: Folklore and Fact," *Harvard Business Review* (July-August 1975): 55.

Chapter 2   Table 2–1 and Table 2–2: James H. Svara, *A Survey of America's City Councils* (Washington, DC: National League of Cities, 1991), pages 23 and 32, respectively.

Chapter 3   Figure 3–2: Adapted from James H. Svara, "Dichotomy and Duality: Reconceptualizing the Relationship Between Policy and Administration in Council-Manager Cities," *Public Administration Review* 47 (January-February 1985): 228. Reprinted with permission. Copyright American Society for Public Administration

(ASPA), 1120 G Street, NW, Suite 700, Washington, DC 20005. All rights reserved.

Chapter 5   Figure 5–4: Jeffrey L. Brudney and Robert E. England, "Urban Policy Making and Subjective Service Evaluation: Are They Compatible?" *Public Administration Review* 42 (March–April 1982). Reprinted with permission. Copyright American Society for Public Administration (ASPA), 1120 G Street, NW, Washington, DC 20005. All rights reserved.

Chapter 6   Figure 6–4: Reprinted from *Site Selection and Industrial Development* (October 1990) by permission of the publisher, Conway Data, Inc., Atlanta, Georgia, USA. No further reproduction permitted.

Index

Municipal Management Series
**The Effective Local
Government Manager
Second Edition**

Text type
Times Roman, Helvetica

Composition
EPS Group Inc.
Baltimore, Maryland

Printing and binding
Edwards Brothers, Inc.
Ann Arbor, Michigan

Design
Herbert Slobin